THE ETHICS OF WAR AND PEACE REVISITED

Also from Georgetown University Press

Biosecurity Dilemmas: Dreaded Diseases, Ethical Responses, and the Health of Nations
Christian Enemark

The Ethics of Interrogation: Professional Responsibility in an Age of Terror
Paul Lauritzen

Ethics Beyond War's End
Eric Patterson, Editor

Human Dignity and the Future of Global Institutions
Mark P. Lagon and Anthony Clark Arend, Editors

Just War: Authority, Tradition, and Practice
Anthony F. Lang Jr., Cian O'Driscoll, and John Williams, Editors

Sovereignty: Moral and Historical Perspectives
James Turner Johnson

War's Ends: Human Rights, International Order, and the Ethics of Peace
James G. Murphy

THE ETHICS OF WAR AND PEACE REVISITED

MORAL CHALLENGES in an ERA of CONTESTED and FRAGMENTED SOVEREIGNTY

DANIEL R. BRUNSTETTER AND
JEAN-VINCENT HOLEINDRE, EDITORS

GEORGETOWN UNIVERSITY PRESS
Washington, DC

Library of Congress Cataloging-in-Publication Data
Names: Brunstetter, Daniel R., editor. | Holeindre, Jean-Vincent, editor.
Title: The ethics of war and peace revisited : moral challenges in an era of contested and fragmented sovereignty / Daniel R. Brunstetter and Jean-Vincent Holeindre, editors.
Description: Washington, DC : Georgetown University Press, 2018. | Includes bibliographical references and index.
Identifiers: LCCN 2017004610 (print) | LCCN 2017008154 (ebook) | ISBN 9781626165069 (hc : alk. paper) | ISBN 9781626165076 (pb : alk. paper) | ISBN 9781626165083 (eb)
Subjects: LCSH: War—Moral and ethical aspects. | Peace—Moral and ethical aspects. | International relations—Moral and ethical aspects.
Classification: LCC U22 .E854 2018 (print) | LCC U22 (ebook) | DDC 172/.42—dc23
LC record available at https://lccn.loc.gov/2017004610

♾ This book is printed on acid-free paper meeting the requirements of the American National Standard for Permanence in Paper for Printed Library Materials.

19 18 9 8 7 6 5 4 3 2 First printing

Printed in the United States of America

Cover design by Jeremy John Parker.

CONTENTS

ACKNOWLEDGMENTS

YEARS AGO, a Chateaubriand Fellowship proved the impetus for the editors to meet at the École de Hautes Études en Sciences Sociales, Centre d'études sociologiques et politiques Raymond-Aron in Paris, in 2005. The idea for the conference and the book emerged from years of intellectual friendship. We would like to thank the Borchard Foundation for the grant that allowed us to host a conference at the Château de la Bretesche in France in 2014. The mission of the Borchard Foundation is to facilitate intellectual exchanges between American and European scholars, and we think that this volume has done so in a very meaningful way. The intellectual rapprochement of the scholars while this volume evolved occurred during a time when France was the victim of multiple terrorist attacks. Given the subject of the book, the ensuing conversations created a special form of critical solidarity as we all responded intellectually and emotionally to the growing angst not only in France but also around the globe.

The chapters were fine-tuned thanks to comments from scores of people over the years: at various iterations of the International Studies Association conference; during engaged conversations with multiple specialists, while Daniel Brunstetter was directeur d'études associé at the Fondation Maison des Sciences de l'Homme in Paris during the summer of 2016; and of course astute comments from reviewers arranged by Georgetown University Press. Special thanks go to Olivier Schmitt, associate professor at the University of Denmark, whose comments at various stages brought added rigor and depth to the volume; and to John Emery, a doctoral candidate in political science at the University of California, Irvine, who graciously did all the formatting, while also providing astute comments that drew links between the chapters. Also, we would like to thank Andrée-Anne Mélançon, a doctoral candidate in politics at the University of Sheffield, for translating Jean-Vincent Holeindre's chapter from French into English in a timely and proficient manner. Final thanks go to Don Jacobs, the senior acquisitions editor for Georgetown University Press, whose faith in the project and guidance along the way were simply priceless.

Introduction

The Ethics of War and Peace in a World of Contested and Fragmented Sovereignty

DANIEL R. BRUNSTETTER AND
JEAN-VINCENT HOLEINDRE

THE PRESENT MOMENT is one of contested and fragmented sovereignty. *Contested* because the norm of territorial integrity has shed some of its absolute nature. The evolution of the Responsibility to Protect (R2P) norm marks a shift toward sovereignty as shared responsibility, empowering humanitarian interventions with mixed outcomes. The notion of preventive force risks further undermining the traditional norm of sovereignty by imbuing states with the ability to use force against distant or emerging threats, thus bypassing diplomatic measures. US drone strikes—based in the view that a threatened state can exercise its right to self-defense against terrorist groups when other states, in whose territory these groups operate, are unable or unwilling to deal with the threat—challenge the notion of Westphalian sovereignty that any given state should be free from outside military interference in its domestic space. *Fragmented* because some states do not control all their territory and cannot necessarily deal with terrorist groups operating within their borders or sliding across them (such as along the Pakistan/Afghanistan border). Or fragmented because the borders have imploded due to civil wars—such as, in the case of Iraq, after the controversial 2003 preventive war; in the case of Libya, after the now-contentious 2011 humanitarian intervention; and in the case of Syria, in spite of no direct foreign intervention in the beginning. Finally, fragmented because of threats from quasi-territorial groups—such as Boko Haram, the Taliban, and the Islamic State group (also known as the Islamic State in Iraq and Syria, ISIS), along with the transnational jihadist activities they inspire. Even as states seek to reestablish territorial integrity by force, their existence itself contests traditional notions of sovereignty. All these uses of force challenge traditional notions of sovereignty, and in doing so, also challenge the ethical paradigms of war and peace to which we turn when international crises erupt.

Humanitarian intervention, preventive war, and drones strikes . . . just war with all it encompasses—all these military actions imply specific framing mechanisms (just war theory, R2P, the Bush or Obama doctrines) aimed to convince domestic and international audiences to go to war (or not), along with a conception of who is justified in legally and ethically killing. This volume explores whether these frameworks are flawed, and if so, how can they be improved. It examines who has the ethical right to kill (and be killed), and asks whether given what the world has become, new frameworks are needed. Finally, it contemplates what all the killing and dying are for if victory may prove, ultimately, to be elusive.

The starting point for this volume was a conference in France during the summer of 2014. The conference brought together scholars from diverse intellectual backgrounds to engage with the following questions:

- Assuming that we live in a world where the notion of sovereignty is, and has been, evolving, what do we really know about the relationship between military intervention and ethics?
- How has the concept of war evolved amid changing notions of sovereignty? And what might war (and war ethics) look like in the future?
- As we look forward, what are the most pressing challenges regarding the ethics of war and peace for the future, and how can the lessons learned from the past (assuming there are any) help us to navigate these challenges in new and innovative ways (or old and time-tested ways)?

Initially, the authors were asked to explore these questions in a post–Cold War context, that is to say, by looking at conflicts since the fall of the Berlin Wall. We suggested this framing to try to add temporal focus to the contributions by encouraging the authors to turn their attention to the wars after the so-called end of history. As became very evident in our conversations, this is a somewhat arbitrary point of departure. It is relevant insofar as one can identify the early 1990s as a period when the norm of sovereignty that had traditionally characterized the Westphalian international system began to seriously unravel. Thus, focusing on wars from the 1990s onward limits the scope of the book and ensures that the contributors' responses to the questions are related in time and geographic space (and thus are in conversation with each other). But it is also somewhat arbitrary because, as some of the contributors to the book suggest, we need to go much further back to make sense of how force is—and should be—used; or because the era since the September 11, 2001, terrorist attacks on the United States is the real timeline that tracks with the dramatic changes in sovereignty, meaning that recent events are much more relevant. Clearly, for those interested in humanitarian intervention, the 1990s are an important part of the story; and for those seeking to understand the use of force against terrorist groups or preventive wars against rogue states, the 2000s are perhaps the more significant time frame (though the twilight of the twentieth century also offers key alternative narratives).

As the reader will soon discover, the authors do not always agree—indeed, we have embraced constructive disagreements. To this end, this book's chapters as a whole seek to offer insight that can reshape old paradigms (just war theory; the Responsibility to Protect, R2P; and the warrior ethos), reconceptualize nontraditional notions of authority to use force (postcolonial responsibility, private military companies, jihadism as an individual duty), offer alternative frameworks to think about military intervention in the future (*jus ad vim* and human security), and reimagine what it means to win an armed conflict. This is not a book about how one should conceive of sovereignty, but rather, its contributing authors explore diverse ways to think about the ethics of force in an era when sovereignty is contested and fragmented.

THE VOLUME'S STRUCTURE

Despite recognizing the significance of the just war tradition as a framework for thinking about war and ethics today, we have deliberately refrained from structuring the volume in the familiar *jus ad bellum*, *jus in bello*, *jus post bellum* format. This framing is, we think, too lineal to adequately address the issues with which the chapter authors have engaged. Moreover, the majority of these authors come from alternative academic backgrounds that have much to contribute to our understanding of the relationship between ethics and the use of force. In a world of contested and fragmented sovereignty, where one interstate war blends into another, with the boundaries between peace and war blurred by the rise of nonstate or quasi-state actors, the temporality of military intervention can no longer be defined as having a set beginning that culminates in victory or defeat.

Instead, the book is divided into four parts, each of which is framed by a question that encourages the reader to think about military intervention as not necessarily being categorically rigid—in terms of the reasons for intervening, the actors taking part, the frameworks we use to think about the use of force, and the fluidity of time. We now turn to a description of the insights the contributors offer to help explain the ethics of war and peace in a world of contested and fragmented sovereignty.

PART I: WHAT FRAMES DECISIONS TO INTERVENE?

The first part of the book explores this question: What frames decisions to intervene? Note that this is not the same thing as asking what just cause under the *jus ad bellum* framework means. Just cause concerns what is morally right, while military decisions involve strategic and legal (as well as ethical) questions. The concern here is to understand what existing frameworks—R2P, elements of the just war tradition, international relations theory—reveal in terms of the reasoning behind decisions to employ military force. Here, the precedents from recent (and sometimes distant) successes and failures loom large. The contributors offer insights into the military fallout that defines our era of contested sovereignty, what we call the *humanitarian intervention hangover* and *the preventive war inheritance.*

The *humanitarian intervention hangover* is the sentiment that, despite all the positive feelings associated with saving strangers in the moment, humanitarian intervention leads to problems in the immediate aftermath. The advent of the R2P norm marries lofty goals—protecting the human rights of innocent populations—with the use of military force. Born from the specter of the non-intervention in Rwanda in the 1990s, there has been a growing sense that if human rights are to have any meaning in the world today, R2P must be a part of global discourse and coordinated action. The intervention in Kosovo—arguably, illegal but moral—raised initial hopes that humanitarian intervention could make a positive impact on global human rights. The 2005 summit placed the rhetoric in the lexicon of world leaders. This rhetoric, long absent from US national security policy, wove its way into the 2006 (under George W. Bush) and 2010 (under Barack Obama) national security strategies. Despite vast differences between these documents, this was a significant point of agreement. However, the current period raises deep questions. The 2011 Libya intervention was initially cited by some as an R2P success story, but success was short-lived, at best. At the time of writing, Libya is in a state of turmoil. The transitional government is struggling to keep its grip on power, while ISIS is gaining a foothold and citizens struggle with daily existence. The specter of Rwanda, at the heart of R2P, weighed heavily on the initial intervention, but now the non-intervention in Syria casts an equally long, if not longer, shadow. Does, or should, R2P still hold moral clout in the world? How could it be saved as a moral framework? These questions are explored by Aidan Hehir in chapter 1 and Thomas Lindemann and Alex Giacomelli in chapter 2.

In chapter 1, Aidan Hehir argues that the record of recent humanitarian interventions evidences five key lessons that must temper the temptation for positive appraisals. First, that intervention has occurred only when the intervening state had key national interests involved in the outcome of the situation. Second, that the UN Security Council has not developed a sufficiently disinterested approach to intrastate conflicts. The respective narrow national interests of the Security Council's permanent members continue to influence their responses, however grave the humanitarian crises. Third, the influence of moral advocacy on the behavior of states—democratic and otherwise—has been greatly exaggerated, and "global civil society" has not developed into the force many hoped it would. Fourth, states have demonstrated a marked unwillingness to deploy their troops in dangerous situations in the course of a humanitarian intervention. Fifth and finally, military intervention and regime change have more often than not failed to precipitate a more peaceful postconflict society. Although these lessons are negative in nature, Hehir concludes by arguing that they collectively highlight the contours of what now needs to be done if the world is to genuinely become more responsive to intrastate humanitarian crises. This new agenda for reform is particularly pressing, he argues, as it can serve to reenergize those who have grown despondent due to interventionism's failings, the shift in the global distribution of power away from the West, and the waning belief in the irresistible spread of liberalism.

In chapter 2, Thomas Lindemann and Alex Giacomelli acknowledge that despite the development of the R2P norm, which presupposes the equal dignity of all people, humanitarian intervention still remains a highly selective affair. The authors seek to uncover a better understanding of where this selectivity comes from. With strategic and economic explanations providing an incomplete answer to the question of when to intervene, they apply recognition theory to humanitarian intervention. Recognition theory offers an alternative logic of war (compared with realism, liberalism, or just war theory) that is more attentive to the emotional issues of war. This theory, the authors argue, illustrates the importance of conceptions of self and other in framing humanitarian (non)intervention. More specifically, self-recognition as a hero-protector and the minimization of the Other can, they assert, offer compelling explanatory potential for understanding the dynamics of humanitarian interventions by illuminating the process of legitimation and selectivity. They draw illustrations from the case of Rwanda to highlight how the triggering or disabling mechanisms of (non)recognition played a key role in the decision not intervene. Turning to the case of Libya, they illustrate the importance of galvanizing positive emotions within domestic populations, given that sympathy is selective and may not emerge easily.

Although R2P is lauded as an ideal norm that ought to be esteemed by the international community if human rights are to have any meaning, the norm of preventive war has had a much more controversial recent shelf life. Preventive war is to be distinguished from preemptive war, with the latter being legal according to international law and moral according to most just war interpretations, while the legitimacy of the former rests on much more shifting sands. Regarding preventive war, the 2003 Iraq War was a watershed moment insofar as it challenged existing notions of international law and controversially expanded the traditional interpretations of the *jus ad bellum* principles. The premise of the 2003 Iraq War was to stop the spread of weapons of mass destruction to rogue regimes, and to stymie the (alleged) link between such regimes and terrorist groups such as al-Qaeda. The war was a democracy-building war, which also raised questions about the *post bellum* intentions and aspirations of the victors. Although much has been written about the war, the hindsight of history serves as a meaningful lens through which to view its normative consequences. The notion of *preventive war inheritance* suggests that, despite the apparent failure of the war to achieve its democracy-building aims amid the instability that has ensued, something of preventive force remains appealing. Thus, much remains to be learned from the normative precedents of the Iraq War. Has (or should) the norm of preventive war been undermined by the Iraq debacle? Has it been transmuted by the advent of drone technology to a norm of preventive force—that is, via drones—to fight nonstate actors? How do we know if preventive war is a bad idea given current threats? What do countries other than the United States make of preventive force, whether at the level of drones or of war? These questions are addressed by Nigel Biggar in chapter 3, Kerstin Fisk and Jennifer Ramos in chapter 4, and Jean-Baptiste Jeangène Vilmer in chapter 5.

In chapter 3, Nigel Biggar looks at recent interventions so as to offer insights into perplexing matters, including how we should understand when injustice is grave enough to amount to a just cause for military intervention, the role of national interest in assessing the ethics of intervention, how we can assess whether an intervention was proportionate in the long run, and whether it makes sense to lay down the formulation of an "exit strategy" as a condition of proportionate intervention. He addresses these concerns through a lens drawn heavily from Christian just war thinking. His conclusions cast a critical gaze on those who are overly critical of recent wars. In doing so, he defends the place of war as a tool of statecraft to respond to grave injustice in the world, but also to pursue the necessarily selective national interest of specific states. This might mean that choosing not to intervene is the most prudent course of affairs. War, he also recognizes, is an imperfect state of affairs, which makes concerns of proportionality difficult to assess and also makes the requirement of an exit strategy problematic. His calculated musings point to the view that recent challenges should not lead us to conclude that war is never efficacious.

Rather, we need to remember that provided the military means chosen are necessary and the cause is just, there is, he claims, no absolute maximum to the collateral damage that may be incurred. Moreover, at the conclusion of a war fought with a just cause, the tides of history may make the prudent choice one of simply leaving. This, he suggests, is not a failure that discredits the concept of just war, but a noble failure that is part of the complex and tragic fortunes of international relations.

In chapter 4, Kerstin Fisk and Jennifer Ramos express worry that the United States is setting a dangerous norm with its foreign policy strategy of preventive uses of force. They investigate this claim in light of the recent war in Iraq and the drone attacks against suspected terrorists in Pakistan, Yemen, Somalia, and beyond. Challenging the views of Biggar, they argue that—ethically, legally, and practically—the United States is setting a precedent that is potentially damaging to its long-term foreign policy goals. Despite the apparent short-term success of a strategy based on preventive force, both the preventive Iraq War and the preventive drone strategy reveal concerns that raise serious questions about the moral and strategic viability of preventive force in general. The preventive war in Iraq failed to produce the stable democracy as hoped for, but created the conditions for a conflict (e.g., the ISIS crisis) that further destabilized the region. The perpetual drone war may be keeping al-Qaeda on the run, but the strikes have not led to definitive victory; arguably, they have deepened anti-American sentiments around the globe, creating conditions where support for al-Qaeda and its affiliates has been bolstered. In this context, Fisk and Ramos discuss the effects of the United States' preventive force strategy and actions on other countries—particularly India and South Korea—and the implications for a possible systemwide shift in norms regarding the use of preventive force. They conclude that preventive military force is a destabilizing norm that challenges the international normative environment that had tended to favor a more restrictive outlook on the use of force.

In chapter 5, Jean-Baptiste Jeangène Vilmer tackles the question of the efficacy of drone strikes. He dismisses the importance of labeling them as preventive or not, focusing instead on the consequences of such strikes. His consequentialist ethics of drone strikes is starkly different from that of Fisk and Ramos. Vilmer's argument is born from a particular context—the debates in France about whether the government should acquire and use armed drones. He begins with a rebuttal of the popular public view in France against drones—the work of the postcolonial theorist Grégoire Chamayou—suggesting that this kind of activist perspective overlooks the strategic and military dilemmas inherent to statecraft and suffers from a selective omission of non-Western abuses of human rights. He offers a consequentialist defense of drones, arguing that they can be used in ethical and militarily effective ways, even if the United States has not always done so. His unique contribution is a look at the nascent debate in France on the ethics of armed drones, and how the US case simultaneously serves as the source of a negative, but potentially misleading, critique in the public domain, while also being an example from which to constructively incorporate this controversial emerging technology into the mainstream of statecraft options.

PART II: WHO SHOULD DO THE FIGHTING—AND WHO, CONSEQUENTLY, BEARS THE RISK OF DYING?

The book's second part explores the two-faced question of who should do the fighting and who, consequently, bears the risk of dying. This question seeks to determine who has the legitimacy to employ military force, who has the right to take up arms, and what this means for those caught in the cross fire whose identity as combatant or noncombatant is blurred. It also problematizes who should bear the risk of dying in nontraditional conflicts. Traditional ways to explore this question could look at legitimate authority from the perspective of the just war tradition or through the lens of the combatant/noncombatant distinction that is also prevalent in debates about *jus in bello*. We do not want to rehash these debates. Rather, the approach of this part of the book is different.

The recent wars fought by the West against state and nonstate actors from Mali to Pakistan raise the following important concerns that the book's contributors seek to address—Deborah Avant in chapter 6, Jean-Vincent Holeindre in chapter 7, John Kelsay in chapter 8, John Emery in chapter 9. Can actors other· than states be legitmate bearers of arms? Do some states have more responsibility than others? Do the great powers, for example, which have the capacity to act and the mantra of human rights on their side? Should others, such as former colonial powers, be stripped of their responsibility, or do their former colonial ties bind them to the fate of their former colonies in a deeper way? Have Western states lost legitimacy, given the debacles of recent military misadventures (Afghanistan, Iraq, the drone wars, Libya)? How do jihadists view the notion of authority and the right to fight, given recent wars and shifting notions of sovereignty? How has their discourse evolved as the West struggles to make sense of, and move on from, recent wars? In a world of contested and fragmented sovereignty, how do we understand risk and security given the perception of uncertainty—of when the next attack might happen and by whom—that the ubiquitous threat of terrorism seems to impose?

Among the recent developments flowing from the war fatigue resulting from contemporary conflicts is the reluctance to send ground troops to fight in distant lands and then occupy them during the *post bellum* transition phase. Drones and prolonged air campaigns are imperfect antidotes—they offer the ability to fight without putting one's own troops in significant harm's way; but placing military emphasis on these tactics raises important concerns about the possibility of long-term victory (concerns addressed in part 4 of this volume). One potential way of circumventing the fear of putting one's own troops in harm's way is to use private military and security companies (PMSCs)—which are controversial at best, though their potential as a means to pursue state security (and perhaps uphold human rights in distant lands) is significant.

Recognizing the decentering of the state's role, Deborah Avant's argument in chapter 6 turns to the just war tradition to provide insight into how one might bring PMSCs into the fold of legitimate bearers of arms. State-based organizations are taken to have a special place as legitimate violent actors and legitimate targets of violence, but the rise of PMSCs has raised questions about who else could hold such legitimacy. Many international legal theorists and practitioners hold tight to the necessity of the state as the proper, or right, authority without which our infrastructure of international law, just war, and the like would be undermined. However, as more violence has been organized outside state bounds, frameworks that extend some privileges of belligerency to nonstate organizations by focusing on what they do rather than what they are have been introduced. The International Commission of the Red Cross first extended the potential for legitimate (or at least more legitimate) violence to rebel groups, while other arguments make similar extensions to terrorists by focusing on what they do (i.e., if they act in line with principles drawn from international humanitarian law) rather than who they are (nonstate actors with no legal or moral legitimacy). Avant examines this claim as it has evolved historically, and evaluates its recent application to PMSCs and its relative usefulness for guiding the moral action of such actors in the future. She argues for a pragmatic approach that can draw PMSCs into established just war norms on the basis of their behavior, not what they are.

In chapter 7, Jean-Vincent Holeindre reflects on the dilemmas of the use of force against the background of France's colonial legacy. His contention is that French reflections on the use of force are strongly determined by the colonial experience. To support its colonial project, France had established a discourse of just war in the name of "civilization" and the values upheld by the French "great nation." Today, whenever France intervenes militarily in its former colonies, echoes of the colonial just war discourse are found in the form of "postcolonial responsibility." What is at stake is no longer justifying colonization but highlighting France's political and moral responsibility toward its former colonies (especially in Africa), which are still part of the French zone of influence.

Holeindre turns to recent interventions (or calls for intervention) in Mali, Libya, the Central African Republic, and Syria, while also paying close attention to France's critical response to the United States–led war in Iraq, to tease out the tensions between the use of force and postcolonial responsibility. A critical reflection on France's postcolonial responsibility reveals that the country faces a recurring dilemma: On one hand, France is accused of intervening and practicing a form of neocolonialism; on the other hand, if it does not intervene, it is blamed for adopting a wait-and-see attitude that neglects the inherent condition of responsibility forged by a shared history between colonizer and former colony. The challenges of this relationship, are, he suggests, compounded by the current threat from Islamist groups. The challenges arising from integrating immigrants from former colonies and their descendants have contributed to serious societal upheaval in France. Insofar as the sentiment of alienation is one element that contributes to radicalization, the problematic colonial legacy may increase the threat of terrorist attacks from within France by those who aspire to the ideology of jihadist groups like ISIS. Postcolonial responsibility is thus a two-edged sword; as France projects its power exteriorly, the very justification it uses risks alienating segments of its own population.

In chapter 8, John Kelsay portrays a different side of the postcolonial coin as he seeks to explain how jihadist notions of authority have evolved in the aftermath of the recent American wars in the Middle East. Kelsay is ultimately interested in promoting a more disciplined attempt at comprehending the dynamic features of this set of particular geopolitical conflicts, which he sees as crucial to the practice of just war thinking. In the context of recent conflicts in the Middle East, Kelsay encourages us to understand the situation through an account of the various groups appealing to the aspect of Islamic tradition whereby jihad becomes an individual duty. This, of course, complicates how we understand both sovereignty and the use of force. Kelsay provides a brief account of the recent history of jihad as an individual duty before discussing the particular challenge presented by ISIS and its adaptation of the idea. In complicating the understanding of jihad through its varied adaptations by different jihadist groups, Kelsay has a parallel goal—identifying the need for a rethinking of the link between statecraft and just war thinking. His overall argument suggests that understanding the particulars of a situation one faces—in this case, combating jihadism in a world of contested and fragmented sovereignty—requires a different notion of timing than that currently associated with the *jus ad bellum* notion of last resort. A return to how the classical just war tradition understands the notion of timing, he proffers, can offer important insights by helping statesmen pursue a more complex understanding of the "signs of the times." This, Kelsay concludes, would engender a deeper, much needed discussion of the range of (morally imperfect) options available to policymakers in a given set of circumstances. This includes the art of compromise for the sake of peace, even if this compromise cuts against the grain of *jus post bellum* and the noble trend of spreading democracy and upholding human right across the globe.

Yet another facet of the West-versus-jihadist entanglement is discussed by John Emery in chapter 9, which examines the ethical and strategic imperatives of fighting terrorism. Emery is the sole contributor to really engage the second part of the question—that is, the concern about who bears the risk of dying. He proposes an updated version of Clausewitz's trinitarian model of warfare based on security, risk, and uncertainty. He explores how to balance these three facets, paying particular attention to the contemporary struggle against ISIS. Emery's goal is to break down the complex ethico-political dilemmas statesmen face when trying to keep security, risk, and uncertainty in balance, and better explain who is at risk of dying when states react too forcefully to terrorist threats. The tendency, he worries, is for states to overreact to terrorism by overemphasizing the need to eliminate uncertainty. Thus, the perceived need to completely eradicate the threat of ISIS to eliminate any uncertainty and provide for perfect security has prompted democratic states to use force abroad without a cohesive strategy and undermine their (alleged) liberal values at home. This view of fighting terrorism, Emery argues, may diminish the security of Western states at home by transferring greater risk to its own civilians as well as transferring perpetual risk to other civilians abroad. Challenging Vilmer's consequentialist ethics approach to fighting terrorism, Emery offers an alternative conceptual framework to supplement *jus ad vim*, by managing uncertainty and diminishing risk, albeit with the recognition that neither can be completely eliminated.

PART III: DO WE NEED NEW ETHICAL FRAMEWORKS?

The book's previous two parts turned mostly to existing frameworks to address pressing questions about the relationship between force and morality in a world of fragmented and contested sovereignty. In part 3, the contributors inquire whether new frameworks that are better adapted to the shifting conditions of sovereignty defining the international system today may be needed. This inquiry is partly driven by the development of weapons that arguably make it easier to challenge traditional norms of sovereignty—drones in particular. But it is also driven by the ever-blurring distinction between zones of peace and zones of war, as states use force in spaces of contested and fragmented sovereignty to pursue security, protect human rights, and project power.

The just war tradition has a storied pedigree, whereas R2P, despite its flaws, offers a powerful vision for global responsibility. But what insight could be gained by asking if these provide adequate ethical leverage to address contemporary challenges? Would doing so help identify weaknesses, limitations, and paradoxes, and, in the process, point to ways to address these concerns to provide better and more pragmatic moral structure for the use of force today?

In chapter 10, Shannon French, Victoria Sisk, and Caroline Bass examine whether the emergence of new technologies requires a dramatic rethinking of military ethics. Every military technological innovation or evolution in tactics—they focus on drones—sparks fresh controversy about the relevance of established ethical traditions to modern warfare. Taking aim at those who argue that we need new rules, the authors assert that because the most compelling motivation to act ethically is tied to the core identity of the warriors themselves rather than the weapons they use or the nature or behavior of their enemies, new modes of combat do not require original ethics. Regardless of the form war takes, soldiers are best served by acting in accordance with a code of behavior that is as clearly delineated as possible and not dependent on too many contingencies. That being said, how ethical codes are communicated to soldiers does matter. In this light, the authors identify some important pitfalls emerging from command structures of armed drone use. Recognizing there are challenges to instilling ethical frameworks in the minds of soldiers, they explore better methods of putting traditional warrior codes into everyday practice. To this end, they hold that while the guiding principles should remain constant, a turn to the infamous Milgram experiments can shed light on the psychological mechanisms that underlie obedience to authority. Lessons drawn from these experiments can foster a greater understanding of the relationship between the context in which drone operators function and, consequently, the ethical choices they make. Moreover, studies of dehumanization can help drone operators to better navigate the specific dilemmas raised by operating killing machines from a safe distance with live feed images. French, Sisk, and Bass express worry that the bureaucratic restraints faced by drone operators—that they are given less freedom than traditional warriors to perform their own mental calculus and decide their own courses of action, in addition to not having access to the "it was either him or me" narrative—cut them off from key sources of psychological comfort. While rejecting the call for new frameworks, the goal of their chapter is to explore the benefits of blending insights from psychological research with our existing understanding of the warrior's code in order to better prepare drone-wielding warriors to endure the rigors of ongoing and future combat without losing their humanity.

In chapter 11, Daniel Brunstetter argues that the ethical use of force lies on a spectrum, spanning a range from the severely restricted use of force that is permitted in law enforcement to the more permissive use of force enabled by the laws of war. Between these two lay a space of statecraft—often used in areas where sovereignty tends to be fragmented and contested—in need of a clearer definition of the rules that govern it. Recent conflicts, he suggests, reveal a space where law enforcement is too restricted, but the rules governing war are too permissive. Although the West has often turned to both war and policing to address humanitarian crises, the proliferation of weapons of mass destruction, and the rise of nonstate actors, it has also turned to limited acts of force (targeted killings of terrorists by drones, the establishment of no-fly zones, limited air strikes, preventive strikes) or has emboldened others to use force (arming rebels, providing military training and air cover for other states fighting insurgents) for political ends. A close examination of these examples reveals the limitations of both the law enforcement and just war paradigms in evaluating current threats to international peace and security, and the need for a framework of *jus ad vim* (the moral use of limited force). Such a framework would, Brunstetter argues, update both the language of the just war tradition to reflect the changing face of international conflict *and* address the ethical, strategic, and bureaucratic dilemmas faced by statesmen and military personnel today. In his concluding section, Brunstetter calls for a deeper engagement with the *jus ad vim* project to theorize about *jus ad vim*, *jus in vi*, and *jus post vim*. This, he hopes, can help us think about how limited force, which is problematically being used under the auspices of just war principles, can be employed in more ethical ways. A secondary goal, he proffers, is to provide practical moral language that can inform statesmen who will wield the power to use such force, but also those who seek to criticize perceived abuses.

In chapter 12, Frédéric Ramel examines alternative conceptions of security that call into question the state-centric perspective that has tended to define security in terms of territorial integrity. His main interest is the concept of human security, defined in the United Nations Development Program's *Human Development Report 1994*. Human security as a framework undercuts traditional notions of state-based sovereignty and thus may offer particular insights into the current international context. Ramel addresses two architectural pillars that arguably change the way we ought to think about the ethics of force—the freedom from want (to prevent persistent and systemic socioeconomic deprivations) and the freedom from fear (to struggle against massive violations of human rights or against states that create chaos). Pondering whether securing freedom from severe want or fear could justify the resort to force, human security (echoing discussions from the previous section) interrogates who, if not states, has the responsibility and authority to act. Ramel considers whether human security embodies a universal set of values or a source of a new imperialism disconnected from local realities. By comparing the place of human security in US and Canadian foreign policy, he highlights the positive potential of thinking according to this framework while also revealing the paradox between the pacific dimension of human security and the resort to force that human security may require from certain actors on behalf of the insecure individual. Though human security has fallen somewhat out of favor, Ramel's chapter hints that a return to viewing conflict through the lens of human security may provide needed insight to help navigate a world where notions of sovereignty are more and more fluid.

PART IV: IS VICTORY REALLY ENOUGH?

If we take the major conflicts discussed by this book's contributing authors dating from the 1990s to today, could we say that victory was achieved in a meaningful way in any of them? The first Gulf War was a victory, and victory was announced. Iraq was driven from Kuwait, and the status quo was restored. But the subsequent no-fly zone was the source of all sorts of complications, and arguably its ultimate failure led to (in the heat of the post-9/11 moment) the second Gulf War of 2003. There was victory in that war, too, as the Hussein regime fell, but the story of postwar chaos is too well known to need rehashing here. Suffice it to say that postwar Iraq was an incubator for ISIS, as many of its leaders were forged in US prisons! Of course, the Afghanistan War of 2001 follows a similar pattern, one of military victory achieved by overthrowing an embattled foe, in this case the Taliban, followed by postwar insurgency movements that have yet to die away. Maybe the humanitarian interventions in the Balkans in the 1990s are the exception, though they resulted in the disintegration of Yugoslavia, with ethnic tensions still seething beneath the surface. The Libya intervention of 2011, however, casts a long shadow on the notion of victory following humanitarian war, given that its *post bellum* phase has been mired in counterinsurgency conflict. The French-led Mali intervention in 2013 that drove back jihadist militants was a victory in the sense that Malian territorial and constitutional integrity were restored, but the militants were driven out, not defeated, and the threat remains. Witness the attack by jihadists on a hotel in Bamako popular with Westerners in 2015.

The struggle against jihadist terrorist groups also suffers from a conceptual lack in understanding what victory means. Drones have, for example, degraded al-Qaeda's ranks and decapitated its leadership. Still, al-Qaeda carries out attacks around the globe—perhaps not in the United States, but certainly in regions where it operates. ISIS will no doubt prove a similar challenge, insofar as each strike that kills its operatives can serve as propaganda to swell its ranks again. Debates about what it would mean to win against ISIS and its affiliates in multiple countries are central concerns of the international community today. We are arguably in a generational war that spans the sovereign borders of states, even contesting these borders in certain regions, and it is hard to know what victory means in this context.

The challenges of understanding victory raise a host of questions that Brian Orend and Cian O'Driscoll address in the concluding chapters of this volume. Much has been written about *jus post bellum*, and Orend and O'Driscoll engage with some of these perennial themes through the lens of the incompleteness, or indeed, elusiveness of victory. How are we to understand *jus post bellum* in a world of contested and fragmented sovereignty? Do the classical models of retribution and rehabilitation, gleaned from the experiences of World War II, still offer insights? What can we learn from the challenges of the postwar phases of recent wars? If wars cannot be won, are they really even worth fighting? If so, what are we really fighting for? If victory is truly elusive, what does this mean for the study of war ethics in the future? Should we think about the relationship between victory-less war and ethics any differently than a war in which victory is possible? Or should the notion of victory be separate from the decision to go to war and how we wage war?

In chapter 13, Brian Orend takes stock of recent *post bellum* situations to reevaluate the promise of the retribution and rehabilitation models. Although he suggests there are significant general reasons for preferring rehabilitation over retribution, especially when one considers the older cases (e.g., the post–World War II reconstructions of Japan and West Germany), more recent cases (Afghanistan, Iraq, and Libya) cast doubt on this conclusion—or, at least, make us wonder about the limits of imposing postwar rehabilitation on defeated states. Given recent history, he argues that we need to focus on the common ground between the two rival theories to better navigate the *post bellum* challenges in the current international climate, what he calls the "Thin Theory of Postwar Justice." Orend offers a frank appraisal of what have we learned about what works, and what does not, when it comes to trying—postwar—to forcibly rebuild a formerly aggressive and decrepit state into one that is stable, productive, internationally engaged, and respects human rights. Exploring *post bellum* dilemmas by looking at recent interventions in Afghanistan, Iraq, and Libya for insight, Orend concludes that because some regulation of the postwar moment would be better than none, the reform of international law and practice should focus on codifying the thin, overlapping consensus between retribution and rehabilitation. We can, he maintains, keep our ultimate values and yet admit that lowered expectations may be more appropriate to today's complex postwar situations.

In chapter 14, Cian O'Driscoll is concerned with the elusiveness of victory in contemporary war. Recent conflicts in Afghanistan, Iraq, and Libya have revealed that, although statesmen make frequent reference to victory, scholars and policymakers alike have no ready answers to what winning really means. Rather, O'Driscoll shows that we suffer today from a lack of analytical clarity regarding the meaning of victory and how it should be ascertained or evaluated in practice. Further, he is concerned that not enough attention is paid to the normative or ethical dimensions of victory. He argues that it is vital that we devote more attention to considering both the concept of victory itself and the thorny question of why it has proven so difficult to apply to modern armed conflict. He contends that the notion of victory is both essential to but also in tension with how we understand contemporary just war. He concludes that charting these particular fault lines is a vital first step toward thinking more clearly about the specific issue of what, if anything, "winning" might mean in contemporary battle zones—from the hot battlefields of Iraq and Afghanistan to spaces where terrorists operate outside declared zones of war—as well as the more general matters of how modern warfare should be concluded and what it can achieve.

CONCLUSION

The contributors to this volume bring into conversation multiple intellectual heritages—including the just war tradition, the Islamic jihad tradition, French critical theory and poststructuralism, international relations theory, and security studies. Their ideas emerge from different formative literatures, with different historical events animating the development of their thought. Although some are focused on and shaped by more traditional aspects of just war, intervention, or the transitional spaces of conflict, others are pivoting from the past to engage with the more recent past, as well as the present and future of conflict, by reinterpreting the theoretical, analytical, and ethical frameworks in which we work. In its collective entirety, this volume seeks to extend our knowledge and understanding of the relationship between ethics and the use of force through a critical examination of recent conflicts that have shaped and driven the contested and fracturing notion of sovereignty that structures international relations. Such uses of force include humanitarian intervention, the struggle against nonstate actors such as al-Qaeda and ISIS (and shifting jihadist discourses), war to spread democracy, preventive war to inhibit the spread of weapons of mass destruction, the advent of drones (and the evolving warrior ethos), the emerging significance of private military companies, the increased use of force short of war, and the challenges of conflicts persisting into and morphing during the *post bellum* phase.

By thinking about the lessons we have learned (or failed to learn) during decades of intervention, the authors provide insight into whether traditional paradigms are sufficient, how they might need to be reimagined and supplemented, and whether new paradigms need to be developed. The hope is that these insights may mark a point of departure on which future advances in the field can build.

PART I

What Frames Decisions to Intervene?

1

Assessing (and Learning from) the Record of Humanitarian Intervention in the Post–Cold War Era

AIDAN HEHIR

THE POST–COLD WAR ERA began with many enthusiastic predictions about the imminent "new world order." One strand of this optimism held that the new era would be characterized by greater international enforcement of human rights and concomitantly more "humanitarian interventions." As noted in the introduction to this book, this emerging disposition and agenda challenged preexisting notions of sovereign inviolability and appeared to herald a new form of "conditional sovereignty."[1]

Compared with the Cold War period, the number of interventions presented as "humanitarian" certainly increased after 1991. Nonetheless, this chapter argues that the record of intervention evidences four key lessons, which must temper appraisals of post–Cold War interventionism. First, intervention has occurred only when the intervening state had key national interests involved in the outcome of the situation. Second, the UN Security Council has not developed a sufficiently disinterested approach to intrastate conflicts; the respective narrow national interests of the council's five permanent members (P5) continue to influence their responses, however grave the humanitarian crises. Third, states have demonstrated a marked unwillingness to deploy their troops in dangerous situations in the course of a "humanitarian intervention." And fourth, the influence of moral advocacy on the behavior of states—democratic and otherwise—has been greatly exaggerated, and "global civil society" has not developed into the force many hoped.

Although these lessons are negative, the chapter will conclude by arguing that they collectively highlight the contours of what now needs to be done—specifically, in terms of UN reform—if the world is to genuinely become more responsive to intrastate humanitarian crises. This new agenda for reform is particularly pressing, I argue, as it can serve to reenergize those who have grown despondent of late due to a combination of the mixed record of intervention, the shift in the global distribution of power away from the West, and the waning belief in the irresistible spread of liberalism.

"THE GREAT ILLUSION"

Perhaps unsurprisingly, the end of the Cold War led many to declare the imminence of a glorious new era for international politics, and specifically human rights. Famously, the dissolution of the Soviet Union constituted, according to some, "the end of history";[2] and the beneficial effects of this triumph of liberalism would, many argued, be spread to all corners of the globe through the exponential acceleration of globalization.[3] In the absence of both the threat of nuclear Armageddon and the East/West division at the Security Council, many heralded the unprecedented possibilities that now ostensibly opened up for the United Nations as the spearhead of this new change.[4] This period, Michael Barnett notes, was characterized by a proliferation of reports and commissions, which "wax eloquent about the transformational possibilities for global politics and about the role of the UN as the prospective global deliverer."[5]

There were certainly empirical grounds for this optimism; as the Soviet Union imploded, President George H. W. Bush spoke not of an era of US dominance but rather of one based on multilateralism, with the UN at its center: "Now, we can see a new world coming into view. A world in which there is the very real prospect of a new world order, . . . a world where the United Nations, freed from Cold War stalemate, is poised to fulfill the historic vision of its founders. A world in which freedom and respect for human rights find a home among all nations."[6] The UN-mandated liberation of Kuwait in 1991, coupled with Security Council Resolution 688 (which unprecedentedly described the plight of the Iraqi Kurds as a "threat to international peace and security"), stoked the optimism, as did the precipitous rise in UN peacekeeping missions; between 1988 and 1994, twenty new peacekeeping operations were deployed, compared with thirteen in the previous forty-three years.[7] The UN-mandated Somalia intervention in 1992 constituted further evidence of a new, more proactive UN and also the increased importance of human security, impelled by the "explosion" in the number of human-rights-oriented nongovernmental organizations (NGOs) that sought to promote the UN's aspirational humanitarian aims.[8]

This belief in the imminence of a new era for the UN did not last, however, and has been described by Mats Berdal as "the great illusion."[9] The optimism dissipated in the face of a number of failed interventions and, indeed, failures to intervene. The operation in Somalia came to an abrupt end when the United States recalled its troops after seventeen Rangers were killed in Mogadishu in October 1993; the implosion of Yugoslavia dashed hopes that the "international community" was now capable of uniting to redress intrastate crises; the 1994 genocide in Rwanda dealt a near fatal blow to the idea of humanitarian intervention as states with the capacity to act willfully ignored the wanton slaughter; and peacekeeping itself lost its appeal as concerns about its efficacy grew. In July 1993 there were 78,444 "Blue Helmets" deployed globally; by November 1998 the number was 14,374.[10] By the middle of the decade, the UN found itself facing an array of dire situations, which were "descending into chaos if not hell."[11]

THE RESPONSIBILITY TO PROTECT

Although the 1990s, therefore, did not witness the dawn of a new era, at the end of the decade NATO launched air strikes against Yugoslavia, thereby catalyzing renewed calls for, and interest in, humanitarian intervention. NATO's "illegal but legitimate" action starkly illustrated the inadequacies of the existing system and impelled a new determination to amend the status quo. In the wake of Kosovo, Kofi Annan asked: "If humanitarian intervention is, indeed, an unacceptable assault on sovereignty, how should we respond to a Rwanda, to a Srebrenica—to gross and systematic violations of human rights that affect every precept of our common humanity?"[12] In response, the International Commission on Intervention and State Sovereignty was established, and in December 2001, it published its report *The Responsibility to Protect*. Vaunted as a means to ensure that there would be "no more Rwandas," the report captured the attention of many scholars, NGOs, and policymakers and quickly became the dominant framework within which discussions of humanitarian intervention were framed; since 2001, the Responsibility to Protect (R2P) has been recognized at the 2005 World Summit and repeatedly affirmed by the UN secretary-general, the UN General Assembly, and the UN Security Council.[13]

Although great contestation surrounds the efficacy of R2P, its content is relatively incontrovertible. It has not in any way altered international law or the institutional procedures of the many UN organs.[14] Nor has it changed the competencies vested in the Security Council.[15] It is best understood as a consolidation and restatement of the existing relationship between the state and its people, and between the state and the international community. It constitutes a means by which pressure to behave responsibly is leveraged and advocacy is focused; indicatively, according to Alex Bellamy, "It is a principle that frames how to think about the prevention of genocide and mass atrocities and respond to the outbreak of these crimes."[16]

Since the eruption of the Arab Spring in late 2010, the efficacy of R2P has been keenly debated; though some heralded the intervention in Libya as evidence of R2P in practice,[17] others argued that there was no evidence that R2P played any causal role in the decision to intervene.[18] Of course, some have cited the disintegration of Libya since the intervention as evidence that humanitarian intervention simply does not work.[19] The crises in Bahrain and, most particularly, in Syria have also been widely cited as evidence that the claims made about R2P were hyperbole and that, in fact, little has changed.

Rather than examine the record of R2P in the contemporary era, the following sections highlight trends in intervention, which emphasize the nature of the systemic flaws that have led to the inconsistent and often morally repugnant record of intervention. Identifying the sources of these flaws helps explain why the strategy underlying R2P cannot hope to achieve the aims it advances.

TRENDS IN THE RECORD OF INTERVENTION

Humanitarian intervention has, of course, a long—if decidedly mixed—history.[20] Identifying trends in this history is beyond the scope of this chapter. Instead, the intention here is to focus on the post–Cold War era; the systemic change in 1992 heralded a decidedly new context in which debates about intervention were framed and, as discussed above, expectations regarding humanitarian intervention were exponentially raised when bipolarity ended. In assessing this period, the following trends are most pertinent.

The Centrality of National Interests

Human rights are by definition universal in nature and transcend state sovereignty. The promotion of human rights, including calls for the forcible protection of these rights, thus stems from a global as opposed to national perspective. The record of intervention, however, demonstrates that though human rights may well be universal, the international system is very much state-based.

The international system, famously, differs from domestic systems in that there is no overarching power mandated to regulate the behavior of states.

International bodies and international laws do exist, of course, but they are controlled by states, and states are the dominant actors internationally, leading to the common conceptualization of the international system as anarchical.

With respect to humanitarian intervention, this means the agents of intervention are states rather than "international" bodies. A humanitarian intervention occurs, therefore, only when states determine that it is in their interests to act. Of course, simply saying that "states act only in their national interests" tells us little; precisely what these interests are varies, and these interests are not, of course, immutable. In the post–Cold War era, it is clear that though states have increasingly felt compelled—for a variety of reasons—to expand their range of foreign policy interests, this has not led to the cultivation of a general disposition whereby the suffering of foreigners has come to be considered a primary national interest.

In assessing the response of the international community of states to intrastate mass atrocities in the post–Cold War era, it is clear that this response at any given time has been a function of relatively parochial national interests; interventions have been launched only when the intervening parties have had key interests at stake, whereas, in the absence of national interests—regardless of the scale of the suffering—intervention has not occurred.[21] This was arguably most apparent with respect to two cases in 1994; in that year, the United States successfully pushed for a UN Security Council mandate to intervene in Haiti. The United States had clear national interests involved in the resolution of the crisis in the country, while other states on the Security Council acceded to the United States' wishes on the proviso that the United States agree to their own requests in other areas.[22] Yet, with respect to Rwanda, the absence of any key national interests led to the unedifying spectacle of inertia at the Security Council and among the international community more generally. Likewise, NATO intervened in Kosovo in 1999, but at the same time it ignored the human rights abuses perpetrated by NATO member Turkey against the Kurds occurring at the same time. During the Arab Spring, this was also clear; while the Arab League called for intervention against Gaddafi, no similar action was suggested with respect to Bahrain; in fact, Saudi Arabia and Qatar actually sent troops into Bahrain to help the embattled monarchy crush protesters.[23] This was essentially ignored by the rest of the international community, most notably by the Western states, which had earlier declared their determination to stop human rights violations in Libya.

This confluence between the national interests of states and their response to particular intrastate atrocities is hardly a revelation; in chapter 3 of this volume, Nigel Biggar makes this point very well, highlighting that states that "act in the national interest" need not feel morally shamed by so doing. However,

Biggar's point—that states continue to have a primary concern with their own interests—does counter any sense that the post–Cold War era catalyzed a wholesale change in the national interests of states; if these interests had expanded in the post–Cold War era to include a determination to prevent and halt intrastate mass atrocities wherever and whenever they occurred, then the relationship between national interests and humanitarian intervention would not be problematic.[24] The record shows, however, that this is not the case.

It is necessary to note that because an intervening state had national interests involved does not necessarily preclude the intervention from being considered "humanitarian." It is widely accepted that an intervention motivated by a mixture of interests and humanitarian concern need not be automatically categorized either as inhumanitarian or cynical.[25] The problem is not that motives must be pure but never are; rather, it is that the compelling rationale for intervention must always involve national interests, and often mass atrocities do not. Hence, we have the prevalence of what Simon Chesterman describes as "in-humanitarian non-intervention," namely, those cases where the need to intervene is clear but, absent any national interests, the will is lacking.[26] This is, as indeed Biggar notes, often a function of the relationship between the government and the people in democratic states; in normative terms, democratic governments will not engage in external military action if the population does not feel that the price to be paid is worth the potential benefits.[27] Of course, when a state engages in a successful overseas intervention, citizens are pleased; in this sense, Biggar's point about popular support in the United Kingdom for the military action in Sierra Leone in 2000 makes sense. However, such retrospective support is of course inevitable; who would not be "proud" that one's state engaged in a benevolent, relatively cost-free external military action? The more important point is that the citizenry has often displayed a marked reluctance to support overseas campaigns when the benefits of such an action appear to be felt only by "foreigners" while the costs are borne by "us." This indeed was evident when US public support turned sharply against the United States' mission in Somalia in 1994—as discussed further below—and indeed, it was reflected in the UK government's failure to win popular and parliamentary support for air strikes against the Assad regime in Syria in August 2013.

In essence, the key point—which Biggar appears to accept—is that states are not moral actors. States have interests, which often inhibit their willingness and capacity to engage in humanitarian interventions, and at other times corrupt interventions legitimized as "humanitarian." These interests are not necessarily immoral, but their existence should temper the overly optimistic conception of Western states as the vanguard of a new "era of human rights enforcement."[28]

The Influence of the UN Security Council

NATO's intervention in Kosovo highlighted the problem at the heart of the international legal system: the veto power of the P5. Both Russia and China were determined not to sanction military action against Yugoslavia, so NATO circumvented the UN Security Council. This led, of course, to heated debate about the legitimacy of the Security Council—and specifically the veto—and yet, surprisingly, the International Commission on Intervention and State Sovereignty reaffirmed the power of the Security Council.[29] As it has evolved, R2P has continued to recognize the Security Council's monopoly over the authorization of military action.

Although the Security Council is mandated under Article 24 of the UN Charter to act on behalf of all the UN's member states, in practice this has manifestly not been the case. The P5 have historically approached issues under their consideration with their respective national interests very much to the fore. This has meant that the council's capacity to sanction humanitarian intervention is severely circumscribed. This has been particularly evident with respect to the crisis in Syria.

There is little doubt that the gravity of the humanitarian crisis in Syria since mid-2011 has warranted remedial international action. However, the manner in which the UN Security Council has responded has been characterized by overt disunity caused by the competing national interests of the P5. On numerous occasions, Russia and China have vetoed resolutions put to the council seeking to impose punitive sanctions against Assad's regime. Although some have argued that a humanitarian intervention into Syria would do more harm than good, and thus nonintervention is in fact prudent, it is important to note that none of the resolutions vetoed by Russia and China came close to calling for military action.[30] The position of Russia has, it is clear, been driven by its own interest in perpetuating the Assad regime, regardless of the human suffering this involves.

The international legal system for promoting and enforcing human rights therefore has at its core a fundamental contradiction: Human rights are universal in nature, and the proscriptions against genocide, war crimes, ethnic cleansing, and crimes against humanity are accepted by all states; yet the enforcement of these proscriptions is dependent on the political interests of five states, of which any one can prevent action otherwise sought by the vast majority of the international community.

Frustration with the UN Security Council's response to the crisis in Syria is widespread. In August 2012 the UN General Assembly formally condemned the Security Council for its inability to act against Assad, while in August 2012

Kofi Annan stepped down as United Nations / League of Arab States joint special envoy for the Syrian crisis, decrying the "finger-pointing and name-calling in the Security Council," which had impeded his efforts.[31] Likewise, in her final speech to the Security Council as UN high commissioner for human rights, Navi Pillay stated, "Greater responsiveness by this council would have saved hundreds of thousands of lives."[32] The council's response to the crisis was neither timely nor decisive, and according to UN secretary-general Ban Ki-moon, it had "fallen woefully short."[33]

The separation of the judiciary and the executive is fundamental to the functioning and legitimacy of any normative polity, yet at the UN, the conflation between politics and law enforcement is embedded in the UN Charter. The Security Council—specifically, the veto power wielded by the P5—thus constitutes a political core in a legal regime.[34] This systemic corruption has not been altered by the rise of R2P, despite its deleterious effects being so obvious in the post–Cold War era, specifically in relation to humanitarian intervention.

"The Somalia Syndrome"

UN Security Council Resolution 794, which sanctioned military intervention in Somalia in 1992, was widely heralded as evidence of the UN's new, more humanitarian disposition prevalent in the post–Cold War era.[35] Indeed, at the time Russia stated that the Security Council had a responsibility, and even in certain cases an "obligation," to save lives.[36] But the operation ended in disaster; in October 1993, seventeen US Rangers died at the Battle of Mogadishu, and US president Bill Clinton, facing a public backlash, pulled all US troops out of Somalia in early 1994. This experience led to what came to be described as the "Somalia syndrome," namely, the belief that "interventions to thwart starvation, genocide, the forced movement of peoples, and massive violations of fundamental rights are no longer politically or operationally feasible."[37] The Somalia case suggested that the public, though supportive of humanitarian intervention in theory, was unwilling to accept the costs associated with helping people thousands of miles away.[38] The failure in Somalia certainly seems to have influenced the United States with respect to Rwanda; sustaining casualties in foreign wars not central to US national interests was deeply unpopular with the American people, and thus the reluctance to engage with Rwanda was a product of the Somalia imbroglio.[39] Indeed, in the immediate aftermath of Somalia, President Clinton passed Presidential Directive 25, which affirmed that the US president will "never relinquish command authority over US forces."[40] This was aimed at assuaging concerns that US troops would be sent to fight at the behest of UN commanders unconcerned with appeasing the American electorate.

This case and its aftermath highlight the fact that states are extremely reluctant to put their troops in danger for the benefit of others. Naturally, in this context the frequency of intervention will be adversely affected and the tactics of those interventions, which are sanctioned, may well have the effect of accentuating the hardship felt by the oppressed. This was readily evident during the Rwandan genocide in 1994, when, after the slaughter began, the UN Peacekeeping Force stationed in the country was immediately stripped of manpower as terrified governments ordered their contingents home.[41] This is discussed in greater detail by Lindemann and Giacomelli in chapter 2 of this book, which highlights the hierarchy of human life induced by the "them" and "us" conception. Likewise, the tactics employed by NATO during its campaign against Yugoslavia in 1999 were explicitly designed to minimize risk to NATO troops; ground troops were immediately ruled out, and NATO planes were ordered to fly at a minimum of 15,000 feet to avoid Yugoslav antiaircraft guns. This strategy worked, insofar as no NATO troops died, but the strategy had the perverse effect of enabling the Yugoslav forces on the ground to accelerate their campaign of ethnic cleansing and murder.[42]

Of course, many argued that this was hardly surprising; states have an obligation to deploy troops only when national interests are involved, and they should have no moral qualms about prioritizing "force protection" in the course of an intervention primarily aimed at alleviating the suffering of foreign nationals.[43] This is, of course, a function of the fact that, unlike the police domestically, states (and their national armies) have not accepted any duty or obligation to imperil themselves for the good of others. As Martin Cook has argued, individuals enter into a "military contract" with their state when they join the army that obliges them to take risks and give their own lives if necessary; however:

> They do these things on the basis of the implicit promise that the circumstances under which they must act are grounded in political leadership's good faith judgment that the defense of the sovereignty and integrity of the nation (or by careful extension, the nation's vital interests) requires their action. The farther a particular engagement or deployment departs from this clear contractual case, the more difficult it is for political leadership to offer moral and political justification for any killing and especially dying that their military forces experience.[44]

As Emery observes in chapter 9 of this collection, a modern manifestation of this concern for self-protection at the expense of the security of innocent others is seen in the current way Western states are fighting ISIS.

The Limits of Moral Advocacy

In the post–Cold War era, human rights advocacy has become a central issue in international politics. The rapid proliferation of humanitarian NGOs coupled with technological advances—most notably the internet and 24-hour news channels—has precipitated a dramatic increase in the general public's exposure to international affairs and, specifically, foreign crises. This was manifested in the emergence of "global civil society" in the early 1990s as a network of activists and writers sought to, as Frédéric Ramel notes in chapter 12, champion "human security," expose state-sponsored oppression, and catalyze remedial state action. Global civil society activists claimed that this movement could exercise pressure on states to save oppressed peoples overseas and also act as a barrier against spurious "humanitarian interventions."[45]

R2P is ultimately predicated on this logic; the absence of any legal reform is mitigated, R2P advocates claim, by the fact that there are now myriad pressure groups calling on states to fulfill their human rights obligations and, when necessary, to take action to help prevent or halt suffering abroad.[46] R2P's efficacy is, therefore, based on an assumption that mass advocacy makes it more difficult for states to say no when called on to act in defense of the oppressed, because they fear the "shame" and "social exclusion" that will result.[47] This strategy is, naturally, held to be particularly effective with respect to democratic states, given that their governments are by definition receptive to public pressure and wary of ignoring mass movements.

In assessing the record of this movement, it is abundantly clear that NGOs have a greater voice today than they did in 1992. Beyond the fact that the sheer number of NGOs has grown exponentially, the discourse of international politics now includes a greater plurality of opinions from non-state actors than ever. These actors have also, fairly incontrovertibly, successfully mobilized global campaigns that have highlighted the plight of people who may otherwise have been ignored. Yet, though the volume of humanitarian advocacy has increased, its efficacy remains in some doubt.

By way of illustration, two cases stand out. The campaign to mobilize international action to respond to the crisis in Darfur was, in terms of generating publicity, a huge success. The Save Darfur campaign achieved sustained and widespread media coverage and cultivated a genuine global grassroots movement. The effect of this campaign on the policies pursued by those with the authority and/or the capacity to act, however, was decidedly less successful.

The Save Darfur campaign was able to bring the suffering of the people in the region to the world's attention to a far greater extent than had been the case with respect to Rwanda in 1994. However, in some respects this publicity's success makes the shameful international response to Darfur almost more damning than the response to Rwanda in 1994. As Thomas Weiss argued, "At least in 1994 there was an attempt to maintain the fiction that no such horror was under way," whereas in 2004 the United States actually declared that genocide was occurring in Darfur yet still did not take effective action.[48] This appears to cohere with Lindemann and Giacomelli's conception, as delineated in chapter 2 below, of Western notions of the African "Other," whereby mass murder and violence in Africa are considered "regrettable but not unusual," and hence remedial action is seen as imprudent.

Likewise, the antiwar campaign preceding the invasion of Iraq succeeded in mobilizing millions of people around the world, and yet this was willfully ignored by a coalition of democratic states. The crisis in Syria has also certainly not suffered from a surfeit of attention; NGOs have again succeeded in pushing the situation to the top of the international political agenda, but this appears to have left Russia and China unmoved. Evidently, generating attention and public pressure is not in itself enough; states—both democratic and nondemocratic—have demonstrated a willingness to ignore eloquent, sustained, and loud calls to take action to alleviate suffering. That the highly visible and extremely vocal campaigns Save Darfur, Don't Attack Iraq, and Do Something about Syria have been in essence ignored must, therefore, temper expectations as to the efficacy of moral advocacy.

LEGAL REFORM: THE PHOENIX FROM THE FLAMES?

In light of the trends noted above, one may well be forgiven for retreating into fatalism. When one adds to these other potentially valid negatives—such as the mixed record of postconflict reconstruction when intervention *has* occurred, as discussed by Brian Orend in chapter 13 below; evidence that the potential for humanitarian intervention may well actually contribute to the escalation of conflicts;[49] and the fact that the era of unipolarity appears to be at an end as new powers with highly dubious human rights records rise to prominence—then the future of humanitarian intervention looks bleak.[50]

However, in the history of ideas, the failure of one proposed alternative to established practices or institutions has not necessarily led to the affirmation or perpetuation of the status quo. Although the alternative most immediately vaunted may well prove to be flawed, the very fact that this alternative is at least advanced helps to generate a consensus around the fact that the status quo is itself untenable.

It is certainly clear that there is a widespread consensus that the existing system has reached the end of its applicability; this is hardly a surprise, given that it was designed more than seventy years ago by Stalin, Churchill, and Roosevelt. The contemporary era is characterized then, as discussed in detail by Ramel in chapter 12, by a jarring disjuncture between the consensus behind the need for greater respect for human security—and a role for the international community in guaranteeing this—and the persistence of a system that habitually obstructs this ideal. Institutions and legal systems do not survive if they are out of step with the prevailing expectations of their constituents; thus, though there are many grounds for pessimism, there is also, arguably, a chink of light. The failure of R2P has surely discredited the idea that states can be *persuaded* to behave better. Therefore, though this is disheartening on one level, it at least narrows the scope of viable alternatives to the issue of legal reform.

Certain theorists—most notably neorealists—have asserted that power politics has always been and will always be the primary determinant on the behavior of states.[51] This certainly appears to have been confirmed by recent events, and with the shift toward a multipolar world order, the capacity for reaching a global consensus on reform has arguably diminished. Yet the primacy of power in international affairs, and the existence of a plurality of powerful states, does not necessitate the perennial constriction of international law. One need only compare today's international legal system with that of a hundred years ago to appreciate the advances that have been made, often at times when the prospects for meaningful progress appeared least propitious, such as in the aftermath of both world wars in the twentieth century.

The legal system designed after World War II has as its primary function the reduction of conflict between the great powers; given the destruction wrought by the two wars in the first half of the century, this was not an insignificant aim. Yet, given this imperative, the system was designed with the interests of the great powers to the fore, as crystallized in the power of the P5.[52] The present system is, therefore, as Hans Kelsen has noted, "primitive," owing to this narrow focus and the related institutional configuration.[53] This explains the lack of mechanisms built into the system regarding human rights protection and the pronounced emphasis in the UN Charter on sovereign inviolability, as manifest in Articles 2.1 and 2.7. As noted in the introduction to this book, this conception of sovereign inviolability is today no longer tenable.

The existing system, as it evolved, evidenced a growing disjuncture between the increasing corpus of human rights laws and the mechanisms through which these laws could actually be enforced. International human rights law is, essentially, a system based on self-regulation that has, unsurprisingly, led states to willfully violate laws to which they themselves have made a commitment.[54] This was apparent, for example, in 2009, when during the UN General Assembly debate on R2P, Sudan affirmed its commitment to the social contract and the protection and promotion of human rights at precisely the same time that it was engaged in the blatant and systemic violation of human rights in Darfur. Those international bodies within the UN charged with overseeing human rights have themselves proved impotent and at times embarrassingly counterproductive; notoriously, in 2003 Libya was elected to chair the UN Human Rights Commission, while the commission's successor, the Human Rights Council, undermined its own credibility when it passed Resolution S11/1 in 2010 congratulating the government of Sri Lanka for its commitment to "ensuring the safety and security of all Sri Lankans" during its 2009 campaign against the Tamil Tigers, which was later described by an official UN investigation as "a grave assault on the entire regime of international law designed to protect individual dignity during both war and peace."[55] The evidence that states cannot be trusted themselves to regulate their own compliance with human rights law is, therefore, clear.

However, within the existing system, the only means whereby the international community can legally overrule state sovereignty and sanction a humanitarian intervention is through Chapter VII of the UN Charter.[56] This requires the consent of the UN Security Council that, as discussed above, makes this a matter of politics rather than law. Additionally, Chapter VII is itself a provision that was actually never intended to be used for human rights enforcement or humanitarian intervention.[57] The inherent systemic deficiencies, inadequacies, and corruptions are, therefore, clear. The need for "something" to be done in response to mass atrocities, however, remains.

In light of the trends identified above and the nature of the existing system, the contours of an alternative system can be determined; this is not to say that a detailed prescription for a new legal order is clear but, rather, that the fundamentals of the required reforms are discernible. Given that any reform needs to treat with the realities of the context in which it operates lest it lapse into utopianism, the following five principles guiding reform emerge.

The First Principle: States Are Not Moral Actors, and Thus Are Not Appropriate Agents of Intervention

In the post–Cold War era, the experience of R2P, and global civil society more generally, demonstrates the limits of moral advocacy. States may well commit themselves to act for the betterment of others, but in practice they will prioritize narrowly defined national interests. This manifests both in terms of the decision to intervene and the manner in which interventions are prosecuted. States are not, it must also be remembered, necessarily acting immorally or amorally if they choose not to come to the aid of oppressed peoples abroad; the state has both legal and moral legitimacy when it commits to act only in its national interest.

The Second Principle: The Security Council Is Not an Appropriate Body to Regulate Human Rights Law

The P5 have consistently demonstrated that they approach issues related to human rights violations in international affairs from a political rather than judicial perspective. The primary determinant of their response is not whether an action is proscribed or the extent to which it has been committed, but rather *who* is committing this act and *where*. In this sense, the UN Security Council's response to a particular intrastate crisis will always be corrupted by the interests of its dominant members, which, armed with the veto, can block remedial action regardless of how pressing or widely supported this putative action is.

The Third Principle: There Is No Shortage of Laws or a Consensus on Inviolable Human Rights

We do *not* live in an era when the rights of the individual need to be defended in principle; myriad laws already exist outlining the limits of what states can do to their own people. The 2005 World Summit's *Outcome Document* clarified the grounds on which a humanitarian intervention can take place—genocide, war crimes, ethnic cleansing, and crimes against humanity—and this, coupled with the vast corpus of supplementary international human rights law, means that we have a firm legal foundation, with universal legitimacy, on which to establish a mechanism for related remedial enforcement action.

The Fourth Principle: Absolute Sovereign Inviolability Is No Longer an Issue

The idea that there is significant support for complete sovereign inviolability is simply not true. Debates at, and resolutions passed by, the UN General Assembly in the post–Cold War era have amply demonstrated that there is a far-reaching consensus that sovereignty is relative and thus limited. Interestingly, even in those cases where state leaders obviously violate the human rights of their citizens on a systematic scale, they do not advance a "we're a sovereign state, we can do what we want" argument. This is simply no longer tenable.

The Fifth Principle: Inconsistency and Selectivity Undermine the Credibility of Legal Systems

Although, as identified in the third and fourth principles, states have accepted legal limits to their sovereign rights, when concerns about intervention have been raised in the UN General Assembly, they have invariably centered on fears about the inconsistent and selective application of the law. This means that the key question is not "Do states have a duty to protect their people?" but rather "Who decides if a state should incur censure—in its various forms—for a violations of human rights?" At the moment, the UN Security Council makes the decision, but clearly this is problematic.

Reform or Die?

Give these five principles, it is possible to imagine the contours of a viable alternative to the status quo. Decisions about when to censure a state for a violation of the human rights of its people should be made by a nonstate actor charged with enforcing preexisting human rights law. This would require the creation of a new judicial body that is independent of states. This body would also require a military force at its disposal, lest its determination that military action is required meet with an unwillingness by states to supply troops, as has often been the case with respect to peacekeeping missions. This reform has the advantage of building on the existing laws regarding human rights, operating within a narrowly proscribed remit—namely, human rights enforcement rather than the resolution of interstate conflicts and so on—and, given its composition, would likely assuage the concerns in the developing world about the politicization of human rights law and inconsistency.

Of course, such a reform would not be a panacea; one can easily imagine a number of scenarios when launching a military intervention even with this system in place would simply be imprudent. Additionally, the resources required to fund this, especially a UN military force, would be considerable. Working out a means by which these reforms could actually be embedded in the existing system and operationalized would also, of course, require a considerably more detailed proposal than the one advanced here. Finally, most obviously, this idea is not likely to be embraced by states and implemented anytime soon; the pace of UN reform is notoriously glacial.

Yet the record of human rights enforcement in the post–Cold War era, and the related fate of R2P, means that we do face a choice—to throw our hands up and declare the world to be a cruel place dominated by heartless states that can never change; or to determine, on the basis of the available empirical evidence, the framework for reform that has the potential to facilitate the progressive evolution of the international legal system. The former option is certainly attractive, insofar as the purveyor of this view does not have to risk the rejection of his prescriptions; the position of the fatalistic cynic is seductive in its simplicity. Those who scoff at new ideas, however, do not make history.

CONCLUSION

The post–Cold War era witnessed exponential growth in expectations about the importance of human rights and the willingness and ability of the "international community" to undertake remedial action to prevent or halt mass atrocities. The heralding of the "age of enforcement" now seems—in light of recent tragedies in Darfur, Sri Lanka, and Syria—to have been sadly mistaken. The most vociferously and widely championed solution to the perennial problem of "in-humanitarian nonintervention," and the related problems experienced during the 1990s—namely, R2P—appears to have failed. Although this coheres with the dismissive outlook of those pessimists who ridiculed the idea of human rights enforcement in a world dominated by power politics, it should serve to compel those who refuse to embrace fatalism to explore alternatives.

Although this chapter has, therefore, advanced a negative analysis of the fate of humanitarian advocacy and R2P in the post–Cold War era, I have sought to forestall resignation by sketching out the parameters of what I consider a viable—though by no means imminent—alternative to the status quo. These ideas are certainly idealistic but, I argue, not utopian; the distinction is surely that the latter constitutes a fantasy that would be impossible to achieve, and the former is an "ideal" that, though fraught with difficulties and by definition aspirational, does retain an empirical basis.[58] The idea—as proffered by R2P enthusiasts—that states can be convinced to act morally if asked enough times by "good" people is surely utopian; and the notion that law can build on existing legal frameworks and establish a means by which the enforcement of preexisting human rights can be made more consistent is certainly ambitious but hardly ahistorical or without some grounding in both legal theory and the actual behavior of states.

NOTES

1. Jarat Chopra and Thomas G. Weiss, "Sovereignty Is No Longer Sacrosanct: Codifying Humanitarian Intervention," *Ethics & International Affairs* 6 (1992): 95–117; and James Turner Johnson, *Sovereignty: Moral and Historical Perspectives* (Washington, DC: Georgetown University Press, 2014).

2. Francis Fukuyama, *The End of History and the Last Man* (New York: Avon, 1992).

3. Michael J. Smith, "Humanitarian Intervention: An Overview of Ethical Issues," *Ethics & International Affairs* 12, no. 1 (1998): 66.

4. Simon Chesterman, *The Outlook for UN Reform*, Public Law and Legal Theory Research Paper 11–55 (New York: New York University School of Law, 2011), 2, http://ssrn.com/abstract=1885229.

5. Michael Barnett, *The International Humanitarian Order* (London: Routledge, 2010), 21.

6. George H. W. Bush, "Address Before a Joint Session of the Congress on the Cessation of the Persian Gulf Conflict," March 6, 1991, www.presidency.ucsb.edu/ws/?pid=19364.

7. United Nations, "List of Peacekeeping Operations, 1948–2013," 2013, www.un.org/en/peacekeeping/documents/operationslist.pdf.

8. Mary Kaldor, "The Idea of Global Civil Society," *International Affairs* 79, no. 3 (2003): 583.

9. Mats Berdal, "The UN Security Council: Ineffective but Indispensable," *Survival* 45, no. 2 (2003): 9.

10. David M. Malone, *The International Struggle over Iraq* (Oxford: Oxford University Press, 2006), 11.

11. Barnett, *International Humanitarian Order*, 21–22.

12. International Development Research Centre, "International Commission on Intervention and State Sovereignty," in *The Responsibility to Protect* (Ottawa: International Development Research Centre, 2001), vii, http://responsibilitytoprotect.org/ICISS%20Report.pdf.

13. See Alex J. Bellamy, *The Responsibility to Protect: A Defence* (Oxford: Oxford University Press, 2015).

14. Carsten Stahn, "Responsibility to Protect: Political Rhetoric or Emerging Legal Norm?" *American Journal of International Law* 101, no. 1 (2007): 99–120; and Bellamy, *Responsibility to Protect*, 13.

15. Aidan Hehir, *The Responsibility to Protect* (London: Palgrave Macmillan, 2012), 75.

16. Bellamy, *Responsibility to Protect*, 11.

17. Paul Williams, "The Road to Humanitarian War in Libya," *Global Responsibility to Protect* 3, no. 2 (2011): 248–59; and Gareth Evans, "The RtoP Balance Sheet after Libya," September 2, 2011, www.globalr2p.org/media/files/gareth-_interview-the-rtop-balance-sheet-after-libya.pdf.

18. Aidan Hehir, "Libya and the Responsibility to Protect: Resolution 1973 as Consistent with the Security Council's Record of Inconsistency," *International Security* 38 (2013): 137–59; and Justin Morris, "Libya and Syria: R2P and the Spectre of the Swinging Pendulum," *International Affairs* 89, no. 5 (2013): 1265–83.

19. Iskandar Arfaoui, "NATO's 'Humanitarian Intervention' in Libya: Transforming a Country into a 'Failed State,'" *Global Research*, April 5, 2014, www.globalresearch.ca/natos-humanitarian-intervention-in-libya-transforming-a-country-into-a-failed-state/5376660.

20. Gary Bass, *Freedoms Battle: The Origins of Humanitarian Intervention* (New York: Vintage Books, 2008); and Simon Chesterman, *Just War or Just Peace?* (Oxford: Oxford University Press, 2002).

21. Nicholas J. Wheeler and Justin Morris, "Justifying the Iraq War as a Humanitarian Intervention: The Cure Is Worse Than the Disease," in *The Iraq Crisis and World Order: Structural, Institutional and Normative Challenges*, ed. Ramesh Thakur and W. P. S. Sidhu (New York: United Nations University Press, 2007), 448.

22. Erik Voeten, "Delegation and the Nature of Security Council Authority," in *The UN Security Council and the Politics of International Authority*, ed. Bruce Cronin and Ian Hurd (London: Routledge, 2008), 51.

23. Aidan Hehir, "Bahrain: An R2P Blindspot?" *International Journal of Human Rights* 19, no. 8 (2015): 1129–47.

24. However, such a worldview would be foolhardy and a grave threat to international order; as Hedley Bull warned: "Particular states or groups of states that set themselves up as the authoritative judges of the world common good, in disregard of the views of others, are in fact a menace to the international order, and thus to effective action in that field." Hedley Bull, *Justice in International Relations: Hagey Lectures* (Toronto: University Publications Distribution Service, 1984), 12.

25. Chris Brown, "Ethics Interests, and Foreign Policy," in *Ethics and Foreign Policy*, ed. Karen E. Smith and Margot Light (Cambridge: Cambridge University Press, 2001), 23; and Thomas Weiss, *Humanitarian Intervention* (London: Polity, 2007), 7.

26. Simon Chesterman, "Hard Cases Make Bad Law," in *Just Intervention*, ed. Anthony Lang (Washington, DC: Georgetown University Press, 2003), 54.

27. The invasion of Iraq in 2003, of course, demonstrates that governments in democratic states are not always mindful of the public's perspective.

28. Geoffrey Robertson, *Crimes against Humanity* (London: Penguin, 2002), xvii.

29. International Development Research Centre, "International Commission," 49.

30. Bellamy, *Responsibility to Protect*, 146.

31. "Kofi Annan Resigns as UN–Arab League Joint Special Envoy for Syrian Crisis," UN News Centre, August 2, 2012, www.un.org/apps/news/story.asp?NewsID=42609#.VBAkIvldWSo.

32. Navi Pillay, "UN Human Rights Chief Criticises UN Over Global Conflicts," *The Guardian*, August 22, 2014, www.theguardian.com/world/2014/aug/22/un-human-rights-chief-criticises-security-council-over-global-conflicts.

33. Ban Ki-moon, "Mobilizing Collective Action: The Next Decade of the Responsibility to Protect," Report of the Secretary-General, A/70/999–S/2016/620 (2016), 2.

34. Nigel D. White, "The Will and Authority of the Security Council after Iraq," *Leiden Journal of International Law* 17, no. 4 (2004): 666.

35. Nicholas Wheeler, *Saving Strangers: Humanitarian Intervention in International Society* (Oxford: Oxford University Press, 2002), 185.

36. UN Security Council, "S/PV.3145," December 3, 1992, 27, http://hdl.handle.net/11176/54686.

37. Thomas Weiss, "Overcoming the Somalia Syndrome," *Global Governance* 1, no. 2 (1992): 176; see also Aidan Hehir, "The Impact of Analogical Reasoning on US Foreign Policy towards Kosovo," *Journal of Peace Research* 43, no. 1 (2006): 76.

38. David C. Hendrickson, "In Defense of Realism: A Commentary on Just and Unjust Wars," *Ethics & International Affairs* 11, no. 1 (1997): 19–53; and James Mayall, "Humanitarian Intervention and International Society: Lessons from Africa," in *Humanitarian Intervention and International Relations*, ed. Jennifer Welsh (Oxford: Oxford University Press, 2006).

39. Timothy W. Docking, "US Foreign Policy towards Africa," in *National Interests and International Solidarity*, ed. Jean-Marc Coicaud and Nicholas J. Wheeler (New York: United Nations University Press, 2008), 215–16; and Gérard Prunier, *The Rwanda Crisis: History of a Genocide* (New York: Columbia University Press, 1997), 274.

40. "Clinton Administration Policy on Reforming Multilateral Peace Operations," White House, May 5, 1994, https://fas.org/irp/offdocs/pdd25.htm.

41. Aidan Hehir, *Humanitarian Intervention* (London: Palgrave Macmillan, 2013), 207–9.

42. Robertson, *Crimes against Humanity*, 402; and Michael Ignatieff, *Virtual War: Kosovo and Beyond* (New York: Picador, 2000), 111.

43. Micahel Walzer, *Just and Unjust Wars* (New York: Basic Books, 2002), 26; and Robert Jackson, *The Global Covenant: Human Conduct in a World of States* (Oxford: Oxford University Press, 2000), 289.

44. Martin Cook, "'Immaculate War': Constraints on Humanitarian Intervention," in *Just Intervention*, ed. Anthony Lang (Washington, DC: Georgetown University Press, 2003), 150–51.

45. Kaldor, "Idea of Global Civil Society"; and Martin Shaw, *Global Civil Society and International Relations* (London: Polity, 1994), 24.

46. Hehir, *Responsibility to Protect*, 120–27.

47. On shame, see Gareth Evans, "R2P: Looking Back, Looking Forward," keynote address in Phnom Penh, February 26, 2015, www.gevans.org/speeches/speech568.html. On social exclusion, see Bellamy, *Responsibility to Protect*, 61.

48. Weiss, *Humanitarian Intervention*, 154.

49. Alan J. Kuperman, "Suicidal Rebellions and the Moral Hazard of Humanitarian Intervention," in *Gambling on Humanitarian Intervention*, ed. Timothy Crawford and Alan Kuperman (London: Routledge, 2006).

50. Aidan Hehir and Robert W. Murray, "Intervention in the Emerging Multipolar System: Why R2P Will Miss the Unipolar Moment," *Journal of Intervention and Statebuilding* 6, no. 4 (2012): 387–406.

51. John Mearsheimer, "The False Promise of International Institutions," *International Security* 19, no. 3 (1994): 5–49.

52. Gerry Simpson, *Great Powers and Outlaw States* (Cambridge: Cambridge University Press, 2004), 68; and David L. Bosco, *Five to Rule Them All* (Oxford: Oxford University Press, 2009), 10.

53. Hans Kelsen, *General Theory of Law and State* (Cambridge, MA: Harvard University Press, 1945), 338.

54. Malgosia Fitzmaurice, "The Practical Working of the Law of Treaties," in *International Law*, ed. Malcolm Evans (Oxford: Oxford University Press, 2006), 205; and Louis Henkin, "Compliance with International Law in an Inter-State System," in *Academie de droit international, Recueil des cours 1989* (Dordrecht: Martinus Nijhoff, 1990), 250.

55. "Report of the Secretary-General's Panel of Experts on Accountability in Sri Lanka," United Nations, March 31, 2011, ii, www.un.org/News/dh/infocus/Sri_Lanka/POE_Report_Full.pdf.

56. Technically, the 1950 "Uniting for Peace" resolution can be employed; but in practical terms, its efficacy is limited. See Jean Krasno and Mitushi Das, "The Uniting for Peace Resolution and Other Ways of Circumventing the Authority of the Security

Council," in *The UN Security Council and the Politics of International Authority*, ed. Bruce Cronin and Ian Hurd (London: Routledge, 2008), 189.

57. Hehir, *Responsibility to Protect*, 60.

58. E. H. Carr, *The Twenty Years' Crisis* (London: Palgrave, 2001), 10; and Ken Booth, "Security in Anarchy: Utopian Realism in Theory and Practice," *International Affairs* 67, no. 3 (1991): 534.

2

Recognition Theory in Humanitarian Intervention

THOMAS LINDEMANN AND
ALEX GIACOMELLI

MOST HUMANITARIAN INTERVENTIONS tend to take place in an environment of contested or fragmented sovereignty, as defined by Brunstetter and Holeindre in the introduction to this volume. *Contested* because the principle of the Responsibility to Protect is often invoked in the attempt to make "sovereignty as responsibility" prevail over more classic notions of sovereignty. *Fragmented* because, on many occasions, interventions occur in failed states (Somalia) or make states lose control over their territory (Libya).

Although one can describe the environment in which humanitarian interventions take place, a more puzzling task is to understand their decision-making process, since selectivity seems to be one of their most striking characteristics. For instance, though intervention came relatively swiftly in Iraq (Operation Provide Comfort, 1991), in Somalia (1991–92), in Kosovo (1999), and in Libya (2011), the same cannot be said of the former Yugoslavia (1991–95), Rwanda (1994), or Syria (since 2011), to mention just the most dramatic humanitarian crises. How can we understand such selective attention to human suffering? In some circumstances, strategic or economic interests can help explain why decision makers opted for certain courses of action. Nevertheless, most of the time these interests do not provide a full explanation. Without dismissing realist or liberal arguments, the objective of this chapter is to show that recognition theory can offer a more comprehensive picture of the factors leading to humanitarian intervention and help explain the reasons for selectivity.

We first make a general presentation of recognition theory emphasizing two factors that have led to military action throughout history: self-recognition as a hero-protector, and the minimization of the Other. We then discuss two case studies applying the theory: Rwanda, where the world did too little too late to stop the genocide, and Libya, where intervention came quickly. As will be seen, although the theoretical framework of recognition theory concentrates on war, it can also be applied to humanitarian interventions.

Most war studies favor utilitarian approaches, reducing war to the quest for security, power (*homo politicus*), or profit (*homo economicus*). Overall, most theorists seem to repeat the Hegelian dichotomy, assuming that once a state is internationally and formally recognized, the analysis of its behavior must be based on the premise that it seeks rationally defined, strategic, and material interests.[1]

Recognition theory, developed over the last two decades, has hinted at an alternative logic of war that is more attentive to emotional and moral issues.[2] These issues are brought about by the nonrecognition of the Self—that is to say, an actor's perception that his or her proclaimed self-image is greater than that which is returned by the Other. Such denials of recognition can produce belligerent effects by encouraging offended leaders or political entities to restore their self-esteem through violent actions against those who offend them. So, unlike reductionist perspectives, the study of recognition makes the expressive assumption that leaders and/or ruled populations of a political entity often reflect strong emotions when they seek to enforce a certain image of themselves and their communities (*homo symbolicus*).

Nevertheless, the literature on recognition also has shortcomings. The most serious one is its inability to take into account the strategic dimensions of war. Recognition scholars, when faced with strategic issues, choose essentially between two options. The first is that of denial: For some scholars, expressive considerations always seem to take precedence over instrumental-strategic ones. This attitude has empirical problems, especially when it must explain what Clausewitz calls "limited war options," such as small-scale interventions where the logic of punishment is secondary and clearly subordinated to instrumental ambitions like seizing territory or energy resources.[3] Thus, the second option, apparently wiser, is to concede that strategic logic may in some situations prevail over expressive ones. However, the risk, in this case, is to turn recognition into nothing more than a residual variable, limited to explaining situations where "normal" assumptions of rationality do not work.

To avoid these problems, it is necessary to question the prevailing dichotomy between "strategy/interest" on one side and "recognition/expressivity" on the other side. Utilitarian models tend to play down the moral and emotional reasoning put forward by recognition theory, but they cannot explain war without referring to some process of legitimation that allows it to happen. Indeed, it is not enough to "want" war; it is also important to "be able" to make it. Although recognition theory does not rule out instrumental approaches, it does oppose their reductionism. War for a cold interest is possible only when emotions of compassion are neutralized by the nonrecognition of the Other: "People go to war because of how they *see, perceive, picture, imagine and speak of* others."[4] It is worth noting that nonrecognition is usually more discrete than hatred, often framing the Other as "insignificant" rather than "evil."

EMOTIONS AND INTERESTS

According to Albert Hirschman, there has been a tendency among political thinkers since the seventeenth century to consider passions as a source of war. Emotions have been identified as harmful to human survival and opposed to reason. This has set up a whole body of thought on how "evil" passions can be tamed. Political thinkers have sought to determine the virtues of an authority able to curb the irrational, "savage," and destructive instincts of the crowd in order to ensure civil peace. As examples, we can mention Hobbes, Burke, and Le Bon.

Nevertheless, some thinkers, such as Montesquieu and Hobbes himself, have recognized the role of "peaceful" passions in counteracting destructive ones: "The passions that incline men to peace are fear of death, desire of things necessary for commodious living, and a hope by their industry to obtain them."[5] Gradually, the bourgeois "passion"—greed—has come to counteract, as the result of a rational "material" quest, the excesses of other passions. The passion for gain has taken over from the excessive pursuit of glory.

Actually, the thinkers of the seventeenth and eighteenth centuries had never thought of reason, rationality, and economic interests on equal terms. The "eclipse of reason," or the forgetting of a collective rationality (common good) greater than the purely subjective aspirations of survival and well-being, is a more recent phenomenon, which is associated with the development of capitalism in the industrial era.[6] The terminological change of the pejorative concept of "passion of gain" into a simple "interest," and then into notions of "reason" and "rationality," has culminated in the current widespread use of econometric models. The former "compensatory passion," capable of overcoming the ravages of honor and glory, eventually became a pure rationality underlying all human behavior: "Indeed, I have come to the position that the economic approach is a comprehensive one that is applicable to all human behavior."[7]

The anti-emotional model of rationality has led us to ignore the pacifying role of certain emotions. Nevertheless, various theories of peace processes have reintroduced the idea of emotional control over dominating or sadistic passions. Freud believes that civilization presupposes a "consciousness of guilt," which is the result of the weakening of the instinct of aggression by the supervision of an inner body, the superego.[8] He also indicates an alternative path to peace through the mobilization of Eros, suggesting that a sense of community can mitigate violence.[9] In his analysis of the civilizing process, Norbert Elias points out that, along with the monopolization of power, certain feelings (shame, repugnance), values (dignity, self-restraint), and social behaviors (courtesy, manners) helped make societies more peaceful.[10] Steven Pinker affirms that empathy is among "the better angels of our nature," that is, among the factors that have contributed to decreasing violence and increasing altruism and cooperation throughout history.[11]

Another alternative and less broadly shared philosophical tradition has highlighted the possible role of empathy and compassion in the pacification of social relations. Rousseau, for instance, states that man is not "greedy" and "thirsty" for power by nature, and that mercy can work as an obstacle to violence: "Pity is a natural sentiment, which, by moderating in every individual the activity of self-love, contributes to the mutual preservation of the whole species. It is this pity which hurries us without reflection to the assistance of those we see in distress."[12] Adam Smith, who is originally regarded as the founding father of economic interest, admits that the principle of "sympathy," which is in the human heart, allows for the existence of social ties and moderate judgments.[13]

The most recent research confirms that human beings have some kind of original capacity for empathy, regardless of their material interests.[14] This capacity is particularly high when an individual feels a similarity with an actual or alleged victim of physical violence. In one experiment, nearly 80 percent of individuals feeling a "similarity" with the victim were willing to help a "friend" who was apparently receiving electrical shocks, even if this victim could easily escape from such a situation.[15] This experiment demonstrates, first, that empathy and compassion are possible, and, second, that these feelings are "channeled," in different degrees, by the recognition of the Other, in that one identifies the Other as one's own Self.

Recognition—or nonrecognition—can take two forms, which we treat in the following sections: the hero-protector narrative, and the minimization of status or existence of the Other.

SELF-RECOGNITION AS A HERO-PROTECTOR

The hero-protector narrative is dichotomous, insofar as the Self is made into the hero, whereas the Other is construed as evil.[16] Four ideal-type characters structure this narrative.

First, the "victim" is any—often a collective—actor who remains passive and is the target of illegitimate aggression by others. He or she is portrayed as not having caused the suffered aggression and as not able to protect himself or herself against it. The victim is generally characterized with attributes such as "innocent," "weak," "suffering," and "oppressed."

Second, the "aggressor" is essentially a perpetrator who pursues his or her advantage without any respect for the life and the rights of others. The aggressor is portrayed as initiating acts of oppression or violence without prior provocation or legitimate cause. He or she is often characterized with attributes such as "evil," "tyrannical," "manipulative," "despicable," and "cynical."

Third, the "hero" is an actor that most often (but not necessarily) emerges from the victim's group. He or she reacts to illegitimate aggression out of a sense of moral obligation and not in the pursuit of egoistic interests. He or she defends the victim and then sets out to eliminate the source of aggression, even if this implies breaking moral rules that would apply in a normative order. In doing so, the hero puts his or her own life at stake and is thus ready to sacrifice himself or herself in order to protect the victim. The hero is often characterized as having a "spirit of sacrifice" and qualities such as "courage," "strength," and "selflessness." Of course, the "hero" is an ideal-type character, whose behavior can contribute to confirm his or her role, or not. For example, the use of air strikes, including with drones, to avoid putting boots on the ground and endangering himself or herself can compromise his or her image. Not surprisingly, the use of drones has been strongly criticized, as mentioned by Fisk and Ramos in chapter 4 of this volume.

And fourth, the "coward" is an actor who, despite having a moral responsibility toward the victim, does not do what is morally right, out of fear for his or her life and material status. He or she is essentially interested in the pursuit of his or her own narrow interests and generally chooses the side of the materially "strongest" actor. As a result, the coward, instead of helping the hero protect the victim, either remains passive or supports the aggressor. In doing so, he or she becomes a legitimate target of the hero's revenge. The coward is often characterized by attributes such as "treacherous," "lazy," "egoistic," "degenerate," "unreliable," and "servile."

In the case of the hero-protector narrative, the acceptance of war is triggered by two factors: a feeling of nonrecognition *of the Self*, and the neutralization of empathy by the nonrecognition *of the Other*. Two oppositions produce such a double effect: the sharp opposition between an innocent victim and an aggressor, and that between the coward and the hero-protector.

THE MINIMIZATION OF THE OTHER

Another narrative linked to nonrecognition and international violence is characterized by the minimization of the Other. In substance, this second narrative "banalizes" and "minimizes" the opponent as well as the use of violence. Although the narrative of minimization can be a manipulation tool for the "elite," it also serves to frame the minds of decision makers.

Existential Minimization

Minimization allows for disengagement and the absence of emotional involvement in the existence of the Other.[17] In the most basic *existential* sense, minimization means denial of the Other's *agency*. Others are not "identified" as actually existing as free actors, because they do not really affect one's own life in a visible manner.[18]

More subtly, minimization of agency can be presented as an "objectification" of the Other (in the sense of not recognizing the Other as a being with needs and capabilities for reaction). This latter form of minimization is also referred to as "reification," which is the act of considering the Other as a mere object or an inanimate thing. Hence, this purely instrumental disposition toward the Other is conditioned by a vision of the world that involves the reification of the Self and the Other, and also the trivialization of violence.

Montesquieu, for instance, despite praising trade for its contribution to peace, blames it for the "monetization of all human relations and the loss of hospitality and of other 'moral virtues.'"[19] This reification can occur with the penetration of market mechanisms in all spheres of society (Marx, Lukacs), along with the increasing technicality of the world and the triumph of instrumental reason (Adorno, Horkheimer).

For Adam Smith, one's sympathy for the Other is selective and depends mainly on the density of a given relationship. Of course, many factors can be responsible for this density, such as geography, nationality, and religion. More generally, in-group dynamics can lead to a lack of consideration for out-group members. After the September 11, 2001, terrorist attacks on the United States, the lives of those who died were presented in detail in daily news, and therefore they were felt very close.[20] In contrast, the pure abstraction of the Other facilitates violence. Everything happens as though the Other had never lived.

According to Christophe Wasinski's study of civilians killed by US forces in Iraq and Afghanistan, the technical discourse on "clean" war is likely to produce an abstract, distanced, and reified representation of the Other, thereby establishing a process of nonrecognition that legitimizes the use of armed violence.[21]

The probability of aggression between political units is higher when there is an "affective" distance between them, and especially when each side believes that the other, insofar as it is politically or religiously different, represents a threat in terms of identity. In fact, empirical research on the causes of war suggests that states with the same political system are much less likely to engage in war than those with different or opposing political organizations. As stated by Doyle, "Even though liberal states have become involved in numerous wars with nonliberal states, constitutionally secure liberal states have yet to engage in war with one another."[22] Peace between democracies, however, may be due not so much to the inherent properties of these political structures as to the perception of dealing with a "similar" Other. The awareness of sharing a similar vision of the world becomes especially significant when it is challenged—that is, in the face of ideological heterogeneity, as in the Cold War. When there is no identification with the Other, the use of armed force is compatible with the valued image of the Self and with the definition of interests that disregard the Other.[23]

Minimization of Status

Minimization of the Other can also be partial and refer to the "reduction" of *status*. The *existence* of the Other can be recognized, but, compared with the Self, the Other is perceived as being hierarchically or morally inferior. According to Judith Butler, interpretive frameworks regulate the influence of affects and indignation. They are expressed in life's "grievability," that is, in the degree in which a life is considered worth weeping over. Thus, "a hierarchy of grief could no doubt be enumerated."[24]

The perception of the Other's inferiority weakens the feeling of compassion, whereas the perception of the Other's superiority strengthens it: "The man of rank and distinction . . . is observed by all the world. Everybody is eager to look at him, and to conceive, at least by sympathy, that joy and exultation with which his circumstances naturally inspire him."[25] The master of Hegel is not responsive to the needs of the "slave," and the Other exists only as a support for an idealized image of the Self. Hegel suggests that the unbridled pursuit of the "consumption" of goods—that is, the master's pure consumption (*reine Genuss*)—implies a negation of the Other.

The actor's power and legitimacy are strong regulators of status. The violence of a "recognized" state is perceived as less shocking than the violence of a less recognized or "irregular" actor. Most of the time, a depreciation of status precedes the outbreak of war. Contempt for enemy regimes, considered as inferior, and its leaders encourages other states to defend their interests through the use of force. Demonization of the Other makes it easier to justify war and neutralize the paralyzing effect of compassion.

Minimization of status could also be seen in dynastic quarrels based on a barely concealed contempt of monarchs for their subjects and for those of rival powers. The same can be said of colonial wars; often attributed to economic interests or social imperialism, they imply a disregard for subjected populations, though Holeindre's argument in chapter 7 of this volume regarding postcolonial responsibility offers an alternative claim.

RECOGNITION OF THE PAIN OF OTHERS

After having made a general presentation of the main aspects of recognition theory, we now concentrate on two case studies of humanitarian intervention in which the question of (non)recognition was a crucial point. We have chosen these cases for various reasons. First, their "outcomes" are completely different. In the case of Rwanda, foreign intervention came too late, as empathy for the victims of the genocide took too long to emerge. As for the Libyan case, there was not only a fast recognition of the plight of the potential victims but also a denial of recognition regarding the Libyan authorities—especially Gaddafi—which were supposed to protect the population. Second, each case fits a model of recognition—or lack thereof—presented in this chapter. While Rwanda illustrates the consequences of minimization of the Other, Libya epitomizes the model of the hero-protector. Finally, each of them represents a particular period in the history of humanitarian interventions. The episode in Rwanda happened in the aftermath of the Cold War, where new contours for these interventions were being defined. The context of the Libyan crisis was different since the international community had already gained some experience in these interventions and had started trying to develop a normative framework for them. We point the reader to other chapters of this volume—for example, Hehir (chapter 1), Holeindre (chapter 7), and Ramel (chapter 12)—that touch on the concepts of the Responsibility to Protect, postcolonial responsibility, and human security and how they have been invoked to justify humanitarian interventions.

As will be seen, humanitarian interventions are a little different from wars regarding the consequences of (non)recognition, although the theory can be applied. Recognition between two countries tends to preserve international peace, while recognition by a country or an international organization of the suffering of another country may lead to conflict. Conversely, nonrecognition between two countries may lead to conflict, but nonrecognition of the suffering of the population of another country tends to preserve international peace (to the detriment of the protection of human rights). Actually, the equation depends in large measure on what is at stake—peace or human rights. In the humanitarian field, "good" emotions, such as compassion, can lead to violence in the form of military intervention.

In our research for the two case studies, we focused our attention on the main actors for the debate on recognition—international organizations such as the United Nations, key countries such as France and the United States, and the press. In spite of the importance of international organizations, nongovernmental organizations (NGOs), and the press, there is no automatic link between the diffusion of news about human suffering and the decision to intervene. Actually, even though being aware of a crisis is an essential first step, it must be accompanied by identification with the Other and the sentiment that one is responsible for his fate. Recognition must be so strong that the Other is nearly perceived as an extension of the Self. We could, for instance, advance the hypothesis that although the campaign "Save Darfur," cited by Hehir in chapter 1 of this volume, achieved the purpose of drawing attention to the crisis in that region, it might not have established a recognition link between the Self and the Other.

It is not our intention to make any moral judgment, but simply to identify factors that led actors to opt for certain courses of action instead of other ones. In order to ensure accuracy of the information, we tried to check different sources. Of course, it is impossible to obtain complete information on the two cases, especially because many documents remain classified; nevertheless, we believe that we offer a fair view of the question of (non)recognition.

Rwanda

The international community took too long to grasp the magnitude of what was going on in Rwanda and to react to the genocide because most of the time it looked at the country through the fog of minimization. In the United States, one of the factors that contributed to minimization was geographical distance, which helped create a psychological gap between the potential hero-protector and the victims. In addition, there were very few Americans of Rwandan origin, and they did not have the capacity to organize themselves and lobby for the causes of that country.

According to Bill Clinton, who considers this episode as "one of the regrets of my presidency," the United States was "so preoccupied with Bosnia, with the memory of Somalia just six months old, and with opposition in Congress to military deployments *in faraway places* not vital to our national interests that neither I nor anyone on my foreign policy team adequately focused on sending troops to stop the slaughter" (emphasis added).[26] Several weeks into the genocide, then–secretary of state Warren Christopher needed the help of a map to locate Rwanda.[27] Geographical and psychological distance could be seen in the press as well. Edgar Roskis, for instance, cites a correspondent saying that Rwanda was in "the middle of nowhere."[28] In sum, this distance contributed to preventing the Self from identifying with the Other and feeling responsible for him or her.

Another factor in the minimization process was relational distance, which can be seen in the dichotomy between in-groups and out-groups. In this case, the lives of in-group members tend to be more valued. The commander of the UN mission to Rwanda, Gen. Roméo Dallaire, asserts that "we in the developed world act in a way that suggests we believe that our lives are worth more than the lives of other citizens of the planet."[29] According to the general, an American officer told him that "one American casualty is worth about 85,000 Rwandan dead."[30] In his memoir, Clinton recalled that his main concern was to protect American citizens in Rwanda and get them out of the country to safety.[31] The Republican opposition did not think otherwise. Senator Bob Dole, the minority leader, said, "The Americans are out, and . . . that ought to be the end of it."[32] The same holds true for other countries.[33]

The dichotomy between in-groups and out-groups was also present in the press. A French journalist recalls that he was sent to Rwanda with specific instructions to cover only the withdrawal of foreign citizens and not stories of "blacks killing themselves."[34] In an analysis of articles published by American news magazines in 1994, Melissa Wall found a tendency toward the minimization of Rwandans' status. The media portrayed them as "little better than animals, ranging from the barbaric to the helpless and pathetic." She refers to animal metaphors such as "mad stampede" of refugees and "human swarm," and also to barbarian imagery, according to which Rwanda was the "Central Africa slaughterhouse," where bodies were "dumped like garbage."[35] Of course, this kind of coverage did not aid in arousing any sympathy for Rwandans. If they had little regard for their own lives, why would other countries think otherwise?

Attributing events to fate was another form of minimization. Not surprisingly, one of the most common words used to refer to the genocide is "tragedy." In fact, what is implicit is not only that bad things happen but also that they run out of control and become unavoidable, as in Greek tragedies. The only thing to do would be to endure it. As Samantha Power notes, US officials talked about conflicts in that African region as something regrettable but not unusual. As a result, human consequences were not duly taken into account. She quotes an American official stating that "these people do this from time to time."[36] President François Mitterrand of France is alleged to have said something similar: "In those countries, a genocide is not too important."[37]

The fatalistic approach can also be found in American newspapers. According to the *Washington Post*, "not much" could be done for Rwanda. For the *New York Times*, "the world [had] little choice but to stand aside and hope for the best."[38] In the same vein, Melissa Wall says that American magazines portrayed events as "beyond human control" by making use of "metaphors comparing the violence to an explosion or conflagration" and concluding that "Rwanda is helpless against its demons."[39] According to the historian Yves Ternon, French newspapers also resorted to expressions such as "blind violence" and "killing madness," as though the genocide was neither planned nor intentionally put into practice.[40]

Linked to this perception—and to the minimization of status—is the ethnic interpretation, which gained ground to the detriment of a closer political assessment of the situation.[41] In her analysis, Wall found out that magazine articles attributed violence to "irrational tribalism." The words "ethnic" and "tribal" appear fifty-nine times in the articles, whereas the word "political" appears only twenty-five times. Wall also identifies expressions such as "tribal meltdown" and "spasm of ethnic violence."[42] To the historians Yves Ternon and Jean-Pierre Chrétien, most French journalists followed the ethnic narrative in their coverage of the genocide.[43] Jean-François Dupaquier offers other examples of ethnic stereotypes published in the French press, including allusions to the recurrent "interethnic massacres" and the "secular antagonism between the two tribes."[44] French television also referred to the "ancestral fight" between the "rival ethnic groups."[45] This ethnic narrative contributed to increasing the distance between Rwandans and those who were able to intervene. There could be no identification with ethnic groups that "killed each other."

Another factor that may explain minimization is the cognitive gap—that is, the difficulty people experienced in making sense of the situation, understanding its dimensions, and acting accordingly. As reported by Gen. Wesley Clark, then director of strategic plans and policy for the Joint Chiefs of Staff at the Pentagon, nobody could give him sensible information about the political consequences of the assassination of Rwanda's president, Juvénal Habyarimana. Actually, people would ask, "Is it Hutu and Tutsi or Tutu and Hutsi?"[46]

One Democratic congresswoman said that "I don't know whether the Hutus or the Tutsis were correct. . . . A lot of people were like me."[47]

The general public did not receive enough information either. In the first weeks, "only a handful of international reporters were on the ground."[48] So, at the very beginning, television channels would resort to archival images.[49] Even human rights organizations did not start alerting the public to the genocide until two weeks after its outbreak.[50] The problem was not only the absence of images but also the way in which the situation was reported, as Wall demonstrates in her above-mentioned analysis.

With regard to the cognitive gap, the United Nations was not in a much better situation. In his first visit to Rwanda, General Dallaire was not given intelligence data. According to one of his aides, "We flew Rwanda with a Michelin road map, a copy of the Arusha agreements [which aimed at putting an end to the civil war], and that was it."[51] The general himself acknowledges that when he was invited to the mission, he "didn't know where Rwanda was or exactly what kind of trouble the country was in."[52]

Another problem of the crisis was the bureaucratic way it was handled. According to Power, the United States concentrated too much on the bureaucratic relations between states and on the agreements reached in Arusha and did not pay sufficient heed to the population's fate. "Abstract" state questions took precedence over real personal dramas, which tended to be minimized or not even considered.

Senior and even midlevel officials did not show much interest in Rwanda, which was relegated to bureaucratic "routine." At the US Department of Defense, an official who tried to put it on a priority list was told, "If something happens in Rwanda-Burundi, we don't care."[53] When the issue was brought up in a conversation with the Belgian foreign minister, Christopher is reported to have said, "I have other responsibilities."[54] This was also reflected in the instructions to US officials: "Delegation is not authorized to agree to the characterization of any specific incident as genocide or to agree to any formulation that indicates that all killings in Rwanda are genocide."[55] The reason for these instructions was spelled out in a discussion paper prepared some weeks earlier: "Genocide finding could commit [the US government] to actually 'do something.'"[56]

UN Security Council deliberations—or the lack thereof—left Dallaire "perplexed."[57] Even after the international community decided to act, signs of minimization persisted. According to Power, it took the United States a month to provide the UN with military equipment because of bureaucratic haggling.[58] As Hutus organized the slaughter and Tutsis started being killed, the UN reiterated its instructions to Dallaire that his troops should not take part in combat except for self-defense.[59] All this was in sharp contrast to the prompt action of the countries that had evacuated their citizens from Rwanda in a few days, and to the permission given to Dallaire, if need be, to go beyond his mandate to facilitate the evacuation of foreign citizens.[60]

Rwanda proved to be a case of minimization. Violence in the country came to be considered trivial and inevitable, which "justified" an attitude of disengagement and aloofness. Actually, to many people even the distinction between the roles of "aggressor" and "victim" became blurred. Very little was known about Rwandans' lives and, for a long while, they remained low in the scale of "grievability." Distance imposed itself in many ways—geographical, political, psychological, emotional—and made it harder for sympathy to emerge.

Minimization is even more puzzling if we take into account that Western countries like to regard themselves as protectors of human rights. The promotion of these rights is also a key element in their respective foreign policies. Although it would not be hard to present the Self as the hero who would save defenseless victims from the evil Other, the image of the hero-protector was not evoked.

According to Brent Steele, when the "sense of self-identity is dislocated, an actor will seek to reestablish routines that can, once again, consistently maintain self-identity."[61] Not surprisingly, in the future this genocide would play an important role in those countries' policy formulation. Any crisis reminiscent of that in Rwanda would give rise to a debate on the need for intervention by the "hero-protector." Libya is a case in point.

Libya

One aspect of recognition theory refers to the attitude toward the elite or the leaders of a country where the population is suffering and is not being protected. The intervention in Libya can be studied as a case of nonrecognition of its leadership and of recognition of the fate of the Libyan population, especially that of Benghazi, which might have suffered a massacre if loyalist troops had taken control of the city.

Actually, even his own people stopped recognizing Gaddafi's leadership, which became apparent with the advent of the Arab Spring. Facing domestic rebellion, he was about to attack Benghazi when the UN Security Council authorized the use of force to protect the civilian population. During the crisis, Cameron, Obama, and Sarkozy published an article saying that they deemed it "impossible to imagine a future for Libya with Gaddafi in power."[62]

Echoes from Rwanda could be heard all along the Libyan crisis. However, contrary to what had occurred in Rwanda, this time everybody paid heed to what was going on in Libya. Governments, the United Nations, NGOs, and the press stressed that human rights were being violated and that genocide could take place. To a great extent, the Libyan government contributed to dramatizing the situation by making use of rhetoric that portrayed the adversaries as despicable people who deserved neither consideration nor mercy. In fact, the Libyan authorities minimized the existence and the status of their own people.

Gaddafi decided to stick to power and did not show any empathy toward the protesters, to whom he referred as "rats and cockroaches," the same language used by the Hutus during the Rwandan genocide.[63] In television broadcasts, he threatened to "show no mercy to collaborators" and to "cleanse Libya house by house."[64] One of his sons said that the regime would fight "to the last man and woman and bullet."[65] And he added that if the opposition insisted on fighting against his father's regime, "rivers of blood would run through Libya."[66]

The presence of the media and NGOs on the ground contributed to drawing the attention of the world to the violations under way. If in Rwanda there were only a handful of foreign journalists, in Libya the world press played a key role in spreading the news of the protests. The government reacted by harassing and arresting some journalists, but the intimidation did not work.

To be sure, the diffusion of these events by itself would not automatically lead to intervention. This was only one step toward recognition. It is worth noting that the Libyan crisis coincided with—and actually was part of—the Arab Spring. A considerable proportion of the international community upheld the same values as this movement and identified with those who were fighting for them in Libya. In addition, contrary to what had happened in Rwanda, events were never treated in the abstract, as many personal stories were told and published. Here are two examples:

> Safai Eddine Hilal al-Sharif, a 41-year-old father of five who worked as a technician in an oil company in Ras Lanouf, was arrested at his home on 24 January 2011. Since then, his family has been unable to obtain any information about him or even an acknowledgement of his detention by the authorities in Tripoli.[67]

> A relative of 14-year-old schoolboy Hassan Mohammad al-Qata'ni told Amnesty International: "I haven't slept since he's gone missing, nobody in my family has slept; we are so worried; he is just a kid; we don't know what to do, where to look for him, who to turn to for help."[68]

In public addresses, political leaders emphasized the gravity of the situation and the importance of intervening. In their article, for instance, Cameron,

Obama, and Sarkozy said that "the people of Libya are still suffering terrible horrors at Qaddafi's hands each and every day. . . . The evidence of disappearances and abuses grows daily."[69] Gaddafi's record was another point that was highlighted in the process of legitimation of the humanitarian intervention. He himself and other members of his government contributed to this process by making use of a vocabulary that not only despised their adversaries but also dehumanized them.

In a conversation with the National Transitional Council, which would soon be recognized as the new Libyan government, Sarkozy argued that Gaddafi had lost all legitimacy since he was attacking—instead of protecting—his own people.[70] Libyan diplomats resigned their posts and accused Gaddafi of hiring mercenaries to commit genocide against the Libyan population.[71] In addition, journalists, government officials, and even the chief prosecutor of the International Criminal Court accused Gaddafi of ordering "the rape of hundreds of women."[72]

One of the factors behind the attention given to events in Libya was the fear of repeating the mistakes made in Rwanda. This fear has certainly contributed to the process of legitimation of the intervention. According to then–secretary of state Hillary Clinton, "We learned a lot in the 1990s. We saw what happened in Rwanda."[73] In the same vein, Anne-Marie Slaughter, then director of policy planning for the State Department, said that "the international community cannot stand by and watch the massacre of Libyan protesters. In Rwanda we watched. In Kosovo we acted."[74] Contrary to what had occurred in the discussions on Rwanda, this time important members of Congress—such as senators Lieberman, Kerry, and McCain—supported intervention, arguing that the United States should not make the same mistake of the 1990s.[75] Even General Dallaire compared Libya with Rwanda and alluded to Gaddafi's "genocidal threats."[76]

This is reminiscent of Ramel's interpretation of Judith Shklar's "liberalism of fear," which he puts forward in chapter 12 of this volume and elsewhere.[77] Liberalism in this case would be instinctive rather than rational, and depend on "an emotion (fear) and not on reason."[78] Shklar emphasizes the fear of cruelty, "the most evil of all evils," which could be perpetrated by any state against any individual.[79] Therefore, recognition can arise from the universal emotion of fear.

The intervention in Libya illustrates the power of moral mechanisms, crystallizing the contrast between the figures of innocent victims (children, women, the elderly, ordinary men) and that of the evil aggressor who knows no compassion. The underlying alternative in this narrative framing is either intervene, playing the role of the hero-protector, or lose your dignity, becoming a coward.

According to Obama: "To brush aside America's responsibility as a leader and—more profoundly—our responsibilities to our fellow human beings under such circumstances would have been a betrayal of who we are. Some nations may be able to turn a blind eye to atrocities in other countries. The United States of America is different. And as president, I refused to wait for the images of slaughter and mass graves before taking action."[80]

The president of the United States is telling Americans that nonintervention is inconsistent with their self-identity ("a betrayal of who we are"). And, as stated by Steele, "actions that contradict self-identity produce shame."[81] Even the vocabulary regarding the intervention in Libya reminds us of the hero-protector narrative. For instance, deliberations in the Security Council were influenced by the principle of the "Responsibility to Protect," adopted by the World Summit in 2005. Moreover, NATO's operation itself was named "Unified Protector."

Obama referred to Benghazi as "a city nearly the size of Charlotte."[82] This comparison certainly contributed to reducing geographical and psychological gaps by helping people not only figure out the size of Benghazi and its population, but also imagine this city as another Charlotte, that is, as an American city. And it enabled them to think of its population not as unknown people but as people similar to those living in an American city.

In opposition to what had happened in Rwanda, this time the United Nations reacted swiftly. The General Assembly suspended Libya's membership rights in the Human Rights Commission. No country had ever been suspended before, not even those with bad human rights records. Moreover, the resolution, cosponsored by seventy-two countries, was adopted by consensus.

The Security Council also made two extremely important decisions. The first one was the adoption of Resolution 1970 (2011), which referred the situation in Libya to the International Criminal Court. Later on, the court's prosecutor accused Gaddafi and other members of his regime of crimes against humanity and requested arrest warrants, which were approved by the judges.

The other decision was the adoption of Security Council Resolution 1973 (2011), which authorized member states to use military force or, in the traditional Security Council language for these cases, to "take all necessary measures" in order to protect civilians. Two days after the adoption of the resolution, NATO countries launched their intervention.

CONCLUSION

Although we concentrate on recognition factors to explain humanitarian (non)intervention, we do not imply that material interests are irrelevant—on the contrary, as argued by Hehir in chapter 1 of this volume, they play an important role in the decision-making process. What we have attempted to demonstrate is the usefulness of going beyond material interests, because they cannot offer a full picture of humanitarian interventions. They must be analyzed in conjunction with recognition factors, such as the minimization of status or existence of the Other, and the self-attribution of a hero-protector role. Instead of an either-or approach, we should pay attention to both interest *and* recognition.

As we have tried to show with the Rwandan and Libyan cases, recognition theory is crucial to fully understand the mechanisms and logics of intervention. A leader is not likely to legitimize intervention if he or she puts emotions aside and adopts the rhetoric of cold interest. To be successful, the leader must galvanize "positive emotions" within his or her own people because sympathy is "selective" and may not emerge easily. As has been seen, triggering or disabling mechanisms of (non)recognition play a key role in deciding whether to intervene.

In conclusion, we believe that recognition theory has a compelling explanatory potential in our objective of understanding the dynamics of humanitarian interventions. Paying attention to recognition factors allows us to rise above the traditional reasons of the *homo politicus* or the *homo economicus*. By including the *homo symbolicus*—that is, by incorporating emotional and moral aspects in the debate—we can understand in a more clear way the process of legitimation and selectivity of humanitarian interventions. And further research on other cases can help shed light on the decision-making process leading to these (non)interventions.

NOTES

1. G. W. F Hegel, *Grundlinien der Philosophie des Rechts* (Hamburg: Meiner, 2013), 331–40.

2. Erik Ringmar, *Identity, Interest, Action* (Cambridge: Cambridge University Press, 1996); Alexander Wendt, *Social Theory of International Politics* (Cambridge: Cambridge University Press, 1999); Barry O'Neill, *Honor, Symbols, and War* (Ann Arbor: University of Michigan Press, 1999); Axel Honneth, *Reification* (Oxford: Oxford University Press, 2012); Thomas Lindemann, *Causes of War: The Struggle for Recognition* (Colchester, UK: ECPR Press, 2010); Thomas Lindemann and Erik Ringmar, eds., *The International Politics of Recognition* (New York: Routledge, 2012); and Reinhard Wolf, "Respect and Disrespect in International Relations," *International Theory* 3, no. 1 (2011): 105–42.

3. Carl von Clausewitz, *On War* (Princeton, NJ: Princeton University Press, 1989).

4. James Der Derian, "The War of Networks," *Theory and Event* 5, no. 4 (2002): 5, https://muse.jhu.edu/article/32644.

5. Thomas Hobbes, *Leviathan* (New Haven, CT: Yale University Press, 2010), 13–14.

6. Mark Horkheimer, *Zur Kritik der instrumentellen Vernunft* (Frankfurt: Fischer, 2007).

7. Gary Becker, "The Economic Approach to Human Behavior," in *Rational Choice*, ed. Jon Elster (New York: New York University Press, 1986), 112.

8. Sigmund Freud, *Civilization and Its Discontents* (New York: W. W. Norton, 1985).

9. Sigmund Freud, *Why War? A Correspondence between Albert Einstein and Sigmund Freud* (New York: Sequoia Free Press, 2010).

10. Norbert Elias, *The Civilizing Process* (London: Blackwell, 2000).

11. Steven Pinker, *The Better Angels of Our Nature* (New York: Penguin, 2011).

12. Jean-Jacques Rousseau, *Discourse on the Origin of Inequality* (Oxford: Oxford University Press, 2009), 32.

13. Adam Smith, *The Theory of Moral Sentiments* (New York: Kessinger, 2004; orig. pub. 1759).

14. Miles Hewstone, Wolfgang Stroebe, and Klaus Jonas, *An Introduction to Social Psychology*, 5th ed. (New York: Wiley, 2012).

15. Daniel Batson, *Altruism in Humans* (New York: Oxford University Press, 2011).

16. John W. Dower, *War without Mercy: Race and Power in the Pacific War* (New York: Pantheon, 1987); and Theo Farrell, "Memory, Imagination and War," *History* 87, no. 285 (2002): 61–73, doi:10.1111/1468–229X.00214.

17. Erving Goffman, *The Presentation of Self in Everyday Life* (New York: Peter Smith, 1999; orig. pub. 1956).

18. Jens Bartelson, "Three Concepts of Recognition," *International Theory* 5, no. 1 (2013): 107–29.

19. Albert Hirschman, *The Passion and the Interests* (Princeton, NJ: Princeton University Press, 1997), 80.

20. Judith Butler, *Precarious Life* (London: Verso, 2004).

21. Christophe Wasinski, "Reconnaître l'absence et dire les responsabilités," *Culture et Conflits* 87 (2012): 97–118.

22. Michael W. Doyle, "Kant, Liberal Legacies, and Foreign Affairs Part 1," *Philosophy and Public Affairs* 12, no. 3 (1983): 213.

23. Wendt, *Social Theory*; and Lindemann, *Causes of War*, 36.

24. Butler, *Precarious Life*, 32.

25. Smith, *Theory of Moral Sentiments.*

26. Bill Clinton, *My Life* (New York: Alfred A. Knopf, 2004), 593.

27. Samantha Power, "Bystanders to Genocide," *The Atlantic*, September 2001, www.theatlantic.com/magazine/archive/2001/09/bystanders-to-genocide/304571/.

28. Edgar Roskis, "A Genocide without Images: White Film Noirs," in *The Media and the Rwanda Genocide*, ed. Allan Thompson (London: Pluto Press, 2007), 238.

29. Roméo Dallaire, *Shake Hands with the Devil: The Failure of Humanity in Rwanda* (London: Arrow Books, 2004), 522.

30. Samantha Power, *A Problem from Hell: America and the Age of Genocide* (New York: Harper Perennial, 2002), 380–81.

31. Clinton, *My Life*, 593.

32. Power, *Problem from Hell*, 352.

33. Roméo Dallaire, "The Media Dichotomy," in *The Media and the Rwanda Genocide*, ed. Allan Thompson (London: Pluto Press, 2007), 13.

34. Philippe Boisserie and Danielle Birck, "Retour sur images," *Les Temps Modernes* 583 (1995): 201.

35. Melissa Wall, "An Analysis of News Magazine Coverage of the Rwanda Crisis in the United States," in *The Media and the Rwanda Genocide*, ed. Allan Thompson (London: Pluto Press, 2007), 267–68.

36. Power, *Problem from Hell*, 351.

37. Gérard Prunier, *Rwanda: le génocide* (Paris: Editions Dagorno, 1997), vii; Boubacar Boris Diop, "La France au banc des accusés," *Courier International*, April 8, 2004, www.courrierinternational.com/article/2004/04/08/dans-ces-pays-la-un-genocide-n-est-pas-trop-important; and Chris McGreal, "France's Shame?" *The Guardian*, January 11, 2007, www.theguardian.com/world/2007/jan/11/rwanda.insideafrica.

38. Power, *Problem from Hell*, 374; and Nicholas J. Wheeler, *Saving Strangers: Humanitarian Intervention in International Society* (Oxford: Oxford University Press, 2000), 229.

39. Wall, "Analysis," 266.

40. Laure Coret and Francois-Xavier Verschave, *L'horreur qui nous prend au visage: L'Etat français et le génocide* (Paris: Karthala, 2005), 169.

41. Faustin Rutembesa, "Écrits sur le génocide des Tutsi: Constat et perspectives de recherches," *Revue d'histoire de la Shoah* 190 (2009): 107.

42. Wall, "Analysis."

43. Coret and Verschave, *L'horreur qui*, 169, 354.

44. Jean-Francois Dupaquier, "Propagande noir et désinformation au cœur de l'engagement militaire français," *Cités* 57 (2014): 45, 47.

45. Danielle Birck, "La télévision et le Rwanda ou le génocide déprogrammé," *Les Temps Modernes* 583 (1995): 184.

46. Power, *Problem from Hell*, 330.

47. Ibid., 376.

48. Dallaire, "Media Dichotomy," 15.

49. Nathan Réra, *Rwanda, entre crise morale et malaise esthétique: Les médias, la photographie et le cinéma à l'épreuve du génocide des Tutsi (1994–2014)* (Paris: Les Presses du Réel, 2014), 43.

50. Alan J. Kuperman, "How the Media Missed the Rwanda Genocide," in *The Media and the Rwanda Genocide*, ed. Allan Thompson (London: Pluto Press, 2007), 238.

51. Power, *Problem from Hell*, 340.

52. Dallaire, *Shake Hands*, 43.

53. Power, *Problem from Hell*, 342.

54. Ibid., 352.

55. Power, "Bystanders."

56. Ibid.

57. Dallaire, *Shake Hands*, 351.

58. Power, *Problem from Hell*, 380.

59. Dallaire, *Shake Hands*, 146, 229; and Wheeler, *Saving Strangers*, 215.

60. Françoise Bouchet Saulnier, "L'ONU et le Génocide des Rwandais Tutsis: Politique Virtuelle et Intelligence Artificielle à l'Épreuve du Monde Réel," *Les Temps Modernes* 583 (1995): 278; and Joel Kotek, "Les leçons du Rwanda: Un Casque bleu peut-il se muer en témoin moral?" *Revue d'histoire de la Shoah* 190 (2009): 124.

61. Brent Steele, *Ontological Security in International Relations* (London: Routledge, 2008), 3.

62. David Cameron, Barack Obama, and Nicolas Sarkozy, "Libya's Pathway to Peace," *International Herald Tribune*, April 14, 2011.

63. Jean-Paul Ford Rojas, "Muammar Gaddafi in His Own Words," *The Telegraph*, October 20, 2011.

64. Sudarsan Raghavan, "Libyans Brace for Gaddafi Offensive in Rebel Stronghold of Benghazi," *Washington Post*, March 17, 2011; and Hebah Saleh and Andrew England, "Defiant Gaddafi Vows Fight to Death," *Financial Times*, February 23, 2011.

65. "Libya: Amnesty International Calls on UN Security Council and Arab League to Act Decisively on Libyan Crimes," Amnesty International, February 22, 2011.

66. David Kirkpatrick, "Qaddafi's Grip Falters as His Forces Take On Protesters," *New York Times*, February 21, 2011.

67. "Libya: Ghaddafi's Forces Are Carrying Out Campaign of Disappearances Inside Libya to Crush Growing Opposition, Says Amnesty International in New Report," Amnesty International, March 29, 2011.

68. Ibid.

69. Cameron, Obama, and Sarkozy, "Libya's Pathway."

70. Bernard-Henri Lévy, *La guerre sans l'aimer* (Paris: Grasset, 2011), 108; and Dirk Vandewalle, *A History of Modern Libya* (New York: Cambridge University Press, 2012), 204.

71. Lindsey Hilsum, *Sandstorm: Libya from Gaddafi to Revolution* (London: Faber & Faber, 2012), 188; Ethan Chorin, *Exit the Colonel: The Hidden History of the Libyan Revolution* (New York: PublicAffairs, 2012), 201; and Maximilian Forte, *Slouching towards Sirte: NATO's War on Libya and Africa* (Montreal: Baraka Books, 2012), 220, 238.

72. Forte, *Slouching towards Sirte*, 254; and Karen Leigh, "Rape in Libya: The Crime That Dare Not Speak Its Name," *Time Magazine*, June 9, 2011.

73. Stephen M. Walt, "More to Read about Libya," *Foreign Policy,* April 14, 2011, http://walt.foreignpolicy.com/posts/2011/04/14/more_to_read_about_Libya.

74. Ibid.

75. Christopher S. Chivvis and Jeffrey Martini, *Libya after Qaddafi: Lessons and Implications for the Future* (Santa Monica, CA: RAND Corporation, 2014), 37–38, www.rand.org/content/dam/rand/pubs/research_reports/RR500/RR577/RAND_RR577.pdf.

76. Forte, *Slouching towards Sirte*, 239.

77. Frederic Ramel, "Political Philosophy and Human Security in the Light of Judith Shklar's Writing," *Human Security Journal* 5 (2007): 28–35.

78. Ibid., 30.

79. Cited by Ramel, "Political Philosophy."

80. Barack Obama, "Remarks by the President in Address to the Nation on Libya," March 28, 2011, www.whitehouse.gov/the-press-office/2011/03/28/remarks-president-address-nation-libya.

81. Steele, *Ontological Security*, 135.

82. Forte, *Slouching towards Sirte*, 242.

3

The Moral Justification for Military Intervention

NIGEL BIGGAR

The costs and mixed results of the past decade's interventions in Iraq, Afghanistan, and Libya have given rise to fatigue and caution in the United States and the United Kingdom. Nevertheless, the crisis in Ukraine caused by Russia's military interference since 2013, together with the crisis in Syria and Iraq provoked by the expansion since 2014 of the Islamic State in Iraq and Syria (ISIS), has pushed demands for intervention back onto Western desks. In the light of recent experience, and building on my recent work in *In Defence of War*,[1] this chapter first of all establishes that, in the Christian tradition of thought, the basic form of a just war is that of the rescue of the innocent from grave injustice and not, as in the philosophical tradition stemming from Michael Walzer, that of national self-defense.[2] This has important ramifications for thinking about how sovereignty can be contested and what role force can play in doing so. The chapter then proceeds to consider five ethical questions raised by military intervention and to offer some answers along certain novel lines. First, when is an injustice grave enough to amount to a just cause for military intervention? Second, what role in assessing the ethics of intervention should national interest play? Third, given the impossibility of an exact and certain "calculation" of costs and benefits, how can we tell whether an intervention is proportionate? Fourth, can military intervention be efficacious? And fifth and finally, how much sense does it make to lay down the formulation of an "exit strategy" as a condition for proportionate intervention?

THE (CHRISTIAN) PARADIGM OF JUST WAR: INTERVENTION TO RESCUE THE INNOCENT FROM GRAVE INJUSTICE

There is a tendency in some reaches of moral philosophy to assume that the paradigm of a just war is national self-defense. Thus, in his excellent critique of what he takes to be just war thinking, David Rodin tells us that national defense "is central to modern international law"[3] and is "one of the lynchpins" of international law's intellectual progenitor, the just war theory.[4] Neither of these assertions is true. International law recognizes as legal *two* forms of the use of armed force—in national defense against attack *and* as authorized by the United Nations Security Council to enforce its resolutions. Rodin does not explain why he thinks that the first is more central than the second. More important, throughout its first millennium and up to the present day, Christian just war thinking has taken as the paradigm of just military action the rescue of the innocent neighbor from grave injustice—and this rescue may take either a defensive or aggressive form.[5] That is, "aggressive" military intervention for humanitarian purposes is prima facie more just, from a Christian point of view, than national self-defense.

That may be so, but why should anyone other than a Christian pay attention to what Christian just war thinking has to say? There are at least two reasons. First, there is no view from nowhere; there are only diverse confessions. What is more, nonreligious views—Aristotelian, Hobbesian, Kantian, Marxist, Nietzschean, and so on—are quite as plural and quite as conflicting as religious ones. Consequently, I do not believe in the possibility of secular language. That is to say, I do not believe that there is a set of terms that is neutral between rival worldviews, which members of a plural society should adopt when communicating with each other about public affairs. Nor do I believe that religious worldviews are irrational per se and that public discourse must be nonreligious in order to be rational.

How, then, can we communicate, and perhaps agree, in spite of our more-or-less radical differences? We can set out candidly and clearly what we think and why; invite others to do the same; engage in the give-and-take of conversation; identify points of agreement; reason together about points of disagreement; and learn from one another.[6] I do not doubt that non-Christians will be puzzled by some things that Christians say and will disagree with other things. But I am equally confident that many of them will find much to which they can consent. After all, the common world that we inhabit does rein in the divergence of our construals. What is more, different traditions are seldom *absolutely* strange to one another: Certain strands of Christianity and Islam both incorporate Aristotle, for example, and both Locke and Kant are more theological than atheist moral philosophers usually care to remember.

In brief, my view of secularity is not that of Jürgen Habermas or John Rawls; it is that of Augustine. In this Augustinian view, secularity is the public space where plural voices put their differences on the table, negotiate, and compromise. That is my first reason for claiming that Christian just war thinking should be granted a hearing by non-Christians.

My second reason is that there is a variety of ways of construing the justification of war, and some are better than others. It might be assumed that Christian thought is passé and that it has been surpassed by modern philosophical versions. In fact, however, I think that Rodin's critique of the just war thinking stemming from Michael Walzer inadvertently illuminates the strengths of the Christian tradition—as I have explained elsewhere.[7]

HOW THE "POLITICAL CENTRALITY" OF GRAVE INJUSTICE DETERMINES LAST RESORT

The issue of when an injustice is sufficiently bad to warrant the costs, evils, and hazards of military intervention is a moot one. Certainly, just war thinking reckons that a measure of injustice is sometimes better borne than addressed by the terrible remedy of war. Therefore, it stipulates that just cause for military action must be a "grave" injustice. What might this be? In the sixteenth century, Francisco de Vitoria proposed the social practice of human sacrifice,[8] to which, in the seventeenth century, Hugo Grotius added the practice of cannibalism.[9] Today, statutory international law stipulates that "genocide" may warrant military intervention and that the doctrine of the Responsibility to Protect would extend that to any "large-scale loss of life" or "large-scale ethnic cleansing."[10] I myself cannot see any good moral reason—as distinct from political reason—to withhold the status of grave injustice from the practice of atrociously inhumane torture:

> [A] man is . . . tied to a chair screwed to the floor, huge crocodile clips attached to his nipples and genitals. His body twitches and shakes as the electric current is delivered, his eyes pop, saliva foams from his mouth. . . . He screams and screams. Some have their arms and legs amputated with an electric saw or an axe; their mouths prised apart until their jaws break; . . . others are secured to a bench with their hands tied behind their

> back, and then hauled up and down until their shoulders snap. A wiry man is tied naked to a gas ring, which is then turned on and burns through his skin. . . . Parents are forced to watch their frantic children running naked around a cell containing a beehive, desperately trying to escape the squadron of stinging insects. . . . One man has his arms broken with iron bars, another has his head crushed between the steel plates of a vice. His skull suddenly collapses with a jolt, and his brain squeezes out like toothpaste.[11]

Such were the activities of the "Special Treatment Department" of Saddam Hussein's regime in Iraq.

In all these instances, injustice is identified as "grave" in terms of its atrocious nature and widespread scale. Note that this is a very different line of argumentation compared with the concerns about preventive war laid out by Fisk and Ramos in chapter 4 of this book. I propose that it should also be identified in terms of what I call "political centrality." Let me explain with reference to the 2011 rebellion against Bashar al-Assad's regime in Syria.

Under Bashar al-Assad's father, Hafiz al-Assad, the Syrian regime was populated largely by members of the Alawite minority and was dominated by the military and security forces, all the while securing and enriching itself through the patronage of business. The regime was also fiercely repressive of dissent, holding that it alone stood between peaceful order and anarchy—anarchy of the kind that would ensue, they argued, if Islamists such as the Muslim Brotherhood were ever to get their hands on the levers of power. Upon Hafiz al-Assad's death and his son's election to the presidency in 2000, there was some hope that Bashar would pioneer both economic and political reform, and indeed he gave some early signals that these hopes would be met.

However, when in 2011 the Arab Spring began to blossom in Syria, the regime reflexively reverted to its customary, repressive mode. In the first week of March 2011, ten children in Deraa, between nine and fifteen years of age, wrote an antiregime slogan (probably more anticorruption than prodemocracy) on the wall of their school: "Down with the system!" For this misdemeanor, the Syrian authorities had them arrested, sent to Damascus, interrogated, and apparently even tortured.[12] On March 15 a few hundred protesters, many of them relatives of the detained children, began demonstrating in downtown Deraa. Their ranks swelled to several thousand. The Syrian security forces, attempting to disperse the crowd, opened fire and killed four people. The next day, the crowd ballooned to about twenty thousand. According to reports, on March 23 the security forces killed at least fifteen civilians and wounded hundreds of others. Thus far, the protests had remained nonviolent. However, when

President Assad subsequently refused to punish the governor of Deraa, who was his cousin, the rebels' patience broke and they resorted to arms. That is, only when it became clear that the state was unrepentant, and that its *very center* was prepared to own the arbitrary repression by refusing to repudiate it, did peaceful protest change into armed rebellion. David Lesch reports that "most opposition elements, if convinced that Bashar was serious about reform, would have been willing to give him one more chance."[13] As it was, Assad's refusal to dismiss the governor of Deraa, and his blaming the unrest on external interference, meant that the "the reckless nature of this act [of arresting the Deraa children] became a potent symbol of the decades of arbitrary oppression."[14] It also made it clear that this oppression was essential, not accidental, to the regime. Since March 2011, the regime has confirmed the indiscriminate ruthlessness of its determination to crush opposition through its use of chemical weapons against rebels in the Ghouta suburb of Damascus on August 21, 2013, as well as possibly on several earlier occasions,[15] and probably on subsequent ones.[16]

To speak of the political centrality of a grave injustice is to locate it at the very heart of an unyielding political regime, and to distinguish it from that which is merely accidental or occasional or peripheral. What is politically central, as I mean it here, is something with which a regime identifies itself and to which it is firmly committed. The moral significance of this feature is that it denotes an injustice from which a regime will not detach itself voluntarily. If the regime is in full control of the state, including the legislature and judiciary, this means that the rule of law has been displaced by arbitrary tyranny and that remedy is not available through peaceful negotiations, peaceful protests, or the courts. In Daniel Brunstetter's terms (see chapter 11 below), *ius* cannot be achieved by any *vis* short of *bellum*. Therefore, the decision to oppose grave injustice by armed force is indeed a "last resort."

THE ROLE OF NATIONAL INTEREST IN *JUS AD BELLUM*

In discussions about international relations, it is commonly assumed that national interest is immoral and that where national interests motivate military intervention, they vitiate it. In chapter 1 of this volume, Aidan Hehir expresses this assumption, insofar as he supposes that the national interests of the five permanent members of the UN Security Council are usually "narrow" and "parochial" and that they "corrupt" the council's response to humanitarian crises within sovereign states.[17]

I think that this popular Kantian equation of genuinely moral action with disinterested altruism is a mistake that seriously distorts the ethics of international affairs.[18] There is, however, a superior ethical alternative: the eudaemonist tradition that found classic expression in Thomas Aquinas. Combining the Book of Genesis' affirmation of the goodness of the created world with Aristotle, Thomist thought does not view all self-interest as selfish and immoral. Indeed, it holds that there is such a thing as morally obligatory self-love.[19] The individual has a duty to care for himself or herself properly, to seek what is genuinely his or her own good.

As with an individual, so with a national community and the organ of its cohesion and decision, namely, its government: A national government has a moral duty to look after the well-being of its own people—and in this sense to advance its genuine interests. As Yves Simon wrote against those who criticized the British government's response to Mussolini's invasion of Abyssinia in 1935 because it was determined by national interests, "What should we think, truly, about a government that would leave out of its preoccupations the interests of the nation that it governs?"[20]

This duty is not unlimited, of course. There cannot be a moral obligation to pursue the interests of one's own nation by riding roughshod over the rights of others. Still, not every pursuit of national interest does involve the committing of injustice, so the fact that national interests are among the motives for military intervention does not by itself vitiate the latter's moral justification.

This is politically important because some kind of national interest needs to be involved if military intervention is to attract popular support; and because without such support, intervention is hard, and eventually impossible, to sustain. One such interest can be moral integrity or self-respect. In chapter 7, for example, Holeindre grounds France's sphere of influence in Africa in its post-colonial responsibility. Nations usually care about more than just being safe and fat. Usually, they want to believe that they are doing the right or the noble thing, and they will tolerate the costs of war—up to a point—in a just cause that looks set to succeed. I have yet to meet a Briton who is not proud of what British troops achieved in Sierra Leone in 2000, even though Britain had no material stake in the outcome of that country's civil war, and even though intervention there cost British taxpayers money and British families casualties.[21] Citizens care that their country should do the right thing. If this were not so, cynical proponents of realpolitik would not feel the need—as they invariably do—to fabricate moral pretexts for their unjust invasions.[22]

There are those, of course, who argue that material motives such as economic prosperity and national security always lie at the bottom of a state's international actions, and that other, apparently nobler, allegedly moral motives can always be reduced to these basic ones, for which they function merely as a cover. Such people call themselves "realists." I consider them, however, to be anthropological ideologues, imposing their dismal Hobbesian, social Darwinist, or Marxist prejudices about human being onto the empirical data. The study of history, untrammeled by such dogma, makes manifest that human motivation is very various, and it furnishes plenty of examples of human beings—and even statesmen—preferring justice to material prosperity and security. I know of no good historical reason to doubt, for example, that in arguing that Britain should take the high risks of continuing the war against Germany after the military disaster at Dunkirk in May 1940, Winston Churchill was very considerably animated by moral horror at the nature of the Nazi regime and by a sense of his own country's moral duty to preserve political civilization.

A nation's interest in its own moral integrity and nobility alone, however, will probably not underwrite military intervention in faraway places that incurs very heavy costs. So other interests—such as national security—are needed to stiffen popular support for a major intervention. But even a nation's interest in its own security is not simply selfish. After all, it amounts to the national government's concern for the security of millions of fellow citizens. Nor need it be private, for one nation's security is often bound up with others'. As Gareth Evans puts it: "These days, good international citizenship is a matter of national self-interest."[23]

Thus, national interest need not vitiate the motivation for military intervention. It is not unreasonable for a nation's people to ask why they should bear the burdens of military intervention, especially in remote parts of the world. It is not unreasonable for them to ask why *they* should bear the burdens *rather than* others. It is not unreasonable for British or American or French mothers and fathers to ask why *their* uniformed sons and daughters should risk the loss of life or limb in the attempt to build a better world in, say, Kosovo, Iraq, Afghanistan, Mali, or Syria. And the answers to these reasonable questions will need to be expressed in terms of the nation's own interests. And these answers could and ought to be presented in terms of the nation's own morally legitimate interests.

The role of national interests in determining the justification for military intervention against grave injustice is one reason why such intervention is irregular—that is, why it happens sometimes, but not always. There are other reasons, too: variable military capability, democratic support, and risk of escalation. A state might have a legitimate interest in intervening but still not do so, either because it lacks effective military means or because its government cannot persuade parliament or people that the national interest is sufficiently strong to warrant the costs, or because the risk of military escalation is too high. As Hehir says in chapter 1, this does create a problem, given that some innocents do not get rescued. That is undoubtedly tragic. However, because I think that the reasons for nonintervention can be good ones, that nonintervention can therefore be prudent, and that prudence is a moral virtue, I am less inclined than he is to view the variable record of intervention as expressive of moral inconsistency and therefore as "morally repugnant." Sometimes, of course, it can be. But whether or not it is so, we must judge according to the facts of each case.

It is quite true that just cause alone does not just military intervention make; it is not enough that there is a grave injustice crying out for redress. Those intervening should intend first and foremost to correct this injustice and not merely use it as a pretext for other intentions—say, to expand territorial control or to seize natural resources. Nevertheless, it might well be the case that the pursuit of national interests can ride on the coattails of the correct primary intention and be consistent with it. Indeed, if military intervention—especially by a democratic state—is to be politically sustainable, it will need to be able to do this. For the more a nation's own interests are involved in military intervention to stop and correct grave injustice, the more the costs and risks of intervening will seem worth bearing—and in this sense, the more the intervention will seem proportionate.

This understanding of the relationship between grave injustice, right intention, national interest, and proportionality helps to illuminate the moral complexity of the United States–led invasion of Iraq in 2003. As I see it, the characteristically atrocious nature of Saddam Hussein's regime constituted a grave injustice, and the Coalition's primary intention in invading was to replace that regime with an altogether happier and healthier political system—for the sake of the Middle East.[24] Bound up with this, of course, was the concern that *such a regime* possessed weapons of mass destruction (WMD) and was on course to acquire nuclear ones. In the aftermath of the September 11, 2001, terrorist attacks on the United States and the consequent climate of heightened anxiety about the possible conjunction of terrorists and WMD, and in light of Iraq's manifest resistance to UN scrutiny during the 1990s, there was good reason to suppose that Saddam's regime posed a substantial, if not immediate, threat to the United States and the United Kingdom.[25] However, when after the invasion no WMD were discovered, it became clear that American and British national interest was in fact *less* engaged than had been claimed. Consequently, the mounting costs in terms of the lives of American and British servicemen and of money made the intervention seem increasingly less proportionate—even though the costs were, frankly, trivial compared with those of previous wars within living memory. Does this diminution of proportionality render the invasion altogether unjust? I cannot say that it does, because, though *less proportionate* than it once seemed, the intervention was still not *simply and manifestly disproportionate*. It was successful in ending the grave injustice of

Saddam's regime, and it was not entirely unsuccessful in substituting a better political system and in realizing some of the national interests of the United States and the United Kingdom. I shall return to the issue of proportionality very shortly.

Before I do that, however, let me add a further illustration of the interaction of national interest and proportionality in terms of Western intervention in Syria and now in Iraq against ISIS. Given the weak or uncertain engagement of national interest in the outcome of the civil war in Syria, it is understandable that Americans, Britons, and French have been shy of direct involvement. Effective intervention would have incurred enormous costs and risks, and the situation there has seemed, frankly, too remote to have made it worth our while. However, if Syria had been geographically located where Mexico or Germany now sits, we would have got stuck in and shouldered all the uncertainties and risks and costs because our own national security would have been directly engaged.

However, now that ISIS has taken control of large swaths of Syria and Iraq, together with considerable resources and sophisticated weaponry, and given its declared hostility toward the West and its capacity to express this hostility by encouraging and supporting acts of terrorist violence in faraway places, Western nations have more of a national security interest in suppressing it. Consequently, military intervention in northern Iraq and even in Syria has become more proportionate now (in 2017) than it was in 2011.

PROPORTIONALITY, ITS PERMISSIVENESS, AND ITS POLITICS

As I understand it, the requirement that a just war be proportionate does constrain but is still permissive. That is to say, without it, justifiable costs would be much higher; but with it, they can still be enormous. This permissiveness troubles me, but I can see no rational way of tightening it. One conceivable way of tightening it is to think of proportionality as a state of affairs that can be seen to obtain when a cost/benefit analysis shows an excess of goods over evils. My problem with this is that, though it may be conceivable, it is not possible. This is because such a cost/benefit analysis would fall prey to the incommensurability of the relevant goods and evils. That is, these goods and evils are so radically different in kind that there is no common currency in which to measure them—they are *in*commensurable. So, for example, how does one weigh, on one hand, the goods of regime change in Berlin in 1945, the liberation of Europe from fascism, and the ending of the Final Solution against, on the other hand, the evils of 60 to 80 million dead and the surrender of

Eastern Europe to the tender mercies of Stalin? Or how does one weigh, on one hand, the loss of 200,000 Iraqi lives to political violence after the 2003 invasion, the country's fragile integrity, the continuing vitiation of its political life by sectarianism, and the extent of Iranian interference against, on the other hand, the fact that Iraq is no longer a military threat to its neighbors and is no longer intent on developing nuclear weapons, that its children are no longer dying by the thousands from the regime's political manipulation of economic sanctions, that power has been peacefully transferred through a democratic process, that the Kurds are thriving, and that the domestic oil industry is booming?[26] In a nutshell, bare human life and political justice are not the same kind of things, so how many instances of the former are worth sacrificing to achieve a tolerable degree of the latter? If there is an answer to this question, it cannot come in the form of either a numerical calculation or a quantitative weighing. The words "calculation" and "weighing" can only be metaphors for a more opaque, complicated, uncertain, and controversial deliberation. Too often, unfortunately, they are used to disguise an intuitive judgment with the authority of mathematical certainty.

Consider another example. Some years ago, the BBC dramatized the memoirs of a Battle of Britain pilot, Geoffrey Wellum. At the end of the dramatization, the real, ninety-year-old Wellum appeared, looking out over the iconic white cliffs of the southern English coastline. And as he gazed out to sea, he said, "Was it worth it? Was it worth it? All those young men I fought and flew with? All those chaps who are no longer with us? I suppose it must have been. I am still struggling with that."[27] Now, did Wellum mean that he doubted that Britain should have fought against Hitler in 1940? I do not think so. Rather, I think he was giving voice to the truth that the loss of each life is an absolute loss, for which there is no compensation. I think that "Was it worth it?" is the wrong question, because there is no sensible way of answering it. Such a "weighing up" of disparate goods and evils cannot be done with genuine, as distinct from spurious, rationality.

Nevertheless, there are other concepts of proportionality that do make sense.[28] One such concept is the aptness of means to ends—or, in the case of disproportion, the inaptness. Thus for NATO to have gone to war against Russia in 1956 to save the Hungarians, or in 1968 to save the Czechs, or even in 2014 to save the Ukrainians, and to risk world-destroying nuclear war, would have been to undercut its goal—a free and flourishing Hungary, Czechoslovakia, or Ukraine. Thus, too, to engage in military operations that cause large-scale civilian deaths, when a vital part of the counterinsurgency strategy is to win civilian hearts and minds, would be self-subverting. Means that undercut their goal are inapt, and in that sense are disproportionate.

At this point, there arises the *political* dimension of military proportionality. Take the case of Israel's Operation Protective Edge against Hamas in Gaza in 2014. It is clear, both in morality and in international law, that Israel had a right to defend its citizens against indiscriminate killing by Hamas's rockets. It is not so clear, however, that its self-defense was proportionate, either in the sense of "strictly necessary" or in the sense of "instrumentally apt to the end."

On one hand, provided that Israel targeted enemy combatants and that such targeting was necessary, there was no upper limit to the number of civilian casualties that may have been incurred, tragically, as "collateral damage." In case this view should appear morally repugnant, let me divert attention for a moment to another case: the Allied invasion of Normandy in 1944. Most people, certainly the vast majority of Anglo-Saxons, regard that military action as morally justified—in spite of the fact that it involved the killing of 35,000 French civilians through American and British bombing. This was undoubtedly massive in scale and terrible and tragic in quality. But if we think that Allied success was worth 35,000 civilian deaths, can we say with confidence that it would not have been worth 70,000 or 170,000? If we are judging simply by numbers, I do not think that we can. Provided that the military means chosen are necessary, there is no absolute maximum to the collateral damage that may be incurred. We see a similar line of reasoning with regard to drones in Vilmer's chapter 5 (contra Fisk and Ramos in chapter 4).

Nevertheless, we should interrogate the claim of necessity by asking about its end: To what end were Israel's chosen military means necessary? If it was to fend off harm to Israeli civilians, then it seems that the country's Iron Dome missile system had already achieved that with, according to its own officials, 90 percent efficiency. It is arguable, of course, that complete defense must extend beyond deflecting the harmful effects to uprooting their cause. This would justify military action against Hamas.

However, if the end was to uproot the cause of attacks on Israel, then military means alone did not suffice. Military means alone, then, were not apt. Although the bombardment of Gaza undoubtedly weakened Hamas's military power, it did not—and could not—uproot it permanently. Without a political solution to the Palestinian question, Hamas will simply revive to fight again.[29] My (controversial) assumption is that it was within Israel's power to undertake diplomatic, confidence-building initiatives without waiting for reliable Palestinian interlocutors. For example, unilaterally, it could have ended the illegal and provocative settlements in the West Bank. If my reading is correct, then, because it did not do this, its military assaults on Gaza were inapt and therefore disproportionate.[30]

WITNESS FROM THE FRONT LINE: MILITARY INTERVENTION CAN BE EFFICACIOUS

In light of recent experience—in Iraq, Libya, and Afghanistan—many doubt the efficacy of military intervention for humanitarian purposes altogether. The interventions in Iraq and Libya are widely regarded as having precipitated unmitigated disaster, and efforts since 2006 at national reconstruction in Afghanistan are frequently pronounced futile.[31] My own view is that such conclusions are lacking in nuance and too definitively pessimistic. There is no doubt that the Iraq and Afghanistan interventions suffered from serious flaws—both of them from an underestimation of the size, complexity, and cost of the task of postwar reconstruction; and Afghanistan also from a chronic lack of coordination, and sometimes even outright rivalry, between different agencies. Certainly, therefore, we should learn from recent mistakes. Despite claims about the elusiveness of victory (e.g., by O'Driscoll in chapter 14 below), we should not learn that intervention is always and everywhere futile.

In support I call, first, two witnesses, both of whom have served as soldiers, diplomats, and politicians; both of whom have had direct experience of responsibility for nation building; and both of whom have written books about it: Paddy Ashdown and Rory Stewart. Ashdown, who served as the international high representative for Bosnia and Herzegovina from 2002 to 2006, argues that "high-profile failures like Iraq should not . . . blind us to the fact that, overall, the success stories outnumber the failures by a wide margin."[32] In support, he appeals to two studies, one of which finds that military intervention by the international community is the best way of stabilizing peace and reconstructing nations after conflict,[33] and the other of which shows that the increasing incidence of intervention has helped to halve the number of wars in the world.[34] Notwithstanding the fact that we got it wrong in Iraq and Afghanistan, Ashdown remains convinced that there is a way of getting it right:

> Remember . . . that an army of liberation has a very short half-life before it risks becoming an army of occupation. Dominate the security space from the start; then concentrate first on the rule of law; make economic regeneration an early priority; remember the importance of articulating an "end state" which can win and maintain local support; but leave elections as late as you decently can. When rebuilding institutions be sensitive to local traditions and customs. Understand the importance to the international community effort of coordination, cohesion, and speaking with

> a single voice. And then at the end, do not wait until everything is at it would be in your country, but leave when the peace is sustainable.[35]

Rory Stewart was the Coalition Provisional Authority's deputy governor of two provinces in southern Iraq from 2003 to 2004. He approached the task of building a more stable, prosperous Iraq with optimism, but experience brought him disillusionment.[36] He now thinks that foreigners' short-term commitment, ignorance of local conditions, and consequent inability to build on local strengths hamstrings many of their well-intentioned efforts.[37] His coauthor, Gerald Knaus, takes direct issue with Ashdown's top-down model of success.[38] Nevertheless, Stewart and Knaus write that

> we both agree that there are certain occasions—such as genocide—that can justify an international intervention. . . . We accept the basic intuitions of many interveners around the world, and a worldview that seems to permit, for example, the intervention in Kosovo, even without the full legal sanction of the UN Security Council, . . . Bosnia and Kosovo were successes. . . . We both believe that it is possible to walk the tightrope between the horrors of over-intervention and non-intervention; that there is still a possibility of avoiding the horrors not only of Iraq but also of Rwanda; and that there is a way of approaching intervention than can be good for us and good for the country concerned. . . . Intervention may be a necessary, indispensable ingredient of the international system. It is certainly capable, as in the Balkans, of doing good.[39]

Ashdown and Stewart know whereof they speak: They have both had first-hand experience of trying to make intervention work. Stewart admits that the experience chastened him, and he disagrees with Ashdown about the conditions for success. Nevertheless, both agree that intervention *can* be done well. Given the right conditions, success is possible. Their consensus, it seems to me, is a powerful testimony against mere academic skepticism (e.g., that expressed by Hehir, Fisk and Ramos, and O'Driscoll in this volume).

To their witness, I add two more. Gen. Sir David Richards, who commanded British troops during their intervention in Sierra Leone in 2000, to prevent diamond-hungry, drug-crazed, limb-chopping rebels from seizing control of the country, has written: "Sierra Leone stands as an important example where overseas intervention was . . . successful. . . . Yes, we need to learn the lessons from Iraq; but in doing so we must not forget those learnt in Sierra Leone."[40] The then head of the object of intervention, President Tejan Kabbah, confirmed

Richards's judgment when he described the British Army as "the architects of Sierra Leone's salvation."[41]

ON THE REQUIREMENT FOR AN EXIT STRATEGY

In reaction against the costs and uncertain success of recent military interventions, some have taken to demanding that any future ones must come with an "exit strategy." What this means is not quite clear. It cannot mean a definite date and plan for withdrawal, because that would be absurd; the appropriate moment for withdrawal is tied to the success or failure of the operation, the circumstances of which cannot be predicted.

More sensibly, the requirement for an exit strategy is a demand for a clear understanding of the goals of military intervention, so that success or failure can be identified, together with the appropriate moment for withdrawal. But if so, what is really required is a strategy tout court. Without such a strategy, means cannot be properly ordered to ends, so the intervention cannot be proportionate.

A second sensible possibility is that the clamor for an exit strategy is an expression of anxiety about so-called mission creep—that is, for the ad hoc expansion of an intervention's goals, which is not accompanied by thorough deliberation and so by a decision to match fresh ambitions with appropriate resources. This appears to be part of what went wrong in Afghanistan in and after 2006. The concern here is entirely reasonable. Again, the failure to match means to ends renders an action disproportionate.

One final possible meaning of the demand for an exit strategy is not so reasonable, however. This is the claim that one should never embark on an intervention without being certain that one is able to finish it successfully.[42] According to this criterion, the 2011 intervention in Libya was disproportionate. NATO intervened to stop rebels in Benghazi from suffering indiscriminate slaughter at the hands of Colonel Gaddafi's state. That done, it was rightly judged that the threat of slaughter came from the heart of the regime, and that therefore the only way of securing the rebels against a future threat was to bring about regime change. In other words, the goal of the mission grew. (Whether or not it "crept" depends on how deliberate the decision makers were.) Then, after bringing down the regime, NATO withheld itself from taking direct responsibility for political reconstruction, leaving this primarily in the hands of the Libyans themselves, while offering support. That seemed prudent. But now, six years later, the political situation in Libya is dire, the authority of the central government is failing, the country is disintegrating, and jihadist groups are flourishing in the vacant space.

Does this mean that NATO should never have intervened in the first place? Not necessarily. It might mean that NATO—and even more so, the European Union—should have furnished the post-Gaddafi state with much more support. Or perhaps, following Orend in chapter 13, that we should lower our expectations and be content with a "thin theory of postwar justice." Either way, guarantees of ultimate success are never available, because success always depends on good fortune as much as on thorough planning—the best laid plans of mice and men, and so on. Victory or defeat can hang on a change in the wind. For sure, in deciding to embark on an intervention, decision makers should satisfy themselves that their means have some chance of achieving their ends, bearing in mind that the more important the ends, the greater the risks worth taking in attempting them. Instructed by the lessons of history, they should also plan for the costs to exceed their estimates. Suppose, however, that fortune happens not to smile on them. Then they might decide, reasonably, to try harder, at greater cost, and with higher risk; or equally reasonably, they might, contra Orend, decide that there is nothing more they can do to succeed, whether because of a lack of resources or diminishing political support. At that point, the most basic exit strategy stands ready to hand: When we have done all that we reasonably can, we leave. The injustice was grave, our cause was just, our intention was right, and our estimation of costs and risks was conscientious. But fortune has looked away. So we fail, but nobly.

NOTES

In this chapter—especially in the subsections "The Role of National Interest in *Jus ad Bellum*" and "Witness from the Front Line: Military Intervention Can Be Efficacious"—I have used some material that was previously published in *In Defence of War*, by Nigel Biggar (Oxford: Oxford University Press, 2014); I thank Oxford University Press for its kind permission to do so.

1. Nigel Biggar, *In Defence of War* (Oxford: Oxford University Press, 2014).

2. For a discussion of the history, see James Turner Johnson, *Sovereignty: Moral and Historical Perspectives* (Washington, DC: Georgetown University Press, 2014).

3. David Rodin, *War and Self-Defense* (Oxford: Clarendon Press, 2001), 1.

4. Ibid., 2.

5. I demonstrate this historical claim in chapter 5 of *In Defence of War*, 153–60.

6. I have written about this at some length—see Nigel Biggar, *Behaving in Public: How to Do Christian Ethics* (Grand Rapids: Eerdmans, 2011); and Nigel Biggar and Linda Hogan, eds., *Religious Voices in Public Places* (Oxford: Oxford University Press, 2009), chap. 7 and conclusion.

7. In *War and Self-Defense*, David Rodin offers a critique of Michael Walzer's account of the just war, mainly as expressed in his modern classic, *Just and Unjust Wars: A Moral Argument with Historical Illustrations* (London: Allen Lane, 1977). In chapter 5

of *In Defence of War*, I argue that Rodin inadvertently vindicates the early Christian tradition of just war thinking.

8. Vitoria, "On Dietary Laws, or Self-Restraint," in *Political Writings*, I.5.5, p. 225. Vitoria makes a point of saying that not *every* violation of the natural law deserves to be stopped by military means, only those that involve *iniuria* to others. Suárez agrees; military intervention can be justified only "in circumstances in which the slaughter of innocent people, and similar wrongs take place"; Francisco Suárez, "On Charity: Disputation XIII," 5:826).

9. Hugo Grotius, *The Rights of War and Peace*, ed. Richard Tuck (Indianapolis: Liberty Fund, 2005), II.XX.XL.3, p. 1022.

10. International Commission on Intervention and State Sovereignty, *The Responsibility to Protect* (Ottawa: International Development Research Centre, 2001), 32–33, s.4.19–21.

11. Justin Marozzi, *Baghdad: City of Peace, City of Blood* (London: Allen Lane, 2014), 351–52. Marozzi is describing the content of a set of videos on which the department recorded its deeds.

12. David Lesch, *Syria: The Fall of the House of Assad* (New Haven, CT: Yale University Press, 2013), 55–56.

13. Ibid., 85.

14. Ibid., 93.

15. For a summary of earlier occasions of the use of chemical weapons, in which the Syrian regime might have been implicated, see the BBC, "Syria Chemical Weapons Allegations," October 31, 2013, www.bbc.co.uk/news/world-middle-east-22557347.

16. See Human Rights Watch, "Syria: Strong Evidence Government Used Chemicals as a Weapon," May 13, 2014, www.hrw.org/news/2014/05/13/syria-strong-evidence-government-used-chemicals-weapon.

17. To be fair, Hehir's view is not without nuance, in that he does concede that it is widely accepted that an intervention motivated by a mixture of interests and humanitarian concern need not be automatically categorized either as in-humanitarian or cynical.

18. The ethics of Immanuel Kant are usually held to be simply "deontological," viewing the only truly moral act as one that is done out of a pure sense of duty or reverence for the moral law. So conceived, the truly moral act stands in stark contrast to a merely prudential one, which seeks to promote the agent's interests. Whether this common, deontological view of Kant fully captures his thought I doubt. I think that a better reading has him argue that truly moral acts are those where the duty of justice as fairness disciplines—rather than excludes—the pursuit of interest.

19. Thomas Aquinas, *Summa Theologiae*, trans. Father of the English Dominican Province (London: R. and T. Washbourne, 1915), Ia IIae, q. 94, art. 2: "Because in man there is first of all an inclination to good in accordance with the nature which he has in common with all substances: inasmuch as every substance seeks the preservation of its own being, according to its nature: and by reason of this inclination, whatever is a means of preserving human life, and of warding off its obstacles, belongs to the natural law."

20. Yves R. Simon, *The Ethiopian Campaign and French Political Thought*, ed. Anthony O. Simon and trans. Robert Royal (Notre Dame, IN: University of Notre Dame, 2009), 55.

21. The British casualties were very light: one dead, one seriously injured, and twelve wounded (www.eliteukforces.info/special-air-service/sas-operations/operation-barras/).

22. E.g., before Germany invaded France in August 1914, its government felt the need to make the entirely false claims that French troops had already transgressed the border and that French planes had bombed Nuremberg; and before Hitler invaded Poland in September 1939, he felt the need to have German troops dress up to look like Poles and attack the German village of Gleiwitz. In both cases, political leaders, notwithstanding their own cynicism, felt the need to satisfy their fellow citizens' need for moral justification.

23. Gareth Evans, *The Responsibility to Protect: Ending Mass Atrocity Crimes Once and for All* (Washington, DC: Brookings Institution Press, 2008), 144.

24. See Biggar, *In Defence of War*, 281–91.

25. Ibid., 258–68.

26. In May 2013, Anthony Loyd, a London *Times* journalist with more than twenty years' experience in Iraq, wrote: "Contrary to the widespread perception among Western publics, . . . the lot of the clear majority of Iraqis today is measurably improved. Many have a better quality of life, greater freedom of expression and more opportunity than during Saddam's era. . . . The killing has stabilized. . . . In the north, the Kurds have never had it so good. . . . The Shia areas of southern Iraq are at the edge of a similar economic renaissance." Anthony Loyd, *Prospect*, May 2013, 41.

27. Matthew Whiteman, director, *First Light*, BBC Television, London, 2010. This film was based on Geoffrey Wellum's memoir *First Light* (London: Viking, 2002).

28. Altogether, I recognize the good sense of three concepts of proportionality. The first is that of necessity: Where the use of force is necessary, it is proportionate; where unnecessary, it is excessive and so disproportionate. The second concept is that of fitness or aptness: A necessary use of military means might be insufficient to achieve the desired end apart from, say, diplomatic measures; so the necessary use of force alone might be inapt and thus disproportionate. The third concept is that of sufficiency of resources: military means might be necessary and apt and yet lack sufficient resources of men, matériel, and political support to be successful; so their continued use would be futile and so disproportionate. See Biggar, *In Defence of War*, chap. 4.

29. In just war reasoning, a tolerably just peace is the proper ultimate end of any justified use of military force. All military action, therefore, ought to be part of a larger, political, diplomatic, and so on, strategy.

30. It goes without saying, I trust, that my moral analysis here depends on a certain reading of the political and diplomatic facts, which is controversial and about which I might be mistaken. Were that shown to be considerably the case, then my moral analysis would have to change accordingly.

31. See, for sobering example, Jack Fairweather, *The Good War: The Battle for Afghanistan, 2006–14* (London: Jonathan Cape, 2014).

32. Paddy Ashdown, *Swords and Ploughshares: Bringing Peace to the 21st Century* (London: Weidenfeld & Nicolson, 2007), 14.

33. P. Collier, V. L. Elliot, H. Hegre, A. Hoeffler, M. Reynal-Querol, and N. Sambanis, *Breaking the Conflict Trap: Civil War and Development Policy*, World Bank Policy Research Report (Oxford: Oxford University Press, 2000).

34. Human Security Centre, *Human Security Report 2005* (Oxford: Oxford University Press, 2005).

35. Ashdown, *Swords and Ploughshares*, 213.

36. Rory Stewart and Gerald Knaus, *Can Intervention Work?* Amnesty International Global Ethics Series (New York: W. W. Norton, 2011), xv. For the full account of Stewart's experience in Iraq, see Rory Stewart, *Occupational Hazards: My Time Governing in Iraq* (London: Picador, 2006).

37. Stewart and Knaus, *Can Intervention Work?* xix, xxi. Stewart's firsthand witness goes a long way toward corroborating Michael Walzer's position: "The common brutalities of authoritarian politics, the daily oppressiveness of traditional social practices—these are not the occasion for intervention; they have to be dealt with locally, by the people who know the politics, who enact or resist the practices. . . . Foreign politicians and soldiers are too likely to misread the situation, or to underestimate the force required to change it, or to stimulate a 'patriotic' reaction in defense of the brutal politics and the oppressive practices. Social change is best achieved from within"; Michael Walzer, "The Argument about Humanitarian Intervention (2002)," in *Thinking Politically: Essays in Political Theory*, ed. David Miller (New Haven, CT: Yale University Press, 2007), 238.

38. Stewart and Knaus, *Can Intervention Work?* xv, xvii–xviii, xxv.

39. Ibid., xii, xiv, xvi, xxvi.

40. David Richards, "Sierra Leone 2000: Pregnant with Lessons," in *British Generals in Blair's Wars*, ed. Jonathan Bailey, Richard Iron, and Hew Strachan (Farnham, UK: Ashgate, 2013), 55.

41. Ibid., 62.

42. It is true that one of the classic criteria of *ius ad bellum* is "the prospect of success." Although this rules out belligerency that has no prospect of success, because it would be manifestly futile, it does not rule out belligerency with poor or doubtful prospects. Sometimes the stakes are so high that it is reasonable to take heavy risks of defeat in going to war or in staying at it. E.g., in May 1940, with its army smashed in northern France, the prospect of ultimate victory for Britain was not good, and some argued at the time that it would be reckless not to come to terms with Germany. Winston Churchill, however, was so convinced of the evils of Nazism that he urged his cabinet colleagues to shoulder the risks of continuing the fight. Not many would now say that he was wrong. And even if Britain had eventually lost the war, he might still have been right.

4

Making the World Safe for Preventive Force

India, South Korea, and the US Precedent

KERSTIN FISK AND JENNIFER M. RAMOS

Is THE US GOVERNMENT setting a dangerous precedent by using force preventively, and, if so, to what extent does this precedent encourage an international—and possibly destabilizing—post–Cold War norm of preventive self-defense? This chapter investigates these questions in light of the recent war in Iraq and drone attacks against suspected militants abroad. It argues that a preventive force norm is rising, and in many ways is further eroding "traditional" conceptions of state sovereignty, as preventive force is increasingly used in the context of fragmented and contested sovereignty outlined in this volume's introduction. For example, the Pakistani government asserts that US drone strikes conducted without its consent—particularly those that target the Taliban—violate its sovereign equality.[1] The United States, meanwhile, operates on the basis that its deference to Pakistan's sovereignty is (1) contingent on the leadership's willingness and ability to address these threats and (2) based on a threat's immediacy.

Despite the debatable upsides to preventive force, even restrained or limited military engagements that draw on preventive logic are legally, ethically, and strategically controversial. In particular, and regardless of their "low-cost" appeal to state policymakers, preventive uses of force are legally contentious because they are not included within the scope of a state's inherent right to self-defense as laid out in Article 51 of the United Nations Charter. Nor are they sanctioned by customary international law, which stipulates that the anticipatory use of force is lawful only if a threat is demonstrably imminent. As US secretary of state Daniel Webster concluded following a British attack on an American ship in 1837, "imminence" describes a condition of extreme urgency, under which a threat of attack is "instant, overwhelming, leaving no choice of means, and no moment for deliberation." When the threat of attack is imminent, or expected in the immediate term, the use of force in response is preemptive and is customarily considered lawful. In contrast, preventive force entails forcefully responding to a threat that is relatively latent—one that is expected to fully develop at an indistinct point in the future. Frequently cast as acts of choice rather than necessity, preventive uses of force are typically not considered legitimate self-defense, and historically have been regarded as not only unlawful but also undemocratic and immoral.[2]

We conceive of preventive force as a broad security strategy that can be viewed along a continuum. At one end is the most extreme form of preventive force—preventive war. The 2003 war in Iraq is one such example of a preventive war because the United States went to war based on concerns that Saddam Hussein possessed weapons of mass destruction, which could pose a threat to the future security of the United States.[3] The midpoint of the continuum encompasses smaller-scale applications of preventive force that are relatively more sustained and expansive, including targeted killing campaigns that employ drone strikes to eliminate individuals considered potential security threats. Although preventive targeted killings via drone strikes entail a relatively more limited use of force compared with preventive war, the United States' heavy reliance on its drone program demonstrates both the draw of preventive logic and an enduring commitment to preventive self-defense. At the opposite end of the spectrum are singular or otherwise exceptional uses of preventive force employed against discrete targets, such as Israel's bombing of the Yarmouk weapons factory in Khartoum, Sudan, in 2012.

In this chapter, we address three key aspects of the preventive force norm. First, we review the US stance on preventive force—a particular type of military intervention—because that has come to the forefront since the end of the Cold War. We discuss how events in the post–Cold War period signal an evolution in the United States' conception of satisfactory self-defense, both in terms of accepted justifications and also technological developments necessary for securing its self-defense. We then discuss some of these concerns in more detail within the context of the United States' preventive drone strikes in countries including Pakistan, Yemen, and Somalia. In the next section, we expand our discussion to more closely explore the beginnings of the diffusion of the preventive force norm in India and especially in South Korea. We assert that the United States' expanded understanding of a rightful response to a threat has paved the way for other countries to follow its lead in using force preventively.[4] Finally, we consider some of the most pressing challenges regarding the future use of preventive force. Even though the United States is currently only using limited preventive drone strikes (and is not engaged in preventive war), its actions have opened up the space for the logic of preventive force to serve as a legitimate basis for states' foreign policies.

A POST–COLD WAR HISTORY OF PREVENTIVE FORCE

The end of the bipolar era, dramatically represented by the fall of the Berlin Wall in 1989, brought forth much speculation about what new threats Western states would subsequently face in the absence of superpower rivalry. The US government soon fixated on threats emanating from so-called rogue states, which it said "exhibit a chronic inability to engage constructively with the outside world, and . . . do not function effectively in alliances—even with those like-minded."[5] It was in this context that the United States prepared to use force to forestall North Korea's nuclear weapons development by waging a "surprise" precision strike on Yongbyon, the nuclear reactor site where North Korea allegedly was attempting to develop weapons-grade plutonium.

Clinton administration officials referred to the intended strike on Yongbyon in the summer of 1994 as preemptive. Yet it was preventive in both its logic and motivation, involving the use of military force by a state in order to counter a nonimminent threat. According to Levy, "the assumption all along was that the United States had the right to *prevent* a 'rogue' third world state from going nuclear, by whatever means were necessary" (emphasis added).[6] This was not the first instance in which senior US officials adopted preventive logic in the context of counterproliferation; however, it was the first time on record that US officials considered a preventive attack without discernible concern for the legitimacy of the act.[7]

In the immediate aftermath of the September 11, 2001, terrorist attacks, the US government maintained the view that "outlaw" states were the predominant threats facing the international community.[8] Later, however, the George W. Bush administration conceptually linked violent nonstate actors and rogue states together, casting them as allied actors united by their antipathy toward the West in general and the United States in particular.[9] This logical (and rhetorical) equivalence of the two threat agents was formally articulated into the 2002 US National Security Strategy, which asserted that "rogue states and terrorists do not seek to attack us using conventional means. They know such attacks would fail. Instead, they rely on acts of terror and, potentially, the use of weapons of mass destruction."[10] President Bush's 2003 State of the Union Address further asserted the perceived severity involved: "Today, the gravest danger in the war on terror, the gravest danger facing America and the world, is outlaw regimes that seek and possess nuclear, chemical, and biological weapons. These regimes could use such weapons for blackmail, terror, and mass murder. They could also give or sell these weapons to terrorist allies, who would use them without the least hesitation."[11]

The Bush administration considered the threat of attack from either of these (allied) actors, both of which were labeled unpredictable and irrational, so grave that the imminence of the threat was assumed. Deterrence and containment were viewed as not only inadequate but also potentially dangerous strategies that would compromise future security. Whether the use of force entails surgical strikes or the initiation of a full-scale war, the basic motive and underlying logic of policymakers are the same for both—"better now than later."[12] These assumptions led to the Bush administration's preventive war in Iraq and also to more-limited uses of preventive force in the form of drone strikes, which President Barack Obama resumed on his third day in office.

Indeed, for all his campaign's criticism of the Iraq War, President Obama maintained the central component of his predecessor's security strategy—carrying out preventive drone attacks against nonimminent threats.[13] The logic behind dealing with unconventional threats therefore remains the same—preventive—although the scale of preventive force that is actually employed has been more limited if we compare Obama's preventive strikes with Bush's preventive war. Whereas President Bush oversaw an estimated 1 drone attack in Yemen and 48 attacks in Pakistan between 2002 and 2008, President Obama oversaw 353 drone attacks in Pakistan and 165 attacks in Yemen during his tenure as president.[14]

How many of these drone strikes can be considered preventive? It is unlikely that even the US government can answer this question accurately. Despite the Obama administration's assurances that its targets were senior-level commanders in charge of the planning and execution of imminent attacks on the United States, leaked US intelligence reports indicate that "hundreds" of low-level terrorists and *unknown individuals* have been targeted and killed in drone strikes. There is evidence of "killings of alleged Afghan insurgents whose organization wasn't on the US list of terrorist groups at the time of the 9/11 strikes; of suspected members of a Pakistani extremist group that didn't exist at the time of 9/11; and of unidentified individuals described as 'other militants' and 'foreign fighters.'"[15] Additionally, the Central Intelligence Agency targets individuals whose identities may be unknown at the time they are killed but whose age, gender, and behavior (fourteen years of age and older, male, carrying a weapon) are thought to suggest affiliation with a terrorist organization. These "signature strikes" were unfortunately to blame for the deaths of the American Warren Weinstein and the Italian Giovanni Lo Porto as they were being held hostage by al-Qaeda in Pakistan.[16]

These targeting decisions suggest that the majority of those killed in American drone strikes have not been operational leaders of al-Qaeda and its affiliates. According to figures from the New America Foundation, an estimated 103 terrorist leaders or "key figures" have been killed in Pakistan and Yemen combined—out of the most conservative estimated total of 3,179 individuals killed in drone strikes in these countries since the drone strikes began.[17] Thus, only about 3.2 percent of those killed in drone strikes have been operational leaders. It is now clear that the US government does not always know whom it is killing, although it insists that its drone policy is lawful because targets are high-ranking members of al-Qaeda and its affiliates, and because its targets pose imminent threats to the United States.[18] This is simply not the case.

Like the Bush administration that preceded it, the Obama administration sought to relax the established criteria for using force in self-defense by altering the meaning of imminence, which, according to customary international law, stipulates that a threat must be "instant, overwhelming, and leaving no choice of means, and no moment for deliberation." It did so in order to claim that its actions are lawful, in line with a state's inherent right to self-defense. According to a 2011 Department of Justice white paper leaked to the press in 2013, the government asserts that it can legally and justifiably use force in self-defense "where there is evidence of further imminent attacks by terrorist groups even if there is no specific evidence of where such an attack will take place or of the precise nature of the attack." At the same time, the memo titled "Lawfulness of a Lethal Operation Directed against a US Citizen Who Is a Senior Operational Leader of Al-Qa'ida or an Associated Force" reinterprets (or reconstructs) the definition of the word "imminent," so that using force "does not require the United States to have clear evidence that a specific attack on US persons will take place in the immediate future."[19]

President Obama's former counterterrorism adviser, John Brennan, has similarly asserted that the imminence standard should be further relaxed in light of terrorists' capabilities. In 2011 Brennan stated, "The traditional conception of what constitutes an 'imminent' attack should be broadened in light of the modern-day capabilities, techniques, and technological innovations of terrorist organizations."[20] This claim is directly in line with the Bush administration's National Security Strategy concerning the threat posed by rogue states and terrorists: The United States "must adapt the concept of imminent threat to the capabilities and objectives of today's adversaries." Thus, the Obama administration's attempt to blur the meaning of imminence in order to justify its drone policy further demonstrates the continuation and pervasiveness of preventive logic across three successive post–Cold War administrations, encompassing both states and nonstate organizations.

Furthermore, as O'Driscoll points out in chapter 14, national leaders increasingly struggle to define the concept of "victory" in the context of modern warfare, which is characterized by protracted campaigns and amorphous battle spaces. Drones can be ideal tools when the point of "victory" is uncertain. Military and governmental leaders can more easily opt to continue to fight because drone strikes are thought to impose relatively fewer costs on the attacker (risks to the attacker's forces are minimized) and the target (drone strikes are generally viewed as precise). Policymakers' perceptions of the nature of rogue state and terrorist threats can therefore contribute to threat overdetermination, which both exacerbates the onset of new conflicts and extends the life of ongoing conflicts—especially asymmetric and low-level ones. Drones make it easier to continue to fight, as the notion of "victory" in contemporary conflicts is more elusive.

In effect, we expect that a combination of preventive logic and unmanned drone technology will lead to a relatively larger number of armed military interventions rather than fewer (in contrast with Biggar's fear that the anticipated costs of a "just" intervention will preclude its possibility). As more leaders acquire drones, preventive force as a matter of just cause will likely be asserted more frequently—both in the national self-interest and as a humanitarian duty (see Biggar, chapter 3). The willingness of states to intervene should increase as a preventive self-defense norm diffuses across the international system, alongside the proliferation of armed drone technology. This could be enhanced even more if, instead of mainly seeing the dangers of preventive force, leaders follow the consequentialist logic outlined by Vilmer in chapter 5 below.

THE DIFFUSION OF THE PREVENTIVE FORCE NORM

So far, we have outlined what we consider to be the major developments in the US leadership's understanding of the most pressing security threats and have discussed preventive force as a mainstay of US security strategy. As we argued above, strategic arguments for the 2003 Iraq War and subsequent drone strikes in the war on terror are highly similar because the underlying logics for counterproliferation and counterterrorism essentially are identical. In this section, we discuss the effects of the US preventive force strategy and actions on other countries, and their implications for a possible systemwide shift in norms regarding the use of force. We do this while recognizing the fact that such a policy has been, and continues to be, controversial both within and outside of the United States.[21] Through its actions, we argue that the United States implicitly acts as a norm entrepreneur, creating a new, preventive self-defense norm by challenging the international community's established understanding of a state's rightful response to an anticipated attack.[22]

Indeed, we now see other powerful states—including those that initially condemned the United States' preventive invasion of Iraq as a flagrant violation of international law, such as India and Russia—affirm the legitimacy of the United States' preventive force policy, in line with their own interests. Certainly, as Vilmer argues in chapter 5, states have not previously *needed the American precedent* in order to act. Obviously, states have violated this norm in the past, but they also suffered international condemnation. What we witness today is these states' ability to unabashedly embrace the norm because of the legitimizing effect of the United States and the new international security context.[23]

Moreover, we argue that technology—the proliferation of drones, in particular—is contributing to the diffusion of this preventive self-defense norm. Diffusion entails "the spread of something within a social system," where "to spread" means to move "from a source to an adopter, paradigmatically via communication and influence."[24] The India case provides one illustration. In 2003 India condemned the Iraq War in palpable terms but has since claimed its right to conduct surgical strikes on suspected terrorists in Pakistan—and not only those implicated in terror attacks. As the former minister for external affairs and current senior leader of India's Bharatiya Janata Party has argued:

> India has been at the receiving end of terrorism for over two decades. India cannot be denied the rights that the US has, including that of surgical strikes. . . . India should reserve the right of surgical strikes and hot pursuit against Pakistan irrespective of the consequences. As and when considered necessary, India should not hesitate to carry out such an attack. . . . The US has been striking at terrorists and terror bases in Pakistan through drone attacks. Even today, 10 terrorists have been killed in drone attacks.[25]

Recent drone strikes by Pakistan against militants on its own soil have further spurred India's armed drones acquisition. In September 2015 the Indian government approved the purchase of ten Heron drones from Israel. India is considering using drones not only internally but also outside its borders. With tensions high between Pakistan and India, and with border disputes with China, it would not be hard to imagine a preventive strike occurring that could spark a larger war. Even if these countries have common enemies—namely, terrorists—they are not likely to allow their sovereign territory to be traversed by armed drones in hot pursuit. But drones also make it easier to cross borders undetected. As one Indian army officer reasoned, "It's risky, but armed UAVs [unmanned aerial vehicles] can be used for counterinsurgency operations internally as well across the borders; sneak attacks on terrorist hideouts in mountainous terrain, perhaps."[26]

Such consequentialist strategic thinking, as illustrated by India, reflects the idea that it is better to strike now than later.[27] Certainly, one could argue that a preventive war against rising Germany in the 1930s could have saved many more lives than appeasement. The argument for signature drone strikes runs parallel—kill the suspected terrorists to save those in harm's way, even if the danger is not immediate. Such is the thrust of the preventive force norm.

To further explore what drives the diffusion of this norm, we now look more closely at a second country case: South Korea. We examine this case for three main reasons. First, states in the region are modernizing their militaries, have a growing interest in developing and/or acquiring armed drones, and are devoting substantial portions of their defense budgets to drone research and development.[28] Second, the country is an intraregional competitor and also has close diplomatic and military relations with the United States. Third, South Korea has tense and competitive relations with China, the rising power in the region.

South Korea

In early 2011, South Korea's defense minister announced Seoul's plans to modernize the country's military by accelerating the planned purchase of UAVs and stealth fighters in order to conduct precision attacks. By many indications, the drone program has unfolded in line with this plan. By November 2011, the military had revealed its own drone, which it called the world's fastest UAV.[29] In 2012, Korean Aerospace Industries (KAI) introduced its plans for the Devil Killer, a "self-destructing drone capable of precision attacks."[30] This drone is marketed by KAI as a "tactical suicide combat UAV" that can hover over a target, can speed toward the target at a maximum of 400 kilometers (250 miles) per hour, and detonates a 2-kilogram payload.[31] In 2014 the South unveiled its new stealth drone, the Remoeye-006.[32] In addition, a South Korean defense official recently announced that the country would spend £276 billion on drone development in the immediate term.[33] South Korea is clearly pursuing drone technology with gusto.

Until about ten years ago, South Korea's national security strategy was based on the notion of passive defense by denial. For instance, in a scenario in which the country was attacked, the military would fight back in order to restore the status quo. If North Korea crossed the border into South Korea but did not fire a weapon, South Korea could not strike. In essence, South Korea could not retaliate in any scenario in which the North did not fire the first shot.[34] In 2005, following its Five-Year Defense Reform Project (1998–2003), South Korea introduced Defense Reform Initiative 2020 as part of an effort to meet future threats. The main task outlined in the reform effort was to build a smaller, more agile, more technologically advanced military by 2020. This included a drive to acquire UAVs. In response to provocations from the North, South Korea's defense minister, Kim Tae-young, claimed in both 2008 and 2010 that his country had a plan to launch a preemptive strike on North Korea to prevent a nuclear attack. In 2010 Kim stated plainly that South Korea "would have to strike right away if we detected that it has a clear intention to attack with nuclear weapons," because waiting for a launch "would be too late and the damage too big."[35]

After North Korea attacked Yeonpyeong Island in November 2010, South Korea took concrete steps to revise its 2005 defense plan. The incident on Yeonpyeong was the first artillery strike in South Korea since 1953 and, according to Rhee Sang-Woo, the head of the presidential committee on defense advancement and the Commission for National Security Review, it "is for South Koreans as 9/11 was for Americans."[36] The attack on Yeonpyeong, combined with an earlier attack on a South Korean warship, was considered a "new threat"—terrorism—by South Korean military analyst Kim Jae-yeop, who argued, "To put it simply, the North has carried out terrorist activities using regular military forces."[37] South Korea's Defense Reform Plan 307, introduced in 2011, includes seventy-three reforms focusing on surgical strikes with high-technology weapons, covert operations in order to deal with asymmetrical threats, and fighting local, limited wars. "Under the South's revised military posture," notes the Nuclear Threat Initiative, "Seoul has left open the possibility of mounting a first strike against the North to prevent new attacks."[38] According to Rhee, "A shift toward a doctrine of 'proactive deterrence' will improve [the] situation. When North Korea is preparing an attack, South Korea will preemptively nullify North Korea's command structure and associated weapons systems through the use of precision-guided munitions . . . and other . . . pinpoint attacks."[39]

Lee Dong-kwan, a spokesman for the president, stated that the basic idea is "to preempt further provocations and threats from the North against the South, as well as simply exercising the right of self-defense."[40] According to

Gen. Jung Seung-jo, however, the South will take military action *if the North tests a nuclear weapon*—a move he views as in line with the South's right to self-defense. Although the general described such a strike as preemptive, this is a preventive move, and it mimics the United States' asserted right to use force preventively based on the presence of nonimminent threats.[41]

South Korea, unlike the United States, does not enjoy a position as one of the world's largest economies; thus the country has "expanded its capacity to the brink of the first rung of global leadership, but has not yet broken into the most exclusive international leadership clubs."[42] In this regard, the South is committed to increasing its prestige. Its 2012 National Defense White Paper asserts that the military is now "fulfilling our responsibility to the international community on a level that is befitting our national power. In the process, we are enhancing our global stature as a defender of world peace." It emphasizes its intentions to "transform into a combat-centric elite military," and a fundamental goal of this transformation is to enhance the country's influence and reputation abroad.[43] Two key centerpieces of this status-building strategy are (1) to obtain "an advanced, globally oriented" elite military and (2) to pursue a "twenty-first-century strategic alliance" with the United States.[44]

South Korea's newly elected president, Park Geun-hye, of the Saenuri Party, has reiterated the salience of the United States–South Korea alliance. However, military advancement is also driven by the South's desire to make its security decisions independently of the United States. General Seung-jo, for instance, maintains that "a preemptive attack against the North trying to use nuclear weapons does not require consultation with the United States."[45] Of course, the United States is also attempting to transfer wartime control to South Korea, which will enable the country to act on its own accord if a conflict arises. Although the initial goal for the transfer was 2015, reports indicate that South Korea also does not consider itself prepared to make decisions regarding the North Korean threat on its own.[46]

The National Defense White Paper of 2012 outlines the most significant threats South Korea perceives for the immediate term. These include provocations from North Korea and its weapons of mass destruction, and sovereignty disputes among powers that surround the Korean Peninsula. South Korea envisions tensions between the key players in the region—China, Japan, Russia, and the United States—increasing as a result of "competition for regional ascendancy."[47] Nevertheless, it is clear that South Korea is most concerned about the North, and this concern has recently been reignited by drones.

In early 2014 South Korea discovered that three rudimentary spy drones from North Korea had entered South Korean airspace undetected and crashed along the border. The drones had been programmed to fly over South Korean military sites and were found with footage of the president's residence in Seoul. South Korea's defense minister, Kim Kwan-jin, now expects the North to use drones to spy and carry out terrorist attacks. If there are any future incursions by North Korean drones, the South has pledged to shoot them down.[48]

Summary of the South Korea Case

It appears to be in South Korea's self-interest to adopt a policy of preventive force. As North Korea's provocations become more frequent and fear inducing, the South increasingly espouses its right to attack in anticipation of a North Korean assault. For instance, in December 2011 word got out that South Korea was working on "bunker busters"—bombs capable of precision-targeting North Korean weapons bunkers. According to a lawmaker on the National Assembly Defense Committee, "the warhead will be equipped with a mid-range GPS device and will be deployed with 500-pound guided bomb units for precision attacks against targets hidden in caves" inside North Korea.[49] The project began after the country reached a major arms agreement—$71 million, to import 150 bunker busters from the United States.[50] Thus, the United States appears to be directly supportive of offensive moves by the South. Sovereignty violations resulting from incursions by North Korean drones, combined with the United States' backing, suggest that South Korea will execute similar plans—precision-targeting threats before they have a chance to fully form—using weapons such as the Devil Killer, which it has labeled an assassination drone, and which is expected to be deployed in the coming years.[51]

Overall, it appears that South Korea has taken steps that put itself in a position to carry out preventive strikes against threats, even if they are nonimminent. The diffusion of its drone policy appears to be a predominantly top-down, elite-driven process. We found evidence of elite learning, whereby state leaders were influenced by the actions of a powerful external actor. The security strategies of the United States are featured prominently in the international news and agenda, "teaching" other states. This makes it easier for elites to increase their knowledge of US policy and strategy. National leaders attempt to enhance their external legitimacy by acquiring the latest advanced military technology and by adopting innovative, corollary policies. These behaviors are "demonstrating the emulating country's modernity" because "governments dread the stigma of backwardness and therefore eagerly adopt policy innovations, regardless of functional needs."[52]

Moreover, competition with other states in the region may affect the desire of South Korean elites to enhance their state's regional status and reputation—not necessarily to identify with the leader in the international system, the

United States, but rather with reference to local rivalries and perceptions. This is also a reference to external legitimacy, but a more localized form of it. Finally, it was evident that leaders adopt security policies in line with their interests, in order to maximize security and economic benefits. If leaders are offered lucrative deals with defense contractors, they may be more likely to adopt the US model. At the same time, the degree to which drone technology meets perceived security needs will likely factor into leaders' incentive structures. Although, in chapter 5 below, Vilmer makes a different case regarding the drone debate in France, we suggest that if leaders expect targeted killing to increase relative security at an acceptable cost, they will rationally justify and choose this policy.

CONCLUSION

The turn toward preventive self-defense in the post–Cold War era was brought about by several developments facing the lone superpower in the international system, the United States. The rise of violent nonstate actors and advances in technology shifted the focus away from traditional state actors and conventional understandings of the use of force. These changes led the United States down the path of open-ended, limited uses of force for preventive purposes. Other states, including South Korea, seem poised to embrace the preventive force norm, while others already have done so (e.g., India and Russia[53]). This norm, as manifested in limited uses of force, is significantly enabled by the concurrent trend toward armed drone acquisition, despite claims that the United States' turn toward the just war tradition could restrict drone use. The question that remains is whether states will similarly limit their preventive use of force or engage in more extreme forms of preventive self-defense. We assert that, for better or worse, the United States has made it acceptable for states to use preventive force logic in their national security strategies, and now it may be nearly impossible to turn back from this precedent.

In light of this, a handful of lessons can be learned from the United States' uses of preventive force, and their impact on the international community, but here we reflect on those we consider the most pressing. First, through ill-transparency and misrepresentation of the threats being targeted, two successive US administrations misled the public to justify using preventive force. By deliberately fostering a climate of secrecy and through outright deception, the Bush and Obama administrations (1) denied the public knowledge of the true severity of the threats that (may or may not) warrant the "war on terror" and (2) directly undermined democratic discourse and accountability. There is a reason that preventive war is more likely to be a tool of dictators rather than democratic leaders: the role of public opinion, and public aversion to the costs of war in democracies.[54] Unsurprisingly, it is hard to convince citizens in a democracy that a preventive war is worth the costs—emphasizing the imminence of the threat and working to temper public perceptions of costs and risks therefore become key to a democratic public's acquiescence. For example, even with rising suspicions about Iran's nuclear weapons program in 2012, only a small portion of the American population was willing to take military action (17 percent) and only 19 percent of Israelis were willing to take unilateral military action.[55] The lack of transparency that has accompanied the use of preventive force, as demonstrated by US drone strikes in Pakistan and Yemen, further inhibits honest assessments of the degree to which international law and ethics are being subverted.

Second and relatedly, if intentions—as they do in law and in the just war tradition—play such a crucial role in distinguishing and evaluating different types of force, how do we discern intentions in the first place?[56] Certainly, the legitimizing discourse for military action comes from those in powerful positions, who have a vested interest in controlling the message. Moreover, there may be multiple motives at play, some of which may undermine the ethical arguments made by administrations. With this in mind, we should be careful about the evidence used to judge "proper intent" and the context within which this is occurring. This creates an even greater imperative for scholars, citizens, and public servants to be conscious of subtexts and multiple perspectives when analyzing and making decisions on these issues.

On this note, there may be room for an alternative approach, whereby the authority to make such decisions is taken out of the hands of states and transferred to another legitimate actor. This transfer of authority may reduce the number of civilians killed—a matter made even more urgent with the revelation of a recent five-month window analysis of US drone strikes in Afghanistan that indicated 90 percent of the targets were unintended.[57] Scholars who allow for preventive force, though with restrictive conditions, consistently point to this issue. After all, in these situations when an attack is not imminent, there would be time to consult and gain authorization. An international institutional authority, such as the United Nations, could set the standards for when preventive force is legitimate, just as it has for preemption.[58] Such approval must be based on meeting criteria identified in the just war tradition as well as appeals to moral norms. If such standards exist, states can be held accountable for their actions, even if sacrificing only their international reputations. Buchanan and Keohane go so far as to suggest institutional models and criteria for preventive force that are necessary both before and after a preventive use of force.[59] Their latest work attempts to translate these ideas into a tangible form, outlining the drone accountability regime, an informal program that could govern drone use.[60]

Although an institution or informal regime may be set up to oversee the preventive use of force, the question remains as to which criteria it would use to judge. As Vilmer acknowledges in chapter 5, though drones have been used in a disproportionate (and thus morally questionable) manner by the United States, it remains possible to use them in a more ethical manner. For example, in chapter 11, Daniel Brunstetter discusses one proposal for an ethical framework that may have promise. Assuming that drone strikes lie somewhere between law enforcement and war, developing the principles of *jus ad vim* could provide a useful way for restraining overly aggressive action without tying states' hands. This may be one way to also avoid the shady ethics of perpetual engagement in low-level war, while benefiting from the limited use of preventive force. *Jus ad vim* would, however, need to explicitly account for the dangerous precedent that preventive force might set, which may not even be possible.

Finally, and perhaps most critically, to what extent are we contributing to the propagation of preventive force by even seeking criteria whereby it could or should be legitimized?[61] This question more fundamentally gets at whether violence is the answer to today's problems. Publics around the world are largely unsupportive of drone strikes against suspected terrorists. A Pew survey of forty-four countries in 2014 found that only three countries indicated more than 50 percent public support for drone strikes against extremists.[62] In many cases, a key reason is the fact that unintended victims are injured and killed as a result of these strikes.[63] This has caused a sharp divide between publics and elites in some countries. In Germany, for example, the "Kunduz bombing affair" sparked public outrage about the use of combat drones when an air strike that killed many innocent civilians was traced back to an order given by a German colonel—under NATO auspices—in 2009.[64] Moreover, citizens are infuriated that Ramstein, the US airbase in Germany, is used as a satellite relay station for drone strikes: "No to the killer terror drones."[65]

Scholars such as Deen Chatterjee urge us to consider alternatives, such as preventive nonintervention.[66] Resisting attempts to reshape traditional just war thinking to fit current threat environments, Chatterjee shifts the focus to "just peace."[67] In his view, how can we expect to build peace if our energy is spent on finding "better" ways to go to war? Trends in global justice and human rights norms suggest that this may in fact be a more humane, and ultimately more secure, path to the goals that just war is trying to achieve.

NOTES

1. "Pakistan Says US Drone Strike That Killed Taliban Leader Violated Its Sovereignty," *The Guardian*, May 22, 2016, www.theguardian.com/world/2016/may/22/pakistan-us-drone-strike-taliban-violated-its-sovereignty.

2. Scott Silverstone, *Preventive War and American Democracy* (New York: Routledge, 2007).

3. Despite the fact that the Bush administration referred to the Iraq War as a "preemptive" war, many agree that the threat did not present an imminent threat, so it is best characterized as a preventive war.

4. Kerstin Fisk and Jennifer M. Ramos, "Actions Speak Louder Than Words: Preventive Self-Defense as a Cascading Norm," *International Studies Perspectives* 15, no. 2 (2014): 163–85.

5. Anthony Lake, "Confronting Backlash States." *Foreign Affairs* 73, no. 2 (1994): 46.

6. Jack S. Levy, "Preventive War and Democratic Politics," *International Studies Quarterly* 52, no. 1 (2008): 19.

7. Marc Trachtenberg, "Preventive War and US Foreign Policy," *Security Studies* 16, no. 1 (2007): 1–31; Also see Silverstone, *Preventive War.*

8. The terrorist bombings in 1993 (of the World Trade Center in New York City) and 1998 (of the US embassies in Kenya and Tanzania) had already drawn international attention to al-Qaeda and had compelled the United States to consider limited force options. However, as Brunstetter (in chapter 11 of this volume) and Zenko articulate, the attempts at limited force against al-Qaeda were viewed as unsuccessful. Micah Zenko, *Between Threats and War: Discrete Military Operations in the Post–Cold War World* (Stanford, CA: Stanford University Press, 2010).

9. In his September 11, 2006, address to the nation, President Bush referred to the clash of civilizations argument explicitly: "This struggle has been called a clash of civilizations. In truth, it is a struggle for civilization. We are fighting to maintain the way of life enjoyed by free nations." See "Text of President Bush's Address to the Nation," www.washingtonpost.com/wp-dyn/content/article/2006/09/11/AR2006091100775.html.

10. Bush administration, "US National Security Strategy of the United States of America," 2002, 15, http://nssarchive.us/NSSR/2002.pdf.

11. President George W. Bush, "State of the Union Address," 2003, www.washingtonpost.com/wp-srv/onpolitics/transcripts/bushtext_012803.html.

12. Levy, "Preventive War," 4.

13. However, President Obama significantly curtailed the number of strikes after the so-called Year of the Drone in 2010.

14. New America Foundation, "Drone Wars: Pakistan," www.newamerica.org/in-depth/americas-counterterrorism-wars/pakistan/; and New America Foundation, "Drone Wars: Yemen," http://securitydata.newamerica.net/drones/yemen/analysis.html.

15. Jonathan S. Landay, "Obama's Drone War Kills 'Others,' Not Just Al Qaeda Leaders," *McClatchy*, April 9, 2013, www.mcclatchydc.com/2013/04/09/188062/obamas-drone-war-kills-others.html.

16. Adam Entous, Damian Paletta, and Felicia Schwartz, "American, Italian Hostages Killed in CIA Drone Strike in January," April 23, 2015, www.wsj.com/articles/american-italian-hostages-killed-in-cia-drone-strike-in-january-1429795801.

17. See note 14.

18. See, e.g., Scott Shane, "Drone Strikes Reveal Uncomfortable Truth: US Is Often Unsure about Who Will Die," *New York Times*, April 23, 2015, www.nytimes.com/2015/04/24/world/asia/drone-strikes-reveal-uncomfortable-truth-us-is-often-unsure-about-who-will-die.html.

19. Michael Isakoff, "Justice Department Memo Reveals Legal Case for Drone Strikes on Americans," NBC News, February 4, 2013, http://msnbcmedia.msn.com/i/msnbc/sections/news/020413_DOJ_White_Paper.pdf.

20. John O. Brennan, "Strengthening Our Security by Adhering to Our Values and Laws," September 16, 2011, www.whitehouse.gov/the-press-office/2011/09/16/remarks-john-o-brennan-strengthening-our-security-adhering-our-values-an.

21. For ethical debates, see Jonathan Barnes, "The Just War," in *The Cambridge History of Later Medieval Philosophy*, ed. Norman Kretzmann, Anthony Kenny, and Jan Pinborg (New York: Cambridge University Press, 1982), 771–84; Daniel Brunstetter and Megan Braun, "The Implications of Drones on the Just War Tradition," *Ethics & International Affairs* 25, no. 3 (2011): 337–58; Daniel Brunstetter and Megan Braun, "From *Jus ad Bellum* to *Jus ad Vim*: Recalibrating Our Understanding of the Moral Use of Force," *Ethics & International Affairs* 27, no. 1 (2013): 87–106; C. A. J. Coady, *Morality and Political Violence* (New York: Cambridge University Press, 2008); Patrick Lin, "Ethical Blowback from Emerging Technologies," *Journal of Military Ethics* 9, no. 4 (2010): 313–31; Avery Plaw, *Targeting Terrorist: A License to Kill?* (Burlington, VT: Ashgate, 2008); Nicholas Rengger, "The Greatest Treason? On the Subtle Temptations of the Preventive Use of Force," *International Affairs* 84, no. 5 (2008): 949–61; Richard Tuck, *The Rights of War and Peace* (New York: Oxford University Press, 1999); and Garry Wills, "What Is a Just War?" *New York Review of Books,* November 18, 2004, 32–35.

22. Fisk and Ramos, "Actions Speak Louder Than Words."

23. For a contrasting view on the Iraq War's effects on the creation of a legal norm for preventive self-defense, see Eric A. Heinze, "The Evolution of International Law in Light of the Global War on Terror," *International Studies Review* 37, no. 3 (2011): 1069–94.

24. David Strang and Sarah A. Soule, "Diffusion in Organizations and Social Movements: From Hybrid Corn to Poison Pills," *Annual Review of Sociology* 24 (1998): 266.

25. "Yashwant Backs Abbottabad-Like Strike by India," *The Times of India*, May 7, 2011, http://timesofindia.indiatimes.com/india/Yashwant-backs-Abbottabad-like-strike-by-India/articleshow/8183300.cms.

26. Sanjeev Miglani, "India Turns to Israel for Armed Drones as Pakistan, China Build Fleets," Reuters, September 22, 2014, http://in.reuters.com/article/2015/09/21/india-israel-drones-idINKCN0RL2EC20150921.

27. David Luban, "Preventive War," *Philosophy and Public Affairs* 32, no. 3 (2004): 207–48; Jeff McMahan, "Realism, Morality and War," in *The Ethics of War and Peace*, ed. Terry Nardin (Princeton, NJ: Princeton University Press, 1996); and John Yoo, "Using Force," *University of Chicago Law Review* 71, no. 3 (2004): 729–32.

28. Saira Syed, "Drone-Makers Target Asia for Growth," BBC, February 16, 2012, www.bbc.com/news/business-17028684.

29. "S. Korea Develops World's Fastest Unmanned Aerial Vehicle," Yonhap News Agency, November 30, 2011.

30. "S. Korea Develops Suicide Combat Drone," *The Chosunilbo*, September 12, 2012, http://english.chosun.com/site/data/html_dir/2012/09/14/2012091400865.html.

31. Ridzwan Rahmat, "Singapore Airshow 2014: KAI Promotes Devil Killer UAV as Maritime Weapon," *IHS Janes Defence Weekly*, February 17, 2014, www.janes.com/article/34025/singapore-airshow-2014-kai-promotes-devil-killer-uav-as-maritime-weapon.

32. "S. Korea Unveils Homegrown Drones," *The Chosunilbo*, September 12, 2014, http://english.chosun.com/site/data/html_dir/2014/04/09/2014040901658.html.

33. Ian Steadman, "South Korea Develops Its Own Kamikaze Combat Drone," *Wired UK*, September 12, 2014, http://www.wired.co.uk/news/archive/2012–09/14/south-korean-drones.

34. See Rhee Sang-Woo, "South Korea's Military Reform in the Aftermath of the Cheonan Incident," 10–11, www.nids.go.jp/english/event/symposium/pdf/2010/e_01.pdf.

35. "South Korea to Launch Pre-Emptive Strike If Threatened, Says Seoul," *The Hindu*, January 20, 2010.

36. See Rhee Sang-Woo, "South Korea's Military Reform in the Aftermath of the Cheonan Incident," 11.

37. "South Korea Adjusts Military Posture after Ship Attack," *Nuclear Threat Initiative*, March 21, 2011.

38. Ibid.

39. Rhee Sang-Woo, "South Korea's Military Reform in the Aftermath of the Choenan Incident," *National Institute for Defense Studies*, 2010, 11–12, www.nids.go.jp/english/event/symposium/pdf/2010/e_01.pdf.

40. "Seoul Halts All Trade with N. Korea," *The Chosunilbo*, May 25, 2010.

41. "S. Korea Warns of Pre-Emptive Strike against North over Nuclear Tests," Reuters, February 9, 2013, http://rt.com/news/south-korea-first-strike-806/.

42. Scott Snyder, "Pursuing a Comprehensive Vision for the US–South Korea Alliance," Center for Strategic and International Studies, April 2009, 12, https://asiafoundation.org/resources/pdfs/SnyderPursuingCompVisionApr09.pdf.

43. "2012 Defense White Paper of the Republic of South Korea," www.mnd.go.kr/user/mnd_eng/upload/pblictn/PBLICTNEBOOK_201308141005219260.pdf.

44. Ibid.

45. S. Korea Warns of Pre-Emptive Strike."

46. Donald Kirk, "US and South Korea Postpone Transfer of Wartime Control to Seoul," *Christian Science Monitor*, April 25, 2014, www.csmonitor.com/World/Security-Watch/Under-the-Radar/2014/0425/US-and-South-Korea-postpone-transfer-of-wartime-control-to-Seoul.

47. See note 43.

48. "President Chides Military for Weak Drone Defense," *Korea Herald*, April 7, 2014, www.koreaherald.com/view.php?ud=20140407001357.

49. "S. Korea Developing 'Bunker-Buster' Bomb," *The Chosunilbo*, December 16, 2011.

50. "US Approves Sale of Earth Penetrator Bombs to South Korea," Nuclear Threat Initiative, December 7, 2011.

51. North Korea is reportedly developing its own suicide-attack drone based on the US Streaker. See www.wired.co.uk/news/archive/2012–09/14/south-korean-drones.

52. Kurt Weyland, "Theories of Policy Diffusion Lessons from Latin America Pension Reform," *World Politics* 57, no. 2 (2011): 270.

53. Fisk and Ramos, "Actions Speak Louder Than Words."

54. Randall R. Schweller, "Domestic Structure and Preventive War: Are Democracies More Pacific?" *World Politics* 44, no. 2 (1992): 235–69; and Levy, "Preventive War."

55. Ruy Teixeria, "Public Opinion Snapshots: Americans and Israelis Urge Caution on Military Action," Center for American Progress, March 12, 2012, www.americanprogress.org/issues/public-opinion/news/2012/03/12/11258/public-opinion-snapshot-americans-and-israelis-urge-caution-on-military-action-against-iran/.

56. For a detailed discussion of the uncertainty inherent in knowing and measuring "intentions," see Brent J. Steele, *Alternative Accountabilities in Global Politics: The Scars of Violence* (New York: Routledge, 2013).

57. Andrew Blake, "Obama-Led Drone Strikes Kill Innocents 90% of the Time: Report," *Washington Times*, October 15, 2015, www.washingtontimes.com/news/2015/oct/15/90-of-people-killed-by-us-drone-strikes-in-afghani/.

58. Allen Buchanan and Robert O. Keohane, "The Preventive Use of Force: A Cosmopolitan Institutional Proposal," *Ethics & International Affairs* 18, no. 1 (2004): 1–22; and Whitley Kaufman, "What's Wrong with Preventive War? The Moral and Legal Basis for the Preventive Use of Force," *Ethics & International Affairs* 19, no. 3 (2005): 23–38.

59. Buchanan and Keohane, "Preventive Use of Force."

60. Allen Buchanan and Robert O. Keohane, "Toward a Drone Accountability Regime," *Ethics & International Affairs* 29, no. 1 (2015): 15–37.

61. Steele, *Alternative Accountabilities in Global Politics*.

62. "Global Opposition to Drones," Pew, July 14, 2014, www.pewglobal.org/2014/07/14/global-opposition-to-u-s-surveillance-and-drones-but-limited-harm-to-americas-image/.

63. Other reasons may include preference to capture rather than kill. See also James Igoe Walsh, "The Effectiveness of Drone Strikes in Counterinsurgency and Counterterrorism Campaigns," US Army War College Strategic Studies Institute, 2014, www.strategicstudiesinstitute.army.mil/pdffiles/PUB1167.pdf.

64. Holger Stark, "Kunduz Bombing Affairs: German Colonel Wanted to Destroy Insurgents," December 29, 2009, www.spiegel.de/international/germany/kunduz-bombing-affair-german-colonel-wanted-to-destroy-insurgents-a-669444.html/.

65. Press TV, "Anti-War Protesters in Germany Slam US Drone Strikes," September 27, 2015, www.presstv.com/Detail/2015/09/27/430902/Germany-US-base-Ramstein-killer-drones.

66. Deen K. Chatterjee, ed., *The Ethics of Preventive War* (New York: Cambridge University Press, 2013), 1–14.

67. Deen K. Chatterjee, "Beyond Preventive Force: Just Peace as Preventive Non-Intervention," in *Preventive Force: Targeted Killing and Technology*, ed. Kerstin Fisk and Jennifer Ramos (New York: New York University Press, 2016).

5

France and the American Drone Precedent

A Consequentialist Response to a Polemical Critique

JEAN-BAPTISTE JEANGÈNE VILMER

One of the manifestations of the current challenges that the traditional notion of sovereignty is facing is the increasing use of armed drones to conduct strikes in contested territories over which states do not have effective control: Waziristan, Yemen, Somalia, and Syria. Roughly eighty states—and even certain nonstate actors—have drones, but only a few currently have armed drones: Israel, the United States, the United Kingdom, Iran, China, Saudi Arabia, the United Arab Emirates, Nigeria, Pakistan, Iraq, and Turkey. But this landscape may quickly be changing. The armament of drones may seem to be a widespread and irreversible trend because of the numerous advantages drones offer—yet drones remain a subject of considerable debate. This is particularly true in France, where the controversial precedent set by the United States (discussed in part in chapter 4 by Fisk and Ramos) is at the center of public debates. As we think about the proliferation of armed drones, it is important to grasp the misconceptions about drones circulating in the public sphere and also to better understand the characteristics specific to armed drones. Reconsidering the misconceptions about drones will allow us to better evaluate whether drones can, indeed, navigate the tension between security, risk, and uncertainty with regard to the terrorist threat that Emery explores in chapter 9 of this volume.

As France contemplates arming its drones, this chapter asks the following question: What have we learned about the specific advantages of drones and their application in foreign affairs from the American precedent? In answering this question, the chapter assesses the legitimacy of armed drones as a means, and targeted killing as a policy, during the past two decades. The chapter is framed as a partial response to correct some of the misconceptions about drones found in Grégoire Chamayou's work *Théorie du drone* (*A Theory of the Drone*; originally published in 2013, and translated into English in 2015). Chamayou has been a critical voice at the center of debates in France surrounding drones; he maintains that drone operators are all "killers" and that the ethics of the drone is that of "executioners."[1] Parallel arguments in the United States have been driven by the antiwar activist Medea Benjamin, as cited by French, Sisk, and Bass in chapter 10 of this volume. Although the literature on drones in the United States is indeed rich, it is beyond the scope of this chapter to fully engage with it.[2] Rather, my examination seeks to incorporate relevant criticisms while meeting head-on the common misconceptions—epitomized by Chamayou's work—about armed drones that permeate the public sphere. Taking a consequentialist approach to evaluate drone strikes by the United States, my primary goal is to argue that, in contrast to Chamayou's claims that drones are part of a "death ethics" projecting Western imperial power, drones provide states with clear tactical and ethical advantages that can, if used properly, satisfy international humanitarian law (IHL) and counter real-world threats. While criticizing elements of the American precedent, I also defend the use of drones for targeted killing as a lesser evil compared with other legitimate alternatives. Challenging Fisk and Ramos's argument in chapter 4, I thus contest the view that the US precedent will necessarily be followed. To this end, I advocate more restrictive policy recommendations for the French to adopt in their future drone policies to address some of Chamayou's more legitimate concerns. A secondary goal of the chapter is to provide a window into some of the elements that shape the debate on the proliferation of armed drones, in France at least, and thus give insight into how the American precedent may (or may not) influence future drone use. Understanding these competing frameworks of the drone debate is particularly pressing given the threat France faces from ISIS, and the measures it might be willing to take in a world of contested and fragmented sovereignty.

CLEARING UP COMMON MISCONCEPTIONS ABOUT ARMED DRONES

The French philosopher Grégoire Chamayou, in his work *A Theory of the Drone*, is guilty of several misconceptions about drones that, if taken seriously, skew the real concerns at stake in the debate about arming drones. As I have elaborated on elsewhere, Chamayou reduces the use of armed drones to a capitalistic weapon enabling Americans to export their imperialism and oppression, a move that succeeds more in placating the views of political activists than engaging the heart of the drone controversy.[3] In what follows, I take issue with four misconceptions that Chamayou puts forth about armed drones.

The first misconception is that what is presented to us as a drone problem is most of the time a problem with American-armed military drones used by the US Central Intelligence Agency (CIA) for targeted killing—that is, a problem with a policy that is of course debatable but to which "the drone" should not be reduced. This policy of targeted killing is questionable, morally as well as legally, but the end and the means must not be confused. It is of course possible to pursue the same end with other means—airplanes, missiles, helicopters, snipers, commandos, killers on foot, polonium 210, and so on. Conversely, it is also possible to use the same means for other ends; the use of drones for targeted killing is highly publicized because it is the most controversial, but quantitatively it remains very minor. There is a legitimate use for drones in situations of armed conflict, which is no more problematic than that of airplanes and helicopters. That the cockpit is not in the vehicle in the air but somewhere else on the ground does not constitute a relevant difference in most situations.

A second point of confusion to avoid is the one between drones and lethal autonomous weapon systems, commonly known in the media as "killer robots." These are weapons that, once activated, are able to independently—meaning without human interference or supervision—acquire and engage targets, adapting to a changing environment.[4] Contrary to widespread belief, the absence of humans *in* drones does not make them free of humans. For example, running four Reapers involves about 160 people on the ground. Chamayou argues that the human-free nature of drones provides a technological solution to the challenge politicians face in mobilizing support for war. With drones and robots fighting wars instead of citizens, politicians would not need to rally citizens to shed their blood, because they would have a risk-free army to do so.[5] I take issue with this point below—as does Emery in chapter 9 of this book, albeit with an alternative argument.

A third, related point is that despite having no human in the machine, this does not mean that the machine is inhumane. Unfortunately, many drone opponents use this homonymy sophism. The fact that in the machine there is no individual belonging to the human species does not mean that that machine cannot be the least likely to cause unnecessary harm. These are two different things, with no logical connection between them. This homonymy sophism also occurs in the British antidrone protesters' slogan: "We don't want to lose our humanity." The humanity in question is humanitarian sentiment, and the contention is that drones threaten it because there is no human being in the cockpit. But there were humans in the Halifax and Lancaster bombers that attacked Hamburg in 1943 and Dresden in 1945, and also in the Tornado aircraft that bombed Iraq, Serbia, Afghanistan, and Libya during the past two decades; yet these British antidrone protesters do not conclude that these British planes were more "humane" on account of being manned.

Behind this homonymy sophism, and the fallacious conclusion that drones are necessarily inhumane because they are unmanned, is often the assertion that drones are necessarily inhumane because they kill. Yet unless one is a pacifist, one must accept the fact that killing is the inevitable essence of war. This assertion is based on a naive view of ethics as a doctrine of the good, whereas it is rather a doctrine of the lesser evil and sometimes characterized by moral disagreements with tragic consequences. Chamayou, for instance, asks: "How can one describe as 'humanitarian' procedures designed to annihilate human life?"[6] In fact, no one says that drones *are* humanitarian. Many—including myself—do say that they *can be more* humanitarian than other weapons. This is a very different statement, a relative position rather than an absolute one.

Chamayou cannot deny that there are degrees of humanitarianism in weapons unless he treats all of them as equal. Yet IHL distinguishes among them, forbidding some, permitting others, precisely on humanitarian grounds. If there were no such degrees of humanitarianism in different ways of killing, a principle like the prohibition of means of warfare of a nature to cause superfluous injury or unnecessary suffering—defined as "a harm greater than that unavoidable to achieve legitimate military objectives"—would never have come about.[7] Introduced in IHL as early as the nineteenth century, this principle serves to condemn weapons like expanding or explosive bullets, poison or poisoned weapons, biological and chemical weapons, antipersonnel land mines, and incendiary weapons. Assuming that Chamayou supports these humanitarian principles, he has no choice but to recognize that some weapons respect them more than others, and therefore that it is possible to say that one weapon is more humanitarian in comparison with another. To understand why drones are more humanitarian, we need to delve more into the specificities of drones.

A fourth common misconception relates to misunderstanding the technological advantages specific to drones (and criticizing them as if they brought some radically new element to warfare). In contrast to a common refrain among critics, it is false to assert that drones are different because they are able to kill at a distance without risk. The power to kill without fear of being killed, the absence of risk reciprocity, the violation of Michael Walzer's rule that "you can't kill unless you are prepared to die"—these are not new to the era of drones.[8] Chamayou invokes the following scenario: Sheltered in a base of Nevada, the drone operator kills from afar (an insurgent, a civilian—can one be sure . . . ?), without being prepared to die himself. The drone thus embodies a dramatic change in the very nature of warfare—combat no longer relies on the concept of shared risk, but on radical asymmetry. What causes moral outrage among drone opponents is the belief that such a fight is "unfair."

But is this really a specificity of the drone? All this is not new. As animals, human beings have an instinct for self-preservation; and as tool-making animals (in Benjamin Franklin's expression), they have always used their ingenuity to protect themselves while killing others. Human capacity for killing at a distance dates back to the Paleolithic era, and always was an engine for the evolution of weaponry (javelins, catapults, bows and arrows, cannons, rifles, revolvers, artillery, machine guns, submarines, airplanes, missiles, drones, and computers).[9]

The first submarines provoked a similar reaction. Before World War I, Adm. Sir Arthur Wilson described them as "unfair, underhand, and damned un-British," and King George V tried to secure their abolition.[10] The French Navy admiral Raoul Castex described them as "invulnerable. For them, the war became a game, a sport, a kind of hunt in which, having dispensed and distributed murder, they needed to do nothing but enjoy the spectacle of the agony of their victims. They, meanwhile, would be sheltered from any attacks and, once back in port, they could busy themselves recounting their hunting prowess."[11] The parallel with the drone debate is striking. Aerial bombing, first from unmanned balloons (the Austrians against Venice in 1849), and then from planes (the Italians against the Ottoman province of Libya in 1911), increased asymmetry, and later made possible the mass killing of civilians at a distance (in Dresden, Tokyo, Hiroshima, and Nagasaki), causing the same outrage.

Therefore, the drone is not the only weapon operating at a distance, just the latest; and it does not change the nature of modern war, which has often been asymmetrical. The drone operator is not threatened by the Afghan insurgent he is killing, but neither is the B-2 pilot dropping his bombs from 8,000 meters, nor the crew of a destroyer launching a missile 1,500 kilometers from the coast, nor that of a submarine hundreds of meters underwater. Remember that in seventy-eight days of bombing and more than 38,000 missions, NATO suffered no loss over Kosovo in 1999. Invulnerability can be obtained with men in cockpits; it simply is much more expensive. The Kosovo intervention provoked the same moral indignation about "riskless warfare," and that had nothing to do with drones.[12]

Some might counter that there is still a difference: The risk taken with a drone is not even infinitesimal (as it can be for pilots and crews in the combat zone) but absolutely nonexistent. Yet, this would still not be applicable solely to the drone, because the chief of staff, at his office in the capital, or those firing intercontinental ballistic missiles, are not taking more risk while making lethal decisions. War has always been safer for some. Moreover, as French, Sisk, and Bass show in chapter 10 of this volume, the risk is never zero for those who operate drones. It is not zero psychologically (studies have found that drone pilots experience mental health problems, in particular posttraumatic stress disorder, not less but at the same rate as manned aircraft pilots).[13] Nor is it negligible even physically, some drones being operated in situ. French surveillance drones were located in Bagram, Afghanistan, a base that has been attacked, and they are currently operated from Niamey, Niger—which could come under threat. The point is that for those on these bases, the risk is real. Moreover, those who speak of a nonexistent risk artificially isolate drones from a more complex system. Drones are not alone; they often support special ground forces, or allied forces (Pakistani and Yemeni, for example), not to mention the launch-and-recovery and technical teams in the zone of combat. Even at home, the US Air Force and CIA operators are at risk; if their identities were to become known, they would be potential targets for a terrorist attack. With drones now becoming airborne symbols of evil, crystallizing terrorists' desire for revenge, this domestic threat for drone operators is real. Therefore, not only is the absence of risk reciprocity not a new phenomenon and not specific to drones, but it is simplistic and false to speak of a "war without risk," as drone opponents often do.

The true specific advantage of the drone is its permanence in the sky—that is, its ability to loiter for long periods—and the intelligence this provides about whom to target. And if drones are armed, the ability to strike is part and parcel of this intelligence. The absence of humans on board permits a massive increase in airborne endurance; manned aircraft must refuel every 90 minutes or so and, due to pilot fatigue, cannot perform long missions (no more than 5 or 6 hours, in general). By comparison, the latest version of the Reaper equipped with additional fuel tanks can fly for 49 hours, and the Zephyr, a solar drone, for 54 hours. Pushing the limits of endurance is one of the areas of research for remotely piloted aircrafts (RPAs) of the future, with plans for solar RPAs and airships that could fly continuously for perhaps several years.

Persistence in flight is the primary operational gain and the true advantage specific to drones. Drones are thus creating the possibility of what some scholars have called "aerial occupation" by replacing the intermittent presence of aircraft with a permanent armed presence over certain zones.[14] Permanently present drones, equipped with sensors, produce actionable intelligence by observing closely what is on the ground for hours, days, or even weeks, which helps in identifying potential targets through an analysis of patterns of life, and seize what might be a narrow window of opportunity to strike a threat.

An unarmed drone depends on the availability of an aircraft to conduct the strike. But in the time period needed for the strike aircraft to arrive in the zone, the target could have moved into an environment where the risk of collateral damage is far higher. If you identified a target's vehicle in the desert, but then need to wait for a combat aircraft to be made available to deal with it, the vehicle could, by the time the aircraft arrives, have moved into town. So it is that the nonarmament of drones reduces choice as to timing and place, and at the same time increases the risk to civilian populations. It also increases the risks to soldiers on the ground. The British quickly realized that their armed drones acted as force multipliers and protectors.[15] Even the drones used today on humanitarian missions, such as that in the Democratic Republic of Congo (DRC) under the UN mandate since December 2014, might someday be usefully armed in an attempt to prevent the abuses that they record.[16]

But even if one gains an understanding of drones in this light, important moral questions about their use remain.

THE MORAL DEBATE: A CONSEQUENTIALIST ANSWER

There is a rich debate about the morality of drones, including about whether they lower the threshold for the use of force, whether they satisfy the *jus in bello* principles, and the extent to which they may undermine democratic accountability. To the extent that Chamayou participates in these debates, it is to completely reject the possibility of drones ever being a legitimate weapon. They are nothing more, to use his words, than "the weapon of an amnesic post-colonial violence."[17] In this section, I explore the legitimacy of drones by taking into account the effects on the ground. My argument is largely consequentialist: I think that the use of armed drones in some situations and under certain conditions produces better consequences not only for "us" (the intervening power) but also "them" (local civilians).

Concerning Civilian Casualties

No one disputes that drones cause civilian casualties, so-called collateral damage. It is inevitable—any weapon used in a civilian area will kill civilians. The debate is, rather, about the number of civilians killed, and more exactly about their proportion. The various reports show an amazing gap in numbers, from 3 percent (of civilian casualties) to 90 percent.[18] Who is right?

The methodological problem of counting the dead is well documented.[19] Thus, we should be very cautious about how we manipulate numbers, and avoid basing any argument on the number of civilian casualties. But in any case, focusing on numbers is misleading.[20] The ethical argument in favor of drones is not that they are *not* causing civilian casualties, or *few*, but *less* than other weapons. There is no point in waving figures on the number of civilians killed, because they cannot prove that the drones are not, all things considered, the least lethal means of conducting the fight. My argument is not absolutist: I am not saying that drone strikes are intrinsically good. It is relative: I am saying they are a lesser evil.

Chamayou writes that "to evaluate it properly, the drones should be set alongside weapons currently available for the same tactical function. . . . If one avoids being misled by some external attribute, the right form of comparison involves not a similarity of forms but an equivalence of functions."[21] He is absolutely right about this. So what does Chamayou compare to the drone? What alternative should we prefer? He has two answers to this question.

His first answer is "troops on the ground," for which "drones are a very imperfect substitute."[22] He remarks that, "for liquidating Osama bin Laden, the choice was between a drone and a commando raid, not between a drone and a Dresden-like bombing of Abbottabad."[23] But in fact, the choice was between the drone, the commandos, aerial bombardment (by modern bombers, not Dresden-epoch ones), and Tomahawk missiles. And the decision was commandos, not to minimize collateral damage but in order to gather intelligence (a "treasure trove" of more than six thousand documents recovered from computers, hard drives, and USB flash drives), to confirm bin Laden's identity and death, and to remove his body (so the Bilal house would not become a shrine).[24]

It is clearly in the realm of ground operations that Chamayou judges drone strikes. For example, he compares them with the use of hand grenades and concludes that drones are imprecise because the lethal radius of their missiles is 15 to 20 meters, while that of a hand grenade is 3 meters.[25] Defenders of drones, conversely, compare them with the Tomahawk missile (which, in its standard version, has a lethal radius of about 30 meters) or to GBU 12 (laser-guided) bombs (with a lethal radius of about 90 meters). From this point of view, drone-fired missiles are much more precise.

So the question is, which comparison is more relevant: the hand grenade in a ground operation, or the missiles and bombs in an air strike? In other words, what would replace drones if they did not exist, or if we were to stop using them tomorrow? Infantrymen armed with hand grenades? That is not very likely, for reasons that Chamayou himself points to: aversion to losses—not to mention the political dimension and issues of sovereignty. Lacking drones, Americans would not have invaded Pakistan, Yemen, and Somalia. Instead, they would have fired missiles and dropped bombs, as they did before they had drones. Or they would have waited until the problem called for a larger-scale air campaign. And then it would be not "one drone strike every four days" to complain about but perhaps 10,484 strikes in seventy-eight days, as over Serbia in 1999—that is, more than 134 strikes per day.[26]

So it is pointless to say that the Hellfire missile is less precise than the hand grenade, because the alternative is not the hand grenade. Instead, it should be noted that Hellfire missiles are more precise than their real alternatives—that is, Tomahawk missiles or bombs dropped from planes.

But let us play Chamayou's game for a moment: If we did replace the drone by a ground operation, would that really be better for the civilians? Chamayou avoids saying this, and with good reason. His nostalgia for conventional war favors ground actions because they involve Clausewitzian duels to express authentic warrior virtues, the ethics "of courage and sacrifice" that drones would corrupt into the ethics of "self-preservation and more or less presumed cowardice."[27] This statement attributes to the drone a transformative role that it does not have (for the drone is a symptom of this older change), and more important, it equates self-preservation with cowardice. Quite paradoxically, Chamayou's model is "the Crusader, a figure who more than any other in European history was enamored with classical armament and a desire to kill at close range."[28]

Chamayou need only look to two recent examples that are difficult to ignore—Iraq and Afghanistan—to see how a poor ground strategy can be disastrous for the civilian population. In criticizing Obama's stealth strategy (the trio of drones, special forces, and cyber warfare), he fails to understand that this "smart power" is a reaction against Bush's "global war," and that its purpose is precisely to move beyond the era of large deployments, which are very harmful both for the occupier (in human, financial, and political costs) and for the occupied (despite the minor gains that Orend describes in chapter 13). This movement away from invasion to sporadic drone strikes reduces the level of violence for many concerned.

Chamayou's second answer to the question of the alternative to drones is very simple: nothing. He argues against the claim "that drone use is justified because it would create fewer collateral victims than other weapons that could have been used in its place. What this argument postulates is that those other means really would have been used—in other words, that the military action would have taken place anyway."[29] History already disproves that nothing would have happened, as the United States did not wait for having drones to strike in the same places, only with other weapons. The only difference is that drones make it somewhat easier and are more accurate. Here, the preventive force norm that Fisk and Ramos point to in chapter 4 is a case in point.

But, for the sake of the argument, let us accept the hypothesis that without drones there would have been no American intervention in Pakistan, for instance. The question that Chamayou does not answer is, would that really have been better for the civilians? In fact, the American actions would not have been replaced by a gaping void, letting terrorism prosper in the region. They would have been replaced by operations that already complement them: actions by Pakistani forces.

For example, from the end of 2008 to the end of 2010, the Pakistan Air Force undertook more than 5,500 sorties and dropped 10,600 bombs on 4,600 targets in the northwest tribal areas.[30] These operations had many casualties. It is even likely that some of the casualties attributed to American drones were in fact casualties of Pakistani aircraft, for village witnesses blaming drones contain some incoherencies (drones do not fly "in pairs sometimes three together," and they do not make a "loud sound").[31]

Moreover, Pakistani forces conducted major ground offensives that caused large population displacements. The Second Battle of Swat (April 26–July 15, 2009) killed nearly 2,000 people and displaced 3.4 million. There is no evidence that drones have this perverse effect, but there is evidence that the Pakistan Army uses indiscriminate weapons in places where combatants and civilians mingle. It is also known for its abuses—thousands of extrajudicial executions, arbitrary detentions, the torture of men and children, and so on.[32]

Drone strikes should not be compared with "nothing," and not even with "peace," but rather, with the imprecise weapons and brutal methods of the Pakistan Army. Obviously peace is preferable to drone strikes, but if they were to stop tomorrow, peace would not descend on Waziristan, because the insurgents would still mount their attacks (as they had before the appearance of drones), and the Pakistani Taliban would still want to overturn the government; the only difference would be that Pakistani forces would redouble their efforts to conduct more anti-Taliban operations.

What the Amnesty International reports unintentionally demonstrate is that actually there are far fewer civilian casualties from American drones than from the armed groups that they are fighting against, or from the Pakistan Army, which is also conducting operations against those groups. However, by taking the absolutist position of denouncing everyone—the armed groups, the Pakistan Army, and the American drones—Amnesty International can express indignation about the civilian casualties of the drones, without noticing the relationship to the others, because their point, like Chamayou's, is simply that *drones are wrong*.

Against this attitude—seemingly noble but in fact supporting a policy that would maximize the misery of those living in the afflicted region—I would appeal to Raymond Aron's more realistic observation: "Politics is never a conflict between good and evil, but always a choice between the preferable and the detestable. It is always so, especially in foreign policy."[33] In the case at hand, this means that one cannot consider two evils equally reprehensible if removing the lesser one means strengthening the greater one; stopping the drone strikes would encourage the Pakistan Army to conduct more operations that would likely produce many more civilian casualties than are currently produced by American drones.

Other Consequences

There are additional issues with the consequentialist approach that are more difficult to resolve. For example, calculating their efficiency: Are drone strikes reducing the security threat or, on the contrary, increasing it? In other words, do drones really make the United States safer? This calculation uses four criteria.

The first criterion is the impact on al-Qaeda. On one hand, drones eliminate terrorists and therefore weaken certain networks. But not all of them are important. It is estimated that only 2 percent of victims are "high-level" targets. Even if immediately replaced, the loss of these leaders disorganizes the network and puts the new leaders on the run, creating additional stresses, and so on. Bin Laden's writings found after his death confirmed that he deplored the impact of drone strikes and recommended that leaders leave Waziristan and find safer havens. On the other hand, the correlation between drone strikes and the decline of al-Qaeda activity has not been proven. The link is not necessarily causal, because there are many other factors to incorporate. Moreover, the dispersal of al-Qaeda away from Waziristan to other regions, like the Sahel or the Middle East, is problematic and raises additional concerns.

Second is the impact on the civilian population: The negative impact of drones on the population is an effective tool for recruitment and motivation of the armed groups. Obama's drones, from this point of view, have the same perverse effect that Guantánamo had for Bush: They have become symbols of oppression. But we need to be careful here, and not simplify the problem; not all local populations are against drone strikes. It depends on the frequency of their use and government propaganda. Yemen and Pakistan are very different in this respect.[34]

Third, as Brunstetter notes in chapter 11, there is an impact on bilateral relations and the effectiveness of international law enforcement mechanisms: Drone strikes affected the cooperation between the United States and Pakistan, making antiterrorist cooperation more difficult and therefore less effective.

And the fourth criterion is the impact on international peace and security: The legality of these strikes is at best questionable when the targets are not related to the 9/11 attacks and do not pose an immediate threat to American security. Therefore, they are dangerous precedents that could be invoked by other powers in the future, especially if the benefits of drones—low cost, endurance, ability to penetrate enemy lines discreetly and safely—could encourage states to conduct armed operations that they would not have conducted otherwise. In other words, are drones a destabilizing factor in the international arena?

What happens, for example, when the Chinese use drones to strike Uyghurs in their own territory or in Kazakhstan, or when the Indians strike in Kashmir, the Russians in the Caucasus, the Turks in Kurdistan? Will they invoke the American precedent? Maybe. In chapter 4, Fisk and Ramos reference evidence that the US preventive force policy is already endorsed by countries, like India and Russia, that condemned the preventive force norm at the time of the 2003 Iraq War but now see it as being in line with their own interest. And yet, I find it hard to believe that countries like the ones cited above *need* the American precedent to justify any lethal actions whose legality and legitimacy are questionable. It is not as if they have never violated international humans rights law before. Iran, to take another example, did not wait for the American precedent to arm its drones; it was already using tactical drones, such as the Mahjer, to deliver unguided RPG munitions during the Iran/Iraq War in the 1980s.[35] Today, Iran is using its armed Shahed 129 drones to strike in Syria.[36] Iran, like Russia and China, does not need to invoke a normative framework to justify its actions. The US policy has not been an encouragement for them; it is very likely that, with or without it, they would have developed these capacities and practices anyway when it suited them. Besides, the fact that the British have armed Reapers has not led them to adopt the American strategy of targeted killing.

In short, it is very difficult to take into account all the consequences of drone use. However, this does not mean we should reject drones outright. Nor does it mean we should not try to better understand their impact. It is in the best interest of the American government to reevaluate its use of drones, doing its best to take into consideration in its utilitarian calculus these criteria. To this end, Emery's objections (in chapter 9 below) against any consequentialist calculation are strong; the difficulty is not to assess the morality of a particular strike, or even a drone warfare campaign in a given area, but rather to understand the long-term effects of such a practice, which are unpredictable. The "epistemic argument against consequentialism"—the ex ante impossibility to know the future, and the correlative post facto impossibility to assess counterfactuals—is probably the most common, although not least potent, objection to consequentialism.[37] I fully recognize this difficulty, but I simply do not see a better normative ethic approach—not even the just war tradition—to assess the morality of drone strikes. Deontologism is impracticable if we do not believe in the sanctity of certain principles, and virtue ethics, as shown below, is useful to explain certain resistance to drones, but it is certainly not sufficient to assess the legitimacy of drone warfare and/or targeted killing in general. Therefore, I consider consequentialism to be the least bad approach.

Drones and War without Virtue?

One of the most troublesome aspects of drone strikes, the moral malaise that is noticeable not only in the public debate but also in some military circles, is a concern with the kind of combatant we want to be. Chamayou, for example, suggests that drone warfare is not even war, that their use has totally changed the face of war. For him, drones are part of a global hunt for presumed terrorists, with the United States killing people whose identity they mostly do not know without taking any risk themselves. Here, it is worth noting that Chamayou totally ignores what the terrorists do, making it seem that drones are the only killers in the region. This is the great cleverness of his book; by erasing the reasons for drone strikes, he makes them illegitimate in the eyes of readers who no longer understand what the Americans are doing in Pakistan. Yet, it is rather sophistic to deplore the consequences without presenting the reasons. Chamayou laments that the means are asymmetrical, without observing that they are a response and that what is being responded to is also asymmetrical. Portraying the problem as "a hunter who moves forward and a prey that flees or hides" paints a false portrait of the relationship.[38] The target of the drone, who in principle is supposed to be a terrorist, is not chosen at random but precisely because of what he or she has done, is supposed to have done, or is potentially capable of doing to the hunter, who kills for self-protection.

Still, what bothers many critics is the absence of reciprocity, the perception that it is "too easy." Can a "desk job" still be combat? And what happened to the martial virtues of honor and courage, among others?[39] The importance of virtue ethics when talking about drones is seen in the so-called drone-medal affair. When then–US defense secretary Leon Panetta announced the creation of an award for service members who remotely launch unmanned military strikes or cyberattacks, and explained that such a distinction would rank higher than the Bronze Star and the Purple Heart, various associations of veterans immediately protested on the grounds that "there is a fundamental difference between those who fight remotely, or via computer, and those fighting against an enemy who is trying to kill them."[40] The Pentagon later suspended the new military medal. What this drone-medal affair reveals is that prestige and military values are still closely linked to the risk taken. That is why many consider drone strikes as acts of cowardice.

What can we answer to such a critique? To begin with, the absence of risk is neither new nor unique to drones, as we saw above. Moreover, such indignation today is based on an outdated premise. War is not conventional anymore—it is no longer a Clausewitzian frontal impact, it is not a duel, and should not be thought of as if it were one. Those who seem to miss the wars of old times where soldiers sacrificed themselves on the field of glory have a romantic conception of war that misses the point that we are now in a post-heroic age.[41] In chapter 9 Emery makes one attempt at reconceptualizing these outdated premises and updating our conceptual understanding of risk with his neo-Clausewitzian model for the contemporary era.

All this to say that there is a gap between the perception of what war should be and the reality of what it has become. The perception is still based on the symmetrical model of conventional war (two armies on a battlefield). The reality is that war is irregular and asymmetric, now based on the avoidance of a frontal confrontation; most of the time, the enemy is not made up of traditional combatants in uniforms organized in battalions, but deterritorialized nonstate actors, part-time civilian bombers. In this respect, drone strikes are an asymmetric response to an asymmetric threat.

Even from a virtue ethics point of view, there is a conflict of virtues. Courage is not the only military virtue. Honor is another one, which can be demonstrated though respect for *jus in bello* principles (distinction, proportionality, necessity, and the prohibition against unnecessary suffering). As French, Sisk, and Bass show in chapter 10, drones do pose challenges for fighting honorably, but this does not make doing so impossible.

However, to take the question in a different direction, what if these two virtues are incompatible? Pakistani soldiers are braver than American drone operators when conducting their ground operations in Waziristan, because they risk their lives. But which of the two are the most honorable? Which better respects the principles of *jus in bello*? If using a drone is more discriminating and causes less collateral damage than a ground invasion, which virtue is more important—the courage of soldiers showing little honor, or the honor of soldiers showing little courage?[42]

Being a consequentialist, my criterion is the harm caused to individuals, not the respect of virtues as if they had intrinsic value; I do not care that a soldier or drone operator is seen as less courageous if the means with which he or she fights requires less risk but also leads to fewer civilian casualties than other means.

CONCLUSION

"Nuclear weapons explode the theory of just war," famously stated Michael Walzer.[43] Tomorrow, autonomy will potentially be a comparable revolution, challenging the applicability of the traditional criteria of just war theory. I do not see this happening with the issue of drones and targeted killing, which do not radically change the nature of warfare. Of course, they do raise questions about certain criteria, like the imminence of the threat (just cause and last resort), but that is hardly new. From this perspective, the issue of drones and targeted killing is part of the larger and much older debate about the prevention/preemption distinction (see Fisk and Ramos in chapter 4).

Provided that we do not confuse the thing with its use, it is quite possible to condemn the abuses of a permissive policy such as signature strikes without calling into question the general idea that, as Walzer argues, "drone warfare could take the form of targeted killing, and it could be justified under tough constraints."[44] This is what Walzer does when he criticizes the excessive use of drones and the abuses of signature strikes, but without throwing out the baby with the bathwater. Here, Brunstetter's *jus ad vim* project discussed in chapter 11 offers one way to think about how to provide ethical constraints for drone use outside the hot battlefield.

The distinction between outright rejection (Chamayou) and criticism (Walzer) is especially useful for a country like France, where a discreet debate is emerging over the possible weaponization of its Reaper, currently based in Niamey, Niger. Unarmed, they are used only for so-called ISR missions (i.e., intelligence preparation of the battlefield, supporting conventional and special operation troops during engagements, monitoring suspected jihadists, and finding or rescuing hostages). The objective of arming them would be to cover the entire kill chain (find, fix, track, target, engage, assess).

The priority for the future naturally needs to be demystifying the machine by explaining again and again what a drone is, and what it is for, and by countering antidrone propaganda, which is proliferating because of ignorance and paranoia. If the French did arm their drones, we would need to stress sufficiently well what separates us from the Americans to refute the confusion of ideas in the public mind, but without doing it too head-on so as not to damage diplomatic relations. It would also be necessary to emphasize that when used in an armed conflict, these machines, which are piloted by genuine Air Force pilots, are subjected to the same rules of engagement and the same constraints as any other aircraft.

After that, we have the issue of targeted killing. First, France would in any case be more discreet and parsimonious in using its armed drones, for the simple reason that it would have very few of them (12 Reapers, while the US Air Force had 346 in 2016). Apart from that, I recommend that France adopt a more restrictive approach to targeted killing, limited to *personality strikes against high-value targets, a very restricted list of leaders of terrorist organizations we are fighting who pose an immediate and demonstrable threat to national security, and when the state in which they are situated does not have the will or the capability to eliminate the threat*. This is very different from the CIA's signature-strike program that has fueled much of the criticism over drones. But drones in general should not be reduced to this controversial policy.

Next, we have to consider the measures needed to satisfy the democratic requirement for transparency and responsibility. This means communicating either before a strike on the processes and standards of targeting (who decides what, how, and according to what criteria) or after a strike has occurred (the identity of the person and the cause of the strike—that is, what constituted the immediate threat, and why it was not possible to capture the person or neutralize him or her in any other way). In a letter to the US federal prosecutor, three members of the Senate Select Committee on Intelligence made a distinction between the list of strategies to combat terrorism (the playbook), of which several sections should stay secret, and the list of rules (the rule book) that the government follows in such situations, which should always be available to the American public.[45]

We might also imagine setting up systems for monitoring. Two types are possible: The first, on the lines of the US Foreign Intelligence Surveillance Act, would authorize strikes before they take place, except in urgent situations, which would be analyzed afterward—in either case, the deliberations would be classified.[46] The second would possibly be along the lines of the Israeli model, which has been operating for several years; by request of the Supreme Court, a thorough poststrike inquiry into a targeted killing would be conducted by an independent body.

The problem with these measures, of course, is that they could affect military effectiveness. The more the process and norms are precise and known, the more the adversary is able to bypass them and restrict our action. Because of this, there is great value in "strategic ambiguity," which means not being clear about one's position. Conversely, excessive ambiguity, a lack of information, risks arousing suspicion and even hostility with regard to an ill-understood policy. The British have grasped this and recommend keeping the public informed as much as possible.[47] The challenge, then, is to make available certain information in order to increase transparency and a feeling of legitimacy, without at the same time affecting national interests. Reveal enough to reassure, but not enough to handicap operations.

NOTES

1. E.g., see his contributions, featured by Alexandra Schwarzbrod, "La guerre devient un télétravail pour employés de bureau," *Liberation*, May 19, 2013, www.liberation.fr/planete/2013/05/19/la-guerre-devient-un-teletravail-pour-employes-de-bureau_904153; Grégoire Chamayou, *France Inter*, July 4, 2013, www.franceinter.fr/emission-linvite-du-57-gregoire-chamayou; Grégoire Chamayou, "Drone et kamikaze, jeu de miroirs," *Le Monde*, April 2013, www.monde-diplomatique.fr/2013/04/chamayou/49004; and Grégoire Chamayou, *A Theory of the Drone* (New York: New Press, 2015), 313, 95, 226.

2. See, e.g., Daniel R. Brunstetter and Megan Braun, "The Implications of Drones on the Just War Tradition," *Ethics & International Affairs* 25, no. 3 (2011): 337–58; Bradley Jay Strawser, ed., *Killing by Remote Control: The Ethics of Unmanned Military* (Oxford: Oxford University Press, 2013); Claire Finkelstein, Jens David Ohlin, and Andrew Altmen, eds., *Targeted Killings: Law and Morality in an Asymmetrical World* (Oxford: Oxford University Press, 2012); Christian Enemark, *Armed Drones and the Ethics of War: Military Virtue in a Post-Heroic Age* (New York: Routledge, 2014); Rosa Brooks, "Drones and the International Rule of Law," *Ethics & International Affairs* 28. no. 1 (2014): 83–103; and Kerstin Fisk and Jennifer M. Ramos, eds., *Preventive Force: Drones, Targeted Killing, and the Transformation of Contemporary Warfare* (New York: New York University Press, 2016).

3. See Jean-Baptiste Jeangène Vilmer, "An Ideology of the Drone," trans. John Zvesper, *Books and Ideas*, www.booksandideas.net/An-Ideology-of-the-Drone.html.

4. Jean-Baptiste Jeangène Vilmer, "Terminator Ethics: Should We Ban 'Killer Robots?'" *Ethics & International Affairs*, Online Exclusive, March 23, 2015, www.ethicsandinternationalaffairs.org/2015/terminator-ethics-ban-killer-robots/; and "Autonomous Weapon Diplomacy: The Geneva Debates," *Ethics & International Affairs*, Online Exclusive, September 27, 2016, www.ethicsandinternationalaffairs.org/2016/autonomous-weapon-diplomacy-geneva-debates/.

5. Chamayou, *Theory of the Drone*, 185–94.

6. Ibid., 135.

7. International Court of Justice, *Nuclear Weapons* case, Advisory Opinion, § 238.

8. Michael Walzer, *Arguing about War* (New Haven, CT: Yale University Press, 2004), 101. See also P. Robinson, "'Ready to Kill but Not to Die': NATO Strategy in Kosovo," *International Journal* 54 (1999): 672–73.

9. Steven E. Churchill and Jill A. Rhodes, "The Evolution of the Human Capacity for 'Killing at a Distance': The Human Fossil Evidence for the Evolution of Projectile Weaponry," in *The Evolution of Hominin Diets*, ed. Jean Jacques Hublin and Michael P. Richards (New York: Springer, 2009), 201–10.

10. A. V. Lowe, "Comments on Howard S. Levie's Paper: Submarine Warfare—with Emphasis on the 1936 London Protocol," in *The Law of Naval Warfare: Targeting Enemy Merchant Shipping*, ed. Richard J. Grunawalt (Newport, RI: Naval War College, 1993), 72.

11. Raoul Castex, *Synthèse de la guerre sous-marine* (Paris: Challemel, 1920), 121, quoted by Chamayou, *Theory of the Drone*, 91.

12. Paul W. Kahn, "The Paradox of Riskless Warfare," *Philosophy and Public Policy Quarterly* 22, no. 3 (2002): 2–8.

13. Jean L. Otto and Bryant J. Webber, "Mental Health Diagnoses and Counseling among Pilots of Remotely Piloted Aircraft in the United States Air Force," *Medical Surveillance Monthly Report* (US Armed Forces Health Surveillance Center) 20, no. 3 (March 2013): 3–8; and Wayne Chappelle, Tanya Goodman, Laura Reardon, and William Thompson, "An Analysis of Post-Traumatic Stress Symptoms in United States Air Force Drone Operators," *Journal of Anxiety Disorders* 28, no. 5 (2014): 480–87.

14. John R. Emery and Daniel Brunstetter, "Drones as Aerial Occupation," *Peace Review* 27, no. 4 (2015): 424–43.

15. Birmingham Policy Commission, "The Security Impact of Drones: Challenges and Opportunities for the UK," October 2014, www.birmingham.ac.uk/Documents/research/policycommission/remote-warfare/final-report-october-2014.pdf.

16. For a more in-depth discussion of the case of the DRC and the UN's use of drones, see, on the pro side, David Whetham, "Drones to Protect," *International Journal of Human Rights* 19, no. 2 (2015): 199–210; and on the contra side, John R. Emery, "The Promises and Pitfalls of Humanitarian Drones," *Ethics & International Affairs* 30, no. 2 (2016): 1–13.

17. Chamayou, *Theory of the Drone*, 59.

18. The Pakistani government said in 2013 that only 3 percent of the 2,227 people killed in US drone strikes since 2008 were civilians, a figure strikingly lower than its previous estimations; Pakistani minister of defense, interviewed at the US Senate, 98th session, October 30, 2013, www.senate.gov.pk/uploads/documents/questions/1383111609_934.pdf. The New America Foundation estimate is between 8 and 11 percent for 2004–February 2016 in Pakistan (http://securitydata.newamerica.net/drones/pakistan-analysis.html); the Bureau of Investigative Journalism between 17 and 24 percent for the same period and country (www.thebureauinvestigates.com/category/projects/drones/drones-graphs/). *The Intercept* finds that "during one five-month period of the operation, according to the documents, nearly 90 percent of the people killed in air strikes were not the intended targets" (https://theintercept.com/drone-papers/the-assassination-complex/). On the discrepancies, see Chris Woods, "Understanding the Gulf between Public and US Government Estimates of Civilian Casualties in Covert Drone Strikes," in *Drones and the Future of Armed Conflict: Ethical, Legal and Strategic Implications,* ed. David Cortright, Rachel Fairhurst, and Kristen Wall (Chicago: University of Chicago Press, 2015), 180–98.

19. Human Rights Clinic, Columbia Law School, "Counting Drone Strike Deaths," October 2012.

20. Compare: Megan Braun and Daniel R. Brunstetter, "Rethinking the Criterion for Assessing CIA-Targeted Killings: Drones, Proportionality and *Jus Ad Vim*," *Journal of Military Ethics* 12, no. 4 (2013): 304–24; and Avery Plaw and Carlos R. Colon,

"Correcting the Record: Civilians, Proportionality, and the *Jus ad Vim*," in *Legitimacy and Drones: Investigating the Legality, Morality, and Efficacy of UCAVs*, ed. Steven J. Barela (Farnham, UK: Ashgate, 2015), 163–89.

21. Chamayou, *Theory of the Drone*, 141.

22. Ibid., 190.

23. Ibid., 141.

24. However, the avoidance of collateral damage was a factor that Obama used to justify the form of the raid to the American public in his very first and dramatic address that Sunday evening in May 2011.

25. Chamayou, *Theory of the Drone*, 141–42.

26. Grégoire Chamayou, "Drones: Comment des milliers de personnes sont exécutées en dehors de tout cadre légal" (interview), *Basta!* October 16, 2013, www.bastamag.net/Drones-comment-des-milliers-de.

27. Grégoire Chamayou, "Un drone, ça ne fait pas de prisonniers," *Télérama*, May 18, 2013, www.telerama.fr/monde/un-drone-ca-ne-fait-pas-de-prisonniers-gregoire-chamayou-chercheur-au-cnrs,97456.php.

28. Victor D. Hanson, *The Western Way of War: Infantry Battle in Classical Greece* (Berkeley: University of California Press, 1994), 14.

29. Chamayou, *Theory of the Drone*, 189.

30. Stephen Trimble, "Dubai: F-16s Powered Up Pakistan's Counter-Insurgency Strikes," *Flight Global*, November 13, 2011, www.flightglobal.com/news/articles/dubai-f-16s-powered-up-pakistans-counter-insurgency-strikes-364727/. See also Avery Plaw, "Counting the Dead: The Proportionality of Predation in Pakistan," in *Killing by Remote Control: The Ethics of an Unmanned Military*, ed. Bradley J. Strawser (New York: Oxford University Press, 2013): 126–53.

31. Amnesty International, "Will I Be Next," October 2013, 19, 31.

32. Amnesty International, "The Hands of Cruelty," December 2012.

33. Raymond Aron, *The Committed Observer: Interviews with Jean-Louis Missika and Dominique Wolton* (Chicago: Regnery Gateway, 1983), 246.

34. C. Christine Fair, Karl Kaltenthaler, and William J. Miller, "You Say Pakistanis All Hate the Drone War? Prove It," *The Atlantic*, January 23, 2013, www.theatlantic.com/international/archive/2013/01/you-say-pakistanis-all-hate-the-drone-war-prove-it/267447/.

35. See, e.g., this video shot in 1984: www.youtube.com/watch?v=uADrXnAHT1Y.

36. Paul McLeary, "Iranian Drones Now Hitting Rebel Targets in Syria," *Foreign Policy*, February 29, 2016, http://foreignpolicy.com/2016/02/29/iranian-drones-now-hitting-rebel-targets-in-syria/.

37. James Lenman, "Consequentialism and Cluelessness," *Philosophy and Public Affairs* 29, no. 4 (2000): 343.

38. Chamayou, *Theory of the Drone*, 52.

39. Robert Sparrow, "War without Virtue?" in *Killing by Remote Control*, ed. Strawser, 84–105.

40. James Koutz (national commander of the American Legion), "Pentagon Calls Off New Medal for Drone, Cyber Warriors," Agence France-Presse, April 15, 2013.

41. Edward N. Luttwak, "Toward Post-Heroic Warfare," *Foreign Affairs* 74, no. 3 (1995): 109–22; S. Scheipers, ed., *Heroism and the Changing Character of War: Toward*

Post-Heroic Warfare? (New York: Palgrave Macmillan, 2014); and Christian Enemark, *Armed Drones and the Ethics of War: Military Virtue in a Post-Heroic Age* (New York: Routledge, 2014).

42. For a more in-depth discussion of and an alternative view of the place of honor in drone warfare, see French, Sisk, and Bass, chapter 10 of this volume.

43. Michael Walzer, *Just and Unjust Wars* (New York: Basic Books, 1977), 282.

44. Michael Walzer, "Targeted Killing and Drone Warfare," *Dissent*, January 11, 2013, www.dissentmagazine.org/online_articles/targeted-killing-and-drone-warfare.

45. Ron Wyden, Mark Udall, and Martin Heinrich, "Letter to the Honorable Eric Holder," November 26, 2013, www.wyden.senate.gov/download/?id=C48CD5E5-EF15-4A44-A1BF-2274E5B1929A&download=1.

46. Diane M. Vavricheck, *The Future of Drone Strikes: A Framework for Analyzing Policy Options*, CNA Occasional Papers Series, September 2014, www.cna.org/sites/default/files/research/COP-2014-U-008318-Final.pdf.

47. Birmingham Policy Commission, "Security Impact of Drones," 83.

PART II

Who Should Do the Fighting—and Who, Consequently, Bears the Risk of Dying?

6

Pragmatism, the Just War Tradition, and an Ethical Approach to Private Military and Security Companies

DEBORAH AVANT

THE JUST WAR TRADITION rests many of its arguments about the legitimacy of violence on who is issuing it. State-based organizations are taken to have a special place as legitimate violent actors and legitimate targets of violence. The decentering of "the state's" role, however, is a prominent feature of violent conflict in the contested and fragmented sovereignty that is typical of the contemporary era. A decentered state is commonly assumed to introduce murkiness into how we think about controlling violence and in how we determine when violence is legitimate. A variety of arguments reflect this assumption. It is part of what underlies some warnings of the dangers of Responsibility to Protect norms.[1] It also lurks behind claims about the difficulties presented by private military and security companies for global norms, and for just war.[2] And it is evident in worries about the role of corporations in limiting violence.[3] Though these arguments make quite different claims, all share a strong commitment to the assumption that the state is *the* right (or proper) authority without which our tools for justifying violence or constraining it will evaporate.[4] Many international legal theorists and practitioners also hold tight to the necessity of the state as the proper, or right, authority without which our infrastructure for international law, just war, and the like will be undermined. Their preferences for hard law and binding treaties as the only appropriate way forward reflect this assumption.

Looking back at the evolution of the broader just war traditions and practice, however, demonstrates that as increasing connections have led to transnational concern with violence organized orthogonally to states, many have nevertheless made just war norms useful by loosening their commitment to the assumption that the state is ipso facto the right authority. Relaxing commitment to the state, per se, has allowed the extension of practices consistent with the just war tradition to nonstate organizations by focusing more specifically on what actors do rather than who they are. The International Commission of the Red Cross and others first extended the potential for legitimate (or at least more legitimate) violence to rebel groups, and some have made similar extensions to terrorists by focusing on whether their actions are more or less consistent with the *jus in bello* principles that underlie international humanitarian law (IHL). A variant of this reasoning has recently informed processes to govern private military and security companies (PMSCs) within IHL and other commitments to human rights.

In this chapter, I examine the logic linking actor and behavior, and the evolution of a historical convention that draws new actors into established just war norms on the basis of their behavior. I suggest that this convention is consistent with a pragmatic approach to change, and then describe its recent application to PMSCs, attending specifically to the pragmatic characteristics of the process. I end with a discussion of the critics and merits of this approach to ethics in the face of change.

JUST WAR AND THE RULES FOR LEGITIMATE VIOLENCE

A long-held assumption in just war theorizing is that we ought to control violence differently based on who is delivering it. Some authorities—states and their soldiers—are legitimate issuers of violence and thus have greater leeway than illegitimate ones—rebels, terrorists, and mercenaries. Alongside this assumption that particular authorities are more legitimate than others are claims that tie legitimacy (and ethics more generally) to behavior or actions rather than assuming that an actor is legitimate or not by virtue of who they are or the position they hold.

There are at least two kinds of reasoning behind moral evaluations based on who or what an actor is. One is focused individually. Historically, an example of this can be found in the divine right of kings. One was born to rule—or serve. Kings answered to no earthly authority. God had bestowed on them certain powers that they used at their will. A king's authority was based on his essence—he was born to be king. If he erred, he would answer to God, but it was the duty of his subjects to obey, no matter what his behavior.

A more modern example of an individual focus is the notion that people are born with particular dispositions—saints or sinners, in religious terms; strong or weak moral dispositions, in secular ones; and the logic of "nature" in the nature-versus-nurture debates. This logic can lead people to trust some rulers more than others on the basis of their essence. Logic rooted in individual essence can leak into claims about institutions through the idea of motivation—good people are drawn to particular types of roles, such as humanitarian ones, that look to serve collective rather than purely individual goals, and can be trusted in them because they are good at their core and their motivations to serve collective ends are likely to lead to good behavior.

The second common type of reasoning assumes no necessary distinction between individuals but rests on what incentives they face. Rational choice arguments about ethics are explicit in this assumption. Institutional arrangements create incentives and sanctions that elicit better or worse behavior. For instance, arguments that heads of state in democracies are more likely to rule well than those in autocracies because they face voters in elections would fall into this category.[5] So would the notion that soldiers can be more trusted than mercenaries because of the chain of command.[6] But constructivist arguments also reflect this reasoning, in that a commitment to particular ideas or norms leads to a set of "appropriate" types of behavior.[7]

The important distinction between the logic of the "divine right of kings" and more modern claims based on institutional reasoning rests on the relationship between behavior and authority. The divine right of kings was based on the authority of God, not the behavior it was likely to elicit on Earth. With more modern claims, however, the claimant assumes that who an actor is tells us something about his or her likely behavior. Although there was significant logical tension between authority rooted in God and authority rooted in behavior in medieval Europe, that tension has eased in modern reasoning. What we assume about who actors *are* is frequently based on what we think that type of actor will *do*.

The just war tradition consists of claims about the justness of the decision to enter a war (*jus ad bellum*) and claims about the justness of behavior undertaken in prosecuting a war (*jus in bello*). *Jus ad bellum* is said to rest on six principles: just cause, right authority, right intention, reasonable chance of success, proportionality of ends, and last resort. The right authority has been most clearly associated with the deference given to states, as actors. *Jus in bello*'s cardinal principles are discrimination between civilians and combatants (targeting only combatants) and proportionality of means (violence should be used proportionately to the injustice suffered). *Jus in bello* has focused more on behavior, though it is informed by the actor categories of combatant and civilian. The just war tradition is full of diversity and debate that is beyond the scope of this chapter. However, James Turner Johnson's interpretation, with its historical richness, offers many examples that illustrate the dynamic relationship between these different logics.

THE JUST WAR TRADITION IN HISTORY

There are tensions between *jus ad bellum* and *jus in bello*—both historically and logically. Historically, *jus ad bellum* crystallized when the Church as well as powerful knights found common reason to restrict the right to take up arms for others but retain it for themselves. The merging of Christian claims with those of the "knightly class" about right authority assumed a distinction between the use of violence for private purposes (*duellum*) and its use for public, or collective, purposes (*bellum*). *Jus in bello*, however, largely grew out of the knights' chivalric code and was sanctioned by the Church, especially as it related to the protection of certain classes of persons. It effectively extended the knightly rules that had governed the individual combat between knights (*duellum*) to more collective efforts (or *bellum*), thus assuming an overlap between *duellum* and *bellum*.[8] Logically, however, *jus in bello* aims at restraint in violence, whereas *jus ad bellum* both offers up violence as a tool for the right cause and authority and limits it only for those without right authority or cause. Initially, the two joined to create something like collusion between the powerful—restraining violence against other states in "war," delegitimizing the use of violence by the less powerful, and keeping the use of violence by the state against less powerful rebels unchecked.[9]

From the beginning, however, chinks in the logic of a ruler's absolute rights created opportunities for describing this collusion as illegitimate. Johnson traces this back to the twelfth century, when Gratian claimed that "a just war is waged by an authoritative edict to avenge injuries."[10] By this definition, not any war undertaken by a ruler would be seen as just. The struggle between the religious and secular authorities over war during the Middle Ages led to competing views on right authority and its limits. The resolution to this tussle, influenced by a variety of developments in Europe and beyond, was a refashioning of just war into the language of natural law.[11] The language of natural law opened the way for further moves away from essentialist claims about actors to claims about actors based on (and predictive of) behavior.

Discussions of states, sovereigns, and what their proper role should be provide evidence that behavior was important for proper authority from the start.[12] The most significant early claims on the proper behavior of states can be found in the logic outlined in the French and American revolutions and the march toward models of state legitimacy based on (1) claims to represent general rather than particular interests, (2) consultation with the governed, and (3) respect for individual human rights. This articulation of a state's proper role had implications for the legitimacy of violence that states could use, as well as the responsibilities of states to protect their citizens from violence. Most recently, this logic has been outlined in the norm of the Responsibility to Protect (R2P); Holeindre offers an interesting version of this based in postcolonial responsibility in chapter 7 of this volume. Weber's definition of the state as "a human community that (successfully) claims the monopoly of the legitimate use of physical force within a given territory" is often taken to mean that juridically recognized states, by definition, are those that can legitimately issue force.[13] But Weber can also be taken to mean that a state's recognition hinges on its successfully claiming to make *legitimate* use of violence. This latter logic informs what Hehir, in chapter 1 of this volume, calls the incontrovertible content of R2P—that states *earn* this right with legitimate behavior.

Tensions in the logic of actor type and behavior can also be seen in discussions of actors that were more traditionally seen as illegitimate: rebels, terrorists, and mercenaries. The definition of a rebel is one that takes up arms against a government or ruler. The term "terrorism" arose out of the "reign of terror" by the (albeit new and revolutionary) state after the French Revolution. The term "terrorist" has typically been reserved for those who use violence to frighten or intimidate people for political ends. A terrorist in the contemporary era is often assumed to be outside the state. The term "mercenary" has been used to describe a wide variety individuals who either fight for a political entity with which they are not affiliated (as the German mercenaries that fought for the British in the American Revolution), fight for money rather than for a cause (motivations often attributed to the condottiere or the military enterprisers), or some combination of the two.[14] Analysts frequently associate (to a greater or lesser degree) the PMSCs prominent in contemporary conflicts with the mercenary category. Any reading of the just war tradition is full of claims about actors by type. What has come to be known as IHL, however, has evolved to pertain differently to similar types of actors depending on the qualities—or behaviors—they exhibit.

A focus on behavior led to innovations in how to treat "illegitimate" actors in ways that would restrain violence. As James Turner Johnson traces the history, whereas war among states was taken to be governed by *jus in bello* principles, violence to put down rebellions was not, and rulers were frequently vicious in their dealings with rebels. He points to the United States' decision during the Civil War to treat the rebel army in the South as if it were a legitimate belligerent as long as it observed the laws of war as a historical turning point.[15] In a sense, the United States offered legitimate status to the rebel force in exchange for behavior that reflected a legitimate force. Though some might suggest that it could have opened the way for more rebellion (by removing the threat of punishing violence against rebels by virtue of their status), it is commonly understood as a decision that put restraints on the use of violence during that war.

This turning point has been built by a variety of decisions, some formalized into international law, that look to the logic of behavior to expand or contract different actor categories:

- The 1907 Hague Convention made it clear that citizens taking up arms in advance of an enemy were to be accorded privileged combatant status, even though they often neither wore uniforms nor were under the army's commands.[16] Though citizens taking up arms did not represent an affront to the state, this convention did extend combatant status to less formal forces.
- The Geneva Conventions of 1949 recognized that members of resistance forces in occupied countries should also be given privileged combatant status (though it required that they wear distinguishing marks and carry weapons openly in ways that few resistance forces would do).
- The Prisoner of War Convention also, in Article 3, extends some protections to fighters in wars "not of an international character."[17] Although not granting privileged combatant status to rebels, this article did restrict the actions that a state might legitimately take against rebels in putting down a rebellion.

Bert Röling traces agreement on Article 3 of the 1949 Geneva Conventions to the gradual and general recognition of human rights that created a baseline level of respect that must be accorded to humans in all circumstances.[18] The acceptance of human rights was also important in generating restrictions on what a state might do to its own population, even in situations short of war—something made clear in the Genocide Treaty of 1948. As Röling expressed this:

> The change in ideas about the nature of a national regime had its effect on notions of rebellion, revolution, and civil war. From the fact that it was made possible to demand armed action in order to end injustice of some sort, it followed that rebellion against such injustice was looked

upon with sympathy. Internal resistance to structural violence of a certain kind came to receive a degree of support which in former times was unthinkable because of the overriding respect for legitimate authority.[19]

Because authority was linked to action, the possibility for a just rebellion became more thinkable. One way rebels could demonstrate their legitimacy was also through action—demonstrating restraint and respect for IHL principles. Nonetheless, there were tensions. One was between what was required of forces in international law and what would be effective for rebel forces with much less strength than their government. Another was between the rather general language of human rights to be accorded to all humanity and the distinctions between different parts of humanity based on the role they played—as residents/citizens of states, rebels, freedom fighters, mercenaries, and civilians.

Michael Walzer's book *Just and Unjust Wars* takes up many of these issues (unsurprisingly, as the book was published in 1977, just as the 1977 Geneva Protocols came into effect). His argument is generally careful to focus on the justice of behavior rather than assuming that particular kinds of actors had essential qualities. First, though he acknowledges the rights of states to territorial integrity and political sovereignty, he explicitly ties these rights to the political community from which they arise, and thus "the rights of states rest on the consent of their members."[20] This logic suggests that a state without the consent of its political community might lose these rights; and Walzer's defense of intervention, and particularly humanitarian intervention under particular circumstances, carries this logic forward by claiming that as states behave in ways that alienate their populace, they also begin to lose their right authority.

A similar logical move is behind Walzer's arguments about individuals, noncombatants, guerrillas, and terrorists. In each case, he examines behavior in the context of choice and holds it up to just war principles or behavior to make determinations about morality. Thus killing a naked soldier taking a bath is akin to murder, while killing that same soldier hours later when he or she is armed and threatening is justified. The threat issued by enemy forces is the key to the degree to which violence is a just response. Similarly, Walzer does not extend the category of noncombatant in a blanket way but as it pertains to an individual's actions. Those who supply military weapons are more justifiably killed that those who supply food. Rather than seeing guerrillas and terrorists as fundamentally immoral or unjust, Walzer examines their cause (those with a more just cause and significant popular support have greater liberty), their capacities (those fighting in a position of extreme weakness have greater liberty), and their behavior (those who target military or political leaders are more justified that those who target uninvolved civilians).

Walzer's discussion of mercenaries is relatively short but retains this nuance. The Italian condottiere, he points out, were not ruthless killers but businessmen. Because their employers depended on them, condottiere were able, at times, to condition the decisions of their employers.[21] This, he suggests, was potentially bad for the people on whose behalf a war was being waged but was not bad for the soldiers themselves (or their "enemies").[22] In other situations, mercenaries were recruited out of poverty for very low wages. This, he suggests, was unjust for these individual mercenaries, for they became merely pawns to be murdered off at will. Finally, he notes that though we think of mercenaries as professional soldiers who sell their services on the open market, the term "professional soldiers" also can apply to those who "though they may earn their bread by soldiering, disdain the name of mercenary."[23] The distinction really is a graded one, where the more a solider fights exclusively for money, the more we see him as a mercenary; or the more he is committed to a common cause and chooses to fight not for private reasons but because he is compelled to do his duty, the less we see this as mercenary activity.

Both the gradation of behavior and the focus on behavior as such also characterize the historical approach that James Turner Johnson takes to drawing out the lessons from the just war tradition and how we might think of them in the contemporary context. Johnson sees the just war tradition as fundamentally one that uses moral judgments as part of "a practical enterprise rooted in community, not an undertaking belonging to the abstract."[24] Rather than seeing this tradition emerging out of a particular idea or principle, he examines them as unfolding from both religious and secular roots in Europe and becoming intertwined in natural law discussions toward the end of the medieval era in Europe as people interacted with particular problems and concerns. From this perspective, right authority—as well as our understanding of sovereignty—are frequently drawn from these various roots but are justified to address the particular concerns of those actors with the power to shape the destinies of others.[25] Those with right authority pledged restraint toward others in a similarly powerful position, in part because it also allowed them to evade restraint against those—rebels—without that same right authority. This approach leads Johnson to a position on rebels similar to Walzer's.

This historical treatment, which is sensitive to the interaction of morals and power, leads to an interesting discussion of mercenaries at different moments in history. Pope Innocent IV wanted to discourage mercenaries in order to constrain the rights of petty princes to wage war (even as he contributed to the flood of these professional soldiers with his crusades). His move, however, was unsuccessful because, though it enshrined the rights of the powerful in the guise of ethics, mercenaries were useful even to the more powerful princes and thus did not go away.[26] Even those who could afford to raise an army of serfs often preferred to use professionals—seeing them as a less dangerous and more effective tool. These professional soldiers served in a variety of roles into the modern era, until the European states settled on the practice of the modern standing army. Johnson's focus on the structure of these roles includes paying attention to how these professionals behaved at particular moments—sometimes leading to less, but other times to more, restraint than alternative mobilization strategies.

Thus, one can trace back to the Middle Ages tenets of the just war tradition that entail particular *behavior* in exchange for right authority. By this logic, no state should automatically be granted right authority; right authority should be granted depending on the degree to which a state takes action that reflects the role we expect it to play. This role has been increasingly tied to issues understood as public—a complex concept in itself, but one that is increasingly best tied to issues of broad or common (rather than narrow or individual) concern. Similarly, the legitimacy of challengers to the state can—and has—been modulated through examining their behavior. This logic requires paying attention to the fact that assertions about who someone is are, in fact, shorthand attempts to determine what they will do, and this is sometimes lost in common discourse (and even in more sophisticated analyses). Within just war analyses, however, one can frequently find a return to the focus on behavior to generate ideas for moral arguments about new or differently placed actors.

C. A. J. Coady's analysis of contemporary political violence is largely consistent with those of both Walzer and Johnson on problematizing states, rebels, and terrorists.[27] Similar to Walzer's insistence that state rights be tied to the goals of the political community, Coady claims that, in today's world, states must be considered to have conditional sovereignty—conditioned on some minimal respect for the human rights of its citizens.[28] In his discussion of terrorism, he joins Walzer in seeing more or less ethical ways of resisting illegitimate state authority and makes the point that states can also commit acts of terrorism.

Most recently, Michael Gross has proposed an ethics for those seeking political change. His sophisticated analysis considers both the relative justice of the resistance as well as the justice of various—hard and soft—tactics. In keeping with the logic here, just resistance depends on its need to generate self-determination and a dignified life and on its level of public consent. Just tactics must reduce potential harm to noncombatants, and "permissible targeting turns on liability."[29]

PRAGMATISM AND THE EVOLUTION OF THE JUST WAR TRADITION

The just war tradition's evolution to begin incorporating nonstate actors, which I have sketched above, is largely consistent with pragmatic action. It neither takes principles (abstractions) as immutable nor abandons them entirely when they run up against obstacles. Rather than forsaking the just war tradition because a particular actor fits awkwardly in its framework or ignoring relevant new actors in the hopes of moving back to those of the familiar tradition, the examples given above drew on experience to develop creative solutions that both drew in new concerns and resonated with experience. This dance between absolutism and relativism is the core of pragmatic ethics.[30] A pragmatic approach to fostering ethical behavior in times of flux focuses on generating imaginative thinking that draws on experience to generate new solutions that work.

Although some might critique just war theorizing by pointing out the degree to which what we see as ethical or appropriate behavior has its roots in power relationships that we find problematic today, a pragmatic approach would be more interested in the potential consequences of how we use the tradition. Rather than looking at the roots of principles, pragmatism would have us look at their potential effects and the degree to which they can be useful for solving problems we see in the world.[31]

In practice, creative thinking often results from gathering stakeholders to solve particular problems. A pragmatic approach notes that problem solving orients people in ways that encourage new connections, that new connections often engender novel ideas, and that novel ideas often take hold—or work—precisely because they resonate with some part of established norms and draw in consequential actors. Thus, this pragmatism seeks creative new solutions through problem solving.[32] And the ethical appeal of this pragmatic approach is generated, in part, by its potential to work, or to move behavior in a more positive direction.

A CASE IN POINT: DRAWING PMSCS INTO THE JUST WAR TRADITION?

Some have argued that PMSCs are a necessary challenge to the just war tradition.[33] Others, like Eric Heinze and Amy Eckert, have suggested that the just war tradition might evolve to take PMSCs into account.[34] Heinze and Eckert make some claims about the conditions under which using PMSCs might be just, but have little to say about how we might expect to see these new actors drawn into the just war tradition. A pragmatic perspective agrees that the just war tradition will evolve and also charts one type of logic whereby this might occur: pragmatic problem solving. The recent effort to pull PMSCs into IHL (and thus into *jus in bello* principles) illustrates this logic at work. As the market for military and security services grew in the 1990s, the initial ethical reactions were mixed. Although many debated what these companies *were* (mercenary or not), from the very start there were calls for holding companies accountable for what they *did*. David Shearer raised the issue of behavior as a way to distinguish among firms in the late 1990s. If these companies say they are professional and are staffed by professional soldiers, he suggested, why not accept that and have them develop and commit to professional practices and then hold them accountable to these practices?

The governments whose nations were home to the majority of PMSCs saw the issue differently—from Shearer, and from each other. US officials maintained that these companies were useful foreign policy tools, but South African officials saw them as inherently illegitimate.[35] Meanwhile, the United Nations largely approached the PMSC issue within the mercenary frame. The UN Commission on Human Rights had appointed a special rapporteur on the use of mercenaries in 1989 to encourage states to ratify the International Convention against the Recruitment, Use, Financing, and Training of Mercenaries.[36] As the industry grew, the special rapporteur insisted on both calling these activities "mercenary" and ratifying the International Convention.[37]

As a counter to the mercenary trope, some companies advocated for various types of self-regulation; but what constituted good behavior was not clear. Sandline claimed to be an "ethical" company, EO said it would work only for legitimate governments, Blackwater claimed to work in the interest of the United States, and MPRI refused to have its personnel carry weapons.[38] In 2001 the International Peace Operations Association (now the International Stability Operations Association, ISOA) was founded and introduced a code of conduct for its companies that focused on a broad array of human rights and legal concerns.[39]

Meanwhile, there were simmering trepidations in civil society, but they were focused on an array of different concerns. Some complained that governments used PMSCs to skirt international norms.[40] Others thought that self-regulation by firms or industry groups was vague and unenforceable,[41] or that regulation could lend legitimacy to an illegitimate enterprise.[42] In response to the highly publicized Sandline affair, the Campaign against Arms Trade published a 1999 paper seeking to abolish all mercenaries.[43] International Alert established a program focused on developing policies to ensure that the activities of PMSCs would have a positive impact on preventing conflicts and building peace,[44] and it investigated the interaction of PMSCs with other clients, particularly humanitarian groups.[45] Events in Iraq brought critical attention from the United States–based Corpwatch, which focused on profiteering, waste, and fraud.[46]

With various states, the UN, different companies, and different civil society groups all approaching the industry from distinct perspectives, there was little moral order surrounding this industry. Even when the International Convention went into force in 2001—ironically, without the support of the United States, the United Kingdom, or South Africa—it had little effect.[47] Percy claims that the ratification of the International Convention actually weakened governance of the industry.[48] As an insurgency rose in Iraq in the spring of 2004, newspaper articles describing the scores of personnel who were mobilized through PMSCs in Iraq demonstrated the industry's growth. At the same time, coverage of PMSCs' participation in abuses at Abu Ghraib and mercenary involvement in a coup attempt in Equatorial Guinea demonstrated its risks. Even some industry officials warned of a race to the bottom.[49]

In the midst of this cacophony, the Swiss government and the International Committee of the Red Cross (ICRC) launched the Swiss Initiative, which sought to bring together all the consequential actors—states and PMSCs, along with critical international lawyers and civil society experts. Their initial goal was to do nothing more than take stock of the international commitments that had already been agreed on (international humanitarian and human rights law particularly) for states when dealing with PMSCs. This goal was shaped by both the degree of disagreement and the ICRC's long-standing approach. The initiative also questioned statements that there was a "vacuum of law" surrounding PMSCs and sought to examine the application of existing law to the industry.[50] Consistent with their approach to other new actors, the Swiss left open the possibility that existing obligations held implications for PMSCs. This claim was appealing to both those who were more complacent about the industry (and were tired of hearing critics say there was a vacuum of law) and those who were more critical of how the industry was being used (and were eager to bring existing obligations to light).[51]

Though participants disagreed on many things, they did settle on a definition of PMSCs at the first meeting. They also recognized that states had different relationships with PMSCs. Few touted these "agreements" as significant, but they established a lowest common denominator and a basis for continued engagement. Building on these small achievements, the Montreux Document was issued in September 2008.[52]

The Montreux Document established an ethical framework for thinking about the industry.[53] It refocused concern on international humanitarian law and human rights and away from either mercenarism or waste and fraud. Concern with IHL and human rights no doubt reflected the inclinations of the Swiss government and the ICRC. But this focus also meant that those involved were embracing the widely accepted principles for governing military forces as well as rebel and other irregular forces that I discussed above. At the same time, this language tapped into linkages among human rights activists who brought with them great legitimacy,[54] and it connected to a more general conversation about businesses and human rights that offered additional normative connections.[55]

The agreement defined PMSCs according to what they did—PMSCs are private business entities that provide military and/or security services (including armed guarding and protection of people and objects, such as convoys, buildings, and other places; maintenance and operation of weapons systems; prisoner detention; and advice to or training of local forces and security personnel).[56] It broke down the obligations of states relative to the industry, contextualizing the various responsibilities of states or right authorities. Some states contract for PMSC services (contracting states), some host PMSCs (home states), and others preside over the spaces where PMSCs operate (territorial states). This separated the concerns of countries like Sierra Leone and South Africa from those of the United States. Articulation of the distinct responsibilities of states dependent on their relationships according to IHL and human rights law allowed more precise cataloguing of responsibilities and concerns, and avoided hyperbolic critiques.[57]

The document also put forth best practices for states in each relationship. Though not legally binding, these practices summed up the thinking of those who were dealing with PMSCs about how they could best ensure their obligations. Some of these were based on laws that were already on the books in the United States and other countries, but others were generated by discussions of problems that the United States and other countries had faced in particular circumstances, in parts of Africa and also in Iraq.

Finally, the Montreux Document broached a statement of PMSCs' responsibilities. It claimed that PMSCs are obliged to uphold international law, even if they are not bound by it; and it called for companies to engage with others to develop general principles for behavior.[58] This call instigated a process to develop an International Code of Conduct (ICoC) for private security providers—that is, those PMSCs providing security services, which are sometimes armed, that pose the most significant potential risk to IHL and human rights. Acknowledging the differences of opinion among the signatory states about whether PMSCs were legitimate, the Montreux Document nonetheless stipulated the importance of engaging with, and providing legal obligations for, the industry: "Like all other armed actors present on the battlefield, PMSCs are governed by international rules, whether their presence and activities are legitimate or not. The Montreux Document follows this humanitarian approach."[59]

Within eighteen months, stakeholders agreed on an ICoC, which developed principles for PMSC behavior based on respect for human rights and humanitarian responsibilities. As paragraph 4 of the preamble states, "The Signatory Companies affirm that they have a responsibility to respect the human rights of, and fulfill humanitarian responsibilities towards, all those affected by their business activities, including Personnel, Clients, suppliers, shareholders, and the population of the area in which services are provided."[60] The ICoC first outlines general provisions and company commitments, and then details specific provisions to regulate the behavior of private security personnel. These include stipulations on the use of force, detention, and apprehension; prohibitions of torture, sexual exploitation, human trafficking, slavery, child labor, and discrimination; recommendations on identification; and various management requirements, ranging from vetting personnel, responsibilities for subcontracts, the treatment of personnel (training and the workplace environment), incident reporting, grievance procedures, and stipulations about meeting liabilities.

The ICoC called for its provisions to be translated into standards (both national and international) and for the development of an association (the International Code of Conduct Association, ICoCA) to govern its application. As the ICoC was issued, the United States expressed its support for an American National Standards Institute (ANSI) process to develop such private security company (PSC) standards, which are now in use. And PSC1 was developed into an international standard (ISO/PRF 18788).[61] As of 2015, the Swiss Initiative had generated the Montreux Document, an ICoC, a multistakeholder association (the ICoCA) to implement it, ANSI and ISO standards based on the Montreux Document and the ICoC, and changes in the laws of particular governments (including the United States) that both reflect best practices and enforce government use of the ICoC and standards.

This initiative has made significant progress in codifying good practices—and ethical principles—for those playing private security provider roles. These practices draw from and are consistent with international humanitarian and human rights law, but they also connect with broader initiatives on the role of businesses in governance. The enforcement of these good practices relies on states (in their various roles), but they also spell out roles for nonstate clients, the management structures of PMSCs, and the populations that private security providers serve.

Five key elements designate the Swiss Initiative as pragmatic, in philosophical terms. First, it created connections among participants to address a problem. Rather than reacting to futuristic scenarios about what might happen, the Swiss drew participants together on the basis of concrete concerns in parts of Africa and Iraq. Second, it engaged relevant stakeholders, including those deemed legitimate (some governments and rights-based nongovernmental organizations) and those considered consequential (important client governments like the United States as well as key industry members). Third, it encouraged open interactions between the members of this newly connected network. Fourth, these connections spurred creative action that participants saw as useful. And fifth, initial accomplishments led participants to greater commitment and began to attract those outside the process. This is consistent with a pragmatic account of how norms develop.[62]

The participants in this process have, in effect, extended *jus in bello* principles to a new set of actors. They have been less focused on *jus ad bellum*. A similar process could, however, be imagined for *jus ad bellum* concerns. For instance, in chapter 11 of this volume, Daniel Brunstetter articulates the problematic tendencies of the spaces in between law enforcement and war, in effect delineating a pragmatic way to identify this problem. Some of his recommendations (for more specificity and particular steps) fall outside the pragmatic logic I have outlined. But gathering stakeholders around the problem of the spaces in between law enforcement and war and generating connections among these stakeholders to agree about what they might draw from both to create principles that develop *jus ad vim* would be a pragmatic way of developing the framework he envisions. And if such a framework proved useful, we would expect it to gain traction.

LIMITS TO THE PRAGMATIC WAY

Though most agree that this pragmatic process has generated progress, skeptics worry about its limits. As I suggest above, the process has addressed ethical behavior for PMSCs, but not whether their use may affect just purposes. It also does little to address potential inequities vis-à-vis those around whom security is mobilized—those who can pay.[63] And it has the potential to reinforce paying attention to security rather than other life concerns.[64] These are reasonable concerns and worthy of continued thought.

Focusing on behavior rather than the essential characteristics of types of actors, however, has been key to translating just war principles into practices that describe more (and less) legitimate behavior for new actors outside the state, along with circumscribing the moral authority of states. These practices have worked to generate restraint in the use of violence and to tie the use of violence to more public or commonly held values—surely among the most pressing human problems in every era, including our own. We need not reconceive just war principles; we have already begun creatively adjusting them (e.g., see French, Sisk, and Bass's discussion of drones and the warrior's code in chapter 10 of this volume).[65]

These kinds of creative responses are most likely to emerge when people engage with one another around a problem, involve all relevant stakeholders, are open to new connections and new ideas, and pay attention to the consequences of their actions. But when debates become so principled that people are not open to new information, when certain stakeholders are left out of processes, and when people are more focused on the type of actor or agreement than their likely effects, the pragmatic path is hard to find. As the concept of war continues to evolve, giving more self-conscious attention to this approach could be helpful in generating answers to many of the important transnational problems this volume addresses.

NOTES

1. Jennifer M. Welsh, "Implementing the Responsibility to Protect: Where Expectations Meet Reality," *Ethics & International Affairs* 24, no. 4 (2010): 415–30.

2. On private military and security companies for global norms, see Sarah Percy, "This Gun's for Hire: A New Look at an Old Issue," *International Journal* 58, no. 4 (2003): 721–36. On just war, see James Pattison, *The Morality of Private War: The Problem of Private Military and Security Companies* (Oxford: Oxford University Press, 2014).

3. Marina Ottoway, "Reluctant Missionaries," *Foreign Policy*, July–August 2001, 44–55.

4. For an exception, see Michael Gross, *The Ethics of Insurgency: A Critical Guide to Just Guerrilla War* (Cambridge: Cambridge University Press, 2015).

5. Michael Doyle, "Kant, Liberal Legacies, and Foreign Affairs," *Philosophy and Public Affairs* 12, no. 3 (1983): 205–35.

6. Niccolò Machiavelli, *The Prince and the Discourses*, with an introduction by Max Lerner (New York: Modern Library, 1950); and Eliot Cohen, *Citizens and Soldiers: The Dilemmas of Military Service* (Ithaca, NY: Cornell University Press, 1984).

7. Sarah Percy, *Mercenaries: History of a Norm in International Relations* (Oxford: Oxford University Press, 2007).

8. James Turner Johnson, *Just War Tradition and the Restraint of War: A Moral and Historical Inquiry* (Princeton, NJ: Princeton University Press, 1981), 44–47.

9. Ibid., 44–49.

10. Ibid., 152–53.

11. Ibid., 173; for an elaboration, see his discussion of Vitoria and Grotius, 172–79.

12. James Turner Johnson, *Sovereignty: Moral and Historical Perspectives* (Washington, DC: Georgetown University Press, 2014).

13. H. H. Gerth and C. Wright Mills, *From Max Weber: Essays in Sociology* (New York: Oxford University Press, 1946), 77–78.

14. Machiavelli calls the former auxiliaries.

15. Johnson, *Just War Tradition*, 49–50.

16. Bert V. A. Röling, "The Legal Status of Rebels and Rebellion," *Journal of Peace Research* 13, no. 2 (1976): 149–63.

17. "Geneva Conventions of 1949 and Additional Protocols, and Their Commentaries," International Committee of the Red Cross, 1949, https://ihl-databases.icrc.org/applic/ihl/ihl.nsf/vwTreaties1949.xsp.

18. Röling, "Legal Status of Rebels," 151.

19. Ibid., 152.

20. Michael Walzer, *Just and Unjust Wars: A Moral Argument with Historical Illustrations* (New York: Basic Books, 1977), 54. However, interestingly, he still talks of global politics as a society of states rather than recognizing the potential for connections among peoples by other means.

21. I could not help but think of this as I read of Blackwater personnel issuing threats to their US State Department investigators. James Risen, "Before the Shooting in Iraq, a Warning on Blackwater," *New York Times*, June 30, 2014, www.nytimes.com/2014/06/30/us/before-shooting-in-iraq-warning-on-blackwater.html?_r=0.

22. By this logic, of course, a military that conditions the goals of its leaders would be seen as also problematic.

23. Walzer, *Just and Unjust Wars*, 27.

24. Johnson, *Just War Tradition*, 329.

25. Johnson, *Sovereignty*.

26. Johnson, *Just War Tradition*, 165.

27. His definition of violence, focused more narrowly than examinations of structural violence would have it and yet broadly enough to account for interstate and intrastate conflicts as well as state repression, is quite useful for capturing together the various elements of violence relevant to the just war tradition. Also in keeping with elements of the tradition (and contemporary sensibilities) is his bias, all things equal, toward limiting violence.

28. C. A. J. Coady, *Morality and Political Violence* (Cambridge: Cambridge University Press, 2008), 77.

29. Gross, *Ethics of Insurgency*, 9. Neither mercenaries nor PMSCs come up in Gross's analysis.

30. Richard J. Bernstein, *The Pragmatic Turn* (Cambridge: Polity, 2010).

31. Helen Kinsella, *The Image before the Weapon: A Critical History of the Distinction between Combatant and Civilian* (Ithaca, NY: Cornell University Press, 2011).

32. Hans Joas, *The Creativity of Action* (Chicago: University of Chicago Press, 1996).

33. Pattison, *Morality of Private War*.

34. Eric A. Heinze, "Private Military Companies, Just War, and Humanitarian Intervention," in *Ethics, Authority, and War*, ed. Eric A. Heinze and Brent J. Steele (New York: Palgrave, 2009); and Amy E. Eckert, *Outsourcing War: The Just War Tradition in the Age of Military Privatization* (Ithaca, NY: Cornell University Press, 2016).

35. Deborah Avant, *The Market for Force: The Implications of Privatizing Security* (Cambridge: Cambridge University Press, 2005).

36. "An Assessment of the Mercenary Issue at the Fifty-Fifth Session of the UN Commission on Human Rights," *International Alert*, May 1999.

37. Percy, *Mercenaries.*

38. Avant, *Market for Force*; and David Shearer, *Private Armies and Military Intervention* (Oxford: Oxford University Press, 1998).

39. IPOA became the International Stability Operations Association, or ISOA, in 2010.

40. Abdel-Fatau Musah and J. Kayode Fayemi, *Mercenaries: An African Security Dilemma* (London: Pluto, 2000).

41. Peter W. Singer, "War, Profits, and the Vacuum of Law: Privatized Military Firms and International Law," *Columbia Journal of International Law* 42, no. 2 (2004): 521.

42. Anna Leander, "The Market for Force and Public Secuirty: The Destabilizing Consequences of Private Military Companies," *Journal of Peace Research* 42, no. 5 (2005): 605–22.

43. Christopher Wrigley, "The Privatization of Violence: New Mercenaries and the State," Campaign against Arms Trade, March 1999, www.caat.org.uk/resources/publications/government/mercenaries-1999.php.

44. "Assessment of the Mercenary Issue."

45. Tony Vaux, Chris Seiple, Greg Nakano, and Keonraad, "Van Brabant, Humanitarian Action and Private Security Companies," *International Alert*, March 2002.

46. Pratap Chatterjee, *Iraq, Inc.: A Profitable Occupation* (New York: Seven Stories Press, 2004).

47. See Fifty-Sixth General Assembly, A/SCH/3600, Third Committee, October 31, 2001, 26th meeting.

48. Percy, *Mercenaries*, 390–91.

49. Richard Fenning, "The Iraqi Security Business Urgently Needs Rules," *Financial Times*, May 27, 2004.

50. This perspective was foreshadowed by comments from Emanuela-Chiara Gillard of the International Committee of the Red Cross, at a conference sponsored by the Institute for International Law, "Regulating the Private Commercial Military Sector," Manhasset, NY, December 2005.

51. See note 41 above on Singer and the vacuum of law.

52. ICRC, *The Montreux Document: On Pertinent International Legal Obligations and Good Practices for States Related to Operations of Private Military and Security Companies during Armed Conflict* (Geneva: ICRC and Swiss Federal Department of Foreign Affairs, 2008).

53. See Swiss Federal Department of Foreign Affairs, "Private Military and Security Companies," December 6, 2016, www.eda.admin.ch/eda/en/home/foreign-policy/international-law/international-humanitarian-law/private-military-security-companies.html.

54. Margaret Keck and Katheryn Sikkink, *Activists beyond Borders: Advocacy Networks in International Politics* (Ithaca, NY: Cornell University Press, 1998).

55. Jessica Banfield, Damian Lilly, and Virginia Haufler, *Transnational Corporations in Conflict Prone Zones: Public Policy Responses and a Framework for Action* (London: International Alert, 2003).

56. Swiss Federal Department of Foreign Affairs and International Committee of the Red Cross (FDFA/ICRC), "Brochure on the Montreux Document," Geneva, 2009, 9, www.eda.admin.ch/etc/medialib/downloads/edazen/topics/intla/humlaw.Par.0078.File.tmp/Montreux%20Broschuere.pdf.

57. See FDFA, *The Montreux Document* (Geneva: FDFA, 2008), www.eda.admin.ch/eda/en/home/foreign-policy/international-law/international-humanitarian-law/private-military-security-companies/montreux-document.html.

58. FDFA/ICRC, "Brochure," 34, 42.

59. Ibid., 41.

60. ICoC, "International Code of Conduct for Private Security Providers," 2010, http://psm.du.edu/media/documents/regulations/global_instruments/multi_stakeholder/icoc/icoc_eng.pdf.

61. For more, see Private Security Monitor, "ANSI/ASIS International Standards," 2014, http://psm.du.edu/international_regulation/global_standards_codes_of_conduct/asis_standard.html.

62. Deborah Avant, "Pragmatic Networks and Transnational Governance of Private Military and Security Services," *International Studies Quarterly* 60 (2016): 330–42.

63. Leander, "Market."

64. Ulrich Beck, *Risk Society: Toward a New Modernity*, trans. Mark Ritter (Thousand Oaks, CA: Sage, 1992).

65. Pattison, *Morality of Private War.*

7

A Certain Idea of Grandeur

French Military Interventionism and Postcolonial Responsibility

JEAN-VINCENT HOLEINDRE

Translated by Andrée-Anne Mélançon

Cette passion générale que la nation française a pour la gloire.
(This general passion that the French nation has for glory.)

—Montesquieu, *Lettres Persanes*, no. 91

THE HISTORY OF COLONIZATION and decolonization has generated an abundant literature, with the most powerful critiques coming from postcolonial and critical studies. These approaches generally focus on the negative impact of imperial domination, and the persistence of this pernicious domination after decolonization.[1] In the case of France, postcolonial domination is commonly seen through the lens of "Françafrique"—a critical term for French interference in the political, military, and economical spheres of formerly colonized African countries.[2] This chapter is not about revisiting the realities of France's interference in its former colonies, the effects of postcolonial dependence, or the aftermath of colonial domination on today's French society (though I do touch on this as it pertains to the current struggle against terrorism).[3] These themes are engaged by others elsewhere.[4] Rather, my intention is to examine the link between France's colonial and postcolonial history and the underlying mentality behind its military interventionism in the post–Cold War era.[5] How has

France's colonial history influenced the French approach to the use of force today? If recent French interventions have predominantly occurred in former colonies—such as Chad, Côte d'Ivoire, the Central African Republic, and Mali—it is certainly because France continues to defend its own political and economic interests in a postcolonial world. And yet, it is also because the colonial experience has marked French military policy, shaping the ideas and norms that govern decisions to intervene. This undergirds what I term a sense of *postcolonial responsibility* that has informed the way France uses military force today.

Postcolonial responsibility designates France's willingness to maintain political and moral leadership over its former colonies, capitalizing on the competences and power relations acquired during the colonial experience to project power to influence regional security. And yet, France is not a global warmonger. It seeks to work within the ambits of the United Nations when using force, and has been notably critical of states—such as the United States in the 2003 Iraq War—that defy the United Nations. In the context of the use of force, postcolonial responsibility offers insights into some of the issues of selectivity and recognition of humanitarian intervention that Lindemann and Giacomelli explore in chapter 2 of this volume.

Following Roland Paris, whose work highlights the link between the idea of the *mission civilisatrice*, or "civilizing mission," developed under the Third Republic and peacekeeping via modern international institutions such as the United Nations, I seek to unpack how France's colonial history underpins its understanding of the responsible use of force.[6] The relationship between the developed and developing worlds is not simple; rather, it is informed by relations of power steeped in history, in the rise of liberal norms governing the international system, and, as I show in the conclusion, challenges of immigrant integration faced by former colonial powers. The notion of postcolonial responsibility highlights the multifaceted ways sovereignty has been contested and fragmented over time, from colonial conquests to postcolonial spheres of influence and the migration- and tension-laden integration into the French Republic of immigrants from former colonies, who are now targets of radicalizations by jihadist groups such as the Islamic State in Iraq and Syria (ISIS) that threaten to strike France (and other countries) with terrorist attacks. As this chapter shows, France's use of force is deeply intertwined with this concept of sovereignty, with France developing a unique outlook of the use of force—what one might call its strategic and security culture—to navigate geographic spaces in and across the international realm.

To develop my argument, I build on a genealogical method that privileges the long term, linking colonial and postcolonial history, as suggested by Frederick Cooper.[7] Unlike the British Empire, which made the economy a lever for power and a vector for liberal norms, the French developed, through the colonial project, a more political ambition based on a certain idea of grandeur in a territorial, moral, and historical sense.[8] The French colonial empire was thus a means for France to project itself as a sovereign "*grande nation*," possessing power and committed to a universal, secular *mission civilisatrice*. In the contemporary era, when transnational actors make trouble for and fragment the international realm, the notion of postcolonial responsibility offers a means for France to preserve some of its power within its sphere of postcolonial influence, despite the disappearance of its empire. Given the controversies regarding the Responsibility to Protect (R2P), the notion of postcolonial responsibility offers an alternative compared with the views expressed by Hehir in chapter 1 of this volume. That said, the colonial legacy poses problems that may fuel the fires of global terrorism. Insofar as the sentiment of alienation is perhaps one element that contributes to radicalization, the colonial legacy may increase the threat of terrorist attacks from within France by those who aspire to the ideology of jihadist groups such as ISIS. Moreover, the use of force abroad, especially in former colonies, can have negative effects, inspiring anti-French sentiments. Postcolonial responsibility is thus a two-edged sword: as France projects its power exteriorly, the very justification it uses risks alienating segments of its own population.

THE ORIGINS OF POSTCOLONIAL RESPONSIBILITY: ARISTOCRATIC GRANDEUR AND THE REPUBLICAN *MISSION CIVILISATRICE*

To understand how France wields force today, it is useful to step back in time, to the nineteenth century, when France was progressively converting itself into a democracy (and the liberal values associated with it), while at the same time developing its colonial project.[9] The tensions between the two are obvious to the modern eye, but it is helpful for our purposes to explore the thoughts of two key figures at the fore of French debates about the colonial project: Alexis de Tocqueville and Jules Ferry. Tocqueville, writing in the early nineteenth century, associated colonization with aristocratic "glory," which in his eyes compensated for the weaknesses of democracy. Ferry invoked, half a century later in the context of the Third Republic, the idea of the *mission civilisatrice* as a form of "grandeur." Their ideas help illustrate the sentiment of French grandeur that would come to undergird the contemporary notion of postcolonial responsibility.

Tocqueville, in his work *Democracy in America*, was opposed to black slavery as practiced in the United States. He was also moved by the plight of Native

Americans in North America. However, he declared himself in favor of the colonial project initiated with the French conquest of Algiers in 1830. His support can be explained essentially with political arguments: As a man in public life—a deputy, and then minister—he believed that colonization could contribute to the standing of France as a "great nation."

Tocqueville defended France's greatness on the international scene as a means to overcome the difficult memory of the 1763 Treaty of Paris. After France's defeat by Great Britain in the Seven Years' War (1756–63), this treaty sealed the transfer of the first French colonial empire (notably, its North American territories) to the British Empire. Given this loss of status, the conquest of Algeria appeared, to Tocqueville, as a way for France to regain its status on the international scene. Although critics, notably Benjamin Constant, saw colonial conquest as an infringement on the sovereignty of others, Tocqueville saw it as a reinforcement of French national sovereignty. For Constant, sovereignty was the expression of *autonomy*, whereas for Tocqueville, sovereignty was the expression of *power* projected abroad that reinforced the domestic image.[10] Tocqueville subscribed to the liberal idea according to which the French and American revolutions initiated an irreversible movement: from war to trade, from aristocracy to democracy. But he distinguished between his general philosophy and his vision of French history. As a philosopher, he was attentive to the irreversible dynamic of democratization. But as a historian and French politician, he sought to temper this by accommodating the vestiges of France's aristocratic heritage, which he sought to preserve. From this point of view, colonization appeared not only as a means to restore some greatness to France but also as a link between the aristocratic heritage of "glory" inherited from the absolute monarchy and democracy's "equalization of conditions." In his view, colonization compensated, via conquests abroad, for the negative effects of democracy domestically by confirming France's stature as an international power.

Regarding the war in Algeria, Tocqueville was at times critical of the methods used by Thomas Robert Bugeaud, the head of the French colonial army in Algeria, but never critical of the war itself. And yet ultimately, he concluded, rather somberly: "For myself, I think that all means of desolating these tribes must be employed."[11] This sentiment of condemning those who are incapable of bending to the yoke of French republicanism to ultimate war is the darker side of the push for French grandeur, even though it arguably was in keeping with just war norms at the time (notably, those expressed by authoritative figures such as Grotius and Vattel). Moreover, this is a sentiment that still haunts postcolonial French society as France struggles with a violent backlash from those who have arguably not been integrated, a point to which I return below.

Tocqueville's stance has been heavily commented on, notably by those who highlight the contradiction between the Tocqueville who admired American democracy and the other Tocqueville who advocated the colonization of Algeria.[12] Although his argument is not exempt from tensions, it was not, from his perspective, contradictory. As Cheryl Welch argues, Tocqueville can be read in the context of his times as both a liberal thinker and an imperialist, who struggles with the tensions between the two.[13] To the extent he resolves them in his own mind, the notion of grandeur lies at the core of his views.

As Jennifer Pitts argues, Tocqueville punctuates political liberalism's conversion to colonization.[14] For Pitts, Tocqueville is part of a historically evolving tradition of liberalism, with liberal norms being affected by the tensions of the times. Tocqueville is less a defender of colonial wars than he is of colonization as a civil and political project. It is important to distinguish between conquest and colonization: Conquest designates the enterprise of military domination, whereas colonization designates the political extension of the nation.[15] Colonization, on the political and civil levels, begins when the conquest is achieved, most often by force. From this point of view, colonial war is a necessary evil for a project that appears legitimate. From the moment the war is considered just with regard to *jus ad bellum*, the methods employed in the war constitute an important but secondary problem as the objective of war prevails over the way it is conducted.

The long-term challenge of colonization for France was not primarily military or economic, but rather social and political. Embedded in Tocqueville's philosophy was the deeper matter of integrating new populations into the French community, with the goal of building a greater nation both geographically and morally. Hence, the importance of grandeur: France would become great again because it would integrate new nationals (Algeria was a settlement colony) and would have more influence in the international realm though its colonial reach.

Fast forward now to the birth of the Third Republic, when the Tocquevillian argument of grandeur was transformed into republican patriotism. In 1870 France was defeated at Sedan at the hands of the Prussians. This defeat brought the fall of Napoleon III and the birth of a new regime. The annexation of Alsace-Lorraine by Prussia was perceived as deeply humiliating, with the revival of colonization at the start of the 1880s appearing as a way to compensate for the loss of French territory to its neighboring enemy. In his 1885 speech at the Chamber of Deputies, Prime Minister Jules Ferry reiterated the "great nation" rhetoric: "To have influence without acting, without mingling in the affairs of the world, keeping out of all European alliances, and regarding as a trap, as an adventure, every expansion towards Africa or towards the Orient, to live in such a way, for a great nation, . . . is to abdicate and, in less time than you may think, to sink from the first rank to the third and fourth."[16]

In the same speech, Ferry also advanced the argument of the *mission civilisatrice*. This moral justification did not figure at the forefront of Tocqueville's discourse; Tocqueville valorized colonial ambition to confront the "decadence" to which national decline would have led domestically. As for Ferry, he returned to a discourse on civilization with racial undertones: "There is one point I must address: It is the humanitarian and civilizing side of the question: There is, for the superior races, a right because there is a duty. They have the duty to civilize the inferior races."[17] This discourse on race, although different from the racialist theories of Arthur de Gobineau, who considered the inequality of races to be based on genetic determinations, nevertheless had social implications. Ferry believed that it was possible to educate the "inferior races" and to propel them toward accepting the republican model, without, however, achieving full equality. Others, such as Paul Bert and Ferdinand Buisson, argued that it was possible to achieve complete equality though republican education.[18] The upshot is that Ferry married the educative ambition of the French Republic with the colonial project. Just as the citizens of rural France, still heavily marked by the aristocratic heritage, were educated to adhere to the values of the republican state, so it was to be abroad. As the radical Albert Bayet reflected in 1931, at the height of the empire, during the League of Human Rights (Ligue des droits de l'homme) congress on colonization: "The country which proclaimed the rights of Man, which brilliantly contributed to the advancement of science, which made education secular, and which is the great champion of liberty . . . has the mission to spread wherever it can the ideas that made it great."[19] For the French republicans, pursuing the *mission civilisatrice* was a way to maintain, or improve on, France's greatness. Moreover, the sentiment that this mission had been bequeathed to France because of its history carried with it notions of duty and responsibility toward the colonized that would create important social ties, despite the power and economic hierarchies.[20] Along with the prestige that came with international power and influence, this marked a key element of the notion of postcolonial responsibility that would later emerge.

AFTER EMPIRE: GAULLIAN GRANDEUR AND POSTCOLONIAL RESPONSIBILITY

Decolonization after World War II marked a new turn in French political history. Under Charles de Gaulle, France strove to maintain its influence in its formerly colonized countries, especially in Africa. It relied on the colonial heritage to perpetuate a certain idea of grandeur, spatially and geographically as well as politically and morally. With this positioning, France aimed to preserve a special status on the international scene, rooted in controversial notions of postcolonial responsibility. Some see in this the preservation of a problematic type of imperial dominance, while others recognize the necessity of maintaining the links for strategic, economic, and security reasons.

Between the Indochina War that began in 1946 and the Algerian War that ended in 1962, France witnessed the crumbling of its colonial structure built over a century, as Indochina, Morocco, Tunisia, Guinea, Sub-Saharan Africa, Madagascar, and, finally, Algeria left the empire and became independent. At a time when the Cold War occupied the American and Soviet superpowers, the decolonization wars diminished France to the status of a medium-sized power. For France, decolonization was synonymous with a decline of influence on the international scene, while also provoking a political crisis at the national level.

During this period, the Fourth Republic oscillated, and then crumbled, following the "Algerian tragedy" of 1958.[21] This regime crisis clearly illustrates the link between the international status of France as a global empire and its internal social and political climate. General De Gaulle returned to power in 1958 to face this crisis. He was opposed to the Fourth Republic and its "party politics," and he drafted a new Constitution, which reinforced executive powers. His main preoccupation was to politically manage the seemingly inevitable decolonization of Algeria and the rest of French colonial Africa while still preserving the project of French grandeur that drove colonization.[22] Through his discourse and his policies, he aimed to demonstrate that decolonization was not synonymous with a decline in France's international status but rather with a renewal. Stanley Hoffmann accurately highlights this sentiment: "When he [De Gaulle] talks to the French about their greatness, then and now, it is in order to get them to adapt to, and to act in, the world as it is, not in order to keep them in a museum of past glories. It is flattery for reform."[23] The Gaullian obsession with grandeur was therefore a political lever to ward off decline, both symbolically and politically.[24]

Unlike the political leaders of the Fourth Republic, De Gaulle was opposed to a Cold War paradigm that pitted the two superpowers—the USSR and the United States—against each other, with France relegated to the status of an "average power" (*puissance moyenne*). If he had been a realist in his view of international relations, he would have simply accepted the security blanket provided by NATO. However, he stubbornly pursued French foreign policy independence in the face of the American and Soviet great powers through economic revival, a strategy of nuclear deterrence, and postindependence cooperation with the formerly colonized countries, mainly in sub-Saharan Africa.

This strategy recognized the reality of independence, and although it relied on realist ideas of power, it also retained the political idealism inherited from France's history of colonization. Thus, France was not only a military and political power; it was also vested with a "global mission" (*mission mondiale*).[25] The rhetoric of "global mission" is a variant of the *mission civilisatrice*. Given that power was no longer what it used to be, this rhetoric allowed De Gaulle to pursue the political ambition of greatness formulated during colonization, but without a colonial empire.

De Gaulle's formulation offered a new way for France to preserve and actualize a certain idea of grandeur within a circumscribed sphere of influence in a postcolonial world. Consequentially, the end of the colonial order did not generate a complete rupture between France and the states formerly under its tutelage. This is particularly true for those countries—such as Chad, the Central African Republic, Senegal, Morocco, and Côte d'Ivoire—with which France had negotiated independence, preserving economic, political, and military cooperation relations after independence.[26]

On the military front, the continuity between the colonial and postcolonial periods clearly outweighed the sense of separation. Between 1964 (the year of the first French intervention in Gabon) and 2016 (the year of Operation Barkhane, still ongoing today in the Sahel Region—comprising Burkina Faso, Chad, Mauritania, Niger, and Mali), the French army has been involved, alone or with partners, in sixty-one military interventions. This represents 44 percent of all the interventions carried out by France since the 1960s. In the majority of cases, these interventions were part of established defense agreements between France and its former colonies to provide assistance to local governments—for example, Operation Tacaud in Chad between 1978 and 1980, during which France came to the aid of the Chadian army to counter rebel groups backed by Libya; and Operation Bonite in Zaire in 1978. However, one can observe a shift after the Cold War, as French operations were carried out under the auspices of the United Nations. As such, defense agreements were combined with UN security resolutions, as with Operation Serval in Mali in 2013.

Since the period of independence, no president following De Gaulle has questioned this interventionism. Moreover, in addition to this military projection of influence, a political and economic presence also exists. It almost goes without saying that this multifold presence has provoked renewed debates on the merits and faults of this postcolonial relationship called "Françafrique."[27]

President George Pompidou and President Valéry Giscard d'Estaing, the immediate successors to General De Gaulle, followed the essential elements of France's global mission and postcolonial African entitlement (*pré carré*) policy.

However, a shift occurred when François Mitterrand, the Fifth Republic's first president from the Left, arrived to power in 1981. The French Left of the time was marked by powerful anticolonialist sentiments and the desire to escape the imperial fantasy associated with the France of the past. Thus, among the promises of the 1981 presidential electoral campaign, Mitterrand pledged to break with Françafrique. But in reality, for a variety of reasons (including corruption), Mitterrand did not really question the government's sphere of influence in former colonial Africa. Indeed, he came to stamp his own version of French grandeur on international affairs after the fall of the Berlin Wall, which would have an impact on France's relations with its former colonies.

During the 1990s, France could no longer rely on the sense of postcolonial entitlement (*pré carré*) with the same confidence. The democratization of the eastern European countries raised questions about the checkered histories of former French colonies with which France still had important relationships. At that time, many of these countries—including Gabon, the Central African Republic, and Cameroon—were under authoritarian rule. France accepted this situation, for it was a way to maintain its direct influence on these countries through personal relations with their individual leaders (e.g., Jean-Bédel Bokassa in the Central African Republic and Omar Bongo in Gabon). But turmoil was on the horizon, as former colonies surfed the wave of global democratization in the post–Cold War context.

Mitterrand captured the "democratic" turn of French foreign policy in a speech on June 20, 1990, during the sixteenth conference of heads of state of Africa and France.[28] Hubert Védrine notes that, following the famous La Baule speech given by Mitterrand in 1990, the entirety of former French colonies in Africa had, by the eighteenth conference held in 1994, converted to multiparty systems and called for elections, with half adopting new constitutions.[29] However, Mitterrand's optimism hid the fact that authoritarian dynamics nevertheless would persist, as in Gabon, which has been formally democratic since 1990 but without any real opposition party. Omar Bongo took power in Gabon in 1967 and negotiated the democratic transition in the 1990s. Yet despite a multiparty system, he was the only candidate in elections. Gabon is just one example of how the shift to a multiparty system with weak opposition parties was often a means for strong parties to hold on to power. Although there were some exceptions—Zambia, the Central African Republic, and Madagascar—many transitions permitted the predemocracy powers to retain their power (e.g., Togo, Côte d'Ivoire, Cameroon, and Guinea).

France thus faced the following ethical and political dilemma: Should Paris relinquish helping African countries so as not to be accused of neocolonialism? Or should it reinforce its privileged relations, established during the colonial period and maintained during the postcolonial transition, insofar as these relations could be a vehicle for development, democracy, and human rights promotion in line with the UN's global agenda? Stated differently, should it reject or embrace the notion of postcolonial responsibility? Perhaps unsurprisingly, the latter option, which was necessarily interventionist because the use of force was sometimes seen as necessary, was embraced.

The 1990s marked the start of military interventionism justified by humanitarian reasons in a post–Cold War context structured around the idea of "democratic peace"—that is, the idea that because democracies do not fight each other, it is strategically beneficial to help the world become more democratic.[30] France played its part in conducting numerous interventions to help the transition to democracy in former colonies; on average, between the 1960s and the 1980s, the number of military interventions in the world conducted by France was never higher than eight, whereas since the 1990s, France has conducted a minimum of twenty interventions per year.

That being said, French discourse changed with respect to the rhetoric of grandeur. Mitterrand advanced a different ideal, that of the "responsibility" of the "richest" countries toward developing countries. In a political climate where the UN promoted democracy through development, Mitterrand denounced the policy of "development without democracy" supported by De Gaulle. Rather, he constructed a different narrative, whereby aid for development and democratization were part of France's "historic" missions. For Mitterrand, "France would remain true to its history." However, to what "history" did he refer, if not to the colonial past? He did not reject the neocolonial criticism that could be levied against France, but he diffused this criticism by touting France's potential role in the democratization trend that followed the fall of the Berlin Wall. Responsibility implied helping former colonies along the path to democratization. Mitterrand argued that democracy was a "universal principle" that would soon be spread around the globe. Yet, in helping former colonies, even via intervention if necessary, France was not simply aiding in their democratization; rather, the "democracy" discourse was justificatory rhetoric that allowed France to maintain its political and economic influence in the postimperial world.

Mitterrand's discourse on democracy and human rights differed in important ways from the UN stance. In his 1990 speech, he presented two propositions that received mixed reception from African nations. First, aid for development was to be conditional on criteria of economic and political good governance. Second was an idea that determined France's "new" African policy—France would intervene only in cases of "exterior threat," but not in the case of "interior conflict." In other words, France would intervene if the sovereignty of African states within its sphere of influence was in danger, but it would not seek to influence internal political processes, such as elections.

The first point paralleled the evolution of aid for development policies as defined at the UN. However, the second point is more problematic because France evidentially continued to be involved in both "international conflicts" in the region *and* the internal affairs of specific African states, whether in 2004 in the Côte d'Ivoire with Operation Unicorn (Opération Licorne) or more recently with Operation Sangaris in the Central African Republic in 2013. But could it be otherwise when the armed conflicts in Africa are often civil wars? Moreover, would the distinction between domestic politics and territorial sovereignty expressed by Mitterrand remain valid even in the evolving international context increasingly defined by contested and fragmented sovereignty?

Mitterrand's distinction intends to respect international law grounded in the notion of territorial sovereignty, but it necessarily clashes with the realities of globalization and the changes to notions of just war. The shift in French policy precedes the new view of multilateral interventionism, which began to emerge in the 1990s and replaced the classic notion of sovereignty defined by territorial integrity. This notion of sovereignty as responsibility has come to justify war for the sake of humanitarian intervention, and forms a key component of the R2P norm (see Hehir's discussion in chapter 1 of this volume). The influence of political figures implicated in humanitarian actions—such as Bernard Kouchner, who founded Médecins Sans Frontières (Doctors without Borders), and the jurist Mario Bettati—was important for how France's military outlook evolved. During the 1980s, in France they helped to impose the notions of both the right and duty to interfere in the sovereignty of other nations, which led to the adoption of a political and moral discourse founded on a sense of responsibility toward former colonies. Regardless of opinions on this normative evolution, Mitterrand's attempt to adapt the narrative of French colonial history to the postcolonial democratizing context intersects with this normative trend, albeit in a way that permitted France to maintain its special relation with postcolonial Africa.[31]

This modified, but broad, vision of French interventionism was not called into question during the subsequent presidencies of Jacques Chirac (1995–2007) and Nicolas Sarkozy (2007–12). For both, the former colonies were an essential vector of French foreign policy, which oscillated between a will to project French power and the desire to diffuse democratic norms in the region where France was implicated during the colonial era. Yet, the controversies related to Françafrique continued during the Chirac and Sarkozy's presidencies. Chirac's discourse was interpreted as having a paternalistic will to maintain the former Gaullian networks, while Sarkozy's "moral" rhetoric was perceived as a mask that hid the private interests of those close to Sarkozy, such as the businessman Vincent Bolloré. Because it failed to clarify relations with former African colonies, French political power found itself in a situation where its discourse on democracy paralleled another discourse, that of the need for French influence. When elected president in 2012, François Hollande tried to break with this ambiguity.

At the start of his presidency, Hollande named Hélène Le Gal as Africa adviser (*conseillère Afrique*); she was determinedly opposed to the Françafrique policy of the past. In October 2012, Hollande chose, as his first foreign state visit, Senegal. There, he delivered a speech in Dakar stating his aim to break with his predecessor Nicolas Sarkozy's paternalism. Several years earlier, Sarkozy had given a speech in the same city, with one phrase that was particularly shocking: "The drama of Africa is that the African man has not entered history enough."[32] The colonial, paternalistic overtones are obvious, with the responsibility of the *mission civilisatrice* lurking in the background. In Hollande's 2012 speech in Dakar, he declared that the hierarchical relations of Françafrique were finished, and that the relationship between the two parties ought to be based on "respect, clarity, and solidarity."[33] Ultimately, however, his administration's deeds have not exactly stayed true to his words.

Since January 2013 and the intervention in Mali, Hollande has fallen in line with his predecessors, who made Africa a place of presidential leadership and an expression of the French vision of international relations. The case of Mali is particularly interesting because it clearly demonstrates Hollande's shift in position. In his speech in Dakar, Hollande had excluded the idea of a military intervention in Mali, which was already the target of attacks from the Islamists of al-Qaeda in the Islamic Maghreb. However, the domestic and international contexts eventually changed France's position. On the domestic front, Hollande's presidential authority was highly contested during the first few months of his presidency. On the international front, the situation in Mali deteriorated significantly. Radical Islamists took control of Northern Mali and were traveling toward the capital, Bamako, threatening to overrun the entire country. When the Malian government asked for international help, France, with UN approval, intervened.

During the intervention in Mali, Hollande discovered, as it were, the military tool of foreign policy. Recall that one of the first measures taken by Hollande when elected president was to disengage the French Army from Afghanistan. In the span of a few days, Operation Serval, as it was called, managed to push back fighters from al-Qaeda in the Islamic Maghreb and prevent the fall of the Malian state. On February 2, 2014, Hollande traveled to Bamako, declaring that this victory marked the most important day of his political career. Several months later, new elections were organized in Mali. At the time of writing, the security situation of Mali remains somewhat precarious; but for Hollande, the operation was a success on the political level. He temporarily gained popularity in the public opinion and credibility on the international level. More important, he demonstrated that he was capable of making decisions in the foreign policy realm, and of achieving rapid results abroad in France's sphere of influence. A trend had been set. Hollande would not shy away from mobilizing the French armed forces—during Operation Sangaris in the Central African Republic, and then with Operation Barkhane again in the Sahel region.[34]

In opposition to the "warrior" rhetoric that gained ascendancy in Hollande's France, certain observers—such as Mitterrand's former adviser Hubert Védrine and foreign affairs minister Lionel Jospin—have accused Hollande's foreign policy of "neocolonialism." It is also not difficult to see the parallels in rhetoric between Hollande and George W. Bush after the September 11, 2001, terrorist attacks on the United States. Can Hollande's military interventionism be seen as a variation of the postcolonial wars of the past or of Bush's doctrine after the 9/11 attacks?

There is clearly a link to colonialism, but one could portray the wars in Africa as a continuation of the marriage between grandeur and responsibility in the postcolonial era that has essentially been a part of French foreign policy since Tocqueville. As for the comparison with the Bush doctrine, perhaps one can make the case for similarity of vocabulary following recent terrorist attacks, but not with regard to actions. It is true that the presidential discourses of Hollande and Bush demonstrate a similar rhetoric that defines an evil military target and seeks to rally a nation traumatized by terrorist attacks. When Hollande spoke to Parliament on November 16, 2015, three days after the terrorist attacks in Paris, he sent a clear message:

> France is at war. The acts committed Friday night in Paris and the Stade de France are acts of war. They killed 129 people, and left many more wounded. They are an act of aggression against our country and its values, against the youth and its style of life. They are the acts of a jihadist army, the group Daesh [another name for ISIS], who fights us because France is a country of liberty, because we are the motherland of Human Rights.[35]

However, the actions that follow from these speeches have been very different compared with Bush. The French military interventions in Mali, the Central African Republic, and Iraq against ISIS have all been multilateral, or had UN backing. They are very different from the quasi-unilateral interventions, such as the United States–led war in Iraq in 2003, which defied the UN, or the controversial US drone strike program outside the hot battlefield against terrorist groups. Recall that France was critically against the United States–led Iraq War, with then–foreign minister Dominique de Villepin delivering a famous speech at the UN as the United States beat the war drum in early 2003. Moreover, as Vilmer demonstrates in chapter 5 of this volume, the French view of the US drone program remains highly critical.

But is France anything more than a middle-level power? Is there anything to be said about French grandeur that translates into a more prominent role in the international realm? France's dominant role in the Libya intervention (under Sarkozy) suggested that France was pursuing a more aggressive role militarily, upholding the norm of R2P, in order to increase its international reputation. But, as Hehir shows in chapter 1, R2P is a problematic norm, with the Libya intervention leading to considerable instability as opposed to a brighter democracy. Thus, despite the French call for intervention in Syria early on in 2013, the world shied away (perhaps in part because of the difficult Libya experience). The inability of France to convince the world to intervene in Syria is characteristic of France's status as a limited power. While trying to uphold global norms as a means to enhance its reputation, it ultimately lacked the political capital to act when greater powers lowered their weapons, as it were. France was in favor of punishing Bashar al-Assad's Syria with aerial strikes after the regime's use of chemical weapons against its own population. Hollande was in contact with US president Barack Obama, who was initially favorable to attacking, as Assad had crossed a "red line" by using chemical weapons. Ultimately, however, Obama decided not to intervene, and he brokered a deal with Russia to facilitate the removal of Assad's chemical weapons. With the American refusal, France also relinquished the threat of intervention. Militarily, the French army was stretched thin, while politically, it was not possible to engage in an intervention without American support. This example demonstrates that France maintained some independence on the military front—the ability to strike Assad's Syria—but politically, it lacked the grandeur of a global power. In Syria (much as in Afghanistan), the French army was only a reinforcement for American military leadership. However, France does maintain a sphere of influence, with the ability to intervene at the regional level, in postcolonial zones (e.g., in Mali and the Central African Republic). This is possible not only because France has the means and competence to do so but also because it has influence and arguably a special legitimacy as a result of its colonial experience. As Hollande recounted to David Revault d'Allonnes, a French journalist for *Le Monde*, the United States allegedly told France with regard to addressing the crisis in Mali: "It's your job."[36] This deferral of power suggests that France is seen, by some at least, as having a legitimate zone of influence, and points to a form of postcolonial responsibility that it can pursue in a concerted manner under the auspices of the UN and in cooperation with the sovereign authorities in the states concerned by these interventions.

Of course, the decision not to intervene in Syria has had repercussions. There is no telling whether punitive strikes against the Assad regime might have helped to end the Syrian civil war; probably not. But the decision not to intervene has invigorated the rise of ISIS, with a backlash in numerous countries across the globe, including France. Although France has embraced its postcolonial responsibility in certain zones of influence in Africa, the question becomes whether it can do so domestically in the fight against ISIS-inspired jihadists.

Since 2013, Hollande and his government have fully assumed the use of the term "war" to qualify the armed conflicts in which France is involved. This war and security rhetoric was reinforced after the terrorist attacks in Paris in January and November 2015, and then with the July 14, 2016, attacks in Nice, and in subsequent attacks. ISIS has declared war on France, so the government has exclaimed in response that, "against the totalitarian Islamism [of Daesh], France will wage a merciless war." This includes waging war in Iraq and Syria, where the ISIS leadership is entrenched, as well as "on our soil," where the group sends suicide bombers and calls for lone wolf attacks.[37] This struggle is something a little different from a classical war, as Brunstetter highlights in chapter 11 of this volume. Although the use of force against ISIS is not specifically in the Françafrique sphere of influence, the struggle to tame the risk of terrorist attacks by those inspired by ISIS's ideology remains a particular challenge that is complicated in the case of France by its colonial heritage. Accepting the other edge of postcolonial responsibility, that of designing a more ethical integration policy, adds a further layer to John Emery's framework, discussed in chapter 9 of this volume, for balancing risk, security, and uncertainty when it comes to fighting terrorism.

In the terrorist context, Hollande and his government insist on the term "war" to demonstrate that the jihadist threat comes from the exterior, not from the interior, and yet there is confusion in the way he portrays the perpetrators. Speaking of the November 13 attacks, he states: "The acts of war on Friday were decided on and planned in Syria. . . . They were organized in Belgium, and perpetrated on our soil with French complicity."[38] On one hand, this implies that the conflict is international—an act of war—as opposed to domestic. And yet the conflict is not just international. Today, the French republican pact is challenged by jihadists who, for the most part, are third- or fourth-generation immigrants from former colonies. Hollande's focus on reinforcing law enforcement measures seems to portray the French jihadists who took part in the terrorist attacks as accomplices in a criminal act, which suggests they are not combatants but rather criminals. There is thus an underlying contradiction in the way Hollande presents matters: If they are accomplices and not combatants, why then does he talk about war? Obviously, there is an uneasiness in considering French jihadists for what they are—that is to say, combatants for an ideological cause that goes well beyond the borders of France but which is also linked to their postcolonial identity. These individuals are the product of the fractured education vision begun with Ferry, albeit in a postcolonial setting. They call into question the politics of integration that France has been pursuing since the early 2000s.[39] The current situation not only demonstrates that colonial history continues to influence French politics today, it also shows how difficult it is to untangle the domestic from the international when evaluating the use of force. As we contemplate the limits of law enforcement, or how it must evolve to deal with this threat (such as Brunstetter's *jus ad vim* framework discussed in chapter 11), one cannot ignore the deeper colonial history that informs social cleavages.

CONCLUSION: TOWARD A NEW POSTCOLONIAL RESPONSIBILITY

Internationally, France has the choice between two strategic and ethical options, both of which are open to criticism, and both of which offer a perilous course in pursuit of the long-sought-after grandeur: interventionism or isolationism. Intervention in former colonies can be criticized because it maintains the dependency dynamics of the "center" toward the "periphery," to use the language of Samir Amin.[40] However, it can help to ensure some level of international influence; and if the Mali case is indeed a success, it can contribute to international peace and security. Isolationism can also be criticized because it can lead to the worsening of humanitarian and political crises while also diminishing France's global stature (though it would shield the country from the neocolonialist critique). The case of Rwanda in 1994, when France put off military intervention, illustrates the costs of a wait-and-see policy. Since then, French diplomacy—through the UN—has sought to avoid the repetition of a similar scenario. The Mali case in particular can be seen as a semisuccessful case of French influence. In response to possible criticism, imagine what could have happened in Mali if France had not intervened? Despite not being the optimal outcome, far worse scenarios could be imagined—for example, ISIS establishing a foothold in Bamako.

The intervention dilemma in a postcolonial context highlights an additional tension underpinning choices about intervention facing some Western democracies in the aftermath of the Cold War. Interventionism clashes with the principle of state sovereignty, but the absence of intervention clashes with the UN aims of spreading democratic norms and peace building. In chapter 1 of this volume, Hehir proposes a means to reform the R2P norm by empowering the UN; however, the French intervention dilemma highlights the ambiguous role of the UN as a multilateral body for collective security over time. The UN was a major craftsman of decolonization and independence after World War II; but it also encourages, through support of military intervention under the auspices of R2P, an interventionist dynamic that can empower former colonial powers to intervene. Given that both the UN's idea of development and R2P have been interpreted by certain postcolonial theorists as a new form of imperialism that reconfigures the colonial idea of the *mission civilisatrice* in contemporary terms of democratization, what lessons can be drawn from the French case?[41]

Above all, the French case illustrates that the colonial heritage, and the postcolonial responsibility it entails, is a two-edged sword. It may prove to be an important factor in the maintenance of international security by providing the kind of legitimacy France benefited from in the Mali intervention. One could imagine how this might undergird the R2P norm in certain contexts in the future. Here, circumscribing the notion of grandeur, as Mitterrand and Hollande attempted to do in their own ways, is important. Delusions of grandeur can be destabilizing. Interventions aimed at expanding France's reputation by intervening outside its sphere of postcolonial influence, such as the one in Libya, may lead to destabilizing outcomes. Managing the scope of grandeur by pursuing some influence, but only where it can be effective, can, as the Mali intervention suggests, ensure that postcolonial influence could play a stabilizing role. Thus, embracing postcolonial responsibility might bolster UN normative initiatives, if navigated carefully—in the case of France, this means with UN and local government support.

And yet at the same time, the postcolonial legacy haunts the domestic French political situation. Colonial history had been, from the early nineteenth century through the crumbling of the empire after World War II, the source of grandeur and the projection of a universalist political project. The fall of the colonial empire put an end to the sense of grandeur that Tocqueville praised and the *mission civilisatrice* that, according to Ferry, carried with it the responsibility of integrating new populations into the French Republic.[42] As the empire began to fall apart, only De Gaulle was able to restore a true sense of grandeur, but that was only temporary. Today, the feeling of discomfort with the colonial past has replaced the idea of grandeur.

The fractured legacy of republican education as the vehicle of the *mission civilisatrice* continues to have an impact on contemporary France as it grapples with the conflict against ISIS. It is impossible to ignore that those implicated in the recent terrorist attacks—in Paris, Nice, and Saint Étienne de Rouvray—were third- or fourth-generation French citizens, whose ancestors came to France as immigrants from former colonies, or foreign nationals from former colonies. How does France deal with these individuals, seemingly lost to the Republic, who have declared war on France by pledging allegiance to jihadist groups such as ISIS? How can it prevent others from following suit?

Recent tragic events in France (and elsewhere in Europe) raise challenging dilemmas, situated in the gray area between wars to fight ISIS externally and taking sufficient domestic measures to deal with sympathizers domestically. For years, France has tried to tame its colonial past, relegating it to the background of the grandeur of the Republic. Today, if it is going to succeed in preserving the republican pact amid the threat of jihadist terrorism, it must bear the responsibility for its postcolonial present.

NOTES

1. For a recent examination on the French case that brings the reader up to date, see Marie-Claude Smouts, ed., *La Situation postcoloniale: Les Postcolonial Studies dans le cas français* (Paris: Presse de Sciences Po, 2007).

2. Jean-Pierre Bat, *Le Syndrome Foccart: La Politique française en Afrique de 1959 à nos jours* (Paris: Gallimard, 2012); and Pascal Airault and Jean-Pierre Bat, *Francafrique, les derniers mystères* (Paris: Taillandier, 2016).

3. These points are discussed with an "engaged" and often military point of view by Pascal Blanchard, Nicolas Bancel, and Dominic Thomas, eds., *La guerre des identités? De la fracture coloniale à la Révolution ultranationale* (Paris: La Découverte, 2015).

4. See, e.g., Dino Constantini, *Mission civilisatrice: Le rôle de l'histoire coloniale dans la construction de l'identité politique française* (Paris: La Découverte, 2008).

5. For a critical approach to this issue, see François Gèze, "L'Héritage Colonial au Cœur de la Politique Etrangère Française," in *La Fracture coloniale*, ed. Nicolas Bancel (Paris: La Découverte, 2005), 155–63.

6. Roland Paris, "International Peacebuilding and the 'Mission Civilisatrice,'" *Review of International Studies* 28 (2002): 637–56.

7. Frederick Cooper, *Africa since 1940: The Past of the Present* (Cambridge: Cambridge University Press, 2002).

8. Mona Ozouf, *Jules Ferry: La liberté et la tradition* (Paris: Gallimard, 2014).

9. For a similar exploration of the British case, see Michael Howard, *War and the Liberal Conscience* (London: Columbia/Hurst, 2008); and David M. McCourt, *Britain and World Power since 1945: Constructing a Nation's Role in International Politics* (Ann Arbor: University of Michigan Press, 2014).

10. Benjamin de Constant, *De l'esprit de conquête et de l'usurpation dans leurs rapports à la civilisation européenne* (Paris: De l'Imprimerie Nationale, 1992; orig. pub. 1813).

11. Alexis de Tocqueville, *Writing on Empire and Slavery: "Essay on Algeria,"* trans. and ed. Jennifer Pitts (Baltimore: Johns Hopkins University Press, 2001; orig. pub. 1841), 71.

12. Olivier le Cour Grandmaison, *Coloniser, Exterminer: Sur la guerre et l'État Colonial* (Paris: Fayard, 2005).

13. Cheryl B. Welch, "Colonial Violence and the Rhetoric of Evasion: Tocqueville on Algeria," *Political Theory* 31 (2003): 235–64.

14. Jennifer Pitts, *A Turn to Empire: The Rise of Imperial Liberalism in Britain and France* (Princeton, NJ: Princeton University Press, 2005), 71.

15. Jacques Frémeaux, *De quoi fut fait l'Empire: Les guerres goloniales au XIXe siècle* (Paris: CNRS Éditions, 2014), 23.

16. Cited by Thomas F. Power, *Jules Ferry and the Renaissance of French Imperialism* (New York: King's Crown Press, 1944), 192.

17. Jules Ferry, *Journal Officiel: Débats parlementaires*, Chambre des députés, July 28, 1885.

18. Pierre-Jean Luizard, *Le Choc colonial et l'Islam: Les Politiques religieuses des puissances coloniales en terres d'Islam* (Paris: La Découverte, 2006), 97.

19. Cited by Charles-Robert Ageron, *France Coloniale ou Parti colonial?* (Paris: PUF, 1978), 70.

20. Adria Lawrence, *Imperial Rule and the Politics of Nationalism: Anti-Colonial Protest in the French Empire* (Cambridge: Cambridge University Press, 2013).

21. Raymond Aron, *La Tragédie Algérienne* (Paris: Plon, 1957).

22. Maurice Vaïsse, *La Grandeur: Politique etrangère du général De Gaulle, 1958–1969* (Paris: Fayard, 1998).

23. Stanley Hoffmann, "De Gaulle's Memoirs: The Hero of History," *World Politics* 13, no. 1 (October 1960): 151.

24. Olivier Schmitt, "Decline in Denial: France since 1945," in *Managing Decline in International Relations*, ed. Frédéric Mérand (forthcoming).

25. Bordeaux speech, April 15, 1961.

26. Lawrence, *Imperial Rule.*

27. Bat, *Le Syndrome Foccart.*

28. "Le discours de La Baule (1990)," *rfi*, June 20, 1990. The full version of the speech (in French) is available at www1.rfi.fr/actufr/articles/037/article_20103.asp.

29. Hubert Védrine, *Les Mondes de François Mitterrand* (Paris: Fayard, 1996), 696.

30. Michael Doyle, "Liberalism and World Politics," *American Political Science Review* 80, no. 4 (1986): 1151–69.

31. François Mitterrand, *Le Coup d'état permanent* (Paris: Plon, 1964).

32. "Le discours de Dakar de Nicolas Sarkozy," *Le Monde*, July 26, 2007, www.lemonde.fr/afrique/article/2007/11/09/le-discours-de-dakar_976786_3212.html.

33. "Discours de M. le Président de la République devant l'Assemblée nationale de la République du Sénégal," *Élysée*, October 12, 2012. The full version of the speech (in French) is available at www.elysee.fr/declarations/article/discours-de-m-le-president-de-la-republique-devant-l-assemblee-nationale-de-la-republique-du-senegal/.

34. David Revault d'Allonnes, *Les Guerres du président* (Paris: Seuil, 2015).

35. "Discours du président de la République devant le Parlement réuni en Congrès," *Élysee*, November 16, 2016. The full version of the speech (in French) is available at www.elysee.fr/declarations/article/discours-du-president-de-la-republique-devant-le-parlement-reuni-en-congres-3/.

36. Revault d'Allonnes, *Les Guerres du président*.

37. "Manuel Valls: 'Venez Nombreux' à la Marche de Dimanche," *FranceSoir*, January 10, 2015. The full version of the speech (in French) is available at www.francesoir.fr/politique-france/manuel-valls-venez-nombreux-la-marche-de-dimanche.

38. "Speech by the President of the Republic Before a Joint Session of Parliament," *France Diplomatie*, November 16, 2015. The full text is available in English at www.diplomatie.gouv.fr/en/french-foreign-policy/defence-security/parisattacks-paris-terror-attacks-november-2015/article/speech-by-the-president-of-the-republic-before-a-joint-session-of-parliament.

39. Daniel R. Brunstetter, "Rousseau and the Tensions of France's Contrat d'Accueil et d'Intégration," *Journal of Political Ideologies* 17, no. 1 (2012): 95–114.

40. Samir Amin, *Neo-Colonialism in West Africa* (New York: Monthly Review Press, 1973).

41. Felwine Sarr, *Afrotopia* (Paris: Philippe Rey, 2016), 21.

42. Ferry, *Journal Officiel*, *Débats parlementaires*.

8

The Signs of the Times

Classical Just War Thinking and the Struggle against Jihadists

JOHN KELSAY

WITH RESPECT TO JUST WAR THINKING, what lessons shall we take from a time of contested and fragmented sovereignty? Particularly with respect to the "war on terror," I suggest that one lesson has to do with the importance of timing—that is, *when* we use force to quell a potential threat. Of course, the *jus ad bellum* is meant to help us recognize the moment when it is just to intervene. However, the way it is currently understood, with emphasis placed on the last resort criterion, is problematic in the struggle against jihadist groups. Insofar as the struggle against such groups is perhaps the defining concern of this new era of contested and fragmented sovereignty, one wonders if it is even applicable. That being said, a return to the Westphalian norm of sovereignty is not necessarily a solution. Even if a collective of states were to somehow take back the land conquered by the Islamic State in Iraq and Syria (ISIS), this would not defeat the threat from jihadist groups. As Emery's chapter 9 argues, ISIS appears very willing to export its terror by operating from zones of both contested and uncontested sovereignty.

Since 2001 there have been several examples that point to how one may get the timing wrong. Policymakers can err on the side of "rushing in"—as was arguably the case in the 2003 war to oust a Saddam Hussein supposedly linked with al-Qaeda. They may also err by missing opportunities—as was arguably the case with President Barack Obama's decision not to assist the Free Syrian Army in 2011. Obama claimed the threshold of last resort had not been crossed to warrant intervention in the Syrian civil war, though intervening in some way might have diminished the global threat of jihadist groups like ISIS that have taken advantage of the space of contested and fragmented sovereignty to project power globally. A typical understanding of last resort asks us to think about when all non-force-based options have been exhausted, but what I am suggesting is different.[1] Following a suggestion from the late Paul Ramsey, we might rather speak of timely (or, perhaps, last timely) resort.[2] Getting the timing right, in the sense of an ability to judge *when* military action is an apt means of statecraft, must be a central concern of those who seek to apply the just war tradition to jihadist threats. Notice that I am not rejecting the criterion of last resort outright but, rather, argue that in some contexts, a return to how the classical just war tradition understands the notion of timing can offer important insights.

So I argue here, in any case. And I suggest that reading "the signs of the times," in the sense of a disciplined attempt to comprehend the dynamic features of particular conflicts, is crucial to the practice of just war thinking in the context where the threat from jihadist groups exacerbates the contested and fragmented sovereignty that continues to destabilize the international system. We are no longer in a system where states can do what they want within their borders; rather, some nonstate actors (with jihadist appeal) seek to impose their will, while sovereign states try to oppose and eliminate their presence.

But this is also about more than sovereignty, as it is understood in modern terms. As an example, I consider the contemporary Middle East, where one of the most significant developments has to do with a controversy over jihad as an individual duty, whereby Muslims across traditional sovereign borders have been—controversially—called to the fight. The number of groups appealing to this notion points to a crisis, in and of itself. According to a report published by the RAND Corporation in June 2014, there are fifty-eight organizations calling Muslims to jihad—up from thirty-nine since 2010.[3] When we consider that these groups understand their fight as a contest with one another, as well as with existing governments, it becomes clear that the current chaos will not be resolved any time soon. In thinking about how to respond, interpreters of the just war tradition must consider what this means. The jihadist phenomenon certainly constitutes a military threat, and in this sense consideration of a military response is appropriate. Even more, however, the appeal to fighting as an individual duty points to a political crisis, in which many people feel that existing institutions work only for the few rather than the many. In the contemporary Middle East, the proper role of military force would seem to involve limiting the impact of jihadist violence, with a view toward creating space for statecraft. Ultimately, the need is for better and more inclusive forms of governance—and that involves hard and sustained political work.

I begin with an account of timing in the classic just war tradition, and then, because I see this as apt for understanding current affairs, move to a discussion of the contemporary crisis in the Middle East. Because one way of understanding the situation is through an account of the various groups appealing to the aspect of Islamic tradition whereby jihad becomes an individual duty, I provide a brief account of the history of this notion before discussing the particular challenge presented by al-Qaeda and ISIS. I close with some comments related to US and allied policy in the region, particularly in terms of the just war tradition and the requirement of reading the "signs of the times." My overall argument suggests that understanding the particulars of a situation one faces—in this case, combating jihadism in a world of contested and fragmented sovereignty—requires a different notion of timing than that currently associated with last resort. In classical just war thinking, the notion I am after is linked to the virtue of prudence.

TIMING AND THE JUST WAR TRADITION

Timing is a central concern of the just war tradition, though it seems important to say that this is not always explicit. Although modern versions of just war tend to reduce timing to last resort, this misses something important. Even if timing does not appear in standard lists of the just war criteria, we have a set of norms designed to help in ascertaining whether particular uses of military force serve in securing the common good. This implies an understanding of when the use of force is prudent. Thus, Thomas Aquinas's well-known summary points to the requirements of sovereign authority, just cause, and rightful intention:

> In order for a war to be just, three things are required. First, the authority of the prince by whose command the war is to be waged. For it is not the business of a private individual to declare war. . . . Moreover, it is not the business of a private person to summon together the people, which has to be done in wartime. . . . Secondly, a just cause is required, namely that those who are attacked, should be attacked because they deserve it on account of some fault. . . . Thirdly, it is necessary that those waging war should have a rightful intention, so that they intend the advancement of good, or the avoidance of evil.[4]

Even in the more expansive lists provided by early modern developers of the tradition, one will not find any mention of timing. For example, Francisco Suárez's discussion echoes that of Aquinas with respect to sovereign authority and just cause; Suárez then glosses rightful intention as right conduct, which includes good faith efforts on the part of the sovereign in judging the balance between costs and benefits to the common good, the likelihood that military force will achieve a just political end, the impact of war on international order, and the possibility that means short of war might provide a better way forward. In contemporary terms, these are the *ad bellum* criteria of proportionality, reasonable hope of success, aim of peace, and last resort. For Suárez, they are joined with the *jus in bello* criteria of discrimination and proportionality in means, so as to provide evidence by which rightful intention may be judged.[5]

Let us dwell for a moment on the concept of last resort, for this has the deepest connection to the notion of timing. Last resort could mean trying everything possible to avoid war. Or it could mean trying just what is plausible, and knowing when other measures are not prudent, and when the use of force is the right option. There is an important question as to the centrality of last resort to the just war tradition; but for present purposes, we have to ask ourselves if these understandings of last resort give us an appropriate criterion for thinking about timing in the current context of the jihadist threat.[6]

I submit that a return to the classical just war tradition can offer important insights into this question. One of the concerns running throughout the accounts of Aquinas, Suárez, and others does in fact have to do with the issue of *when* military action is justified. To put it another way, the logic of the just war criteria is such that the vocabulary serves to enable us to answer the question "When is war an apt means of statecraft?" To reiterate, this is not the same question as "Is intervention a last resort?"

This distinction becomes clear when one considers the way such classical interpreters connected the practice of statecraft with the virtue of prudence. Aquinas, for example, describes prudence or practical wisdom as an intellectual and a moral virtue. In relation to justice, temperance, and fortitude, prudence involves a habitual focus on the assessment of facts, so as to determine the form these other "cardinal" virtues should take in a given circumstance. As we look at Aquinas's account of the matter, it seems clear that the virtue of prudence is supposed to travel with action that is timely.[7]

Aquinas thus proceeds to distinguish the role of prudence in political and military activities. The former is related to the work of rulers crafting policy for the common good, the latter to the work of those who plan strategy. Both share the feature Aquinas considers most significant in prudence—"taking counsel." In the end, of course, one whose behavior is characterized by prudence makes judgments about various courses of action and issued directives "concerning the means of obtaining a due [that is, a just] end."[8] Prudence is first of all a matter of listening, of gaining knowledge of the particulars of a situation. Let us remind ourselves what this means in today's world—trying to understand the way in which jihad transcends traditional notions of sovereignty, and how force could be used to combat the subsequent threat.

With respect to just war thinking, prudence serves to direct the desire for justice. After all, a decision to employ military force is not only a matter of responding to provocation, in the sense associated with a just cause. It is also a matter of statecraft whereby those entrusted with governance seek to secure the common good. Such persons rightly "take counsel" as they try to ascertain the matters related to overall proportionality, reasonable hope of success, and aim of peace, as well as to learn whether war may be waged in ways that respect the criteria of discrimination and proportionality. In all, the classical just war tradition can provide a framework within which we attempt to ascertain *when* military action constitutes a timely approach to a particular problem. This is the essence of the just war tradition before the shift to Westphalian sovereignty that Johnson seeks to recover, one that deserves our particular attention in the current era (and arguably merits being put into dialogus with Brunstetter's *jus ad vim* approach, described in chapter 11).[9]

THE CRISIS OF THE CONTEMPORARY MIDDLE EAST

Recent developments in the Middle East provide a case in which the importance of such deliberation seems clear. Beginning with its declaration of a caliphate in June 2014, the military successes of the group variously known as ISIS or ISIL inspired heated debates over the possibility that the United States and allied forces might once again be drawn into fighting. Many of the arguments were retrospective: Did the rise of ISIS demonstrate once and for all the foolishness of the George W. Bush administration's war to oust Saddam Hussein? Or was it rather the result of President Obama's failure to sustain American influence with the government in Baghdad? And in either case, what should be done now? Given that ISIS held territory on either side of the border between Iraq and Syria, would military intervention necessarily involve actions in Syria as well as Iraq? Would air power be sufficient, or would success require "boots on the ground," particularly in the sense of US forces?

Much discussion of these questions seemed to focus on *how* the United States and its allies should proceed. From another perspective, however, what was (and is) needed is an assessment of *when*, in the sense of prudent or timely action. In this connection, most commentators seemed to neglect the kind of analysis mentioned by former defense secretary Robert Gates in a February 2015 interview on *Meet the Press*. Responding to questions from Chuck Todd, Gates suggested the need to step back for a moment and to think about the "complexity and historical magnitude of the challenge" before us. As the secretary had it, fighting in Syria, Iraq, Libya, and elsewhere is only one piece of a multifaceted struggle regarding the shape of political order. Conflicts between Sunni and Shia Muslims, "authoritarians and reformers," Islamists and secularists are set in the context of questions about the viability of the states currently claiming a monopoly on the legitimate use of armed force. This, he said, is "a generational conflict."[10] To return to the themes of this volume, what we have here is a conflict simultaneously contesting sovereignty and rendering sovereignty more fragmented.

What is going on in a particular setting? Getting an answer to this question is always the first step in encouraging timely action. Recalling Aquinas's discussion of prudence, one might say that obtaining an account of developments in the Middle East is an aspect of "taking counsel." Secretary Gates's brief comments were on the right track. If anything, the situation is even more far reaching than he suggests. This is actually a multigenerational conflict, and the region is teetering on the brink of anarchy, as Turkish, Russian, and other forces, each with a distinctive agenda, suggest that the fighting might now be characterized as a kind of miniature world war rather than as a civil war or even regional conflict.

One can bring this into focus in a number of ways. John Emery's chapter 9 focuses on counterterrorism in relation to the balancing of security, risk, and uncertainty. He rightfully attempts to de-homogenize the idea of cohesive terrorist organizations that takes on the simplistic notion of jihad against the West. Here, I concentrate on the ways various groups in the historically Muslim lands are applying the notion of jihad as an individual duty. As I argue, appeals to this idea point to a deep crisis, in which there is little or no agreement regarding the form of a legitimate political order.

ON FIGHTING AS AN INDIVIDUAL DUTY

A little background may be helpful. The notion of jihad as an individual duty is an aspect of a larger war convention. The judgments pertaining to armed struggle represent the opinions of members of the learned class, developed in connection with questions about resort to and conduct of war. Thus, war is justified (1) when authorized by officials charged with protecting and preserving the common good; (2) for the purpose of extending, maintaining, and defending a polity considered legitimate, in the sense that Islam is established in accordance with God's directives; and (3) when those fighting adhere to norms of honorable combat, including avoidance of direct harm to noncombatants and observance of proportionality in means.[11]

These are the criteria for just war in ordinary circumstances, and in such times, fighting is classed as a "collective" duty. It is the responsibility of those who hold office to maintain a military force sufficient to secure just political ends. As long as enough people volunteer to serve, others may go about the business of ordinary life, supporting the military and other institutions of the state by paying taxes.

In an emergency, however, the duty to serve takes on a different cast. If a foreign power makes incursions into the territory of the Islamic state, or if its preparations and placing of troops suggest that an invasion is imminent, fighting becomes an "individual" duty. In such cases, Muslim scholars compared the duty to fight with the duty to pray or to fast.[12] These are obligations every individual must fulfill. No one can perform them in place of another; each person stands alone in the presence of God and will give an account of what he or she has done. The opening sections of Yusuf al-Qaradawi's 2009 discussion provide a convenient summary. In response to the question "When is Jihad an individual obligation?" Qaradawi writes:

> If the enemy attacks a Muslim country, or if such an attack is feared and its signs are manifest, . . . then it does not suffice for some Muslims of that land [to fight] but not others; rather, all must rise up to resist the invasion, each to the extent to which he is able, each to the best of his abilities. . . . This is in contrast to the jihad in which it is Muslims who seek out and attack their foe. For God and His Prophet have granted permission to one who would stay behind from such expeditions, . . . although he is denied the grace and merit of those who do participate. . . . As for that jihad involving resistance to invasion, it is as described by the Shaykh al-Islam Ibn Taymiyya, a defense of the faith, of holy things, and of life. It is a kind of necessity, while other forms of jihad involve fighting by choice for the building up and exaltation of the faith.[13]

Shaykh Qaradawi continues, identifying several other conditions when the notion of individual duty applies to military activity: when the head of state calls on a specific person or group to serve; when a believer possesses particular skills or training needed by the armed forces; or, in the context of battle, when one is not allowed to abandon an assigned post. Along the way, he cites numerous precedents, not least the great Ibn Taymiyya (d. 1328), whose various opinions on the matter show the influence of the Crusades as well as of the Mongol invasion.[14]

In a similar fashion, Qaradawi's account is intended as a contribution to Muslim discussion of conditions in the contemporary Middle East. In particular, he offers an alternative to the version of jihad as individual duty set forth by Osama bin Laden, Ayman al-Zawahiri, and others associated with al-Qaeda. As well, looking at developments since the publication of Qaradawi's summary, one should say that he offers an alternative to the way ISIS interprets the notion. In either case, however, the claim is that the Muslim community faces an emergency. That is the point of an appeal to fighting as an individual duty; as we shall see, even Qaradawi's discussion of the matter suggests this.

With respect to al-Qaeda, the World Islamic Front's 1998 *Declaration Concerning Armed Struggle against Jews and Crusaders* begins with an account of political conditions in the historically Muslim regions. Describing the continuing presence of US forces on the Arabian Peninsula as an occupation, bin Laden, al-Zawahiri, and others connect this with sanctions imposed on Iraq by the international community and the continued existence of Israel to support the judgment that the United States and its allies are engaged in war against Islam. Given the circumstances, the authors assert that an overwhelming consensus supports the claim that in such circumstances, jihad becomes an individual duty, so that "the ruling to kill the Americans and their allies—civilians and military—is an individual duty for every Muslim who can do it in any country in which it is possible to do it, in order to liberate the al-Aqsa Mosque and the holy mosque [Mecca] from their grip, and in order for their armies to move out of all the lands of Islam, defeated and unable to threaten any Muslim."[15]

Subsequent statements by al-Qaeda spokespersons reinforce the notion that jihad is an individual duty that authorizes Muslims to carry out attacks on a global scale. Ultimately, the organization's goals were and are political, so that the point of such operations is to convince the United States and its allies that the costs of maintaining influence in the historic territory of Islam outweigh the benefits. Once such foreign powers withdraw, then the community of believers will be free to dispense with the existing state regimes and to engage in "true reform." A June 2005 statement by al-Zawahiri provides a convenient summary. Here, Zawahiri argues that "true reform is based on three principles." These are (1) the rule of Shari'a, or Islamic law; (2) the "freedom of the lands of Islam" from foreign domination; and (3) correlatively, self-determination for the Muslim community. This, he adds, can only be "accomplished by fighting for the sake of Allah."[16]

Al-Zawahiri and others certainly supported organized resistance in Afghanistan, Iraq, Somalia, and elsewhere. Over time, however, it became clear that the favored tactic of the group would be "lone wolf" attacks, in which individuals or small groups operating in the United States and other countries strike at airlines or other modes of public transportation, buildings, or spaces where large numbers of people gather, or at people who represent targets of interest. Thus the first issue of *Inspire*, the online magazine associated with al-Qaeda in the Arabian Peninsula, urged Muslims to attack restaurants or to drive automobiles into groups of pedestrians in US cities, and subsequent issues praised the Fort Hood shooter and the Tzarnov brothers' operation during the 2013 Boston Marathon.

In a sense, these are preferred to operations in Yemen or elsewhere in the Middle East.[17] Thus, readers are exhorted to do their part—they need not wait for further orders or ask for permission from recognized authorities. The emergency condition allows, and even requires, that any believer who understands the situation should do his or her part, using whatever tools might be available.

Back to Qaradawi: When the summary account cited above was published, Qaradawi had already offered a number of criticisms of al-Qaeda's emphasis on lone wolf attacks. Many of these focused on the indiscriminate nature of the operations. For example, Qaradawi's response to the September 11, 2001, terrorist attacks declares that "all Muslims ought to be united against all those who terrorize the innocents, and those who permit the killing of non-combatants without a justifiable reason. . . . [It is] a duty of Muslims to participate" in the effort to bring such people to justice.[18] Similarly, with respect to the London bombings in July 2005, Qaradawi described himself as "dumbfounded" by the carnage, especially because it included women, children, elderly persons, and other noncombatants.[19]

In 2009, Qaradawi offered some additional critiques. These went to the heart of what sorts of efforts may be authorized under emergency conditions. Jihad as an individual duty, Qaradawi wrote, is a matter of defense only. Its purpose is to repel an invading force. Once this goal is achieved, further action must follow the pattern of "normal" war. Those "ordinary" citizens who took up arms at a critical moment must now put them down. Jihad as individual duty does not authorize hot pursuit, reprisals, or attacks on foreign soil. Otherwise, the conduct of a few individuals may in the end increase the danger to the whole—for example, by involving the Muslim community in a wider conflict or by encouraging an enemy to respond in ways that increase the degree of harm to believers.[20]

Qaradawi's statement thus aims at reining in a group that is exceeding its mandate. Resistance in places like Iraq, Afghanistan, and Israel/Palestine might be framed as a matter of individual duty. Attacks on the "far enemy" in Britain, Europe, or the United States ought not be thought of in this way.

By the time Qaradawi published his views, political conditions in the Middle East were changing, however. The United States' plans to disengage from Iraq were on the table from the beginning of President Obama's administration. And even though the president would commit additional troops to Afghanistan, he did so with a timeline, by which reductions in US forces would begin in 2014, with a view toward 2016 for the end of the allied combat mission in that country. In December 2010, the developments that people came to call the Arab Spring surprised some in Washington. For someone like Qaradawi, however, the appropriate response was less a matter of surprise and more along the lines of "It's about time." At various points, he spoke of participation in demonstrations as an individual duty, and in 2011 he called on "any Libyan soldier or officer who has the opportunity to shoot and kill" Libyan president Muammar al-Gaddafi to do so. And, as things went from bad to worse in Syria, Qaradawi's language certainly reflected something close to the idea of fighting as an individual obligation. Particularly when Hezbollah forces entered the fray, he interpreted the conflict in sectarian terms, proclaiming that any Sunni Muslim trained and able to bear arms should come to the aid of their coreligionists.[21] Even as he criticized the particulars of al-Qaeda's program, Qaradawi's rhetoric thus confirmed the idea of an emergency. The Arab Spring and its aftermath pointed to a crisis of authority, which al-Qaeda and others were trying to exploit.

THE CHALLENGE OF ISIS TO TRADITIONAL NOTIONS OF SOVEREIGNTY

By 2014, Qaradawi and other members of the learned class would be responding to ISIS.[22] Originally cast as al-Qaeda's affiliate in the "land between the two rivers" (that is, Iraq), ISIS established its independence through a series of operations in Syria. When Ayman al-Zawahiri ordered ISIS leaders to focus on Iraq and to leave Syria to the Nusra Front, they refused, announcing that the group would henceforth be called "the Islamic State in Iraq and Greater Syria." Having obtained control of considerable portions of western Iraq and eastern Syria by June 2014, the group then proclaimed the establishment of a caliphate, and summoned all Muslims to migrate to the territory of ISIS. This was, of course, a defiant challenge to the way sovereignty had been organized to date in the international system. The following excerpt from a speech by one of the leading spokesmen for ISIS is instructive.

> The time has come for the umma of Muhammad, . . . to wake up from its sleep, remove the garments of dishonor, and shake off the dust of humil-

> iation and disgrace. . . . The sun of jihad has risen. The glad tidings of good are shining. Triumph looms on the horizon. The signs of victory have appeared.
>
> Here the flag of the Islamic State, the flag of *tawhid*, rises and flutters. Its shade covers land from Aleppo to Diyala. Beneath it, the walls of the *tawaghit* [tyrants] have been demolished, their flags have fallen, and their borders have been destroyed.

All this (and more) indicates that, while the struggle continues, the group's success is sufficient, so that "there only remained one matter, a [collective duty] that the ummah sins by abandoning. It is a forgotten obligation. The ummah has not tasted honor since they lost it. . . . It is the *khilafah*—the abandoned obligation of the era."[23]

As the statement proceeds, the author informs us that the leadership organized a *shura* council, indicating a gathering of those with credentials in the religious sciences (and perhaps some others) in order to deliberate. Those assembled determined that there was "no *shar'i* [legal] constraint or excuse" for delay, and thus "resolved to announce the appointment of a *khilafah*." Abu Bakr al-Baghdadi, at that time the political leader of the group, was deemed to satisfy the traditional criteria for leadership and is now "the imam and *khalifah* for the Muslims everywhere." The obligation to recognize his leadership and to swear loyalty to him is now "incumbent upon all Muslims," and the "legality of all emirates, groups, states, and organizations becomes null by the expansion of the *khilafah*'s authority and arrival of its troops to their areas."[24]

In the context of the general crisis of authority outlined above, the identification of a caliph is clearly an attempt at resolution. The declaration received a mixed reception, however. Not only did al-Zawahiri and others associated with al-Qaeda reject al-Adnani's report; scholars at al-Azhar indicated that ISIS had exceeded its authority, as did Yusuf al-Qaradawi and others associated with the Muslim Brotherhood. Still, there were those who responded positively to al-Adnani's announcement; some of these paid heed to al-Baghdadi's subsequent call to emigrate to the lands of ISIS:

> We make a special call to the scholars, *fuqaha'* [experts in Islamic jurisprudence], and callers, especially the judges, as well as people with military, administrative, and service expertise, and medical doctors and engineers of all different specializations and fields. . . . We call them and remind them to fear Allah, for their emigration is *wajib 'ayni* [an individual obligation], so that they can answer the dire need of the Muslims for them.[25]

Here, the language of individual duty is of interest. Al-Adnani described the establishment of Islamic government as a "collective duty" (*wajib kifa'i*), here in the sense that this is an obligation that requires consultation. Elsewhere, leaders of ISIS referred to jihad or armed struggle as an individual duty, as did those associated with al-Qaeda; the point of such language is to indicate that the influence of non-Muslims in the territory of Islam constitutes a crisis of such magnitude that any and all able-bodied believers should take part in fighting, without waiting for authorization from an existing government.

Now, however, al-Baghdadi is speaking as the head of an Islamic government. His call to Muslims able to emigrate to do so reflects historic judgments that, given the choice between living in lands governed by Muslims and others governed by non-Muslims, believers should avail themselves of the former option. By contrast, the special order to people with certain kinds of expertise reflects precedents indicating that the leader may declare that the needs of the state are such that certain individuals or groups are required to follow his directive. This may be in terms of fighting, or (as here) in the sense that building ISIS requires a particular set of skills.

In any case, there is no question that al-Baghdadi's call stood in sharp contrast to al-Qaeda's suggestion that believers who carry out attacks in the United States and Europe make contributions that are equal, or perhaps even superior to, those who are active in Yemen, Afghanistan, Iraq, or Syria. A number of analyses immediately focused on this, suggesting that the change indicated a new dynamic in the global jihadist movement, with important policy implications. For example, a "backgrounder" published under the auspices of the Institute for the Study of War focused on al-Baghdadi's call for believers to make the journey to the territory of the caliphate (which is indeed a challenge to existing norms of sovereignty): "[The] request that international supporters perform *hijrah*, rather than form remote attack cells in their own countries, shows a caliphate-centric foreign policy for ISIS. . . . This approach is markedly different from that of al-Qaeda's central leadership, which oversees a global network of semi-independent groups that will join together in the far future. ISIS seems intent to succeed in Iraq and Syrian before pursuing contiguous expansion."[26]

An assessment offered by analysts associated with the Middle East Media Research Institute puts the point even more sharply. Arguing that a focus on atrocities (beheading journalists and the like) has led some to view ISIS as "simply a more vicious version of al-Qaeda," the authors suggest that "unlike al-Qaeda, [ISIS] places priority not on global terrorism, but rather on establishing and consolidating a state, and hence it defers the clash with the West to a much later stage. . . . [The group's] ideology, discourse and conduct thus demonstrate that terror attacks in the West are at the bottom of its order of priorities." Still, once the group fulfills its aim of deposing and replacing existing regimes in the historic heartland of Islam, "the West's turn will arrive," so that US and other policymakers are advised to take action now, because "postponing the clash with the West serves the [ISIS'] interests rather than the West's."[27]

A close reading of the first two issues of the ISIS magazine *Dabiq* provides much evidence that supports these analyses. For that matter, even *Dabiq* 3, which begins by acknowledging the beginnings of the air campaign ordered by President Obama in August 2014, nevertheless maintains the focus on state building.

One month later, however, the focus of the magazine changed.[28] *Dabiq* 4 begins with encouragement to believers to remember that even in the midst of the American-led "crusade," this "religion is one that is promised with victory."[29] Excerpts from a long speech by al-Adnani congratulate the soldiers of ISIS on their success, and warn the United States and its partners not to expect such fighters to fail in resistance: "O Americans, and O Europeans, the Islamic State did not initiate a war against you, as your governments and media try to make you believe. It is you who started the transgression against us, and thus you deserve blame and you will pay a great price, . . . as you walk on your streets, turning right and left, fearing the Muslims. You will not feel secure even in your bedrooms."[30]

This paragraph in *Dabiq* 4 concludes with the warning that once the crusade is defeated, ISIS will turn to attacks on the American-led coalition—a statement very much in line with the analysis offered by the Middle East Media Research Institute. The next paragraph, however, offers a different thought. Speaking generally to believers, al-Adnani's exhorts them:

> Do not let this battle pass you by wherever you may be. You must strike the soldiers, patrons, and troops of the [tyrants]. Strike their police, security, and intelligence members, as well as their treacherous agents. . . . If you can kill a disbelieving American or European—especially the spiteful and filthy French—or an Australian, or a Canadian, or any other . . . citizens of the countries that entered into a coalition against the Islamic State, then rely upon Allah, and kill him in any manner or way however it may be. Do not ask for anyone's advice and do not seek anyone's verdict. Kill the disbeliever whether he is civilian or military, for they have the same ruling.[31]

At this point, al-Adnani's rhetoric is strikingly similar to that of bin Laden and other signatories of the World Islamic Front *Declaration*: "The ruling to fight the Americans and their allies, civilians and military, is an individual obligation for every Muslim who can do it in any country in which it is possible to do it." It is instructive, then, that the same issue includes a two-page article featuring bin Laden and Anwar al-Awlaki, in which the point is to argue for the imperativeness of attacks in the homelands of those participating in the "crusader coalition."[32]

The change here seems significant. Without abandoning the program of state building, the leadership of ISIS is clearly making a strategic shift. Thus, *Dabiq* 6 claims credit for attacks by individuals in Australia, Canada, the United States, and France. Praising those who carried out these operations, the idea is that these "warriors" acted alone, "striking the [unbelievers] where it would hurt them most—in their own lands and on the very streets that they presumptively walk in safety."[33]

CONCLUSION: "READING THE SIGNS OF THE TIMES"

The analyses sponsored by the Institute for the Study of War and the Middle East Media Research Institute were not so much wrong as incomplete. The focus on state building featured in the first three issues of *Dabiq* correlates with success on the ground. Why not? In June 2014, territorial gains led to the declaration of the caliphate. Throughout July and into August, ISIS' forces expanded their range, at one point threatening to take the Baghdad airport. Al-Baghdadi and his associates could afford to leave the United States and other "far" enemies alone, save for attempts to extort money in exchange for journalists and humanitarian aid workers unfortunate enough to become captives.

When the US bombing campaign began to take its toll, and even more when Kurdish fighters took back territory in the north of Iraq and Syria, ISIS leaders turned elsewhere. Showing a strongly pragmatic tendency—or, perhaps better, an opportunistic tendency—the group began to urge the kind of individual attacks typically associated with al-Qaeda. Again, why not? As al-Zawahiri and al-Awlaki stressed, any cost/benefit analysis of this tactic points to a ratio favorable to the jihadist cause.[34]

Given such convergence, it did not seem strange when journalists presented evidence that those carrying out the January 2015 attacks in Paris included people with ties to both organizations. At the operational level, ties of kinship, friendship, or other relations indicative of trust sometimes carry more weight than the differences of doctrine or judgments about the proper way to establish Islamic government so important to the leaders of al-Qaeda and ISIS. People like the Kouachi brothers and their colleagues want to strike a blow for Islam, and against those societies that allow insults to Islam to go unpunished, or that join in fighting against Muslim resistance groups. If the differences between such groups are important to such people, they seem at least willing to set them aside for a time.

This is not to say that the differences between ISIS and al-Qaeda should be ignored. These are sufficiently serious for the former to describe the latter as outside the circle of Islam, and thus subject to attack. Even as ISIS continues to lose territory and its spokesmen begin to speak of a "return to the desert" (i.e., going underground), the distinctive visions of these and other jihadist groups suggest continuing strife.

In this, such groups exacerbate the broader conflict outlined by Secretary Gates in the interview cited above. The appeal to jihad as an individual duty deals with military matters. It is a general call to arms, whether the emphasis is on lone wolf attacks or on operations intended to build a state. It is also, however, a political act that defies traditional notions of sovereignty. One might say that it exacerbates these contested and fragmented notions. In claiming the right to use force, groups like al-Qaeda and ISIS assert that existing governments in the region, along with current arrangements in the international arena, are illegitimate. Their insistence on a state governed by God's law—at least, as they understand it—is intended as an alternative.

With respect to the question of timing, let us return to a point made several times in this chapter. The jihadist phenomenon is best understood as an attempt to exploit the generational conflict about which Secretary Gates spoke. In this sense, al-Qaeda and ISIS are symptomatic of a much broader crisis of authority. Those who joined in protests in Egypt, Yemen, and Syria as part of the Arab Spring did not, by and large, do so in the name of jihad as an individual duty. They did say something about the current state of governance in the region, however. The message was that the institutions of government are working only for the few and not the many. And now, in late 2016, with authoritarians back in charge in Egypt, and gaining momentum in Syria and elsewhere, the kinds of political reform that might address this perception seem even further from reality than a few years back.

To defeat or at least diminish ISIS, in other words, provides only a partial solution to the turmoil in the Middle East. We are in a time when a serious discussion about political institutions, religious education, and other matters related to the ongoing crisis of legitimation in the Middle East is important. To quote Gates once more, the "military is clearly one tool, but it is by far not the only one." Although Vilmer focuses on consequences in chapter 5, a just war analysis of current circumstances should thus point to the limits, as well as the necessity, of military force. In particular, any discussion of the use of armed force requires thinking about issues of timing and the goals of statecraft. And in the contest of jihadism, this is not necessarily a question about contemporary understandings of the last resort criterion, but more a question of the classical just war emphasis on prudence.

As this suggests, the just war tradition ought to encourage discussion of the range of *prudent* options available to policymakers in a given set of circumstances. Diplomatic, economic, and other initiatives (including, perhaps, those under the purview of *jus ad vim* discussed by Brunstetter in chapter 11?) ought always to be in play in ways that suggest that these often work together with the threat or use of military force. This is so, not least because ultimately the solution to most conflicts is political; military force may help to move matters in the direction of political resolutions, but it seems that military force is truly decisive only in rare circumstances. Witness O'Driscoll's concerns about victory raised in chapter 14. It must also be said that at least some uses of military force work against political resolution. This, I take it, is a possibility that motivates some of the arguments advanced by Fisk and Ramos in their discussion of preventive force in chapter 4, and by Emery in his discussion of balancing risk in chapter 9.

Timely action—that is, with respect to military force—is thus connected with thinking about wider, strategic issues in the context of jihad that I have laid out. Where do we—that is, the United States and its allies in the international community—want to go in response to ISIS, the chaos in the Middle East, and more generally with respect to the growth of global militancy for which ISIS and al-Qaeda provide important examples? The short answer is, we want peace, not least in the sense of an end to the violence, which is damaging so many people's lives.

At the same time, the institutions of the current international system are built on the notion that real peace requires something more. The vision of those crafting the United Nations Charter, the Universal Declaration of Human Rights, and the associated conventions dealing with civil, political, social, and economic rights point toward liberal, democratic values. Together with the International Monetary Fund, the World Bank, and other organizations aimed at strengthening or developing the economies of states in need, the idea was to encourage the building of local, state, and regional institutions reflective of such values. Respect for human rights, and the articulation and enforcement of constitutional norms able to secure broad participation in political and economic life—these were the aspirational goals of the UN system, which was built with strong input not only from the United States, the United Kingdom, and the western European states but also from a broad array of states emerging in the aftermath of colonialism.

To say that this did not prove easy is to state the obvious. During the Cold War, the United States and its allies engaged in a number of compromises, many of which involved acceptance and even encouragement of authoritarian regimes. In the Middle East, one thinks of the shah of Iran, of military rule in Turkey, and of the Sunni monarchies in the Gulf region. Even when Soviet influence began to wane, the liberal democracies preferred the order of authoritarians in Egypt; and when the revolution of 1978–79 displaced the shah, the emergence of the Islamic Republic of Iran provided a new reason for dealing with rulers whose price for cooperation with the United States and its allies included tolerance for domestic policies that ran afoul of liberal norms. When President George W. Bush argued that one of the lessons of the 9/11 attacks ought to be that support for authoritarian regimes did not necessarily deliver security, he had a point. The Freedom Agenda proposed a new direction, by which the goal of democracy promotion would take center stage, not least in Afghanistan and Iraq.

There is much to be said about this, though at this point one would have to say that the difficulties of building democracy loom very large, despite the positive undertones expressed by Orend in chapter 13. Not least important is the reemergence of authoritarian players in the region with little to no interest in cooperating with the United States. Despite its agreement on nuclear weapons with the Group of 5 + 1, the goals of the Islamic Republic of Iran are very different from those of the United States and its allies, as are those of Russia. In this connection, though there is a way that the argument advanced by Brian Orend, by which we may have to settle for suboptimal *post bellum* solutions, makes good sense, one must also say that accession to the Iranian-Russian goal of maintaining a compliant regime in Damascus would constitute rather very far down the scale of suboptimal—a third-, fourth-, or fifth-best solution, or even an outright defeat.

The great realist E. H. Carr comments that

> it cannot be too often repeated—for it is still not widely understood—that neither security nor peace can properly be made the object of policy. . . . A generation which makes peace and security its aim is doomed to frustration. The only stability attainable in human affairs is the stability of the spinning top or the bicycle; . . . the condition of security is continuous advance. The political, social, and economic problems of the postwar world must be approached with the desire not to stabilize, but to revolutionize.[35]

Carr had in mind the failure of Great Britain and its allies to recognize the need for revision of the terms of the Treaty of Versailles in a timely fashion. The lesson is more general, however. Those who seek peace must adapt to changing conditions. And sometimes—perhaps most of the time—this will involve compromise, second-best solutions, and even partial defeats, in the interests of limiting the occasion of war.

At the same time, one ought to say that without a sense of where one wants to go, there is a risk that the short-term compromises Carr envisioned could lead to injustice, which in turn would undermine the goal of peace. In matters of statecraft, success is a matter of finding a fit between long-term goals and the requirements of the moment. What is clear in the present moment is that eliminating the ISIS caliphate and reestablishing the territorial integrity of traditional states (Iraq and, eventually, Syria) is not a solution to the jihadist threat. Insofar as this threat is real, the norm that Fisk and Ramos identify in chapter 4 is at greater risk of coming into being. Perhaps Emery's musings about risk management in chapter 9 point us in the right direction. But these scenarios do not make the classical just war tradition obsolete. It seems useful to emphasize, in response to the searching questions raised by O'Driscoll in chapter 14, that the just war tradition may favor "success" over the concept of "victory"—or at least to suggest that the latter is meaningful only where it stands in for the former.

Matthew 16:1–3 relates a memorable encounter between Jesus and those skeptical of his claims: "The Pharisees and Sadducees came, and to test him they asked him to show them a sign from heaven. He answered them, 'When it is evening, you say, "It will be fair weather, for the sky is red." And in the morning, "It will be stormy today, for the sky is red and threatening." You know how to interpret the appearance of the sky, but you cannot interpret the signs of the times.'"

As in this text, we have ample evidence that reading the signs of the times is a difficult task. With respect to just war thinking and the desire to foster timely action, however, such "reading" is not only recommended. It is required, as an aspect of that disciplined activity characteristic of the kind of statecraft that aims at policies both wise and just—that is, as a timely response, matched to particular conditions, but not necessarily a last resort.

NOTES

1. My arguments also challenge recent claims to eject last resort altogether from the *jus ad bellum*; see Eamon Aloya, "Just War Theory and the Last Resort," *Ethics & International Affairs* 29, no. 2 (2015): 187–201.

2. Paul Ramsey, *Speak Up for Just War or Pacifism*, with an epilogue by Stanley Hauerwas (University Park: Pennsylvania State University Press, 1988), 51–77.

3. Seth G. Jones, *A Persistent Threat: The Evolution of al-Qa'ida and Other Salafi Jihadists* (Washington, DC: RAND Corporation, 2014).

4. Thomas Aquinas, *Summa Theologiae*, II-II, q. 40, as presented in *The Ethics of War*, ed. Gregory Reichberg, Henrik Syse, and Endre Begby (Oxford: Blackwell, 2006), 177.

5. See the selection in ibid., 339–70.

6. James Turner Johnson, "Contemporary Just War Thinking: Which Is Worse, to Have Friends or Enemies?" *Ethics & International Affairs* 26, no. 1 (2013): 25–45.

7. Aquinas, *Summa Theologiae*, II-IIae, 61.1. See the translation by the Fathers of the English Dominican Province (Westminster, MD: Christian Classics, 1981).

8. Ibid., q. 47.10.

9. James Turner Johnson, *Sovereignty: Moral and Historical Perspectives* (Washington, DC: Georgetown University Press, 2014).

10. February 1, 2015. Transcript available at www.nbcnews.com/meet-the-press/meet-press-transcripts-n51976.

11. In his contribution to this volume (chapter 3), Nigel Biggar proffers the view that humanitarian intervention provides the paradigmatic case for the Christian just war tradition. In this, Biggar's argument may be compared with Paul Ramsey's in *The Just War* (Savage, MD: Rowman & Littlefield, 1983) and other works. I find myself more in agreement with James Turner Johnson's account in the above-cited *Sovereignty*, which is that the framework of *jus ad bellum* and *jus in bello* developed as a resource for rulers charged with the protection of the common good; as the account of Muslim tradition presented above suggests, I think this holds for the judgments pertaining to jihad as well.

12. I provide some examples of such scholars below. The argument is one that is widely shared, so any list will be very long. Some historical perspective is provided by Michael Bonner, *Jihad in Islamic History* (Princeton, NJ: Princeton University Press, 2006), 106–8.

13. Yusuf al-Qaradawi, *Fiqh al-Jihad* (*The Jurisprudence of Armed Struggle*) (Cairo: Maktabat Wahba, 2009), 90–107. The quotation here is from the translation of *Fiqh al-Jihad* by Aziz El-Kaissouni, portions of which appear in *Religion, Ethics, and War: A Sourcebook of Textual Traditions*, ed. Gregory Reichberg, Hendrik Syse, and Nicole M. Hartwell (Cambridge: Cambridge University Press, 2014), 379–80.

14. The reference to Ibn Taymiyya, who lived in Damascus and Cairo (and, incidentally, spent years in the prisons of the Mamluk sultan), is standard in contemporary invocations of fighting as an individual duty, not least because those who appeal to this notion see an analogy between the Crusaders' and Mongols' incursions into Islamic territory and the current situation.

15. World Islamic Front, "Declaration concerning Armed Struggle against Jews and Crusaders," 1998, http://fas.org/irp/world/para/docs/980223-fatwa.htm.

16. Middle East Media Research Institute, "Latest Al-Zawahiri Video on Al-Jazeera: 'Reform and Expelling the Invaders from the Lands of Islam Will Only Be Accomplished by Fighting for the Sake of Allah,'" June 19, 2005, https://www.memri.org/reports/latest-al-zawahiri-video-al-jazeera-%E2%80%98reform-and-expelling-invaders-lands-islam-will-only-be.

17. *Inspire* 11 (Spring 2013): 34.

18. Statement of September 27, 2001, at http://kurzman.unc.edu/islamic-statements-against-terrorism/.

19. See "Muslim Voices: Part I—Fatwas & Statements by Muslim Scholars & Organizations," May 13, 2015, compiled by Sheila Musaji, http://theamericanmuslim.org/tam.php/features/articles/muslim_voices_against_extremism_and_terrorism_part_i_fatwas/.

20. See note 7 above.

21. For the statement on Libya, see www.digitalislam.eu/article.do?articleId=6243; on Syria, see www.bbc.com/news/world-middle-east-22741588.

22. This would also be true for a number of journalists, analysts of terrorism, and scholars of Islam. See, e.g., Michael Weiss and Hassan Hassan, *ISIS: Inside the Army of Terror* (New York: Regan Arts, 2015); Patrick Cockburn, *The Rise of the Islamic State: ISIS and the New Sunni Revolution* (London: Verso, 2015); Jessica Stern and J. M. Berger, *ISIS: The State of Terror* (New York: HarperCollins, 2015); and William McCants, *The ISIS Apocalypse* (New York: St. Martin's Press, 2015).

23. Abu Muhammad al-Adnani al-Shami, "This Is the Promise of Allah," Al-Hayat Media Center, http://jihadology.net/2014/06/29/al-furqan-media-presents-a-new-audio-message-from-the-islamic-states-shaykh-abu-muhammad-al-adnani-al-shami-this-is-the-promise-of-god/.

24. Shaykh Abu Muhammad al-Adnani al-Shami, "This Is the Promise of Allah," June 19, 2014, http://triceratops.brynmawr.edu/dspace/bitstream/handle/10066/14242/ADN20140629.pdf?sequence=1. To speak of al-Baghdadi as a caliph is, as the quotations suggest, to assert his claim to the loyalty of all Muslims. For background on him, see William McCants, "The Believer," www.brookings.edu/research/essays/2015/thebeliever.

25. "A Call to All," *Dabiq* 1 (Ramadan 1435): 10. Note that ISIS made (and still makes) use of various media in order to publicize its message. *Dabiq*, an online magazine published in several languages, was until late 2016 or early 2017 one of the most prominent of these.

26. Harleen K. Gambhir, "Dabiq: The Strategic Messaging of the Islamic State," Institute for the Study of War, August 15, 2014, available at www.understandingwar.org.

27. Y. Carmon, Y. Yehoshua, and A. Leone, "Understanding Abu Bakr al-Baghdadi and the Phenomenon of the Islamic Caliphate State," Inquiry and Analysis Series Report 1117, September 14, 2014, www.memri.org/report/en/print8147.htm.

28. A more recent analysis from the Institute for the Study of War acknowledges the changes outlined below. See Harleen Gambhir, "ISIS Global INTSUM," www.understandingwar.org/backgrounder/isis-global-intsum.

29. *Dabiq* 4 (Dhu'l-Hijjah 1435): 3.

30. Ibid., 8.

31. Ibid., 9.

32. Ibid., 43–44.

33. *Dabiq* 6, 3.

34. I originally wrote this in June 2014; a survey of subsequent issues of *Dabiq* indicates that the trend has continued.

35. E. H. Carr, *Conditions of Peace* (New York: Macmillan, 1942), xxiii–xxiv.

9

Balancing Security, Risk, and Uncertainty in a World of Contested and Fragmented Sovereignty

JOHN R. EMERY

WHAT ARE THE ETHICAL and strategic imperatives of counterterrorism operations in the world since the September 11, 2001, terrorist attacks on the United States? In an age of globalization, and contested and fragmented sovereignty, how can policymakers, military personnel, and academics conceptualize what it means to wage a "just" counterterrorism "war"? Carl von Clausewitz offered what many considered to be a timeless, trinitarian model of warfare—one that balances the triangular relationship between the people, government, and army. If one seeks to intertwine justice into the calculation, the just war tradition has a deep pedigree in guiding the use of force. However, both the Clausewitzian framework and the just war tradition may be insufficient to address the threat posed by terrorist organizations, which, some argue, lies in the space in between law enforcement measures and war.[1] With regard to the former, insofar as war is no longer defined by a clash of armies on the battlefield (see Vilmer's chapter 5 above), the government may be more isolated from public critique because there is less need to send the armed force to full frontal battle. The notion of combat as defined by decisive battles, though central to Clausewitzian thought, does not fit the paradigm of war on terrorist groups.[2] Regarding the just war tradition, questions about so-called new wars—against nonstate actors—raise serious concerns about the framework's applicability to such contexts.[3] To quote Ian Clarke, the challenge is this: "The ethics of war do not apply to anything that is 'non-war,' and hence we need to resolve the war/nonwar issue before the ethics can get fully down to business."[4] I assert that the traditional Clausewitzian and *jus ad bellum* frameworks fail to capture the essence of contemporary terrorist activities and counterterrorism measures, which are not exactly war.[5] But if we cannot turn to just war frameworks, where can we turn? The fact that, fifteen years after 9/11, there remains little consensus on which counterterrorism measures are effective demonstrates the need for a more rigorous development of frameworks for thinking about counterterrorism, and how common strategies have been effective or detrimental to the security environment.[6]

To better navigate the challenges the threat of global terrorism poses both domestically and internationally, I propose an alternative trinitarian model that seeks to balance security, risk, and uncertainty.[7] This framework can be viewed as complementary to the *jus ad vim*—just use of force short of war—paradigm developed by Daniel Brunstetter in chapter 11 because it questions the resort to war to counter the threat from terrorism while emphasizing both measures short of war and potential law enforcement mechanisms that are available to fight globalized terrorist networks.[8] As a framework, it can help us to think through what is at stake in countering terrorism with specific means, which can in turn help inform our ethics.

The challenge for states to keep security, risk, and uncertainty in balance in the fight against terrorism should not be underestimated. It is difficult for a leader to publicly accept that the state—and its citizens—can never have complete security, achieve true certainty about eventual threats, or be completely free from risk. Thus the danger of getting the balance between them wrong is all too real. Recent examples—the United States after the terrorist attacks by al-Qaeda on 9/11, and France after the ISIS terrorist attacks on 11/3—are all too illustrative. Being subject to dramatic terrorist attacks almost inevitably leads to an increase in uncertainty, which in turn—in these cases, at least—prods the affected states to act firmly and swiftly militarily, believing that this will decrease risk and increase security. A military reaction to the crisis of the moment could be justified as an act of self-defense against a continuous threat, insofar as terrorist groups are rarely in the business of isolated attacks.[9] However, as the creation of ISIS and the expansion of terrorism in the chaos resulting from United States–led wars in Afghanistan and Iraq demonstrate, the impulse to respond militarily can be counterproductive. Could the same be true for the reaction of various states—especially France—to attacks perpetrated by ISIS? These questions get at the heart of the challenges associated with balancing uncertainty, risk, and security.

In this chapter, I pursue the idea that states acting on an increased perception of uncertainty, and that thus are compelled to "do something"—usually, act firmly and swiftly *militarily*—may actually increase risk and decrease security while doing little to overcome uncertainty. Therefore, the tendency is for states to overreact to terrorism by giving uncertainty too much emphasis. The angst of uncertainty—when and where the next attack may occur—coupled with the perceived need to completely "eradicate" or "destroy" the enemy in order to eliminate any risk and provide for perfect security, prompts states to use force abroad while undermining their (alleged) liberal values at home. But what if, as O'Driscoll intimates in chapter 14, victory in such conflicts may be impossible? What does this imply for the balancing act I view as being at the heart of the fight against terrorist groups?

I suggest, first, that there is a wrong way of balancing. The fight against ISIS is illustrative here, and I return to it throughout the chapter. It captures the challenges of using force in an era of contested and fragmented sovereignty. ISIS is involved in a battle for sovereignty in Iraq and Syria, while its reach transcends traditional borders as its operatives communicate with would-be recruits in foreign lands to establish terror cells. Meanwhile, Western states are called on to manage refugee flows and tighten border security, which has even led to questions about the viability of the European Union's free travel zone. And of course, nations like the United States, the United Kingdom, and France are using force abroad to combat ISIS. The use of force abroad and more draconian measures at home gives the impression that the risk of terrorist attacks against "our" civilians in the future is reduced, thus increasing the security of "our" civilians, but I want to suggest that such a strategy may actually have opposite affects. In terms of uncertainty, the use of force probably does little to affect the lingering doubt that some attack will come sooner or later. By transferring greater risk to one's own civilians, who become subject to retaliatory attacks, such a strategy may serve to diminish the security of Western states in the long run, especially in a perpetual conflict against jihadist groups. Finally, absent the possibility of final victory, what must amount to a perpetual campaign to preserve "our" security transfers greater risk to those living under the yoke of the targeted terrorist group—in this case, civilians living under ISIS now, or those who may be subject to its rule if the group spreads (or flees to other spaces of contested and fragmented sovereignty, e.g., Libya).

What, then, is the answer to balancing risk, uncertainty, and security? In this chapter I do not seek to propose definitive answers to the complex challenges of neo-Clausewitzian balancing in counterterrorism operations. However, I do strive to offer key insights drawn from recent counterterrorist operations against ISIS in order to provide guiding questions for a possible path forward in debating and discussing the contemporary ethics of counterterrorism. Ultimately, this chapter is the first step in developing an alternative conceptual framework to supplement *jus ad vim*, a framework that strives to manage uncertainty and diminish risk, albeit with the recognition that neither can be completely eliminated.

RISK-TRANSFER WAR IN AN ERA OF CONTESTED AND FRAGMENTED SOVEREIGNTY

How does engaging in counterterrorist activities make an impact on risk? To address this question, we need to think about *who* is being put in positions of *risk* by what kinds of activities. In this section, I sketch the ways in which the risk of being killed or injured in counterterrorism operations has been transferred from Western belligerents to civilians, both those on the ground living under ISIS and those at home living in the West (in addition to other places around the globe, from Mali to Lebanon and beyond, who have also been targeted). The term "risk-transfer war" is borrowed from Martin Shaw to describe the new Western way of war, whereby soldiers are kept free of risk by keeping boots *off* the ground, relying on high-altitude air campaigns and on local allies.[10] The blame for civilian casualties is already deemed always accidental, although Shaw argues that this is "hardly accidental," for it is "the product of political choices in the refinement of Western military power."[11] Shaw concludes that the risks have been transferred from Western combatants to civilians, and that civilians "being directly killed is deliberate and systematic."[12] Although I may not go as far as Shaw, his discussion of risk transfer raises important questions that deserve further exploration in the fight against ISIS: What might due care look like today, given that ISIS essentially uses entire populations as human shields? What level of risk are we willing to impose on them to increase our level of security, and for how long—indefinitely?

Understanding Risk in an Era of Blurred Civilian/ Combatant Distinction

If due care is difficult to enact in warfare where the enemy wears a uniform, soldiers are interacting on the ground, and civilians are easy to distinguish, it is even more challenging in a counterterrorism campaign operated from the skies.[13] The fight against ISIS serves to illustrate just how blurred the distinction can become. In Raqqa, the self-proclaimed capital of the Islamic State, ISIS has subjected civilians to harsh and inhumane treatment, instilling fear in the population, and forcing many to participate in their cause. The fate of children in Raqqa is equally troubling. ISIS members befriend children playing in the streets, enticing them with gifts like candy or a mobile phone, and then send them to ISIS training camps, where they are radicalized with an extremist form of Islamic teaching.[14] Finally, there are the hundreds of thousands of civilians who are practically the equivalent of human shields living among ISIS military positions.

Keeping all this in mind, what is the West to do? How should calculations of risk transfer be balanced with the struggle for our security, insofar as bombing ISIS in Syria serves more to diminish their power than to defeat them? Although the only likely way to defeat ISIS in Syria would be to send in ground troops—a problematic assumption by all accounts, and especially given what Orend shows us in chapter 13 below about the *post bellum* experiences in Iraq and Afghanistan—is more bombing the answer? The answer seems to be yes.

Just six days after the Paris attacks, the Pentagon changed its rules of engagement, acknowledging that the coalition was seeking to increase air strikes by changing the standing policy that had aimed at protecting against civilian casualties in ISIS-held territory.[15] This marked a conscious decision to intensify the bombing—transferring more risk onto civilians *over there*—when the perception was that ISIS was a great threat to *our* security in the West after the Paris attacks. Following the Paris attacks, there was an increased outcry from the West to push for targeting ISIS's oil infrastructure, including tanker trucks, which were previously not struck due to concerns about civilian casualties. According to Operation Inherent Resolve spokesman Col. Steve Warren, this had not previously taken place, because "we assessed that these trucks, while they are being used for operations that support ISIL [another name for ISIS], the truck drivers, themselves, probably not members of ISIL; they're probably just civilians. So we had to figure out a way around that. We're not in this business to kill civilians, we're in this business to stop ISIL—to defeat ISIL."[16] In order to minimize civilian casualties in striking these civilian-driven trucks, forty-five minutes before striking, the air force would drop leaflets stating: "Get out of your trucks now, and run away from them" along with a show of force, having aircraft "essentially buzz [above] trucks at low altitude." However, there is always a problem of interpretation, which we have seen previously in Afghanistan, where the assumption is that all these truck drivers are literate (which is a problematic assumption) and that the "show of force" will be interpreted in the way it is intended by US forces.

There are two further problems in the targeting of the oil infrastructure beyond the issue of civilian truck drivers. Daniel Glaser, the assistant secretary for terrorist financing at the US Treasury Department, acknowledged that oil was in fact the third-largest source of income for ISIS, whereas extortion was the largest source.[17] Although, with the leaflets being dropped, one could say that the United States is exercising "due care" to prevent civilian casualties (if we assume the drivers are literate and interpret our actions the way we expect them to), there is still a concern that targeting oil infrastructure is not the panacea politicians claim it to be. Furthermore, there is a concern about how this would negatively affect the postwar environment (if and when that occurs), which emphasizes the importance of *jus post bellum* (see the lessons proffered by Brian Orend in chapter 13 of this volume). Such a short-term policy assessment indicates that although the postwar climate may be in the back of the minds of policymakers, it is a concern of the secondary order.

At the time of writing (late 2016), the United States has promised to provide air support to Kurdish forces intent on taking Raqqa. This strategy obviously transfers a huge risk to civilians living there (witness what is happening in Mosul today, as Iraqi forces move in to liberate the city street by street). Perhaps this is a necessary part of any war, but even this assumption does not mean we should ignore the interplay between risk, security, and uncertainty. This is especially true given some of the arguments presented in this volume. We should, as O'Driscoll shows in chapter 14, be wary of assuming that victory is even possible in these kinds of wars. And in chapter 8 Kelsay points to a deeper problem, that the struggle against jihadist groups will outlive whatever happens on the battlefield. If there is no concept of victory against groups like ISIS because we are fighting a generational, transglobal struggle, how do we evaluate whether to intensify the fight? Here is where thinking about the balance between risk, security, and uncertainty can be helpful, and especially to keep in mind whose risk and whose security are being increased or decreased.

Risk Transfer to Civilians in the West

Perhaps some individuals reading this chapter would argue that the fact that Iraqi and Syrian citizens die in these bombing raids is tragic, yet unavoidable, given the way ISIS operates. However, it is important to realize that while the risk has been transferred from Western combatants to foreign civilians, the risk has also been transferred to Western civilians in the process. The uncertainty brought about by a sophisticated ISIS propaganda campaign and the horror it incited in the West, accompanied by a territorial acquisition that was previously thought impossible for a terrorist group to achieve, were key factors that led to a United States–led coalition to act militarily to retake land occupied by ISIS. It is easy to forget that, initially, ISIS was solely focused on gaining geographic territory and establishing a caliphate in the vacuum created by the ongoing Syrian conflict and the instability left in "postwar" Iraq. However, in

August 2014, after the United States–led coalition began launching air strikes against ISIS targets, ISIS made a major policy shift, from that of territorial acquisition to attacks against the West. As a consequence, the group's spokesman, Abu Muhammad al-Adnani, responded with a call for supporters to carry out lone-offender terrorist attacks targeting the West.[18] Citizens of the coalition, he warned, will "pay the price as you walk on your streets, turning right and left, fearing the Muslims. You will not feel secure even in your bedrooms. You will pay the price when this crusade of yours collapses, and thereafter we will strike you in your homeland."[19]

The Guardian interviewed two ISIS members, who discussed a meeting before the Paris attacks, where the ISIS leaders met in the Syrian town Tabqah near Raqqa in order to discuss the evolution of the group. At that meeting, the leaders acknowledged that they could not continue to hold territory, given that fourteen air forces were constantly bombarding them—by the end of 2015 and early 2016, ISIS lost roughly 30 percent of the territory it had once controlled.[20] Instead, the group decided to export its terrorism to Europe, as geographic control in Iraq and Syria became less of a priority than influencing faraway societies. Allegedly, a handful of foreign fighters were sent back to their home countries to form classic sleeper cells and to prepare and wait for orders; this new wave would place emphasis on wreaking havoc in Italy, Belgium, France, Germany, and the United Kingdom. According to the two ISIS members interviewed, "[the leaders] said the UK was the hardest to get to. But Belgium was easy."[21] Furthermore, the leaders expressed a deep understanding of European political architecture: "At the meeting, they talked about which societies would crumble first and what that would mean. They thought big attacks would lead to pressure on the European Union and even NATO. This would be ideal for them."[22]

Thus, what is clear is that ISIS did make a conscious shift from controlling territory in the Middle East to exporting terror to the West. The leaders now contend that controlling geographic territory was only ever a means to the ultimate ends of spreading its influence far and wide.[23] In addition to recruiting fighting from abroad to strike abroad, there is another problem. Assuming, for the sake of argument, that ISIS could be defeated in Syria and Iraq, we would likely see an exodus of existing fighters who would carry out suicide missions elsewhere. This would probably start to occur even before this hypothetical "victory," if the coalition force were able to strangle ISIS holdouts. ISIS operatives would move out to stage the fight from somewhere else—that is to say, by transferring the risk to other populations. This may already be occurring in Libya. And if Kelsay's analysis in chapter 8 is correct, the struggle against and risk from jihadist groups will not be abated even if the caliphate is dismantled.

Within the counterterrorism literature, the shifting of ISIS's modus operandi from territorial acquisition to attacks in the West is termed the "substitution effect." The idea that the West can deter terrorists from attacking by bombing instead of doing diligent police work at home is political—in the call to "do something" militarily as a show of force (explored below)—and simultaneously increases risk and decreases security at home. As Isabelle Duyvesteyn notes: "The idea of deterring terrorists is indeed problematic, because if the deterrence is successful, it can promote a 'substitution effect' where terrorists shift their mode, venue, or country of attack. There is indeed strong empirical evidence for the substitution effect of terrorism."[24] Although there may be evidence against responding militarily, this is something politicians *do* in order to not appear weak at a time of psychological vulnerability and uncertainty. However, it is times such as these where *jus ad vim* calls us to take a step back and evaluate the situation through the lens of possible law enforcement measures before escalating to even limited military force abroad. As we know empirically, "military measures against terrorist activities have been indicated to possess a high risk of escalation"[25]

As ISIS exports terror to the West (and beyond), police work and intelligence sharing between countries are imperative to help prevent Paris- or Brussels-style attacks from occurring again. Diligent police work can combat these sleeper cell individuals and groups. However, those who are simply inspired by ISIS, like the San Bernardino couple who attacked a holiday party in California and the perpetrator of the Orlando massacre, are almost impossible to prevent. This is not a small point. The fact that there can *never* be complete *security*, zero *risk*, or complete *certainty* is essential to understanding the nature of the contemporary threat posed by nonstate actors and keeping the triangle in some sort of balance. Although the uncertainty caused by ISIS prompted a military response that is showing signs of success, in the sense that much of the territory acquired by ISIS has now been retaken, this success has been met with increased risk and insecurity at home. Even though the threat posed by lone-wolf attacks against the West remains statistically small, if uncertainty is given too much space, the psychological impact is indeed as Abu Muhammad al-Adnani had explained above: People are afraid as they walk down the streets, and are fearing Muslims in their own communities. Needless to say, alienating, marginalizing, and making Muslims feel like second-class citizens in their own homes in the United States, France, Belgium, and the United Kingdom is exactly what ISIS had hoped for, exasperating the sense of fear, leading to a knee-jerk reaction to do something that ultimately may reduce security.

MANAGING UNCERTAINTY TO REDUCE RISK AND INCREASE SECURITY

I have argued above that the increased uncertainty from threats by terrorist groups such as ISIS has led to a military response that has been successful in diminishing the territorial control of ISIS, but has had the unintended consequences of increasing risk and decreasing security for civilians both living under ISIS and going about their daily lives in the West.[26] As I have alluded to in the introduction, and as Daniel Brunstetter discusses in chapter 11, a military response is sometimes, but not always, the best means to fight terrorism, because law enforcement can often be sufficient. His framework of *jus ad vim* recognizes that there is an in-between space (as Michael Walzer termed it) that is neither a state of war nor a state of peace. Such spaces are typical of the uncertainty that the fight against terrorism produces, not simply in faraway places but also—if we are to take the threat by al-Adnani seriously—walking the streets at home. Who is the enemy? When will the next attack occur? What rules do we fight by? When will we "win"—if ever—so we can get on with our normal lives?

In this section I offer one possible path forward to manage—as opposed to decreasing or eliminating—uncertainty, which can in turn reduce risk (for some) and increase security (again, for some). As a first step, we need to conceptually understand the nature of the enemy that we face in order to, borrowing a phrase from Kelsay in chapter 8, better read the "signs of the times" to ascertain when, and with what kind of force, we should act. Echoing what Kelsay argues—that just war thinking needs to take better stock of the complexity of the context, and consequently the nature of the enemy—I suggest that exploring the psychological process of "Othering" illuminates the negative impact of treating ISIS as a homogeneous and cohesive organization, like a state, as opposed to a loosely affiliated terrorist network plagued with infighting, suspicion, and divergent goals among its own members. Beyond the rhetoric of "good versus evil," "the clash of civilizations," and so on, there is a real security threat posed by ISIS-like terrorism; however, this threat is magnified, based in part on our reaction to it. When we homogenize the enemy into a state-like entity or a civilization, instead of recognizing the fact that these are loosely affiliated terrorist organizations, one misunderstands the enemy. To base further decisions on how to "defeat" this enemy—really, an ideology that can never be "defeated"—is a false premise. Again, I point the reader to Kelsay's illuminating discussion of jihad as an individual duty in chapter 8. What I hope to demonstrate below is a way to de-homogenize the enemy and recognize them for who they are and the realistic threat that they pose. This can, in turn, put the psychological uncertainty that terrorism presents into perspective. The goal is to clear the ground for a counterterrorism framework that, by managing uncertainty, reduces the risk and security threat posed by such groups.

Constructing the Enemy

The psychological processes of in-group and out-group formation are essential to how one tends to construct the enemy, especially loosely affiliated terrorist organizations. The constructivist Paul Kowert discusses the psychological components in identity formation of groups. In essence, "people tend to exaggerate their perceptions of others in order to make memory and categorization easier."[27] As a result, distinctions between members of different groups are often exaggerated, while simultaneously there is greater perceived intragroup homogeneity. In other words, because out-groups are perceived as homogeneous, their behavior is more easily explained as the result of positive intent. This bias leads to the tautological perception that all behavior of powerful out-groups is intentional ("since they are powerful, they can do whatever they want").[28] Thus, in the United States one tends to view the out-group of terrorists as far more homogeneous than their loosely affiliated network is in reality. Furthermore, ISIS propaganda is so powerful *because* the members of the out-group view power through their professed intentions rather than their situational constraints. For example, the *uncertainty* arising from individuals acting in the name of ISIS with no physical connection to the group (like the Orlando shooter) creates a feeling that ISIS is omnipresent and that it intends to plant sleeper cells everywhere. Now, this is part of its expressed policy; however, it also capitalizes on the psychological impact that terrorism has in making the stronger enemy destroy itself from within by sparking fear and overreaction. In chapter 2 of this volume, Lindemann and Giacomelli's discussion of recognition theory, particularly the construction of the Other, is useful to supplement the discussion here of the construction of ISIS as the homogeneous enemy.

It is true that ISIS is far more organized and "homogeneous" than al-Qaeda was in the post-9/11 era. At a superficial level, al-Qaeda was concerned with its war against the West, utilizing whatever safe havens it could to launch and coordinate its operations, whereas ISIS's initial intention was more that of a traditional military power—that is, conquering territory and amassing military weaponry by capitalizing on the volatile situations of contested and fragmented sovereignty in Syria and Iraq. There are consequences to failing to read the enemy accurately. Seth Jones recognizes that in the early 1990s, the United States failed to capitalize on internal divisions within al-Qaeda in its initial law enforcement and military measures against them. For example, as Ayman al-Zawahiri called for a military jihad against the Egyptian government, others such as the leaders of the Egyptian Islamic Jihad and the Muslim Brotherhood advocated for "a return to *da'wa* and a move away from violence,"[29] believing that Zawahiri had "grossly misinterpreted Islam."[30] Even after the 9/11 attacks, Sayyid Imam Abd al-Aziz al-Sharif—the former leader of the Egyptian Islamic Jihad and a friend of Osama bin Laden—condemned the attacks, calling them "barbaric and un-Islamic." Al-Sharif wrote that bin Laden had betrayed Mullah Omar and the Afghan people by orchestrating an international terrorist attack while living on Afghan soil, thereby condemning "Afghanistan and its people . . . [to] pay the price" with America's military response.[31] Recalling Kelsay's point in chapter 8, which I wish to highlight here, the United States tends to misread the context and see black and white where there are many shades of gray; thus, the problematic tendency is to create homogeneous groups of outsiders when the reality is much different. Although this homogenization may score political points—both in rhetoric and in notching small victories in the so-called war on terror—it is a false portrait of the enemy and undermines ways in which one could conceivably have the best chances of mitigating risk while undermining terrorist organizations from within.

I do not want to suggest that ISIS and al-Qaeda are the same type of organization or possess the same military power or global reach; nevertheless, the West's war against al-Qaeda should provide some lessons learned for how to fight ISIS. Current strategies against ISIS allegedly have had some success in diminishing the territorial gains the group had made during the years 2014–15. In January 2016, US Army colonel Steve Warren, the US Coalition spokesman, told a press briefing in Baghdad that ISIS had lost about 40 percent of it territory in Iraq and in "Syria, harder to get a good number, we think it's around 20," together losing "30 percent of the territory they once held."[32] At the time of writing, more territorial loss happens almost on a daily basis. Nevertheless, the loss of a substantial amount of territorial control by ISIS is a "victory" that should be taken with a grain of salt. As the terrorist attacks in Paris, San Bernardino, Brussels, and Orlando demonstrated, bombs realistically cannot defeat the ideology and broader appeal of ISIS, which feeds off such a military response.

The group homogenization process I have described, along with the attribution of positive intent, has created in the Western psyche a barbaric ISIS that is as powerful as its propaganda videos would make one believe. However, the reality on the ground for ISIS fighters is allegedly quite different. A recent video taken from the body camera of an ISIS fighter after being defeated by Peshmerga forces outside Mosul demonstrates utter disarray and a lack of fighting skill.[33] Not only were the ISIS fighters in improvised armored vehicles, but also they argued with one another about how to fight, and one almost launched a rocket into their own truck, as he did not want to expose himself to enemy fire. We are beginning to gain more and more insight from ISIS foreign fighters who went to join the movement abroad and then returned home after realizing that they had made a mistake, such as one UK citizen named Harry Sarfo who is currently facing terrorism charges in the United Kingdom after fleeing the group's brutal regime.[34] Sarfo believed the "daily life" propaganda videos when he decided to join the fight in Syria, but he found that the reality was "astonishing hardship and brutality," where many Westerners who wanted to flee home were trapped and faced execution for attempted desertion.[35] The point here is that spreading this message and funding anti-extremist Muslim organizations at home may be a more effective use of funds in preventing homegrown terrorists from either joining the fight in Iraq and Syria, or being inspired to undertake lone-wolf attacks. By capitalizing on infighting and discontent, we can begin to de-homogenize the Other.

De-homogenizing the enemy helps us to manage, but not eliminate, uncertainty about when the next attack might come or who is likely an enemy among us. This is an important step in not giving in to fear, in avoiding the reaction to act forcefully at the level of war that may have unforeseen—and perhaps destabilizing—security and risk consequences.

THE TRINITARIAN MODEL AND MILITARY ETHICS

In the aftermath of a terrorist attack, there is often the urge, and public outcry, to "do something." In the post-9/11 era, and after the experiences of Iraq and Afghanistan, that "something" to be done has been expanding a military campaign abroad—whether with bombing campaigns, drones, or special forces—as well as expanding law enforcement privileges that undermine alleged "liberal democratic values" at home. However, some academic research questions the effectiveness of privileging both the military strategy and the challenge to democratic values at home.

For example, Isabelle Duyvesteyn explores the military effectiveness of counterterrorism; she views the prioritization of military means as problematic, because it undermines other "soft measures" such as traditional law enforcement. When you approach your enemy from a military manner, "the effectiveness of subsequent 'soft measures' can be questioned," such that the former reduces the effectiveness of the latter.[36] In the face of terrorism, both ethically and strategically, all measures short of war must be reasonably attempted before engaging in or escalating to significant military engagement abroad. The problem lies in the fact that "counterterrorism has a strong tendency for *reactive* rather than *proactive* measures. This fits with the 'something must be done' calls after terrorist attacks" (emphasis added).[37] It also plays into the dangerous norm of preventive force (especially with drones) discussed by Fisk and Ramos in chapter 4.

Regarding law enforcement, David Luban argued after 9/11 that because the war on terror appears as though it will go on perpetually, "the suspension of human rights" characteristic of US policy "is not temporary but permanent."[38] Among other things, Luban's critical remarks were referring to the refusal, to suspected terrorists, of the right to due process, as the George W. Bush administration instead pursued a problematic preventive force doctrine to fight terror (see chapter 4, by Fisk and Ramos). Although law enforcement in a time of terror may be difficult, given the perception of uncertainty that permeates society, it should not, however, be discarded. Mark Hamm emphasizes that by focusing on the small-scale crimes that facilitate complex terrorist organizations, "investigators may well preempt larger operations designed to kill thousands of innocent people."[39] This is a different risk-management strategy compared with the prolonged—some might say permanent—emergency measures taken after 9/11 and 11/13 that have undercut democratic values and arguably have led to social profiling that exacerbates the alienation of certain populations within society and thus potentially increases perceptions of uncertainty and security in society.

In the remainder of this chapter, I seek to begin a discussion of what specifically this trinitarian model and managing uncertainty may do, both strategically and ethically. First and foremost, I assert that insofar as it informs ethics, it offers a counter to the consequential model that permeates some analyses of war. The fundamental flaw with the consequentialist model (as promoted by Vilmer in chapter 5) is that though it is difficult enough to predict the short-term consequences of our counterterrorist actions, grasping the long-term impact—of equal or greater importance—is even more difficult. Given that "we simply know too little about whether force works against terrorists, apart from indications that there are real drawbacks," it may be prudent to take a step back from consequential ethics and rethink our traditional frameworks of the ethics of war and peace.[40]

Vilmer makes the consequentialist case for targeted killing by drones as the lesser of evils in contemporary warfare—thus reducing uncertainty and increasing our security with limited risk (compared with alternatives) to civilians. While acknowledging that the United States' practice has been far too lax, with signature strikes and the like, he argues that civilian casualties by drones ought to be compared with the alternative—for example, the Pakistani troops in the

Battle of Swat. However, I would argue that such consequentialist calculations are a dangerous game to play. When asking "What is better for Pakistani civilians?" Vilmer argues for drones, but he does not seriously engage with the question of risk transfer.[41] Nor does he take into account concerns regarding the broader kind of uncertainty that define the struggle against terrorist groups—namely, that the enemy is out there somewhere hoping (ready?) to strike; drones are simply assumed to reduce uncertainty, based on the observation that al-Qaeda has not struck the United States since 9/11, though it has struck many other populations, especially locally, where it is based. Again, the question of risk—whose risk?—comes to the fore. This also raises questions about the efficacy of military measures that privilege our security over others' security in the long run. As ISIS shifts its strategy to targeting Westerners, these concerns will become more and more significant, even as we turn to drones to hunt ISIS operatives down wherever they may flee.

To the extent to which one may agree with Vilmer that consequentialism may indeed be the least-bad option in evaluating drone strikes, the trinitarian model I suggest adds the following caveats to think about. By thinking more about risk transfer, we turn our attention to the major concerns about the impact drones are having on the next generation of Pakistanis who live under the risk of "a strike from the blue," and the impact this might have on the possibilities for future terrorist recruitment. Thinking about managing uncertainty also requires us to imagine the possibility of a never-ending drone campaign, and to consider how this fits into a consequentialist ethics. It is hard to be a consequentialist unless one thinks only of the short term; balancing uncertainty with risk and security in the framework I propose, however, proffers an alternative conception of temporality that is perhaps more appropriate for a generational struggle against groups like al-Qaeda and ISIS.

As a counter to consequentialism, the trinitarian model can, I suggest, complement an ethics based in *jus ad vim*. By managing uncertainty, and diminishing the drive to "do something" militarily, space is provided for a more holistic understanding of what security means in an era of nonstate terrorist networks that privileges measures short of war. As Andrew Silke has argued, "Ultimately harsh, aggressive policies in response to terrorism fail so often in their stated aims, because they so badly misunderstand and ignore the basic psychology of the enemy and of observers. Strength and power alone are not enough to defeat terrorism."[42] Both my trinitarian framework and *jus ad vim* (discussed by Brunstetter in chapter 11) begin with the premise that contemporary terrorist actions often take place in the space between law enforcement and war—something must be done, but perhaps war is too much and law enforcement is not enough. That said, the *jus ad vim* framework's ethical machinations can benefit by paying more attention to the relationship between risk, security, and uncertainty.

There remain many barriers to effective law enforcement, such as a lack of intelligence sharing, as well as the threat of undermining liberal values at home by establishing permanent emergency powers over your populations; nonetheless, this must be a part of the counterterrorism discussion. To quote one scholar: "It is clear that ideas and conceptions held about terrorism influence the choice for a particular counterterrorism strategy. When terrorism is seen as war, counterterrorism favors repressive measures; when terrorism is seen as criminal, it favors judiciary responses."[43] Hence, the ethical frameworks that we utilize have a real impact on the sorts of doors that we open and close in response to the contemporary terrorist threat, and ultimately on *managing* uncertainty. Through the lens of *jus ad bellum*, the United States, France, Belgium, and the like have a just cause to engage with ISIS militarily in Iraq and Syria; yet *jus ad vim*, if informed by the trinitarian model, suggests an alternative framing of the issue: Is escalating to an air campaign the necessary and proportionate way to manage uncertainty and risk at home? If coalition forces are successful in reestablishing territorial integrity in Iraq and ISIS is driven from Syria, how would the morphed ISIS threat be managed? Answering these question asks us to balance the level of force with the level of risk (at home and abroad), without placing too much emphasis on eliminating uncertainty or seeking perfect security.

CONCLUSION

The "war on terror" may never be "won," because victory is a notion whose time perhaps has passed (see O'Driscoll in chapter 14). However, recognition that one can never have complete security, but that risk can be minimized and uncertainty can be managed, ought to be the foundation on which we build a coherent counterterrorism strategy. By decreasing the psychological uncertainty that terrorism produces through de-homogenizing the Other, risk can start to be mitigated through diligent police work at home and intelligence gathering abroad. For example, following the most recent attacks in Brussels, the French government released an eighty-point plan to combat homegrown terrorism that included setting up dozens of de-radicalization centers.[44] Young would-be ISIS recruits at home need to hear the experiences of those who come back from radicalization—like the UK citizen Harry Sarfo mentioned above—because the de-radicalized understand the appeal that ISIS propaganda has and what it is really like to be there when the cameras are not on. Furthermore, focusing on policing actions where feasible—and treating terrorists as criminals, as the West did in the pre-9/11 era—all ought to have a positive impact on security at home, even if uncertainty cannot be not eliminated altogether. By concentrating on stopping criminal activity, such as breaking up funding and arms trafficking rings, one can hope to disrupt the operations of these organizations before they can carry out attacks, but not necessarily "win" the generational struggle against them. Regarding managing uncertainty, terrorist attacks will still occur; no amount of spying by the National Security Agency or ethnic profiling could prevent some ideologically driven individuals from carrying out such acts. However, with a more cohesive guiding framework, we can at least aim to not further exacerbate bad situations by placing too much emphasis on reducing uncertainty by undertaking actions that increase risk and insecurity at home in the long run.

Unlike actions following the terrorist attacks in Paris, the trinitarian model seeks to avoid both perpetual imminence and a constant state of emergency at home as well as increased bombing campaigns abroad; let us not forget that the threat posed by ISIS and like-minded organizations to the West remains relatively small (only 2 percent of those killed by ISIS in 2015 were Westerners).[45] Recognizing this means that in cases of *lagged imminence*—where there is lower risk, yet an element of uncertainty remains—law enforcement must be the primary means to disrupt terrorist activities.[46] Ultimately, attempting to keep security, risk, and uncertainty in balance is necessary to avoid a detrimental overreaction to terrorism. A knee-jerk reaction—the "we must do something!" effect—to quell uncertainty too often undermines liberal democratic values at home, while also increasing the risk to alternative populations both at home and abroad.

Balancing security, risk, and uncertainty at home as well as abroad in an era of contested and fragmented sovereignty contextualizes the natural urge to create a permanent state of emergency, which ultimately undermines liberal values at home, in light of the terrorist threat. Such a balancing act recognizes that we can never eliminate all risk or uncertainty, no matter how much we compromise our values—a point David Luban made after the 9/11 attacks that is worth repeating in the era of ISIS.[47] Rosa Brooks is right in recognizing that we need to move beyond the political posturing that characterizes most public debates about counterterrorism and instead speak honestly about the costs and benefits of different approaches. Most important, we need to "stop viewing terrorism as unique and aberrational as the more we panic and posture and overreact, the more we decrease our security and increase our risk of terrorism."[48]

Where, then, are we left with an incoming Trump administration and a few years into the war against ISIS? After 17,005 coalition air strikes in Iraq/Syria (at an average cost of $12.6 million per day), ISIS has lost about half the territory it once controlled; yet it has inspired more attacks in the West, such as those in Paris, Nice, and Berlin.[49] These coalition strikes have killed an estimated 45,000 "enemies" with a suspiciously impressive 188 civilian casualties.[50] There are, of course, many questions that remain to be answered. I recognize, for example, that my conclusions leave the question of "liberating" ISIS-controlled cities unanswered; in Iraq, this is ultimately the challenge that the Iraqi government must face, and to the extent to which it needs international help, the framework I provide could still prove useful to help discern what level of help with what consequences regarding risk and security. In Syria, it is perhaps an international problem, with all the challenges that reaching a consensus that would work for the concerned parties entails. However, rebuilding the conceptual apparatus we have for engaging in counterterrorism, both strategically and ethically, is a first and crucial step on which we can build a coherent strategy that, by managing uncertainty, increases security while reducing risk—to some, at least.

NOTES

1. See Daniel Brunstetter, chapter 11 of this volume. Also see Daniel Brunstetter and Megan Braun, "The Implications of Drones on the Just War Tradition," *Ethics & International Affairs* 25, no. 3 (2011): 337–58l; and Daniel Brunstetter and Megan Braun, "From Jus ad Bellum to Jus ad Vim: Recalibrating Our Understanding of the Moral Use of Force," *Ethics & International Affairs* 27, no. 1 (2013): 87–106.

2. Antulio J. Echevarria II, *Clausewitz and Contemporary War* (Oxford: Oxford University Press, 2007), 6; also see Clausewitz's emphasis on great battles as decisive in warfare: Carl Von Clausewitz, *On War*, ed. Michael Howard and Peter Paret (Princeton, NJ: Princeton University Press, 1976), book IV, chap. 11, 260.

3. See, e.g., Terrence K. Kelley, "The Just Conduct of War against Radical Islamic Terror and Insurgencies," in *The Price of Peace: Just War in the Twenty-First Century*, ed. Charles Reed and David Ryall (Cambridge: Cambridge University Press, 2008); and Michael L. Gross, *Moral Dilemmas of Modern War: Torture, Assassination, and Blackmail in an Age of Asymmetric Conflict* (New York: Cambridge University Press, 2010). For a discussion of the obsession with "new wars" and "post-Clausewitzian" wars, see Mary Kaldor, "In Defense of New Wars," *Stability: International Journal of Security and Development* 2, no. 1 (2013): 1–16.

4. Ian Clarke, *Waging War: A New Philosophical Introduction* (New York: Oxford University Press, 2015), 131.

5. For a more in-depth rationale for the necessity of rethinking of the *jus ad bellum* framework and making the case for *jus ad vim*, see Brunstetter, chapter 11 of this volume, and also John R. Emery and Daniel Brunstetter, "Restricting the Preventive Use of Force: Drones, the Struggle against Non-State Actors and *Jus ad Vim*," in *Preventive Force: Drones, Targeted Killing, and the Transformation of Contemporary Warfare*, ed. Kerstin Fisk and Jennifer Ramos (New York: New York University Press, 2016). Here, Brunstetter and I address criticisms of *jus ad vim*, as we sketch a theory of last resort in

relation to the US Central Intelligence Agency's drone strikes in Yemen and Pakistan for the space that lies in between law enforcement and war, which is where many counterterrorism operations lie today.

6. Rebecca Freese, "Evidence-Based Counterterrorism Flying Blind? How to Understand and Achieve What Works," *Perspectives on Terrorism* 8, no. 1 (2014), http://terrorismanalysts.com/pt/index.php/pot/article/view/324/651.

7. Ole Wæver, of the University of Copenhagen, originally presented these three concepts in unpublished papers at various International Studies Association annual conferences. In one of his visits to the University of California, Irvine, he briefly discussed these three elements with me as a possible avenue to provide a framework for my research. The following discussion of the model is solely my own and may depart significantly from Wæver's conception and theorization surrounding these three elements.

8. See note 1.

9. E.g., see Christian J. Tams, "The Use of Force against Terrorists," *European Journal of International Law* 20, no. 2 (2009): 359–97.

10. Martin Shaw, "Risk-Transfer Militarism, Small Massacres, and the Historic Legitimacy of War," *International Relations* 16, no. 3 (2002): 343–59.

11. Ibid., 348.

12. Ibid., 349.

13. For a classic account, see Michael Walzer, *Just and Unjust Wars: A Moral Argument with Historical Illustrations* (New York: Basic Books, 1977), 152. For a more up-to-date account, see Michael Gross, *The Moral Dilemmas of Modern War: Torture, Assassination, and Blackmail in an Age of Asymmetric Conflict* (New York: Cambridge University Press, 2010), esp. part II.

14. David Remnick, "Telling the Truth about ISIS and Raqqa," *The New Yorker*, November 22, 2015, www.newyorker.com/news/news-desk/telling-the-truth-about-isis-and-raqqa.

15. Micah Zenko, "The US Air Campaign in Syria Is Suspiciously Impressive at Not Killing Civilians," *Foreign Policy*, November 25, 2015, http://foreignpolicy.com/2015/11/25/the-u-s-air-campaign-in-syria-is-suspiciously-impressive-at-not-killing-civilians/.

16. US Department of Defense, "Department of Defense Press Briefing by Col. Warren via DVIDS from Baghdad, Iraq," November 18, 2015, www.defense.gov/News/News-Transcripts/Transcript-View/Article/630393/department-of-defense-press-briefing-by-col-warren-via-dvids-from-baghdad-iraq.

17. David Francis and Dan de Luce, "Hitting the Islamic State's Oil Isn't Enough," *Foreign Policy*, November 17, 2015, http://foreignpolicy.com/2015/11/17/hitting-the-islamic-states-oil-isnt-enough/.

18. Matthew Levitt, "The Islamic State's Lone-Wolf Era Is Over," *Foreign Policy*, March 24, 2016, http://foreignpolicy.com/2016/03/24/the-islamic-states-lone-wolf-era-is-over/.

19. "The Failed Crusade," *Dabiq*, issue 4, https://azelin.files.wordpress.com/2015/02/the-islamic-state-e2809cdc481biq-magazine-422.pdf.

20. Martin Chulov, "How ISIS Laid Out Its Plans to Export Chaos to Europe," *The Guardian*, March 25, 2016, www.theguardian.com/world/2016/mar/25/isis-plans-export-chaos-europe-paris-brussels.

21. Ibid.

22. Ibid.

23. Ibid.

24. Isabelle Duyvesteyn, "Great Expectations: The Use of Armed Force to Combat Terrorism," in *Modern War and the Utility of Force: Challenges, Methods, and Strategy*, ed. Jan Angstrom and Isabelle Duyvesteyn (New York: Routledge, 2010), 73.

25. Ibid., 77.

26. Of course, I recognize that the counter to this is that regardless of US actions, ISIS would have eventually turned to emphasizing attacks against the West. However, counterfactual arguments are simply ex post facto conjecture. It is interesting to note however, that al-Qaeda had the opposite modus operandi of ISIS in what we could call a mirror image. Al-Qaeda was a terrorist organization with no territorial ambitions other than having a safe haven for planning attacks against the West. Today, however, in the mayhem of Northern Syria, al-Qaeda is set to establish an emirate as its first sovereign state. Charles Lister, "Al-Qaeda Is about to Establish an Emirate in Northern Syria," *Foreign Policy*, May 4, 2016, http://foreignpolicy.com/2016/05/04/al-qaeda-is-about-to-establish-an-emirate-in-northern-syria/.

27. Paul Kowert, "Agent versus Structure in the Construction of National Identity," in *International Relations in a Constructed World,* ed. Vendulka Kubálková, Nicholas Onuf, and Paul Kowert (New York: Routledge, 1998), 107.

28. Ibid.

29. In Islamic theology, the purpose of *da'wa* is to invite both Muslims and non-Muslims to understand and worship Allah, as expressed in the Qur'an.

30. Seth G. Jones, *Hunting in the Shadows: The Pursuit of Al Qa'ida since 9/11* (New York: W. W. Norton, 2013), 41.

31. Ibid., 72.

32. "ISIS Lost 40 Percent of Territory in Iraq, 20 Percent in Syria: Coalition Spokesman," NBC News, January 5, 2016, www.nbcnews.com/news/world/isis-lost-40-percent-territory-iraq-20-percent-syria-coalition-n490426.

33. "What It's Really Like to Fight for the Islamic State," Vice News, April 27, 2016; full video at www.youtube.com/watch?v=aM3ElTvF52I.

34. Lizzie Dearden, "Former ISIS Militant Reveals Reality of 'Staged' Propaganda Videos and Brutal Life under Islamic State," *Independent*, April 30, 2016, www.independent.co.uk/news/world/middle-east/former-isis-militant-harry-sarfo-uk-reveals-reality-of-staged-propaganda-videos-and-brutal-life-a6982831.html.

35. Ibid.

36. Duyvesteyn, "Great Expectations," 78.

37. Ibid., 68.

38. David Luban, "The War on Terrorism and the End of Human Rights," *Philosophy and Public Policy Quarterly* 22, no. 3 (2002): 13–14.

39. Mark S. Hamm, *Terrorism as Crime: From Oklahoma City to Al Qaeda and Beyond* (New York: New York University Press, 2007), 16. Mary Ellen O'Connell also believes that law enforcement methods are the proper means to employ in suppressing terrorism. Mary Ellen O'Connell, "Unlawful Killing with Combat Drones: A Case Study of Pakistan, 2004–2009," Notre Dame Law School Legal Studies Research Paper 09–43, July 2010, www.law.upenn.edu/institutes/cerl/conferences/targetedkilling/papers/OConnellDrones.pdf.

40. Duyvesteyn, "Great Expectations," 77.

41. For further elaborations, see John R. Emery and Daniel Brunstetter, "Drones as Aerial Occupation," *Peace Review* 27, no. 4 (2015): 424–43.

42. Ibid.

43. Duyvesteyn, "Great Expectations," 68.

44. Kim Willsher, "France to Set Up a Dozen Deradicalisation Centres," *The Guardian*, May 9, 2016, www.theguardian.com/world/2016/may/09/france-to-set-up-a-dozen-deradicalisation-centres.

45. Rosa Brooks, "The Threat Is Already Inside," *Foreign Policy*, November 20, 2015, http://foreignpolicy.com/2015/11/20/the-threat-is-already-inside-uncomfortable-truths-terrorism-isis/.

46. The notion that there is a real threat always on the horizon, albeit not immediate, and statesmen lack the ability to pinpoint the precise moment when such a threat will be actualized, but cannot simply ignore it. This was originally utilized by John R. Emery and Daniel Brunstetter; see note 5.

47. Luban, "War on Terrorism."

48. Brooks, "Threat Is Already Inside."

49. "Operation Inherent Resolve," US Department of Defense, October 15, 2016, www.defense.gov/News/Special-Reports/0814_Inherent-Resolve.

50. Micah Zenko, "US Airstrikes in Iraq and Syria," Council on Foreign Relations, November 10, 2016, http://blogs.cfr.org/zenko/2016/11/10/us-airstrikes-in-iraq-and-syria-versus-drone-strikes-in-pakistan-yemen-and-somalia/; and Operation Inherent, "CJTF-OIR Monthly Casualty Report," January 2, 2017, www.inherentresolve.mil/News/Article/1040262/cjtf-oir-monthly-casualty-report/.

PART III

Do We Need New Ethical Frameworks?

10

Drones, Honor, and Fragmented Sovereignty

The Impact of New and Emerging Technology on the Warrior's Code

SHANNON E. FRENCH, VICTORIA SISK, AND CAROLINE BASS

EVERY TECHNOLOGICAL INNOVATION, evolution in modes of combat, or rise of a previously unseen group of combatants sparks fresh controversy about the place and continued relevance of ethical traditions in war. As the contributors to this volume attest, conflicts arising as the result of or in reaction to threats against entrenched concepts of sovereignty produced several waves of advanced military technology to be applied asymmetrically against unconventional forces. Yet these "new" forms of warfare do not require new ethics. The classical just war principles, which include restrictions on the conduct of war, such as the requirement to respect noncombatant immunity, do not dissolve with the introduction of new tactics. Contra some of Brunstetter's claims regarding the *jus ad vim* project in chapter 11, distance in warfare is nothing new, and the traditional just war principles remain the best evaluative framework for assessing the morality of war. They apply as much to the use of drones as they once did to the targeting of a crossbow or canon.[1] Even when strategies change, the principles remain relevant.[2] While consequentialist accounts such as the one argued for by Vilmer (chapter 5) offer some insights, they cannot replace, from the warrior's perspective, the guiding value of just war principles. Nor should traditional just war restrictions be lifted solely because the enemies are non-state actors that violate international law. The original authors of these rules were not unfamiliar with nonstate actors or unlawful combatants, though they may have called them barbarians or pirates.

This is not to say, however, that nothing more can be added to our present-day understanding of military ethics. There remains much work to do concerning the best ways to put the existing ethical principles into practice. Empirical research can be fruitfully applied to the analysis of the effects of current conflicts on combatants. Findings from fields such as psychology and neuroscience can be paired with established ethical frameworks to better enable troops to sustain ethical behavior in the field and minimize psychological trauma.

Many of the drone-related debates focus on the legal, ethical, and strategic implications of drone use.[3] To the extent that the impact of the experience on the drone operators themselves has been studied, the concern has been mainly about the supposed "Playstation effect" or levels of posttraumatic stress disorder. This chapter looks at how operating drones affects the warriors who pilot them, focusing specifically on the psychological effects the chain of command has on drone operators' ability to follow a consistent warrior's code that provides them with the grounds to distinguish what they are asked to do from murder and other ethically irreconcilable actions. Although the guiding principles of a robust and coherent warrior's code to guide drone operators can readily be established from the well-worn principles of *jus in bello* found in the Western just war tradition, there are human factors that can interfere with a drone operator's ability to remain constant to such a code. Established and emerging empirical research can provide valuable insights into how these human factors operate and how their more pernicious aspects might be countered. For example, as discussed below, the infamous Milgram experiments shed light on the psychological mechanisms that underlie obedience to authority. Lessons drawn from these experiments can foster a greater understanding of the relationship between the context in which drone operators function and their actions and experience. And both psychology and neuroscience can teach us about the dehumanizing effects of distance warfare. There is much to be gained from the marriage of ancient codes with modern discoveries to supplement our understanding of the ethics of war.

THE NEED FOR A WARRIOR'S CODE

War imposes heavy psychological and physical burdens. Soldiers are asked to overcome the most basic lessons of their moral development and kill fellow human beings. Although observers have touted the advancement of military technology as a means to lessen bloodshed and save the lives of troops, removing operators from the battlefield and placing them in controlled conditions may deprive them of the psychological support of a warrior's code of honor. This is not meant to imply that the role of, say, an armed drone operator is inherently dishonorable. Rather, the concern is that unless proper care is taken, these operators may not have the internal narrative necessary to contextualize their place within a meaningful warrior's tradition and thus reconcile their actions.

All troops who kill on behalf of their societies need the mental and emotional armor provided by the warrior's code. As explained in *The Code of the Warrior*:

> Warrior cultures throughout history and from diverse regions around the globe have constructed codes of behavior, based on that culture's image of the ideal warrior. These codes have not always been written down or literally codified into a set of explicit rules. . . . These codes tend to be quite demanding. They are often closely linked to a culture's religious beliefs and can be connected to elaborate . . . rituals and rites of passage. . . . The code is not imposed from the outside. The warriors themselves police strict adherence to these standards; with violators being shamed, ostracized, or even killed by their peers. . . . The code of the warrior not only defines how he should interact with his own warrior comrades, but also how he should treat other members of his society, his enemies, and the people he conquers. The code restrains the warrior. It sets boundaries on his behavior. It distinguishes honorable acts from shameful acts.[4]

Troops who lack the armor provided by a robust warrior's code are at greater risk of experiencing severe combat trauma and of violating the laws of war. This point is perhaps best made in Jonathan Shay's contemporary classic, *Achilles in Vietnam: Combat Trauma and the Undoing of Character*. Drawing from decades of interviews and analysis with combat veterans, Shay extols us to recognize "the specific nature of catastrophic war experiences that not only cause lifelong disabling psychiatric symptoms but can *ruin* good character."[5] Shay's work and that of many others who study combat-related posttraumatic stress disorder come to the same conclusion—that it is not exposure to violence alone that produces the most severe psychological trauma, but rather what Shay terms the "betrayal of 'what's right.'"[6] Troops who take lives, by any means, need to feel like they are honorable warriors, not murderers or monsters. They need to be able to make sense of their actions in a way that is consistent with the values around which their identities were formed. A US Navy SEAL may have a somewhat different warrior's code than a US submariner, but both will have to be reconcilable with fundamental American values and the US Constitution, which they both have sworn to defend.

The stakes are very high. The reasons for troops to act ethically under the pressures of combat must be internal and cannot depend on the nature or behavior of their enemies or the weapons or tactics used by them or against them. Regardless of what form war takes, troops are best served by acting in accordance with a code of behavior that is not determined by contingencies beyond their control. As Daniel Brunstetter observes in chapter 11 of this volume, the "renegotiation of *jus ad bellum* principles [during the George W. Bush administration] was the cause of considerable consternation in just war circles." But Brunstetter also seeks to renegotiate the just war principles with his theory of limited force—the *jus ad vim* project—which he claims could curtail drone abuses. Renegotiations of the rules, however well intended, can put troops at risk, unless they are clearly and explicitly tied back to familiar values the warriors already accept.

It is essential to make some kind of consistent warrior's code accessible to all troops who participate in killing, including drone operators. Upholding timeless standards of martial honor requires an active moral imagination and careful reflection when death can be delivered digitally, but it must be done. A warrior's code exists to protect the very humanity of the troops. It cannot be constructed merely of shifting rules of engagement, redesigned by each wave of leadership. A word of warning also about Vilmer's consequentialist approach to drones (chapter 5): Honor does matter when fighting with drones, not just the logic of consequences. There must be strong threads connecting every rule closely to an emotionally accessible warrior identity that runs deep and addresses the existential agony that can accompany any kind of intentional killing.

HOW DISTANCE CAN DEGRADE THE PSYCHOLOGICAL COMFORT OF A CODE

Drone operators experience the same signs and symptoms of posttraumatic stress disorder as traditional combat troops, despite working in a "safe" environment.[7] Perhaps this is a reflection of the unique challenges of their command climate and the psychological complications of technologically mediated warfare. The better we understand their experiences, the more effective we can be in providing them with insights and lessons from other warrior cultures. There is no need to reinvent the wheel. However, some adaptations may be required.

The fundamentals of war have not changed in millennia, or arguably across all of human history. Wars are essentially large, organized groups of people attempting to settle political disputes through the use of force. Whatever new means are devised, the same old questions apply. Did a legitimate authority authorize this use of violence? Did they have just cause to do so? Do they have noble intentions? Is violence the last resort—were all less devastating options truly exhausted?

When it comes to the actual deployment of new weapons of war, the two core principles of *jus in bello* (just conduct of war) established by ancient and medieval scholars remain relevant and indispensable: proportionality and discrimination. Proportionality refers to the magnitude of the response to the actual threat. It requires that the response be only enough to neutralize the threat and not devolve into mere vengeance. Discrimination requires that all possible care be taken to target only those who pose a legitimate threat and to minimize the harm to noncombatants. The hard work of determining how these and other criteria apply to new technology often necessitates identifying the correct analogy and capturing the spirit behind each principle in order to shape these into practical guidance for the use of a new technology such as drones.

Much has been made of the fact that drone operators are able to pilot their drones from thousands of miles away, incurring no immediate physical risk themselves. Yet distance warfare is hardly a paradigm-shattering new concept. It is, however, one that has consistently raised ethical concerns. Face-to-face combat is much less problematic to process and evaluate, both from the point of view of external judgment and the perspective of the warriors themselves. The psychology is straightforward, even primal. Put simply, if I have been ordered to kill you and you have been ordered to kill me, and we fight it out face-to-face, it looks and feels *fair*. As Ginger Rogers' character explains to Cary Grant's in *Once upon a Honeymoon* after she fights with and kills a Nazi, "He said it was him or me; . . . and, I don't know, in my mind, it just dwindled down to him."[8] There is a sense of shared risk and even a flavor of mutual respect: two humans, struggling with each other for survival. Certainly, there is still significant trauma associated with such a struggle. But the feeling of necessity—that even if the overall justification for the war is questioned, few would question that, in that moment, it was kill or be killed—provides solace to the surviving warrior and helps him or her come to terms with the gut-wrenching reality of having ended another person's life. For scholars such as Michael Walzer and Christian Enemark, the risk of being killed is ethically essential, perhaps even necessary, for a person to be considered a "warrior." As Enemark argues, the drone pilot's moral status is diminished as he or she is not put at risk, and "[mutual] risk is an indispensable characteristic of war."[9] But, as Vilmer argues in chapter 5, this goes a step too far in denying warrior status to too many, though it has undeniable intuitive appeal.

Distance strips away a key element of that comforting kill-or-be-killed rationale. If I kill my enemy without giving him at least some chance to kill me, I cannot tell myself it was either "him or me." To reconcile myself to having intentionally and directly caused his death and not to feel myself guilty of a form of murder requires more sophisticated reasoning. Murderers kill for personal reasons and with a certain mind-set (what the law terms "*mens rea*," or the "guilty mind"). In contrast, troops kill for a cause and on behalf of an authority (for example, conventional members of the military are agents of the state). If I kill from a distance but the target of my attack was a threat to others to whom I owe special duties (such as fellow troops or citizens I have sworn to protect), I defend my action as defending a third party and saving lives. Note that the evidentiary and justificatory bar has been raised significantly from the case of face-to-face combat. Distance warriors will naturally ask themselves questions it would rarely occur to close-combat troops to ask. In face-to-face combat, the combatants are usually in no doubt that they killed from grim necessity. But in distance warfare, the case has to be made, and it must be compelling. Why did you have to kill that particular person who was *not* at the time also trying to kill you?

Again, this is an old problem, brought up centuries ago by the use of such cutting-edge military technology and tactics as longbows and hiding in ambush behind a copse of trees. Is the experience of the drone operator different in a meaningful way from that of a well-concealed sniper, or a military pilot operating in a region where his or her forces enjoy air superiority, or a submariner launching missiles at a land-based target? All distance warriors depend on assurances that the actions they have been ordered to take are proportional and discriminant—that there is good justification for the killing they are asked to do. For example, in recent asymmetric conflicts, one might expect these kinds of orders: "Take out these targets, because they are planting IEDs [improvised explosive devices] that are shredding our convoys." "Destroy that building, because the men inside it are plotting terrorist attacks on the US and her allies." However, even when these justifications are provided, other concerns remain.

THE DEHUMANIZING EFFECTS OF DRONES

Beyond distance, relative safety, and concealment, another potentially psychologically troubling aspect of advanced-technology-enabled distance warfare is the (often radical) asymmetry of it. There still is nothing new under the sun here. Asymmetric warfare is well documented in the West from at least the Roman era. From the standpoint of military strategy, radical asymmetry is a strongly desired goal. The faster you can "shock and awe" your enemies and overwhelm them with superior force, the quicker the conflict can be resolved.

However, historically, sharply asymmetric conflicts have seldom been the swift, decisive routs anticipated by the more advantaged side. Some of the reasons for this raise concerns that apply to drone warfare. The apparently "weaker" side in asymmetric conflicts can be unexpectedly tenacious and find ways to prolong the conflict, or even triumph over the "stronger" side. Thus what begins with shock and awe and seemingly overwhelming force becomes the quagmire of a counterinsurgency campaign. There are several notable exceptions, but generally the response of those meant to be shocked and awed into submission is intense anger and deeper resolve not to give in to the will of the "stronger" enemy. It also has the potential to foster generations of new enemies, a point made by both Kelsay and Emery in their chapters (8 and 9, respectively).

Some of the remarkably tenacious responses to strikes by a technologically superior force can be explained simply as any group's natural desire to fight to the end in its own defense. But there is also the fact that being on the receiving end of superior weapons technology—especially that which can kill you with great efficiency while simultaneously protecting those launching the attack from you—is a uniquely dehumanizing and, for lack of a better word, insulting experience. The disrespectful attitude of the "stronger" enemy appears to be, "Our conflict is not really worth risking many lives on our side for, but I am perfectly willing and happy to kill you and your people over it." This perceived attitude becomes a perfect rallying point for the opposition.

Peter Singer highlights this aspect of drone warfare in *Wired for War*. His research concludes that far from making its less-technologically-advanced enemies feel demoralized with fear, America's use of drones has emboldened its opponents:

> [Rami Khouri, director of the Issam Fares Institute of Public Policy and International Affairs at the American University of Beirut] describes how, instead of cowing the populace, these sorts of attacks were reinforcing the position of radical groups like Hezbollah. The use of such technologies was "spurring mass identity politics. . . . The new combination of Islamist, Arab nationalist and resistance mentality is seen as an antidote to the technology discrepancy."
>
> Instead of receiving a message that they were overmatched, "it is enhancing the sprit of defiance." [The response was] that "the enemy is using machines to fight from afar. Your defiance in the face of it shows your heroism, your humanity. . . . [They] are also cowards because they

> send out machines to fight us; . . . they don't want to fight us like real men, but are afraid to fight. So we just have to kill a few of their soldiers to defeat them."[10]

The effects of dehumanization in war can now be examined with the context of a richer understanding of neuroscience. Shannon French and Anthony Jack explain some of the ways dehumanization occurs in the brain in "Dehumanizing the Enemy: The Intersection of Neuroethics and Military Ethics":

> We can identify four broad cognitive modes that humans use to think about other people, which are distinct in terms of the extent and type of cognitive effort involved: (1) When we think of people as objects, we barely engage any effortful cognitive processing. We remain indifferent, including to their suffering, and have cognitive resources to spare. (2) When we think about people as biological machines, as a doctor or neuroscientist does, we engage analytic but not empathetic reasoning areas. (3) When we humanize people (i.e., when we think about their experiential point of view), we engage empathetic but not analytic reasoning areas. (4) When we animalistically dehumanize people, or engage in Machiavellian thinking, we engage both networks. In this mode we think about the person as an agent driven by beliefs and desires, but we refuse to recognize the other as a truly feeling being similar to ourselves. We recognize it if the other person is suffering, but we do not feel concern about it—we may even take sadistic pleasure in it.[11]

Technologically enhanced distance warfare breeds dehumanization on both sides of the conflict. In describing a case study based on an incident in Afghanistan involving Australian troops, the military ethicist and veteran Dan Zupan noted how the soldiers, dressed in their advanced body armor, appeared to the Afghans: "They do not see soldiers. They see anonymous figures, clad in armor, wearing helmets, and bearing weapons. They see black shields where human eyes should be. In short, they really do not see human beings."[12] Zupan argues persuasively that this dehumanization causes the Afghans to "detest" the Australian troops more than they otherwise would, which aids in the recruitment of Afghans willing to fight against the Australians and other coalition troops.

As the philosopher and expert on dehumanization David Livingstone Smith explains in *Less Than Human*: "We are innately biased against outsiders. This bias is seized upon and manipulated by indoctrination and propaganda to motivate men and women to slaughter one another. This is done by inducing men to regard their enemies as subhuman creatures, which overrides their natural, biological inhibitions against killing. So dehumanization has the specific function of unleashing aggression in war."[13]

This dehumanizing effect is amplified in the case of drone warfare, when those being targeted not only cannot see the eyes of their attackers but also cannot see their attackers at all. The source of the threat is decidedly nonhuman, a menacing object hovering in the sky above them. It is only human to want to shout in response, "Don't send your damn robots! Come and fight me like a man!" or to quote some version of William Faulkner's famous line, "Tell that bastard to come down here and say that to my face."[14] The nature and form of the attack galvanize an impassioned resistance whose members may feel justified in using any means available to undermine their enemy's advantages and shatter its seemingly smug sense of security.

Two quick points of clarification are needed here. First, though we, like many others, note that the use of tactics such as drone warfare may produce more enemies for countries like the United States and inspire some of those enemies to employ terror tactics and attack so-called soft targets (e.g., civilians), this is in no way to say that any such attacks are justified. The intentional targeting of civilians is a clear violation of the principle of discrimination that must never be condoned, even by implication, and we certainly do not do so. All such victim blaming is abhorrent. Second, we readily acknowledge that people who believe themselves to be unjustly occupied by foreign powers are likely to resist that occupation with great passion, regardless of what weapons or tactics are employed by those foreign powers. Nevertheless, insofar as there is any truth to the idea that a successful counterinsurgency strategy requires "winning the hearts and minds" of those on the ground, that cannot be achieved through distance warfare.

DRONES AND DISCRIMINATION

Returning, then, to the principle of discrimination, a considerable amount of the international uproar over the use of drones has focused on the deaths of noncombatants—or so-called collateral damage.[15] Collateral damage is always one of the bitterest tragedies in war. It is also hard to reconcile with a warrior's code that depends on maintaining the distinction between just and unjust targeting. It is often difficult for troops to hold on to the belief that they are acting for the good and the right when they see the broken bodies of innocents, struck down by their actions.

Is the outrage any greater because of the nature of the weaponry? If so, the reason is quite comprehensible: Drones are recognized to be a weapon of precision. Appeals to the inherent *precision* of the drone *technology* itself are rampant both among scholars and policymakers—for example, President Barack Obama repeatedly referred to "very precise precision strikes."[16] Enemark has noted that "technology alone cannot be a determinant of legitimacy, but rather what matters is the ethical use of technology by humans."[17] Furthermore, Brunstetter and Braun also address the fact that drones, specifically, "are only discriminate to the extent that their human operators choose to employ them discriminately."[18] Here we have a case of can implying ought, rather than the reverse. Because drones are seen as capable of carefully picking out specific individual targets, it is felt to be more egregious if excessive collateral damage occurs. It is construed almost as criminal carelessness. Again, from the perspective of those receiving the attacks, it adds insult to injury. The read on it is, "You (i.e., the United States) *could* have targeted only person X, but you *chose* to kill others, as well."

To argue from analogy again, imagine a highly skilled military sniper who fires indiscriminately into a crowd of people instead of targeting only combatants within the crowd. Because the sniper is *capable* of much greater precision and discrimination, we are inclined to judge him harshly for his failure to do so—for his decision not to exercise that restraint. The same should be the case for drone strikes, though this does not rule out the possibility of human error or a system of checks and balances that does not allow drone operators to choose not to fire. In the end, discrimination depends on target selection and good intelligence about potential targets. Both of these may be hampered by overreliance on distance technology.

As Michael Ignatieff argued eloquently back in 2000 in his book *Virtual War: Kosovo and Beyond*: "Virtual reality is seductive. . . . We see war as a surgical scalpel and not a bloodstained sword. In so doing we mis-describe ourselves as we mis-describe the instruments of death. We need to stay away from such fables of self-righteous invulnerability. Only then can we get our hands dirty. Only then can we do what is right."[19]

In other words, even if new tools of war allow the military to be more precise in its targeting, they may at the same time encourage civilian leaders to jump more readily to the use of deadly force, and perhaps even to be more callous about who is targeted. John Kelsay reminds us in chapter 8 of this volume that leaders should rightly "take counsel" as they try to ascertain the matters related to overall proportionality, reasonable hope of success, and aim of peace, as well as to learn whether war may be waged in ways that respect the criteria of discrimination and proportionality. It is all too easy to "send in the drones" (or, in future, the robots)—not for members of the military, perhaps, who are fully invested and more able to grasp the true costs of such moves—but for political policymakers, who pressure the Pentagon to rely more and more on distance warfare solutions.[20] The worry is that in an era of contested and fragmented sovereignty, turning to drones will become all the more frequent. Without really understanding the psychological constraints that affect drone pilots, this could be a morally problematic turn.

THE POTENTIAL TO EXERCISE MORAL JUDGMENT

A former colleague at the US Naval Academy, Cdr. Bob "Sprout" Proano, often used to speak of one of the best leaders under whom he ever served as a Navy pilot. When this officer sent his pilots off to do any mission, he briefed them on their targets and then always added the caveat, "Unless it doesn't look right." This simple phrase, "unless it doesn't look right," gave his pilots both the freedom and the responsibility to make their own in-the-moment decisions to reject any target that, for example, appeared (in contradiction to the intelligence) to be a civilian target or to include too many innocent civilians as potential collateral damage. If the proverbial school bus full of children started to roll across a bridge they had been told to destroy, the pilots could exercise judgment and hold their fire. The pilots could also react in real time to any fresh intelligence gathered and conveyed by troops or other operators on the ground. This kind of allowance for changing conditions on the ground or mistaken or outdated intelligence enhances the ethical conduct of war.

This level of control and opportunity for moral judgment may not be available to drone operators. The antidrone activist Medea Benjamin shares a heartbreaking example of unintended civilian casualties, in which a strike could not be called back in time, reported by the pilot Matt Martin:

> [He] had carefully planned to blow up a group of supposed rebels who were standing around a truck. Suddenly, two kids on a bicycle appeared on the screen. There was an older boy, about ten, and a younger one balanced on the handlebars. They were laughing, talking—and riding alongside the truck. Panicking, Martin wanted to stop the missile, but it was too late. The sensor operator had already released it: "Mesmerized by approaching calamity, we could only stare in abject horror as the silent missile bore down upon them out of the sky. When the screens cleared, I saw the bicycle blown twenty feet away. One of the tires was still spinning. The bodies of the two little boys lay bent and broken among the bodies of the insurgents."[21]

Note that the vivid nature of the imagery used by the drone operators only caused greater psychological trauma for the operator, who was forced to witness the awful tragedy unfold. As the investigative journalist Mark Bowden observes,

> A B-1 pilot wouldn't learn details about the effects of his or her weapons until a post-mission briefing. But flying a drone, the pilot sees the carnage close up, in real time the blood and severed body parts, the arrival of emergency responders, the anguish of friends and family. Often the pilot has been watching the people he or she kills for a long time before pulling the trigger. Drone pilots become familiar with their victims. They see them in the ordinary rhythms of their lives with their wives and friends, with their children. War by remote control turns out to be intimate and disturbing. Pilots are sometimes shaken.[22]

Many drone operators complete their missions in an environment more akin to corporate America than a traditional battlefield, with their actions closely monitored in real time by their superiors. Traditional "boots on the ground" troops are also, of course, supervised in combat and operate within a strict hierarchy. However, a certain amount of chaos often obscures the exact details of their tactical moves and weapon use. Although high-technology gear and weapons may include Global Positioning System trackers, microphones, and recording devices, troops must still rely on their training and individual judgment to assess situations with high physical and moral risks. Individual warriors frequently make the final call to fire their weapons or not. Even if their actions will ultimately be reviewed and possibly second-guessed or even condemned, it will almost always be after the fact, once the "dust settles." The so-called fog of war offers some limited protection from the prying eyes of the military hierarchy—warriors can sometimes ignore or creatively reinterpret orders they consider unjust, illegal, or contrary to their intuition. There can be a mild degree of moral privacy that drone operators may not experience.

Adm. Jerry Miller told a "Code of the Warrior" class of midshipmen at the US Naval Academy about how he was ordered to do a bombing run near the end of the Korean War over an area of land that he and his squadron had only the day before covered in leaflets declaring that there would be no more combat operations in that area. Admiral Miller (who was not yet an admiral) tried everything he could to get the orders changed before the mission, but to no avail. However, he held firm to the belief that it would be unethical to bomb that area. Therefore, he defied orders—in secret—and led his men to deliver their deadly payloads in an unpopulated area adjacent to the one they had previously papered with leaflets, to ensure the safety of those on the ground. Afterward, he was called on the carpet for what he did (although, as he pointed out to the midshipmen, he still eventually made flag rank), but the timing and conditions were such that he succeeded in preventing bombs from being dropped on the proposed targets.[23] It is doubtful that a drone operator could ever pull off such a stunt in the name of acting ethically.

Like traditional warriors, drone operators must navigate a rigid institutional hierarchy. But every step in their mission, from their decision-making processes to their actual maneuvering, is potentially visible in real time. Each keystroke and click of a mouse controls important military functions: the flight of an unmanned aircraft, or the launch of a missile. It is possible for each individual action to be scrutinized, measured, and evaluated as it happens. This environment of comprehensive supervision and collective action places pressure on operators to follow orders unquestioningly while simultaneously distancing them from the actual act of killing (though not shielding them from the impact of that act, as they must still view the bloody aftermath with high-pixel clarity).

When faced with an order that is illegal, unjust, or in conflict with one's best judgment, traditional warriors are sometimes (although, it should be emphasized, not always) able to physically distance themselves from their commanders to consider their orders and act on the conclusion of their analysis. In contrast, drone operators experience a work climate akin to two infamous experiments from psychology: the Milgram experiments, which explored the negative aspects of obedience to authority; and the Asch experiments, which explored individual conformity to group beliefs. These classic psychological experiments can be used to spark a discussion on what accountability mechanisms and defenses against the abuse of authority ought to be in place to preserve some moral autonomy for drone pilots.

In 1961, Stanley Milgram set out to explore the role of authority and obedience in unethical behavior. Three months earlier, the Nazi war criminal Adolf Eichmann's trial had reignited the worldwide debate about the ethical responsibilities of soldiers and civilians under a genocidal regime. Milgram intended to explore the power of authority under controlled conditions. He devised a protocol for testing the extent of an individual's obedience to a malevolent authority.

In the original study, the participant believed himself to be joining an experiment on learning and memory. He met a fellow participant (actually an actor) and was "randomly selected" to be the "teacher," whereas the actor was made the "learner." The experimenter connected the fake learner to electrical wires in front of the teacher, and he was then taken to an adjacent room and told to administer a learning and memory task to the learner. If the learner made a mistake, the teacher was ordered to deliver electric shocks of increasing voltages. The machine was labeled with voltages and intensity of shocks, from "slight shock" to the frightening "XXX."[24] In the first variation of the experiment, Milgram believed that "the verbal and voltage designations on the control panel would create sufficient pressure to curtail the subject."[25] But he was wrong. Despite Milgram's expectation that the vast majority of participants would refuse to comply well before the final voltage, only fourteen of forty participants stopped the experiment early, and none of them stopped before delivering 300 volts.

After receiving the astonishing results of the initial experiment, Milgram and his team conducted a set of twenty variations on the original experiment in order to identify which factors influenced the number of participants who resisted authority. Though factors such as the gender of the participant (variation 20) and the prestige of the university (variation 23) did not affect the number of participants who resisted authority, others, such as the physical proximity of the learner (variations 3 and 5), had a significant effect.[26]

Though many variations reduced the percentage of fully obedient participants, only one variation led all participants to resist. In this variation, number 15, there are two experimenters in charge. One tells the subject he may stop, while the other urges him to continue. When a conflicting authority was present, none of the participants continued delivering shocks. This and other variations (including one where the conflicting authority left the room after objecting to the experiment) appear to indicate that the best antidote to a malevolent authority is an equally overbearing benevolent authority. Participants were not empowered to resist authority so much as they were allowed to choose which authority to obey. Participants also resisted authority well when a faux "peer" (in the "peer rebels" variation) steadfastly refused to obey the authority figure.

Likewise, Solomon Asch's early experiments on conformity demonstrated that people (or at least, in this case, white male American college students) are willing to go along with a group's decision even when it is manifestly wrong. In Asch's 1956 experiment, the participant sat in a room with seven actors pretending to be other participants. The group viewed images of three lines of varying lengths labeled A, B, and C. They were then shown a fourth line and asked to identify which of the other lines was the same length. They said their answers aloud and in order, with the true participant always last. In the first two trials, the actors gave the correct answer. In the third trial, every actor identified the wrong line as matching the fourth. The participant faced a dilemma: agree with the group and state the obviously wrong answer, or be the only person to deviate. In preliminary tests of the task, participants' error rate was less than 1 percent. However, in trials where participants faced a dilemma to conform, their error rate was 33 percent. Overall, 75 percent of participants gave at least one incorrect answer during the experiment.

Like Milgram, Asch performed variations on his original paradigm to determine what factors influenced the conformity of his participants. His most relevant finding involved a simple deviation from the paradigm; in these variations, one other "participant" gave a different answer from the rest of the group for some or all trials. Even if this individual gave a different wrong answer, the true participant was far less likely to conform to the group. Thus, as with Milgram's findings, participants were better able to defy one person if they could side with another.

Though there is some evidence that norms have changed since these experiments, they are nevertheless excellent starting points to examine the experience of a drone operator facing orders to fire on an uncertain target. The parallels between the experience of a drone operator and the Asch and Milgram experiments are clear. Drone operators are in a high-pressure situation, in close contact with the expectations of their peers and at least one higher-ranking authority. There are many people involved in a single operation: the pilot, the sensor operator, the mission intelligence coordinator, a safety observer, multiple video analysts, and a ground force commander.[27] Though they are not all physically together, they are in constant communication. These individuals influence one another through their attitudes and their expectations of the situation and of their team. Several of them also carry the weight of their rank and their authority. If seven people say they see rifles and no evidence of civilians riding with a convoy, the remaining person is faced with a hybrid, real-life version of the dilemmas Asch and Milgram created in the safety of their labs.

The question becomes how to apply Milgram and Asch's findings. One of the challenges, of course, is linked to concerns over transparency regarding some of the drone programs, such as those involving the Central Intelligence Agency. If we do not know how they operate, then it is difficult to draw decisive conclusions.[28] Notwithstanding this obstacle, we can still infer some conclusions based on what we know from leaked documents about how the agency's drones operate, as well as the way in which the US Air Force employs them. Returning to the physiological experiments, both Milgram and Asch found that individuals are best able to hold true to their initial beliefs when they are not alone in their actions. Milgram's participants most effectively resisted a corrupt authority when they could side with a benevolent authority or ally. Likewise, Asch's participants were able to give the correct answer when the group was not unanimous, even if the other deviator gave a different answer. In both scenarios, participants were able to take solace and courage from another person. They experienced doubt about the actions of the group from the beginning, but were mostly unable to follow through on their moral (or perceptual) convictions until a rebellious other gave them a socially acceptable way to do so. In the circumstances of drone operations, an individual's ability to express doubts about the group's consensus could mean life or death for civilians on the ground.

Fortunately, the administrative structure of US Air Force drone operations is designed to include numerous checks and balances. The issue becomes ensuring that these checks and balances serve their function. Such a system, created with good intentions, can easily become only a mindless routine that must be checked off before the real action can begin. On the opposite extreme, this practice could serve as an echo chamber in which a false consensus is reached. Ideally, however, each check on drone operations would provide an opportunity for any individual involved to voice doubt. If the culture of the unit is created such that moral concerns are genuinely welcomed and encouraged, drone operators will be better able to resist the pull of group unity and authority. The command climate must be open to moral discussion—and the protocol designed to foster objections—so that one person can deviate from the group. As Milgram and Asch have demonstrated, any others with similar doubts will then feel free to follow.

In addition to potentially fostering moral debate, the current administrative system serves a logistical purpose. Technologically mediated warfare demands a bureaucracy to manage information flow to the operators. Bureaucracy is not an inherently worrisome instrument in this context. If managed well, it supports a climate of accountability that can be helpful in executing high-stakes military operations while adhering to basic ethical codes. However, the operational bureaucracy also regulates information flow to operators in such a way that they may not have enough information to know when to object to unethical orders. Operators are sometimes assigned a specific target person and asked follow them for days or weeks, without being aware of who this person is or how he or she relates to wider enemy activities. Due to the constricted information flow, operators cannot be called on to act as a meaningful check on the power of the military institution in such cases. They may not be in a position to judge if it "doesn't look right," let alone have the autonomy to act in line with their conscience if they do have qualms.

An incomplete flow of information has dire psychological implications. Warriors are often required to kill and to view the ghastly consequences of their killing, which causes trauma. However, as noted above, warriors in combat are more likely to feel that their actions were necessary, proportionate, and discriminate. Although operators may seem remote from the battlefield, high-resolution cameras and lightning-fast connections force them to view the gruesome details of the carnage their actions have caused, without helping them place it in context. The focus of the cameras is at once too clear and too narrow. All troops must execute missions that have been justified by a hierarchy, with little say in whether the larger missions are ethical. But if drone operators are given even less freedom than traditional warriors to perform their own mental calculus and decide if and when to rebel against an order, in addition to not having access to the "it was either him or me" narrative, then they are cut off from key sources of psychological comfort to help them process what they have done.

CONCLUSION

In conclusion, technology-enhanced distance warfare is nothing new, and the ethics of its use can and should still be evaluated using the established principles of just war theory. Troops who employ lethal force today face the same challenges as those from other historical periods to maintain their sense of being part of an honorable endeavor and acting as warriors, not murders. Having a warrior's code anchored in core values with which warriors can deeply identify is as relevant as ever. At the same time, it cannot be denied that certain traditional considerations of military ethics are magnified by the new technology. There is a greater risk of dehumanization on both sides of the conflict. The response to asymmetric assaults may be more severe. The increased distance and capacity for precision put greater pressure on policymakers to improve discrimination and carefully calculate proportionality. Civilian and military leadership owe it to the troops who operate these technologies to take additional care to provide clear and compelling justifications for their missions and, if possible, allow them some autonomy to (on rare occasions) resist authority and group dynamics to reject targets that "don't look right." These steps may not be easy to take, but they are required both by the principles of just war and by the warrior's psychological need to be allowed to follow a coherent code of honor.

NOTES

1. For the purposes of this chapter, we use the term "drone" to refer to unmanned aerial vehicles/systems (UAVs/UASs). The literature on drones is vast; for good overviews, see Frank Sauer and Niklas Schörnig, "Killer Drones: The 'Silver Bullet'of Democratic Warfare?"*Security Dialogue* 43, no. 4 (2012): 363–80; James DeShaw Rae, *Analyzing the Drone Debates: Targeted Killings, Remote Warfare, and Military Technology* (New York: Palgrave Macmillan, 2014); and Sarah E. Kreps, *Drones: What Everyone Needs to Know* (Oxford: Oxford University Press, 2016).

2. On the evolution of rules governing aerial force, see Matthew Evangelista and Henry Shue, eds., *The American Way of Bombing: Changing Ethical and Legal Norms, From Flying Fortresses to Drones* (Ithaca, NY: Cornell University Press, 2014).

3. As a case in point from a vast literature, see two recent edited volumes structured by this frame: Steven J. Barela, ed., *Legitamacy and Drones: Investigating the Legality, Morality, and Efficacy of UCAVs* (Farnham, UK: Ashgate, 2015); and David Cortright, Rachel Fairhurst, and Kristen Wall, eds., *Drones and the Future of Armed Conflict: Ethical, Legal, and Strategic Implications* (Chicago: University of Chicago Press, 2015).

4. Shannon E. French, *The Code of the Warrior: Exploring Warrior Values, Past and Present*, 2nd ed. (Lantham, MD: Rowman & Littlefield, 2016), 4.

5. Jonathan Shay, *Achilles in Vietnam: Combat Trauma and the Undoing of Character* (New York: Simon & Schuster, 1994), xiii.

6. Ibid.

7. James Dao, "Drone Pilots Are Found to Get Stress Disorders Much as Those in Combat Do," *New York Times*, February 22, 2013; and Wayne Chappelle, Tanya Goodman, Laura Reardon, and William Thompson, "An Analysis of Post-Traumatic Stress Symptoms in United States Air Force Drone Operators," *Journal of Anxiety Disorders* 28 (2014): 480–87.

8. Ginger Rogers and Cary Grant, lead performers, and Leo McCarey, director, *Once upon a Honeymoon*, RKO Radio Pictures, 1942.

9. Christian Enemark, *Armed Drones and the Ethics of War* (New York: Routledge, 2014), 96.

10. Peter W. Singer, *Wired for War: The Robotics Revolution and Conflict in the 21st Century* (New York: Penguin Books, 2009), 308–9.

11. Shannon E. French and Anthony I. Jack, "Dehumanizing the Enemy: The Intersection of Neuroethics and Military Ethics," in *Responsibilities to Protect: Perspectives in Theory and Practice*, ed. David Whetham (Boston: Brill / Martinus Nijhoff, 2015).

12. Dan Zupan, "The Child Soldier: Negligent Response to a Threat," *Journal of Military Ethics* 10, no. 4 (December 2011): 321.

13. David Livingstone Smith, *Less Than Human: Why We Demean, Enslave, and Exterminate Others* (New York: St. Martin's Griffin, 2012), 71.

14. William Faulkner, *Snopes: The Hamlet, The Town, The Mansion* (New York: Random House, 1994; orig. pub. 1957), 512.

15. *New York Times* Editorial Board, "The Trouble with Drones," *New York Times*, April 7, 2013. For an overview of the debate, see Chris Woods, "Understanding the Gulf between Public and US Government Estimates of Civilian Casualties in Covert Drone Strikes," in *Drones and the Future of Armed Conflict*, ed. Cortright, Fairhurst, and Wall, 180–98.

16. Scott Shane, "US Said to Target Rescuers at US Drone Strike Sites," *New York Times*, February 5, 2012.

17. Enemark, *Armed Drones*, 96.

18. Daniel Brunstetter and Megan Braun, "The Implications of Drones on the Just War Tradition," *Ethics and International Affairs* 25, no. 3 (2011): 351.

19. Michael Ignatieff, *Virtual War: Kosovo and Beyond* (New York: Picador USA, 2000), 214–15.

20. On the need to better understand the military perspective on use-of-force issues, including that of aerial power, see Martin L. Cook, "Drone Warfare and Military Eth-

ics," in *Drones and the Future of Armed Conflict*, ed. Cortright, Fairhurst, and Wall, 46–62. See also Charles J. Dunlap Jr., "Clever or Clueless? Observations about Bombing Norms Debates," in *The American Way of Bombing: Changing Ethical and Legal Norms, From Flying Fortresses to Drones*, ed. Matthew Evangelista and Henry Shue (Ithaca, NY: Cornell University Press, 2014), 109–30.

21. Medea Benjamin, *Drone Warfare: Killing by Remote Control* (London: Verso, 2013), 90–91; this includes an excerpt from Matt J. Martin and Charles W. Sasser, *Predator: The Remote-Control Air War over Iraq and Afghanistan: A Pilot's Story* (Minneapolis: Zenith Press, 2010), 211.

22. Bowden, Mark. "The Killing Machines: How to Think about Drones," *The Atlantic*, September 2013, 7.

23. This story was shared by Adm. Jerry Miller in Shannon E. French's course, "NP232: Code of the Warrior," at the US Naval Academy in 2004.

24. Don and Sandra Hockenbury, *Psychology*, 5th ed. (New York: Worth, 2008), 501.

25. Gina Perry, *Behind the Shock Machine: The Untold Stories of the Notorious Milgram Psychology Experiments* (New York: New Press, 2012), 305–8.

26. Stanley Milgram, *Obedience to Authority: An Experimental View* (London: Tavistock, 2009).

27. Benjamin, 91–93.

28. *New York Times* Editorial Board, "Transparency in the Drone Wars," *New York Times*, March 19, 2016, www.nytimes.com/2016/03/20/opinion/sunday/transparency-in-the-drone-wars.html?_r=0.

11

The Purview of State-Sponsored Violence

Law Enforcement, Just War, and the Ethics of Limited Force

DANIEL R. BRUNSTETTER

ETHICAL DEBATES about a state's use of force have long distinguished between the conditions of peace and war, with different ethical frameworks governing each.[1] In the former, the ethical constraints of law enforcement shape the extent to which a state can use force against a suspected criminal, whereas in the latter the laws of war apply against combatants of the enemy's armed forces. The distinction is important because the scope of force that is justifiable in a situation of law enforcement is much more restricted than what is permissible in the context of war. In other words, depending on the context, the legitimate use of force is governed by different standards, which have an impact on decisions about when to use force, how much force to use, and the ethical responsibility regarding these decisions.

In a world of fragmented and contested sovereignty, force is used in ways that seem to fall in between law enforcement and full-scale war. The post–Cold War era has seen its fair share of interstate wars in which the distinction was very clear, but changing international conditions (the rise of nonstate actors, and the implosion of certain authoritarian states leading to pockets of lawlessness) combined with technological advancements (especially drones) have led to a blurring of the lines between peace and war. Thus, political violence between states and nonstate actors, within states, and in failed states has come to characterize the international realm.[2] The chapters in this volume regarding drones (chapter 5, Vilmer), preventive force (chapter 4, Fisk and Ramos), and humanitarian intervention as related to human security (chapter 12, Ramel) all attest to ways in which force is used in ways that contest and potentially fragment sovereignty; the discussion of the transnational threats from jihadist groups (chapter 8, Kelsay) and the challenges of victory (chapter 13, Orend; and chapter 14, O'Driscoll) suggest that these challenges will be enduring, meaning that sovereignty will remain fragmented in certain parts of the globe, and thus contested.

What does this mean with regard to how we evaluate the use of force? James Turner Johnson has argued that as notions of sovereignty evolved over time, so too did the meaning of moral responsibility with respect to the decision to use force.[3] For Johnson, the international system is at a crossroads, with recent shifts that challenge the Westphalian system marking a point of departure for reflecting on the relationship between force, moral responsibility, and political order in the international system. Although he argues that we should seek to recover the core element of the classic just war tradition—sovereignty as responsibility for the common good—that was lost when we moved to the Westphalian system centuries ago, my purpose here takes a different angle.[4] Building on the pragmatism discussed by Avant in chapter 6, I seek to chart an ethical via media between law enforcement and war applicable to limited force. To this end, I explore the following questions: Are the law enforcement and just war paradigms sufficient to guide our ethical thinking? What are the strengths and weakness of each? Do we need a new paradigm? Drawing on cases from the last two decades, I illustrate the limitations of both, and argue that a new paradigm—what I have called *jus ad vim*, or the ethics of limited force—is not only warranted but can also contribute to the essence of moral responsibility for the common good that is central to Johnson's view of the just war tradition.

THE LIBERAL LAW ENFORCEMENT PARADIGM AND ITS LIMITS

In the literature on the ethics of force, the liberal law enforcement paradigm is often used as a foil for the rules-of-war paradigm. It is juxtaposed with the laws of war to illustrate the different kinds of actions that are permissible in the context of war, but not in peace—that is, in the domestic setting.[5] At its most basic level, the law enforcement paradigm denotes how a state upholds its laws, and in particular, deals with those believed to be breaking them. It is important to qualify from the beginning that we are really talking about a liberal law enforcement paradigm based on adherence to human rights. The distinction is important because we reject the kinds of law enforcement typical of authoritarian regimes, such as torture, detention without trial, and extrajudicial execution. In addition, the law enforcement paradigm is very much an ideal; in reality, racial profiling—especially in the aftermath of terrorist attacks, but also because of latent, racially fused inegalitarianism—erodes the idealized restraints. Moreover, the fight against terrorism has further eroded these restraints, pushing statesmen to employ unliberal means such as torture and controversial forms of detention as necessary modifications of the rules governing peacetime.

The crux of the liberal law enforcement paradigm assumes that every individual is equal to the extent that each has certain rights, including the right to life and a fair trial. This is manifest in a set of agreed-on laws that a sovereign authority has the duty to enforce, as well as an institutional foundation—including agents of enforcement, a system of courts, and localities of incarceration—operated with a transparent process. Individuals cannot be arrested randomly (or simply because he or she has an affiliation with a nefarious group); rather, there must be a burden of evidence that suggests transgression of the laws.

The liberal law enforcement paradigm severely restricts the legitimate use of lethal force. Because there is a presumption of innocence until proven otherwise in a court of law, lethal force cannot be the first option, regardless of the past actions of an individual, which may even include a history of violent crime. In other words, a suspect has the right not to be killed (unlike soldiers, who, under the rules of war, can be killed). The task of law enforcement agents is to protect citizens and uphold the laws. Although this may require the use of lethal force in rare circumstances, capturing suspected criminals is the preferred course of action unless there is an imminent threat to the security of citizens or law enforcement agents. In such circumstances, lethal force can be used because the rights of those put in danger by a violent criminal take precedence over the criminal's rights. Of course, herein lies the rub. In today's world, the limits of law enforcement are exposed in the now-ubiquitous struggle against global terrorist organizations.

Law Enforcement in an Age of Terror

The law enforcement paradigm is particularly useful in the thinking about the use of force against nonstate actors. But it may not always be the most appropriate moral framework in this context. The decades-long struggle against al-Qaeda, in which the United States has combined law enforcement, limited force, and war to combat the perceived threat, is an illuminating example of the emergent parameters of the law enforcement paradigm.

Following the 1998 US embassy attacks in Kenya and Tanzania, which announced the arrival of al-Qaeda on the international scene, the United States relied mostly on law enforcement, but also conducted limited missile strikes against presumed al-Qaeda targets. The goal of these attacks was to destroy what the Central Intelligence Agency's intelligence had preliminarily identified as a chemical weapons plant in Sudan and to decapitate the al-Qaeda leadership, which was supposed to be gathering at a specific location in Afghanistan, while avoiding the need for a wider war. But, as Micah Zenko notes in his detailed case study, the lasting effect of this political and military failure was that it "deterred the Bill Clinton and George W. Bush administrations from using limited force against al-Qaeda again until after the attacks of 9/11."[6]

The terrorist attacks on September 11, 2001, were a watershed moment. As Fisk and Ramos argue in chapter 4, fears and uncertainties related to the proliferation of weapons of mass destruction, concerns about imminence, and presumed links between states and terrorist groups led to the development of a problematic view of preventive war. The so-called Bush doctrine exploded the law enforcement paradigm by authorizing the use of force, broadly speaking, against the perpetrators of 9/11, along with all those presumed to be associated with it (including states such as Iraq). This meant that lethal force could justifiably be used to pursue the so-called war on terror anywhere in the world, although in reality there were clear limits. Such a view came to erode the constraints of the law enforcement paradigm in the struggle against terrorist organizations. Since 9/11, the United States has seen itself as being at war with al-Qaeda and its affiliates, thus creating what scholars have referred to as "a new category of armed conflict (that is, a 'transnational' armed conflict without geographical limitation)."[7] Following the advent of drones, this policy extended the erosion of sovereignty norms by enabling the targeted killing of suspected terrorists in areas where law enforcement mechanisms are notably weak (e.g., parts of Yemen, Pakistan, and Somalia).[8]

Although drone strikes have claimed countless lives outside the traditional battlefield and arguably have redefined an era in which the use of lethal force is more permissive than what was traditionally permitted by the law enforcement paradigm, the law enforcement paradigm has served, in certain areas, as the paradigm of choice to pursue al-Qaeda. The use of law enforcement has led to numerous arrests, foiled terrorist plots, and captured intelligence around the globe, both before and after the advent of drones. To explore the scope and limits of law enforcement, I examine four different contexts where law enforcement has been—to various degrees—a viable paradigm that will help us to understand its parameters.

First, individuals accused of having links to terrorist groups affiliated with al-Qaeda and seeking to conduct terrorist attacks against Western targets have been arrested in the United States, Canada, and many European countries, including the United Kingdom, Norway, Belgium, Germany, France, and Switzerland. The arrests were frequently the result of international cooperation. None of them entailed the killing of suspects, though the legal systems that would process the suspects differed from country to country. However, one of the major challenges of the law enforcement paradigm is accentuated when the urgency of stopping a seemingly imminent attack builds. The case of France's response to the threat from ISIS is an illustrative example.

After the *Charlie Hebdo* attacks in early 2015, there was a general feeling that it was not a question of whether another attack would occur but rather when it would. In hindsight, one could criticize the French for not being aggressive enough in pursuing potential threats. When the attack did come in November 2015, the government called for a state of emergency, giving greater powers to law enforcement to combat what was seen as a situation of imminent peril. This included the power to make warrantless searches and increased surveillance capabilities. Paris lived under a siege mentality as law enforcement officials pursued the masterminds and eventually thwarted another attack. There were hundreds of raids on individual dwellings, and countless arrests. The culmination was the firefight in Saint-Denis (just north of Paris), where one of the masterminds, Abdelhamid Abaaoud, had holed up and was allegedly planning to carry out another attack. In an operation that lasted several hours, 110 commandos and police fired more than 5,000 rounds of ammunition, and also threw about 20 grenades; two suspected terrorists were killed, and several others arrested when attempting to flee. Parts of the building were reduced to rubble, but no bystanders were injured, though many described the scene as one from a war zone.[9]

I raise this example to illustrate what the future may look like: What if the Saint-Denis raid is not an exception to the general trend of law enforcement pursuits but rather the beginning of a new era in which law enforcement officials race to stop impending attacks by employing greater and greater force against heavily armed people with links to international terrorist groups that are actively planning terrorist attacks and who do not want to be captured? In France, there was a sense that the ISIS operatives were bringing the zone of war to European cities, with European law enforcement operatives, acting in a context defined by an impending sense of peril, reacting out of necessity. In the case of the Saint-Denis raid, law enforcement officials attempted first to apprehend the suspects before a firefight ensued. But if Saint-Denis is not an isolated event, and other such raids ensue in the future, will the rules of engagement for law enforcement remain so constrained? The continued threat from ISIS—as the Brussels and Nice attacks, along with multiple thwarted attacks, demonstrate—raises serious questions about the efficacy of the law enforcement paradigm. How much force can be used to quell the domestic terrorist threat? When does capture become unfeasible in a domestic context? Are suspected terrorists different from other kinds of criminals? Do law enforcement officials have to show the same levels of restraint when trying to apprehend them? Could there be a context when it is legitimate to shoot first and ask questions later? Some have likened the French response to a problematic shift that challenges the democratic foundation of the French Republic, whereas others see it as a needed step to update antiterrorism laws that were forged in the 1970s against a different kind of threat. In either case, it is significant that the domestic law enforcement paradigm in France (as in the United States after 9/11) has not remained stagnant but has sought to adapt by investing law enforcement agents with greater power. As confrontations with domestic terrorist cells increase, the contexts in which lethal force—as in the Saint-Denis raid—may be used will also increase. The challenge lies in finding a balance between restraint and efficacy on one hand and democratic values and security on the other hand.

Second, key nondemocratic allies that also reject the ideology of groups like al-Qaeda or ISIS, and have a monopoly on the use of force within their borders, have aided in apprehending terrorist suspects. In the months following 9/11, war—that is, the invasions of Afghanistan and Iraq—was not the only US strategy. Al-Qaeda suspects were arrested in Indonesia, Singapore, and Malaysia, while US Special Forces trained local operatives in the Philippines to combat local extremist groups.[10] All these arrests occurred before the incorporation of drones as a major tool of statecraft. But even after drone technology took off, the United States continued to pursue law enforcement activities within the borders of key allies.[11]

Third, even in countries where the government does not have full control over its territory (including Pakistan and Yemen), arrests still do occur.[12] Finally, the United States has used Special Forces to capture suspected terrorists, either in transit in international waters or in so-called safe havens that exist in places where there is a security vacuum. This includes the controversial practice of sending Special Forces into the sovereign territory of other states without these governments' consent. For example, in 2013, Abu Anas al-Libi—under federal indictment in New York for more than a decade for his suspected role in the US embassy bombings in Kenya and Tanzania in 1998—was captured by US Special Forces on the streets of Tripoli.

These examples identify several conditions needed for law enforcement to be effective. Law enforcement is viable in places where a government has the will to uphold laws that prohibit the kinds of acts called for by those who espouse the ideology of groups like ISIS or al-Qaeda. This cuts across regime type, as it is feasible in both democracies and authoritarian regimes. Law enforcement requires clearly identifiable agents of the law who possess the authority to arrest suspected criminals, and a court system by which individuals could be fairly tried, and, if found guilty, the appropriate punishment rendered. It is worth noting that different views of human rights and the legal rights of terrorists, corruption, and varying prison conditions lead to clear distinctions. One might venture that the ideal form would be one in which arrested suspects are housed in safe prison establishments before and during their trial, are not subject to torture or harassment, and have access to a lawyer and a fair trial to ascertain their innocence or guilt. If found guilty, the level of punishment then raises moral dilemmas—notably, whether the death penalty is justifiable. Moreover, any deviations from this ideal form—of which there are many, including incarcerating "enemy combatants" in the controversial US prison in Guantánamo instead of federal prisons in the United States proper—also raise moral quandaries.

In addition, law enforcement is effective in places were governments have a monopoly on the use of force within their borders *and* the will to pursue suspected terrorists to the letter of the law. This means that pockets of territory where individuals or groups can live outside a state's laws, pursuing threatening interests under the protection of their own arms, do not exist. Jordan is a good example of such a state, where there is systematic implementation of the law enforcement paradigm—and, consequently, no perceived need for limited force by the United States. When a state does not have both, then the viability of law enforcement is diminished. If, for example, a state is involved in a counterinsurgency struggle, the police may not be fully effective. Or if a state does not have full control of its rugged borderlands, this can provide safe havens in areas where arrest is difficult. When a state lacks the will to pursue terrorists—because of corruption, perceived domestic costs, or geopolitical factors—this also undermines the systematic implementation of law enforcement. Pakistan is a good example of such a case: A shifting will, coupled with the lack of a full monopoly on the use of force, diminishes the viability of law enforcement measures, and, consequently, creates a context where alternative means may need to be pursued. The question then becomes what level of force, used by whom, could dislodge or diminish the capacities of terrorist groups in such places.

Hence, the moral and strategic trade-offs between, for example, Pakistani military operations and US drones.[13]

International cooperation—especially the decision to share intelligence—contributes to the effectiveness of law enforcement. When intelligence gathering is shared between governments, the chance of the authorities being tipped off to terrorist plans is enhanced. This contributes to making terrorist groups more cautious, thus restricting their movements and the scope of their activities, unless they are willing to risk greater exposure. Cooperation creates geographical spaces—Europe comes to mind—where diminishing the capacity of a common enemy can be accomplished through law enforcement mechanisms (although Emery reminds us in chapter 9 that states should never assume they could actually take measures to reduce the risk to zero). That said, the use of limited force such as drone strikes has, because of the lack of shared norms governing this type of force, arguably diminished cooperation. As Anthony Dworkin argues in a recent brief from the European Council on Foreign Relations, some European states (Germany and the United Kingdom, in particular) have been reluctant to share intelligence with the United States because of fears that doing so might facilitate the targeted killing of suspected terrorists instead of following law enforcement procedures.[14]

The major challenge, however, lies in places where relations between states are not based on mutual trust. In these places, such as Pakistan and Yemen, a delicate game is played between short-term cooperation, plausible deniability, and self-interest that reduces the effectiveness of law enforcement, thus making the use of limited force, such as drones, appear to be a necessary alternative. As with the previous condition, cooperation is not a black-and-white affair. To the extent that there is nearly full cooperation and intelligence sharing, law enforcement is likely to be more viable (though this does not ensure it will be successful); on the flip side, diminished cooperation reduces the capacity to apprehend suspects and bring them to trial, while the absence of cooperation makes law enforcement very difficult.

The Limits of Law Enforcement

The conditions delineated above, when examined in relation to real-world situations, reveal limitations of the effectiveness of law enforcement. Even in states that do have a monopoly on the use of force, challenges cast a long shadow over the ideal of liberal law enforcement and the delicate balance with national security. Leaders are not simply concerned with bringing terrorists to justice, but also in preventing future attacks. As Jeff McMahon notes, terrorists "lack some of the defining characteristics of combatants and are considerably more dangerous than ordinary criminals." Thus, he proffers, antiterrorist actions "cannot be well governed within either the law enforcement paradigm or the war convention."[15] This is particularly relevant in countries such as France (or Belgium), which have terrorist cells in suburbs where law enforcement has difficulty penetrating effectively. Following current law enforcement procedures may not be enough to prevent future attacks if innocence is presumed and one has to wait for imminence as the standard to act with the lethal force. But broadening the powers of law enforcement is also problematic. Concerns about giving the government greater surveillance powers, and arresting and holding suspects preventively (or deporting them), have been raised in France as the country comes to grips with the ISIS threat. The worry is that the government gets it wrong too often, arrests the innocent, and thus undermines the rule of law. Again, parallels with the United States post-9/11 loom large. Moreover, as Holeindre intimates in chapter 7, abusive law enforcement practices may actually increase the level of terrorist threats in the current international climate.

Nevertheless, it may be the case that one can successfully employ law enforcement in most geographic spaces, but this may not be enough to quell the threats posed by terrorist groups operating in failed states or so-called in-between spaces. The post-1998 US embassy bombings should serve as a stark reminder of the limits of law enforcement. Capturing and bringing to trial the perpetrators was arguably a success, but this did not ultimately eliminate the threat of an emerging al-Qaeda.[16] The persistence of al-Qaeda in parts of Pakistan and Yemen, along with the rise of ISIS in US prisons in Iraq, also raise concerns.[17] Even though one may wish to see law enforcement as the "good" alternative to the "bad" alternative of more permissive uses of force (i.e., missile strikes or targeted killing by drones), such a black-and-white view glosses over the limitations of the former.

In conditions where a state does not have a monopoly on the use of force within its borders and/or does not have the will to pursue terrorist groups within its borders, a perceived threat exists, and cooperation with that state is limited, then statesmen must weigh various options. They can attempt to build trust and create better conditions for effective law enforcement (which leaves the threat smoldering). Alternatively, they could pursue law enforcement scenarios that target the threat but violate the territorial integrity of that state and risk further diminishing the chance of cooperation—that is, the Abu Anas al-Libi raid in Libya. Another option would be to abandon the law enforcement paradigm altogether and opt for a more permissive use of force through extended drone campaigns, missile strikes, or full-scale war.

These trade-offs point to the major limitation of the law enforcement paradigm that becomes apparent when one looks at the terrorist threat in a world of contested and fragmented sovereignty—that in some circumstances, the ethical constraints of law enforcement are too strict to quell the threat posed by terrorist groups. Relying solely on law enforcement ties the hands of statesmen because the enemy can find safe havens in geographic spaces where the effectiveness of law enforcement is severely curtailed. Given that traditional state-to-state methods of curtailing such a threat—sanctions, deterrence, and so on—do not work against nonstate actors, one can see the rationale behind choosing to pursue lethal actions that would not be permissible under the law enforcement paradigm (especially drone strikes, as Vilmer argues in chapter 5). However, framing the morality of these actions in terms of the just war paradigm, as the United States has done, is ultimately problematic.

THE LIMITATIONS OF THE JUST WAR PARADIGM

Even as the US global war on terror accelerated, Michael Walzer wrote that "the triumph of just war theory is clear enough; it is amazing how readily military spokesmen during the Kosovo and Afghanistan wars used its categories, telling a causal story that justified the war and providing accounts of the battles that emphasized the restraint with which they were being fought."[18] His point was that the *jus ad bellum* and *jus in bello* categories had succeeded in making war a moral sphere, as opposed to one where the strategic ends justify any violent means.

There is a large body of literature on the significance of the just war tradition today, with considerable ink spilled examining many varieties of conflict through the lens of the tradition's principles. Although some scholars are critical of just war principles as facilitating the turn to war, there is a strong consensus that they form a moral framework that can provide guidance "to all those involved in war, from the highest to the lowest level."[19] However, a rich critical literature on the post 9/11 era contests the meaning of the *jus ad bellum* principles by exploring the distinction between preemptive and preventive war, the legitimacy of regime change, the meaning of last resort, the legitimacy of humanitarian intervention, the use of drones, and how the precepts of the just war tradition can be adapted to asymmetric warfare against nonstate actors or in the context of civil wars. These debates remain, for the most part, anchored in the historical category of *jus ad bellum* to explore the ethical issues associated with the use of force. However, as I have argued elsewhere, states are, with greater frequency, turning to limited uses of force that do not neatly fit within the purview of just war principles.[20]

Contested and Fragmented Sovereignty and the Jus ad Bellum *Framework*

In this section, I identify three trends in the use of force in the twenty-first century that raise concerns about the applicability of the principles of *jus ad bellum* to evaluate the entire spectrum of force that statesmen can employ. These trends of limited force not only challenge traditional notions of sovereignty but have also contributed to the contested and fragmented state of international affairs in which we live.

The first trend is the partial erosion of the principle of sovereignty that has opened the path to humanitarian intervention. The 1990s saw the beginning of a shift in the view of sovereignty as being protected by the norm of nonintervention to sovereignty as a moral responsibility.[21] The major cause of this shift was the humanitarian crises in Africa and the Balkans that shook the moral conscience of the world. And yet, as Lindemann and Giacomelli show in chapter 2, there were nevertheless inconsistent responses from leading states and a lack of credible commitment from the United Nations to uphold human rights in the aftermath of the humanitarian awakening. Later, the norm of the Responsibility to Protect (R2P) emerged. R2P allows for various levels of force—ranging from peacekeeping missions to establishing no-fly zones to bombing campaigns to full-scale invasion—to be employed by the international community (with UN support) to protect vulnerable populations from significant state-sponsored violence. These options employ very different levels of military force, and it is not clear whether the *jus ad bellum* principles are sufficiently calibrated to work through the ethical dilemmas posed by each (as well as the dilemmas associated with moving from one option to the next).

Proponents say that force can prevent what would surely be grave humanitarian catastrophes—Kosovo, Libya, and ISIS are all cases that come to mind. Critics, including Hehir in chapter 1 of this volume, provide evidence that these campaigns (at least Kosovo and Libya) cause significant civilian casualties, damage vital infrastructure, and fail to ensure long-term respect for human rights in the respective regions.[22] Thus, one of the key concerns is reconciling the ever-escalating levels of force seemingly required for humanitarian intervention to be effective with the fear that, in the long run, too much intervention fails to uphold human rights in a satisfactory way.

The Libyan intervention proves to be an illuminating case that points to how protecting the human rights of civilians from the aggression of a state can problematically escalate to long-term instability. The initial call for limited force authorized the establishment of a no-fly zone to prevent the imminent mass killing of civilians by government forces. In defending the decision to support the no-fly zone, Obama referenced the Libyan regime's escalation of violence, and the need to act.[23] The decision to employ limited force thus had the purpose of preventing or halting violence that would immediately escalate absent such strikes—a use of force that ultimately upholds human rights. Nevertheless, intervening on behalf of rebel groups is a different matter because this implies the goal of regime change. The escalating mission creep helped turn the tide of the civil war, but the result has been significant posttransition instability and a country on the verge of plunging again into civil war, with ISIS ascendant. The problem, it seems, was not the initial authorization of limited force (which had global support) but rather whether the escalation of force to support loosely connected rebel groups was justified or whether a semipermanent no-fly zone scenario was a just outcome of limited force.

These scenarios raise a host of questions. How should we evaluate the shift from one level of force (no-fly zones) to the next (rebel-aiding air strikes)? How do when know when to widen (or restrict) the rules of engagement? Stated more broadly, when do we enter a state of war and gain the full privileges of belligerency? Imagine, for a moment, a counterfactual scenario in Libya—what if no allied escalation had occurred, and the no-fly zones had been kept in place? Perhaps we would have had a situation similar to Iraq during the 1992–2003 period, when the Iraqi regime was partially kept at bay. Or perhaps we would have a Kosovo-type solution that, despite underlying tensions, has endured. Would this have been a "better" outcome than the current situation? Would this respond to the postwar rehabilitation limits that Orend discusses in chapter 13?

The second trend in the use of force in the twenty-first century is the rising threat of nonstate actors or rogue states acquiring and using weapons of mass destruction. The 2003 Iraq War sparked considerable debate about how to deal with such a threat. In the buildup to the war, just war precepts were employed by the George W. Bush administration as a language of persuasion to convince the American public and the world at large that the coming war was legitimate. In an assessment by the US State Department's Bureau of Intelligence and Research Intelligence dated August 29, 2002, the "problems and prospects of 'justifying' war with Iraq" were explored. The document revealed how "traditional just war theory" could serve as a platform for critiquing the decision to go to war. While recognizing the moral value of just war principles, the administration was convinced the just war tradition needed to be stretched in order to tackle the new threats posed by terrorism.[24] Doing so required a more expansive (and dangerous) view of the just cause criterion to include preventive war and regime change, along with a significantly relaxed standard of last resort.

This renegotiation of *jus ad bellum* principles was the cause of considerable consternation in just war circles; some scholars argued that the Bush doctrine successfully reflected the changing international conditions, and others argued that it was a significant departure from the tradition.[25] In chapter 4 of this volume, Fisk and Ramos argue that the turn to preventive force marks a dangerous trend, whereas in chapter 3 Biggar challenges us not to be overly critical of preventive war despite imperfect outcomes in recent cases (notably Iraq). Of particular interest for my purposes, however, is the following observation by Michael Walzer: "The Iraqi case invites us to think about the use of force-short-of-war; the containment regime of 1991–2003 is only one possible example of this use. Despite the French argument at the UN in 2002 and 2003 that force must always come as a last resort, force-short-of-war obviously comes before war. The argument about *jus ad bellum*, therefore, needs to be extended to *jus ad vim*. We urgently need a theory of just and unjust uses of force."[26]

The implication of Walzer's observation is that a theory of *jus ad vim* could have helped statesmen better assess the situation. Walzer's subsequent discussion of how limited force could have been used to curb the threat of Saddam Hussein's Iraq and eventually lead to regime change without having to resort to full-scale war demarcated a distinction between limited force and war that invites us to think about how the ethical dilemmas and moral requirements differ in each context.

The Iraq case highlights the containment system as one possibility; the ongoing Syrian debacle highlights a host of other uses of limited force. President Obama's interpretation of the principles of just war led him to the conclusion that waging war against Syria—a full-scale war similar to the one waged in Iraq to topple Saddam Hussein's regime, or a humanitarian intervention like that in Libya—was not justified. Wary of escalation to a wider conflict, he nevertheless threatened limited air strikes to punish the Assad regime's use of chemical weapons on its civilians: "I will not put American boots on the ground. I will not pursue an open-ended action like Iraq or Afghanistan. I will not pursue a prolonged air campaign like Libya or Kosovo. This would be a targeted strike to achieve a clear objective, deterring the use of chemical weapons and degrading Assad's capacities."[27] What is interesting here is the distinction Obama makes between war and something of a lesser intensity, and that he bases this distinction on the lessons he drew from previous wars that many considered just at their commencement (Iraq being the exception).

But if such a use of force is not war, what moral rules ought to govern it? Are there specific moral dilemmas or requirements? How should we morally evaluate the risks of escalation? Can as much latitude be tolerated with regard to civilian casualties in the context of limited force as is permitted by the rules of war?

The third trend is the terrorist threat from nonstate actors, such as al-Qaeda (including affiliates such as al-Qaeda in the Arabian Peninsula and al-Qaeda in the Islamic Maghreb) and ISIS, which operate in the disputed border regions of sovereign or failed states. As Kelsay argues in chapter 8, the problem lies in the way these groups defy traditional notions of sovereignty by relocating to places where sovereignty is contested while projecting a global threat. The use of force in these spaces, such as drone strikes and Special Forces raids, is clearly not law enforcement but does not neatly fit the just war paradigm either. These activities have "a different feel" from war because, as Walzer observes, they happen "outside the moral and legal conventions of ordinary warfare."[28] Critics claim such acts are illegal because they are outside the traditional battlefield, meaning that only law enforcement should be used. However, the level of restraint inherent in the law enforcement paradigm, as the previous section demonstrated, means that such measures are not feasible around the globe. Should this mean that the war paradigm automatically applies?

The drone controversy points to one of the troubling characteristics of the fight against terrorist groups that makes it difficult to apply just war principles—that the struggle is seemingly without end. Although policymakers have spoken about the mythical tipping point, when these groups will be so degraded that "the law enforcement and intelligence resources of our government are principally responsible" for dealing with the threat, the lessons of past wars suggest that this point is far off on the horizon.[29] As O'Driscoll illustrates in chapter 14 of this volume, the military victories in the Afghanistan, Iraq, and Libya wars were not really victories at all, but rather transitioning phases to new conflicts as al-Qaeda shifted its operations to Pakistan and ISIS began its meteoric rise in the postwar turmoil. These groups, and the perceived threat they pose to existing states, contribute to the contested and fragmented sovereignty that characterizes the international realm today.

If, indeed, the conflict is perpetual, how does one even apply the *jus ad bellum* principles? What does last resort mean with regard to a looming threat? How does one interpret proportionality in a never-ending conflict? Or how can the probability of success be determined if there will not be a concrete victory? In chapter 5 of this volume, Vilmer offers a consequentialist-based account of drone use against terrorist groups; but as Fisk and Ramos point out in chapter 4, thinking of consequences can be shortsighted if doing so sets a dangerous precedent for the preventive use of force. My own view of drone use, which I have expounded on elsewhere, is that the legal ambiguity, muddled notion of imminence, and misplaced use of just war principles that characterized the Obama administration's justification of drones points to the need for a hybrid moral framework that is calibrated specifically to limited force and lies somewhere between law enforcement and just war, but combines elements of both.[30] That being said, there remains much to be explored with regard to the morality of limited force if one is to answer the host of questions, emerging from the limitations of the just war paradigm, that I have raised in this section.

CONCLUSION: THE GOLDILOCKS DILEMMA AND *JUS AD VIM*

In this chapter, I have argued that both the law enforcement paradigm and the just war paradigm have important shortcomings given the spectrum of force that states employ in the contemporary world against the threats they face. This "Goldilocks dilemma"—the former does not allow for enough force, whereas the latter allows for too much force—suggests that what is needed is a more calibrated theory of force, what scholars have been calling a framework of *jus ad vim*. In the words of Rosa Brooks, "The international community needs to develop a *jus ad vim* to occupy the space between war and peace: a law and ethics relating to ongoing but discrete smaller scale uses of force."[31]

As we think of what such a framework might look like, it is worth taking a critical gaze at the wrong ways of imagining *jus ad vim*, and then set out the path forward. In the wake of 9/11, David Luban identified the emergence of a "hybrid war–law model" that came to govern the United States' use of force, especially against nonstate actors. The crux of the model lies in the United States' claim that it possesses the right to wage war against terrorist groups (which gives them a wider latitude to use lethal force compared with criminal law enforcement), while adapting the logic of law enforcement that denies terrorists the right to fight back or to have the legal status of prisoners of war. This model, as Luban describes it, assumes that law enforcement does not always work, while recognizing that there is a different feel to the "war on terror" compared with traditional wars. But instead of upholding peacetime human rights or constraining the use of force, it borrows elements from law enforcement and the war paradigm—hence the hybrid nature—to justify a wider scale of violence against terrorist suspects: "By selectively combining elements of the war model and elements of the law model, Washington is able to maximize its own ability to mobilize lethal force against terrorists while eliminating most traditional rights of a military adversary, as well as the rights of innocent bystanders caught in the crossfire."[32] Luban is absolutely correct in identifying this type of hybrid model as problematic. The major consequence—which *jus ad vim* must avoid—is that such a hybrid model "depresses human rights from their peacetime standard to the wartime standard" in the in-between spaces where terrorists hide by permitting levels of force that are too high.[33]

One worries that accepting a moral space in between law enforcement and the just war paradigm will lead to an overly permissive theory of force that can easily be abused. This is the critique of C. A. J. Coady, who recognizes the important distinction between *jus ad bellum* and *jus ad vim*, that "there should be greater reluctance to engage in wholesale invasion than, for example, to send in a small armed unit to effect a minimal objective," but is skeptical that such a distinction will reduce the turn to violence.[34] Coady thinks that a theory of *jus ad vim* would lower the threshold of last resort for using lethal force too much—though, as Fisk and Ramos argue in chapter 4, this is happening regardless. By distinguishing morally between force-short-of-war and war, states would be provided a greater array of "moral" options to counter threats that would make nonviolent options seem less attractive and increase the frequency of political violence. Coady thus concludes that "we do not need some more permissive theory quite distinct from just war thinking," because this would erode its restraints, only serving to promote unnecessary and unjust uses of force.[35] Such a theory would, he predicts, reinforce power distinctions in the international realm, thus sowing the seeds for increased asymmetrical conflict as strong states engage in more frequent "correcting" operations that fall short of war but exceed what would be permitted by the law enforcement paradigm.[36] But it is precisely just war principles' lack of precision that gives statesmen the moral leeway to impose wartime standards on contexts when limited force is employed, when perhaps more restrictive standards should guide their decisions.

Although one may wish to remain wedded to the law enforcement / just war dichotomy and reject any uses of force that fall in between, to do so marks a disconnect between theory and practice that will lead to the kinds of abuses that both Luban and Coady warn against. Indeed, without a framework of *jus ad vim*, statesmen can continue to operate in the moral ambiguity that reigns instead. It is better, I think, to explore the moral space in between law enforcement and the just war paradigm in order to identify the ethical dilemmas associated with limited force and elucidate ethical constraints that respond to the instances when law enforcement falls short, but where a resort to war would be unjustified. This is the moral space where *jus ad vim* can bridge the gap between law enforcement and the morality of war, and between theory and practice.

The scholarly debates about what *jus ad vim* might look like have only just begun. Both Luban's and Coady's critiques remind us that the development of *jus ad vim* cannot diminish the ethical burden of a state seeking to use limited force. Although they fear a theory that is too permissive, a robust *jus ad vim* should be capable of doing the opposite. As I have argued elsewhere, permissiveness must be circumscribed by clear restraining mechanisms that limit when and how a state uses limited force and that protect human rights in more robust ways than the hybrid model that Luban claims functions today, while also permitting the necessary force to respond to threats in the in-between zones described by Walzer and against threatening states.[37]

In these concluding words, I want to raise a call to arms, as it were, to challenge scholars to think about the specific challenges linked to using limited force, and take part in what I call the *jus ad vim* project. There are three steps to developing this project. First, we must ask in earnest: Do we need a framework for *jus ad vim*? I recognize that there will be more challenges to my argument and invite them—indeed, a number of my colleagues have expressed their skepticism at recent conferences and workshops—but whether one thinks a framework for *jus ad vim* is needed, the debate does not end with a yes or no answer to this question.[38] The second step is identifying the most salient ethical questions related to the use of limited force, some of which I have raised in this chapter's previous sections. The third step can lead in multiple directions. If one answered "no" to the need for a framework for *jus ad vim*, then the challenge is to show how existing paradigms answer the relevant questions and resolve the most pressing ethical dilemmas. If one thinks a framework for *jus ad vim* is warranted, then one must decide what kind of theory is best suited. There are several possibilities. One could imagine a deep moral theory that parallels some of the claims of revisionist just war theorists or an applied ethics suitable for nonideal situations, or a set of alternative moral principles to just war thinking, or perhaps simply a recalibration of just war principles combined with new principles that are specific to contexts of limited force. Perhaps the focus should, instead, be on understanding how to reconfigure the liberal law enforcement paradigm to meet the challenges of the threat from terrorism.

The primary goal of the *jus ad vim* project as I see it lies partly in the process itself—in the act of theorizing about *jus ad vim*, *jus in vi*, and *jus post vim*, which can help us think about how limited force, which is problematically being used under the auspices of just war principles, can be employed in more ethical ways. This could help us to better understand the challenges of R2P and connect to some of the recommendations proposed by Hehir in chapter 1. It may also become even more urgent to discern the extent to which O'Driscoll is right in arguing in chapter 14 that victory in war is always elusive, leaving states to wield limited force on a more frequent basis to deal with persisting security threats. A secondary goal is to provide practical moral language that can inform statesmen who will wield the power to use such force but also those who seek to criticize perceived abuses. Just war principles already serve this purpose when it comes to war. As I have argued elsewhere, in the US presidential debates and beyond, the *jus ad bellum* principles served John Kerry and Barack Obama as a way to criticize and depart from President Bush's expanded view of just war.[39] But just war principles are, as I have argued here, problematic when it comes to limited force, and may even provide moral leverage legitimizing decisions to use limited force when greater restraint ought to be observed.

Jus ad vim can provide a more calibrated moral framework to address the security concerns for which some level of force is used, but not war. Echoing Walzer's conclusion about the triumph of just war, theorizing about the moral precepts of *jus ad vim* is the first step in a process of updating the moral vocabulary with which ethicists and military practitioners think about the use of military force now and in the future. It remains to be seen whether *jus ad vim* could enter into the warrior's code and address some of the issues discussed by French, Sisk, and Bass in chapter 10. However, in a world of contested and fragmented sovereignty, limited force will only increase as states seek to protect themselves and/or provide for the common good. Thus, I think the development of *jus ad vim* is a step toward clarifying the spaces of moral ambiguity that lie in between law enforcement and just war, restraining the turn to limited force that occurs there, and setting realistic expectations regarding the achievement of the common good through the use of force.

NOTES

1. Michael Walzer, *Just and Unjust Wars: A Moral Argument with Historical Illustrations* (New York: Basic Books, 2006), 51–52.
2. C. A. J. Coady, *Morality and Political Violence* (Cambridge: Cambridge University Press, 2008), 4.
3. James Turner Johnson, *Sovereignty: Moral and Historical Perspectives* (Washington, DC: Georgetown University Press, 2014).
4. I nevertheless recognize the importance of the (classical) just war tradition in shaping the moral vocabulary we employ today. See Daniel Brunstetter and Cian O'Driscoll, eds., *Just War Thinkers: From Cicero to the 21st Century* (New York: Routledge, 2017).
5. Daniel Statman, "Can Just War Theory Justify Targeted Killing? Three Possible Models," in *Targeted Killings: Law and Morality in an Asymmetrical World,* ed. Andrew Altman, Claire Finkelstein, and Jens David Ohlin (Oxford: Oxford University Press, 2012), 90–112, at 94.
6. Micah Zenko, *Between Threats and War: US Discrete Military Operations in the Post–Cold War World* (Stanford, CA: Stanford University Press, 2010), 53.
7. Craig Martin, "Going Medieval: Targeted Killing, Self Defense, and the *Jus Ad Bellum* Regime," in *Targeted Killings*, ed. Altman, Finkelstein, and Ohlin, 223–52, at 249.
8. Scott Shane, "Targeted Killing Comes to Define War on Terror," *New York Times*, April 7, 2013, www.nytimes.com/2013/04/08/world/targeted-killing-comes-to-define-war-on-terror.html?pagewanted=all.

9. "Paris Attacks: How the Saint-Denis Raids Unfolded," BBC, November 19, 2015, www.bbc.com/news/world-34867205.

10. Jane Corbin, "Al-Qaeda Strikes Back," BBC, October 20, 2012, http://news.bbc.co.uk/2/hi/programmes/panorama/2329661.stm.

11. E.g., in Jordan: Joby Warrick and Taylor Luck, "Jordan Disrupts Major al-Qaeda Terrorist Plot," *Washington Post*, October 21, 2012, www.washingtonpost.com/world/national-security/jordan-disrupts-major-al-qaeda-terrorist-plot/2012/10/21/e26354b4–1ba7–11e2–9cd5-b55c38388962_story.html.

12. Yassin Musharbash, "The Arrest of Younis al-Mauretani: On the Trail of the al-Qaida Phantom," *Spiegel*, September 6, 2011, www.spiegel.de/international/world/the-arrest-of-younis-al-mauretani-on-the-trail-of-the-al-qaida-phantom-a-784724.html; Mohammed Ghobari and Aboudi Sami, "Yemen: We Foiled Al-Qaeda Plot to Seize Oil, Gas Plants," NBC, August 7, 2013, www.nbcnews.com/news/other/yemen-we-foiled-al-qaeda-plot-seize-oil-gas-plants-f6C10865627.

13. Compare: Avery Plaw, "Counting the Dead: The Proportionality of Predation in Pakistan," in *Killing by Remote Control: The Ethics of an Unmanned Military*, ed. Bradley J. Strawser (Oxford: Oxford University Press, 2012), 126–53; with Megan Braun and Daniel R. Brunstetter, "Rethinking the Criterion for Assessing CIA Targeted Killings: Drones, Proportionality and *Jus ad Vim*," *Journal of Military Ethics* 12, no. 4 (2013): 304–24.

14. Anthony Dworkin, "Drones and Targeted Killing: Defining a European Problem," 3, www.ecfr.eu/page/-/ECFR84_DRONES_BRIEF.pdf.

15. Jeff McMahan, "Targeted Killing: Murder, Combat or Law Enforcement?" in *Targeted Killings*, ed. Altman, Finkelstein, and Ohlin, 135–56, at 155.

16. Zenko, *Between Threats and War*.

17. Martin Chulov, "ISIS: The Inside Story," *The Guardian*, December 11, 2014, www.theguardian.com/world/2014/dec/11/-sp-isis-the-inside-story?CMP=fb_gu.

18. Michael Walzer, *Arguing about War* (New Haven, CT: Yale University Press, 2004), 11.

19. David Fisher, *Morality and War: Can War Be Just in the Twenty-First Century?* (Oxford: Oxford University Press, 2011); for a critique of the just war tradition, see Robert Myers, "Notes on the Just War Theory: Whose Justice, Which Wars?" *Ethics & International Affairs* 10 (1996).

20. Daniel R. Brunstetter and Megan Braun, "The Implications of Drones on the Just War Tradition," *Ethics & International Affairs* 25, no. 3 (2011): 337–58.

21. Nicholas J. Wheeler, "The Humanitarian Responsibilities of Sovereignty: Explaining the Development of a New Norm of Military Intervention for Humanitarian Purposes in International Society," in *Humanitarian Intervention and International Relations,* ed. Jennifer M. Welsh (Oxford: Oxford University Press, 2004), 29–51, at 36–37. For another view, see Nicholas Onuf, "Humanitarian Intervention: The Early Years," May 5, 2000, www.cgpacs.uci.edu/files/docs/2010/working_papers/nicholas_onuf_humanitarian_intervention.pdf.

22. For an excellent overview of the crucial questions, see the introduction to *Humanitarian and International Relations*, ed. Welsh. For a more recent critical examination of R2P, see Jennifer Welsh, "Implementing the Responsibility to Protect: Where Expectations Meet Reality," *Ethics & International Affairs* 24, no. 4 (2010): 415–30.

23. "Obama's Libya Speech: Full Text as Delivered," *Politico*, March 28, 2011, www.politico.com/news/stories/0311/52093.html.

24. US Department of State, Bureau of Intelligence and Research, "Problems and Prospects of 'Justifying' War with Iraq."

25. Compare, e.g., Nigel Biggar, *In Defense of War* (Oxford: Oxford University Press, 2013); James Turner Johnson, *The War to Oust Saddam Hussein: Just War in the Face of New Conflict* (Lanham, MD: Rowman & Littlefield, 2005); and Craig M. White, *Iraq: The Moral Reckoning* (Lanham, MD: Lexington Books, 2010).

26. Walzer, *Just and Unjust Wars*, xv.

27. Zeke J. Miller, "Obama Makes Case for Strike on Syria," *Time*, September 10, 2013, http://swampland.time.com/2013/09/10/obama-makes-case-for-strike-on-syria/.

28. Michael Walzer, "On Fighting Terrorism Justly," *International Relations* 21 (December 2007): 480–84, at 482.

29. Jeh Charles Johnson Jr., "The Conflict against Al-Qaeda and Its Affiliates: How Will It End?" Speech to the Oxford Union, November 30, 2012, www.lawfareblog.com/2012/11/jeh-johnson-speech-at-the-oxford-union/.

30. Daniel Brunstetter and Megan Braun, "From *Jus ad Bellum* to *Jus ad Vim*: Recalibrating Our Understanding of the Moral Use of Force," *Ethics & International Affairs* 27, no. 1 (2013): 87–106.

31. Rosa Brooks, "Drones and the International Rule of Law," *Ethics & International Affairs* 28, no. 1 (2014): 83–103, at 99.

32. David Luban, "The War on Terror and the End of Human Rights," *Philosophy and Public Policy Quarterly* 22, no. 3 (2002): 9–14, at 10.

33. Ibid., 14.

34. Coady, *Morality and Political Violence*, 93.

35. Ibid.

36. Ibid., 6–7.

37. A more fully developed argument is made by Brunstetter and Braun, "From *Jus Ad Bellum* to *Jus Ad Vim*," 95–103.

38. In terms of published work, see Christian Enemark, "Drones, Risk, and Perpetual Force," *Ethics & International Affairs* 28, no. 3 (2014): 365–81; also see Avery Plaw and Carlos R. Colon, "Correcting the Record: Civilians, Proportionality, and the *Jus ad Vim*," in *Legitamacy and Drones: Investigating the Legality, Morality, and Efficacy of UAVs*, ed. Steven J. Barela (Farnham, UK: Ashgate, 2015), 163–89.

39. Daniel R. Brunstetter, "Trends in Just War Thinking during the US Presidential Debates 2000–12: Genocide Prevention and the Renewed Salience of Last Resort," *Review of International Studies* 40, no. 1 (2013): 77–99.

12

Contesting Sovereignty

Human Security as a New Justification for War?

FRÉDÉRIC RAMEL

> The genie cannot be put back in the bottle: The admittedly limited and sometimes too slow movement on human security is irreversible.
>
> —Laura Neach, "The Future of Human Security"

"I MAY HAVE COINED THE WORD, but I am sure that many others thought similarly. It could become a question of our collective imagination. . . . This idea came to my mind in 1989. It was the end of the Cold War and the Third World. We needed a new paradigm."[1] Jorge Nef, one of the founding fathers of the European International Studies Association, was among the first to use the term "human security" (HS) at the end of 1980s. He established the link between the end of bipolarity and the emergence of HS. Does this represent a paradigm shift or simply hot air? Roland Paris offers two ideas: HS as a rallying cry between heterogeneous actors, or a political campaign that could entail international progress, similar to the antipersonnel land mines convention or the International Criminal Court. For Paris, HS is more a "label for a broad category of research" than a relevant concept because of its inherent ambiguity:[2] "As a new conceptualization of security, or a set of beliefs about the sources of conflict, human security is so vague that it verges on meaninglessness—and consequently offers little practical guidance to academics who might be interested in applying the concept, or to policymakers who must prioritize among competing policy goals."[3]

In other words, hot air more than a paradigm shift! Many scholars share this point of view because HS remains analytically weak,[4] is obviously linked to an outdated notion of neoliberal peace,[5] or is a source of new Western domination of the developing world.[6] This chapter does not follow these research programs, even though my conclusions merge with concerns about domination. Instead, it aims at considering the normative effects of HS in the international arena, paying particular attention to the link between HS and the resort of force in Canadian and US foreign policies. These states have different diplomatic postures toward HS. Canada was a proactive promoter of HS in the 1990s. At the same time, the United States was reluctant to accept HS's promotion outside the American hemisphere. Despite this initial gap between the two countries, their strategic decisions, from Kosovo to Afghanistan and Iraq, highlight normative tensions within HS. This chapter does not aim at exploring the intellectual roots of HS, but rather how HS as a new paradigm nourishes paradoxically new perspectives on military interventions. In doing so, it also highlights two processes connected with the main core of this volume—the present moment as one of contested and fragmented sovereignty. HS calls into question the principle of sovereignty by deepening notions of security beyond the state-centered military perspective—that is, with a focus on the individual and a call for enhanced multilateral cooperation. However, it also seems to unwittingly contribute to reinforcing Western spheres of domination over non-Western states and terrorist groups that may reside within or across them.

This chapter is divided in five sections. In the first section, after explaining the method of conceptual history in order to understand the emergence of a new idea, I describe the shift promoted by the United Nations Development Program (UNDP) in 1994.[7] *Human Development Report 1994* was dedicated to the notion of HS and aimed to change international policies in the security field. In the second section, I set up a link between the components of HS and the intentions of the UNDP, as well as several states that defended this new conception, especially Canada. Nevertheless, these good intentions can have a darker side. Canada's discourse and practices reveal a restrictive conception of HS that focuses on freedom from fear, which paradoxically provides explicit justifications for war, as explained in the third section; US discourse and practices show peripheral acceptance of HS's main intentions, even though these intentions are also the source of implicit justification for war, as delineated in the fourth section. Finally, the fifth section explores how the link to war calls into question the backbone of HS—namely, emancipation from fear and want—and contributes to a new form of domination of non-Western countries in world politics.

CONCEPTUAL HISTORY: A RETURN TO INTENTIONS OF NEW IDEAS

Conceptual history takes the opposing view of what has constituted for decades, if not centuries, the core approach to the study of ideas. The latter approach relies on two major assumptions: The first is the importance of study of great texts, which may be qualified as canonical; the second is that these great texts are addressed to audiences across time, regardless of when they were produced. While focusing on what the authors wrote and applying the concepts universally, regardless of the period when they were conceived, political thought turned its back on a more refined conceptual history. In doing so, we fell into the trap of myths—that is to say, the alleged consistency and unity of concepts throughout history. This is what some would call the mythology of doctrines.[8]

Helge Jordheim and Iver Neumann identify two major approaches to conceptual history.[9] The first aims at bringing to the fore the historical fresco—that is, the study of a concept in a long-term perspective throughout the centuries. Reinhart Koselleck's work epitomizes this approach (Koselleck is one of the main authors of *Geschichtliche Grundbegriffe: Lexikon zur historish-sozialen Sprache in Deutschland* [*Basic Historical Concepts: Encyclopedia of Historical-Social Language in Germany*]). Koselleck pursues a double aim. On one hand, conceptual history is directly linked to present-day preoccupations "in that it is concerned with how the modern world is conceptualized."[10] In other words, it aims at developing an "increased awareness of the concepts we use.'"[11] On the other hand, conceptual history consists in tracing the slow transformations of concepts, and identifying long-term changes. Historical sequences are drawn out in order to link the content of the ideas to the varied social and political processes at play. Conceptual history therefore favors long periods of analysis so as to identify the sometimes multiple shifts in the uses and definitions of a concept.

The representatives of the Cambridge School develop a second position. Unlike a diachronic fresco, which locates the use of concepts in the long term, this school favors to focus on prominent moments in time. This is because concepts, they argue, do not present any unity over time, and therefore must be considered only at particular periods in time. The scholar must first and foremost identify the precise moment when a new concept (or a new use of an existing convention) emerges. He or she must also discern the author's intention. Indeed, the text is defined not only as a discourse but also as an act. The author does something when addressing his or her readers: "The question we accordingly need to confront in studying such texts is what their authors—writing at the time when they wrote for the specific audience they had in mind—could in practice have intended to communicate by issuing their given utterances."[12] Hence, Quentin Skinner concludes with respect to the purpose of conceptual history: "There is no history of the idea to be written. There is only a history of its various uses, and of the varying intentions with which it was used."[13] One must therefore clarify the author's intentions (and precisely clarify the author's participation in the debates of his or her time).

Skinner identifies the main pitfalls the scholar may encounter: anachronism and the error in interpreting the author's intentions. These two risks meet in the mythology of prolepsis—that is, "the type of mythology we are prone to generate when we are more interested in the retrospective significance of a given episode than in its meaning for the agent of the time."[14] Furthermore, texts encompass more than just the great works, according to Skinner. The scholar must also take into account secondary texts and visual or artistic productions.

These insights, I think, are important to keep in mind when examining the concept of HS. In the next section, I employ the main ideas of Skinner's framework to explore the conceptual history of HS. By focusing on intellectual contexts, circulation of conventions, and intentions of agents, I do not use other possible means—that is, scientific or critical approaches—when dealing with concepts in international relations.[15]

A NEW INTENTION FOR SECURITY POLICIES IN THE 1990S

With the second chapter of the UNDP's 1994 report, HS was promoted for the first time in the international arena.[16] The new international configuration after the fall of the Berlin Wall, along with multiple intrastate conflicts, helps to explain the emergence of HS, which focused on dealing with the uncertainties of everyday life.[17] The concept of HS includes a focus on the individual and a call for enhanced multilateral cooperation.[18]

Enlarging and Broadening Security

For the UNDP, "Human security is not a concern with weapons—it is a concern with human life and dignity."[19] This short sentence reveals the core of the concept, which defines people as the source, object, and purpose of security policies. HS relies on two architectural pillars: freedom from want, to prevent persistent and systemic socioeconomic deprivations; and freedom from fear, to struggle against massive violations of human rights or against states that create chaos. The first pillar is broad in order to handle structural violence, while the second is more restrictive and linked to direct physical violence.

HS relies on autonomy in relation to other concepts that appear closely linked. The UNDP emphasizes the distinction between human security and human development, even though the two are interconnected: "The concept of human security stresses that people should be able to take care of themselves: All people should have the opportunity to meet their most essential needs and to earn their own living. This will set them free and help ensure that they can make a full contribution to their own development and that of their communities, their countries and the world."[20]

HS is different, insofar as it must manage two main sources of insecurity: "chronic threats such as hunger, disease and repression," on one hand, and "protection from sudden and hurtful disruptions in the patterns of daily life—whether in homes, in jobs, or in communities"—on the other hand.[21]

But the report goes further. It describes the structure of the concept as consisting of seven components: (1) economic security, for the guarantee of a minimum income that comes from paid work; (2) food security, allowing each individual to have at all times a base allowance; (3) health and safety, which includes the eradication of infectious and parasitic diseases; (4) environmental safety, in order to prevent or to counteract the effects of intensive industrialization and rapid growth of the population; (5) personal security, which corresponds to the protection of human life against various forms of violence; (6) safety of the community, which covers the protection of individuals against oppressive practices imposed by authority figures; and (7) a security policy having as its basis the preservation of fundamental rights. The UNDP stresses the interrelated nature of these various components, in the sense that a threat against one of them is likely to spread to the others, "like an angry typhoon."[22]

These components call into question the centrality of states in the security realm. On top of that, they suggest that states could embody a source of human insecurity. The UNDP defines the individual as the new standard of value in the security field: "Human security is a child who did not die, a disease that did not spread, a job that was not cut, an ethnic tension that did not explode in violence, a dissident who was not silenced."[23]

The report insisted on different measures to promote this new conception at the national level, but also in the international arena. It proposed several indicators that assess human insecurity: the worsening of the food situation, the high rate of unemployment coupled with a fall in wages, violations of human rights, outbreaks of ethnic violence, the strengthening of regional disparities, and the excessive weight of military expenditures. These indicators were considered essential instruments for the implementation of preventive diplomacy to ensure human security. The report then offered a set of recommendations for governments and international institutions to prevent chronic situations and especially to take into account "the indivisibility of global human security—that no one is secure as long as someone is insecure anywhere."[24] Finally, the UNDP focused on direct assistance to the poor. It considered preventive diplomacy to be the major way to handle HS—to avoid, inter alia, the aggravation of situations of instability that could turn into bloody conflicts.

In other words, the UNDP's report intended to break from the classic representations of security in the international relations arena—that is, state-based security. The UNDP also aimed at enlarging the scope of security policies. Military issues thus, in theory at least, became less central, as new, interconnected sectors of security became the more central focus.

Diplomatic Dissemination

Some states took notice of this new concept of security. For instance, the Canadian minister of foreign affairs, Lloyd Axworthy, exclaimed: "We need new approaches and new tools. We need a new form of diplomacy. It will have to be based on collective efforts of a variety of actors, inside and outside of government. It will depend upon our ability to raise people's awareness of fundamental human security needs, and it will require a new and broad-based consensus to address squarely basic human needs and rights affecting the daily lives of millions."[25]

Canada and Norway were the main states that promoted HS at the end of the 1990s. They decided to create a partnership in 1998, with the Lysøen Declaration setting up a coalition of governments that cooperated on a wide range of issues related to peace, conflict, and the protection of human lives. Austria, Chile, Greece, Ireland, Jordan, Mali, the Netherlands, Slovenia, Switzerland, Thailand, and South Africa (as an observer) joined the group. The Canadian government—and, above all, Lloyd Axworthy, who was minister of foreign affairs between 1996 and 2000—played a fundamental role in the development of this partnership.[26] Some scholars go so far as to identify it as a manifestation of the "Axworthy Doctrine."[27] All the coalition members shared the same conception of multidimensional security aimed at protecting people, as well as the same diplomatic practices relying on inclusivity and transparency. We must also bear in mind that the Japanese government played a major role in the evolution of HS. Japan was instrumental in creating the UN Trust Fund for Human Security, which financed more than 170 projects around the world.[28] The shift embodied by HS may be illustrated by the matrix given in figure 12.1.

What is the source of the security threat?

	Military	Military, nonmilitary, or both
States	NATIONAL SECURITY (Conventional, realist approach of security studies)	REDEFINED SECURITY (Environmental and economic security)
Societies	INTRASTATE SECURITY (For example, civil war, ethnic conflict, and genocide)	HUMAN SECURITY (For example, environmental and economic threats to the survival of societies, groups, and individuals).

Figure 12.1 A Matrix of Security Studies

The movement from national security to HS relies on a deep denunciation of Hobbesian political philosophy and all that it embodies for international relations. Hobbes's view of security was born out of the context of the English Civil War. If the state wished to end wars, he argued, it *must* provide security. Hobbes's description of a "state of nature" (a fiction where all people live without political authority characterized by a quarrelsome people) is an allegory for a state of war, which stands for "Hell on Earth." This description allows Hobbes to assert human nature as egoistic, with all people afraid of each other. Hobbes sought to emphasize the properties of fear.[29] How was it possible to overcome fear? The answer, for Hobbes, lies in establishing a Leviathan—an overarching power that provides security by enforcing the rule of law. People decide to end the state of war by alienating their natural rights to a sovereign who provides security; they "unite themselves into a body politic, for their security, both against one another, and against common enemies."[30] This "social contract" entered into between the people and the sovereign is submissive. This "freedom from fear" is a fundamental step toward the modern era of state sovereignty and the conceptions of security this entails. On one hand, it must be borne in mind that Hobbesian thought has been responsible for formulating the main functions of states. Yet, simultaneously, this function has increasingly come to be questioned. Hobbes's concept of security was fairly circumscribed. Since the seventeenth century, new kinds of threats have evolved. Some of these are not a result of deliberate human action, but have developed unexpectedly. Natural disasters are one such kind of threat that humans must face. Furthermore, Hobbes trusted the state. The UNDP report calls into question this perspective because states may have become a source of threat. The main intention of HS is to offer an alternative to this Hobbesian conception of security, even if the Leviathan can be interpreted as the first contribution of a people-centered conception of security.

Finally, the movement from national security to HS seeks "to engage the wide variety of nontraditional threats to the state. Whatever the term, these threats are challenging the traditional views and forcing states to change their perspectives on what may or may not constitute a security risk."[31] This intention aims at enlarging and broadening the concept of security:

- To focus on peoples.
- To reinforce institutional multilateralism.
- To improve the association of societal actors in negotiation and decision processes.

All these require "a rethinking of state sovereignty."[32] Do international events post-1994—the conception of HS—confirm this shift? Some evidence suggests the implementation of this new diplomatic design—for example, the Ottawa Treaty on the prohibition of land mines and the International Criminal Court. Moreover, the discourse of HS has circulated across the globe, from eastern Europe and the post-Soviet countries to Africa and Asia.[33] That said, whereas actors like the European Union include it on their political agenda, other states and even the United Nations seem to have lost their enthusiasm for the concept.[34] Beyond these trends, new dilemmas have emerged that limit the emancipation hopes of HS. These dilemmas are essentially linked to its first pillar: freedom from fear.

CANADA AND HS AS AN EXPLICIT JUSTIFICATION FOR WAR

According to Michael Ignatieff, "Human rights, tolerance, multiculturalism, human security have all served as guiding values for Canadian foreign policy."[35] He links HS with another tenet of Canadian international action, the importance of multilateralism, but then suggests embracing HS could lead Canada down a different path: "Supporting multilateral institutions doesn't always mean singing in the choir. Sometimes we have to take a solo, and we should not be afraid to let our voice ring out. We sang solo on land mines, on human security, and on the Responsibility to Protect."[36] Nevertheless, Canadian governments have adopted a restrictive approach to HS that privileges freedom from fear, which in turn offers explicit reasons to justify war.

The Kosovo Case and the Military Version of HS

In 1999, the discourse of the Canadian government suggested that viewing international relations through the lens of HS helped to legitimize the intervention in Kosovo. According to Prime Minister Jean Chrétien, intervention was justified: "To alleviate poverty in the world or to promote stability and prevent conflict by participating in peacekeeping missions of the United Nations or NATO, Canadians are committed to their responsibilities as citizens of the world."[37] Although HS and cosmopolitanism were interconnected, Chrétien underlined its Canadian dimension. HS was embedded in Canadian tradition and history. He added: "Our participation in this mission of NATO is only the most recent manifestation of a foreign policy dictated not only by our interests, but also by our values. Our values as Canadians. Our fundamental human values."[38]

The same arguments are used in Lloyd Axworthy's discourses. As Canadian minister of foreign affairs, he explained the legitimacy of resorting to force, even though the UN Security Council did not ratify such action, by arguing that there was a duty to protect the Albanian community, which lived in "fear of terror": "NATO is engaged in the conflict in Kosovo to give the Kosovars a safe country. The Alliance was driven by a humanitarian imperative, and is still. Some strategic considerations have certainly played a role in this decision. Indeed, the spread of the conflict in the Balkans, Albania, and the former Yugoslav Republic of Macedonia particularly was, and always is, a risk. However, NATO is essential to ensure respect for the rights and welfare of the Kosovars."[39]

We may add two comments. First, the Canadian government promoted the restrictive concept of HS—freedom from fear—at the expense of prevention and development, even though Canada had significant experience in the field: "Canada, with its reputation as a noncombatant mediator of disputes and innovator of United Nations peacekeeping, might have offered high-level leadership on conflict prevention, development support, and diplomatic alternatives to bombing campaigns to resolve disputed issues, not just in Kosovo but throughout the Balkans and at a much earlier stage."[40]

Second, the government did not see the tension between armed force and the peaceful core of the concept.[41] In Canadian foreign policy, HS was developed in response to nontraditional sources of insecurity in Central America during the 1980s, including organized crime, drug trafficking, environment degradation, disease, and antipersonnel land mines.[42] HS embodied an alternative to American imperialism in the region and was designed to offer solutions to threats that kill people outside classic warfare. The military machine, as it were, was not the backbone of the HS concept initially adopted by the Canadian government. Instead, following the Kosovo crises, freedom from fear and a greater appreciation of military solutions to human security challenges have prevailed over "freedom from want."

From the Kosovo example, we can infer a tension inherent to HS: "A human security regime would require an increase of military interventions to accomplish the humanitarian ideal. Ironically: power for the benefit of justice inexorably increases the use of armed force."[43] Such a trend raises interesting questions about the link between HS and the potential development of *jus ad vim* (as proposed by Brunstetter in chapter 11 of this volume) to guide limited force that could have the potential to enhance HS. Or another way of thinking about this could be discerning how the quest for HS could make the need for limited force obsolete by overcoming the shortcomings of the law enforcement paradigm that Brunstetter elucidates. Originally, HS implicitly was a way to constrain the use of force by focusing instead on pacific operations in order to protect peoples and provide security. With the Kosovo crisis, Canada's government unwittingly revealed the limits of this ideal.

HS as a False Tenet of Canadian Foreign Policy?

Arguably, HS has been "obfuscated" since 2000 in Canadian foreign policy.[44] A first episode that points to this is John Manley's redefinition of Canadian federal foreign policy in 2000, in which domestic economic issues prevail. The conservative turn following Stephen Harper's election reinforced the elimination "of the concept from Canada's foreign policy memory."[45] Today, there is "no explicit mention of the concept" of HS.[46] HS no longer embodies the main area of concern in Canadian foreign policy. Rather, the focus is on Canadian economic sanctions, human rights, international organizations, international security, religious freedom, stabilization, and reconstruction. Even in the human rights section, HS is not cited as a dimension of Canadian action. Furthermore, the dimension of international security does not incorporate the language of HS, as HS was "squeezed out of the governmental discourse."[47]

This squeezing out is also seen at the bureaucratic level. The Human Security Policy Division changed its name and became the Human Rights and Democracy Bureau. The Human Security Program was integrated into a new structure in 2005 called the Global Peace and Security Fund. It was also renamed in 2007 as the Glyn Berry Program: "This program supports the development of Canadian and international policies, laws and institutions that embed core human security objectives of freedom, democracy, human rights and the rule of law into international peace and security efforts in countries outside the [the Global Peace and Security Fund's] priority country envelopes."[48] The Glyn Berry Program is less people centered and more state centered.[49]

Several reasons explain this shift in Canadian foreign policy.[50] These include the possibility of a conscious decision by politicians to distance themselves from Axworthy's concept—or perhaps because the era since the September 11, 2001, terrorist attacks requires deeper diplomatic relations with the United States focused on border control, intelligence, and military capacity.[51] But ideological factors must also be taken into account. The new Liberal government elected in the fall of 2015 may revitalize Canada's HS-centric identity. If this happens, the conservative era would then appear as a parenthesis in the history of the country's foreign policy. The speech from the throne on December 4, 2015, by Prime Minister Justin Trudeau does not refer explicitly to human security. However, some elements are part of the extension of the HS "tradition" initiated by the Liberal governments during the 1990s: the efforts to provide development aid and assistance to the poorest and most vulnerable, and the renewal of Canada's commitment with respect to UN peacekeeping operations. Several favorable signs seem to attest to a return to the diplomatic culture of HS. The new prime minister, Justin Trudeau, appointed Harjit Singh Sajjan and Stéphane Dion to, respectively, the Ministry of Defense and the Ministry of Foreign Affairs. The former is considered to be a specialist on human security; the latter has made the fight against climate change one of the priorities of his political involvement. In addition, the hosting of Syrian refugees by the prime minister himself at the Toronto Airport on December 11, 2015, was a strong symbolic gesture placing the protection of vulnerable populations at the heart of governmental concerns. All these decisions suggest a revival of Canada's reputation as a leader in HS (to which the first press conference of the prime minister also attests). But bureaucratic and financial measures must confirm this trend in the future.

THE UNITED STATES AND HS AS AN IMPLICIT JUSTIFICATION FOR WAR

In contrast to Canada, the United States has not officially adopted HS as a central tenet of its foreign policy. However, after 9/11 and despite HS being on the margins of public discourse, it is implicitly interwoven into the United States' justifications for the war on terror as well as its counterinsurgency campaigns in Afghanistan and Iraq.

HS on the Margins of US Foreign Policy

The United States is not hostile, a priori, to HS. In 1994, the undersecretary of state for global affairs, Timothy Wirth, underlined its relevance.[52] Several speeches by members of the State Department subscribe to this value. Moreover, some even consider HS a part of the American political identity: "Although the term is new, human security describes one of the ideas on which are based the United States: the dignity and worth inherent in the individual. . . . In a sense, we have always been proponents of human security."[53]

However, the application of HS to US foreign policy has been limited. First and foremost, the concept does not frame US foreign policy. The sphere of influence of HS is confined from a geographical point of view, to the American hemisphere especially, and to only certain regions of the world where the US national interest is at stake. The State Department refers to HS when new threats against individuals may affect the security of the United States (e.g., the Colombian question, organized crime, and trafficking in drugs in Latin America). The Charter of the Americas of 2003, as well as various declarations adopted by the summits of the Americas (including the one in Quebec in 2009), refer to HS. Another privileged area is the Arabian Gulf region. For example, the then-secretary of state Hillary Clinton employed the language of HS in her speech at the Manama Dialogue in 2010: "True security is not just the absence of violence. It is also the presence of opportunity. Like the opportunity to receive an education or find a job, to live in a safe environment, to have access to the basics of life—food, water, health care, and housing."[54] In short, HS remains confined to a regional dimension, and it does not entail a reinforcement of universal intergovernmental organizations. Rather, pursuing the ideals of HS comes after national sovereignty.

Regarding the substance of the HS concept, US policy remains state-centric insofar as the best way to fight against human insecurity is to fortify state structures. The state is seen as the true standard for providing security, unlike the paradigm proposed by the UNDP, which prioritized relevant international actors. As a result, HS is approached from the standpoint of the state and not from international institutions. In this sense, any reference to HS is questionable, given that it does not translate into broad partnerships between the United States and foreign states. The struggle for HS does not entail a strengthening of multilateral designs, nor the development of bilateral procedures. Rather, it is a pseudo-multilateralism, which mostly supports the traditional interests of the United States.

HS and the War on Terror

For the United States, the reference to HS is not explicit, because no federal official documents have relied on HS, even though "the US military increasingly finds itself operating in non-war-fighting environments attempting to alleviate human suffering brought on by natural disaster, civil war, and insurgency."[55] Nevertheless, by considering terrorism as the main threat to the United States, the George W. Bush administration implicitly recognized several elements of HS, especially concerning its reasons for waging war—against terrorist groups and certain rogue regimes. Failed or weakened states became a source of new armed conflicts. They also benefited terrorist networks, which operate in these regions and threaten the United States (and the West in general). It is not far of a jump to see how the "war on terror fits easily into the framework that has already been established by HS."[56] Emery's discussion in chapter 9 of the balancing act between security, risk, and uncertainty is illuminating in this regard, even if the notion of security nominally has more to do with "our" security at the expense of others'.

The US intervention in Afghanistan was, somewhat ironically, an opportunity to implicitly implement major tenets of HS. The language of HS is articulated in the main aim of the campaign: "HS is in the end what is going to win this for the government of Afghanistan, and there is a long way to go until, not only that is provided, but people are convinced that it is going to endure. And that's the scale of the challenge."[57] HS is also used officially in the doctrinal documents related to counterinsurgency campaigns in Iraq and Afghanistan. Military action is not an isolated policy but is seen as a way to create the political context for the development and maintenance of public services and individual rights: "The Security Component. Providing physical security against insurgent violence, though often imperative, is only one step in progressing toward Human Security which also encompasses the maintenance of laws, human rights, freedom to conduct economic activity, public safety and health."[58] A campaign of counterinsurgency will be accepted by the local population only if it provides "human security to the population and improve[s] the political and economic situation at the local level."[59] In other words, though US officials do not wield HS as an explicit justification for war, it is worth noting that the concept implicitly underpins US decisions to wage war—and how it does so. It is also worth noting that HS is vital to the *jus post bellum* requirements discussed by Orend in chapter 13 of this volume, though the lack of HS—or, perhaps, the impossibility of truly attaining it—may contribute to the elusiveness of victory discussed by O'Driscoll in chapter 14.

HS AND DOMINATION

One of the risks of linking war to HS is that doing so may link HS to a new form of domination in world politics. The pillars of HS—freedom from fear and freedom from want—could be interpreted as universal values. As the UNDP report pointed out, "Human security is a *universal* concern. It is relevant to people everywhere, in rich nations and poor."[60] HS is based on a strong connection to cosmopolitanism: "HS is not only about the shift of referent object away from a focus on states and raisons d'état, toward individuals, groups and communities. It is about cosmopolitan ideas, transnational movements, and the idea that a universal humanity should frame decisions about who is vulnerable and should be protracted."[61]

However, the language of HS is also part of the normative debate about the Westernization of values. By focusing on individuals, many governments and non-Western scholars see HS as a product of the liberal democratic ethos. Struggling for HS means enlarging the Western conception of human rights. Stated differently, HS is a mechanism of domination through which the West imposes its own norms. In the Asian context, HS has been connected to the Asian values debate, which opposes such universalism. Some Asian governments have sought to differentiate between Asian and Western conceptions of human rights: a communitarian ethos based on a "society-before-self" tradition versus an individualist ethos. They also have been opposed to Western campaigns that are limited to political rights by promoting the principle of "nonselectivity." I have explored elsewhere a way of reconciling these challenges by focusing on the liberalism of fear developed by Judith Shklar.[62] According to Shklar, fear is a *universal emotion*.[63]

Shklar underscores the fact that all people can be victims. The "liberalism of fear" does not have a specific origin. It does not result from a particular culture or tradition. And its opposite—the absence of fear—is a desirable end that is shared globally. All people refuse the fear of fear, and proactively seek to reject the conditions of such a feeling, regardless of the times when they live or their geographical locations. Lindemann and Giacomelli underline this in chapter 2 of this volume, referring to the impact of fear on the decision to intervene in Libya. Many political leaders and soldiers had in mind the tragedy of Rwanda during the 1990s. They tried to avoid the same phenomenon when observing Gaddafi's practices. In other words, the liberalism of fear became a justification for intervention. But this dimension is also a source of normative tension, especially with regards to the Responsibility to Protect (R2P).

HS and R2P are interconnected, even though they must also be distinguished. On one hand, HS is "encapsulated" in R2P.[64] The International Commission on International Intervention and State Sovereignty puts HS at the center of the issue. Also, a report on R2P argues: "There is a growing recognition worldwide that the protection of human security, including human rights and human dignity, must be one of the fundamental objectives of modern international institutions."[65] On the other hand, R2P is not the only way to ensure HS.[66]

The rise of R2P highlights a current, problematic trend vis-à-vis sovereignty and the role of international law in upholding international peace and security. Historically, international law relied on the right of coexistence in the international realm as applied to states (regardless of what they did within their borders). Its main function was to ensure the negative freedom of states. International law did not intervene in the domestic affairs of states, and especially not in the choice of domestic rules.[67] This principle of tolerance produced international law that served only as a "law *between* states."[68] In the postcolonial and post-bipolar era, this classic understanding of international law as pluralist has come under great scrutiny. The development of socioeconomic inequalities along with armed conflicts within nation-states has tended to modify the initial project of international law, which cannot be reduced to only coexistence. Rather, it now must deal with dimensions that had been monopolized by states for decades, such as the protection of human rights and development. HS resonates with this transformation. But it also entails a normative cleavage between states. For instance, the promotion of such new values by Western states is perceived as a form of domination or as the practice of holding double standards. NATO's intervention in Libya was a major event that demonstrates this divide. Emerging powers proposed alternatives: responsibility while protecting (Brazil) or responsible protection (China). The proponents of these conceptions of intervention distanced themselves from a maximalist interpretation that confounded the "regulation and reinvention of political regimes."[69] But they relied on several ideas that would ultimately weaken the development of a robust R2P, as described by Hehir in chapter 1 of this volume. This is because they did not, as Hehir might hope, step back from the old-fashioned architecture of states as moral agents.

FROM FEAR TO WANT: POSTCONFLICT RECONSTRUCTION AND THE DILEMMAS OF HS

The dynamics caused by the emergence of HS led to a broad discussion within the United Nations at the end of the 1990s. This had consequences for the conception of sovereignty. Sovereignty was not marginalized but was reformulated in articulation with the requirements of HS. In 2001, the International

Commission on Intervention and State Sovereignty shifted states' objectives from controlling territoriality to protecting peoples. The 2005 summit endorsed a concept of R2P through the use of force articulated in paragraphs 138 and 139 of the final declaration. States retain the first level of responsibility to protect their populations against genocide, war crimes, ethnic cleansing, and crimes against humanity. The responsibility of the "international community," and more specifically the UN Security Council, remains secondary. These various texts have contributed to a change in the design of sovereignty. They emphasize the pivotal and major role that states play in providing for human security (whereas before, sovereignty did not carry this duty with it). A report of the UN secretary-general in 2012 goes in the same direction by stressing the initial role of states regarding HS. To improve HS means to increase state capacities: "Human security calls for comprehensive, people-centred, context-specific and prevention-oriented actions that help to improve the capacities of governments and peoples."[70]

This idea of capacity building materialized with the programs for security sector reform that are essential in postconflict situations: "The HS discourse has also played a pivotal role in the development of the concept and practice of [security sector reform], as well as providing justification for greater involvement of the development community in security-related issues."[71] But these programs entail two consequences linked to the theme of domination. First, they are imposed from outside, even if the imposers hail the appropriation of the values and political and social instruments of the local population.[72] Paradoxically, these populations are more exposed to normative pressures than before—that is, within the framework of an international law limited to the coexistence of the states: "Citizens in weak or unstable states may arguably have even less freedom or power than under the old pluralist security framework."[73] Sometimes, nongovernmental organizations or other interveners become the substitutes for the established institutions in postconflict periods.[74]

Second, focusing on the state enables these programs to avoid the legal definition of HS, which would radically constrain governments. This allows states to follow their own interpretations of HS, and insulates them from any sanctions in the event of failure. The UN secretary-general's report prefers to qualify HS as an "operational and policy framework"—that is, a more flexible definition.[75] This loose conception is particularly worrisome, in part because it reaffirms the discrepancy between the need for more HS and the incapacity of the current world system, despite calls for multilateralism and empowerment of the UN, to achieve the emancipatory goals of HS.

CONCLUSION: FROM INTERVENTION JUSTIFIED TO EMANCIPATION DENIED

Security is an essentially contested concept. This contestation results from the fact that the meaning of security changes over time. Since the end of the Cold War, new conceptions of security have been promoted in order to call into question the state-centric perspective and military dimensions often associated with achieving security. As defined in the United Nations Development Program's *Human Development Report 1994*, HS illustrates this critical trend by focusing on people as individuals. The main intention of this concept is to challenge classic representations of security: "It appears to be one of the central categories through which the changing nature of security discourses and policy practices is understood and analysed."[76] That being said, despite all these good intentions, HS generates strategic and conceptual tensions:

- Between a pacific dimension of HS and the resort to force that HS may require for state representatives in specific situations (*the paradox of instrumentality*) and
- Between the responsibility of powerful states as primary moral agents for HS and a new dependency of peoples in the Global South on external actors that implement HS policies (*the paradox of dependency*).

The Canadian and US cases illustrate these two paradoxes. HS disappears from the horizon as a central tenet of Canadian foreign policy. The promise of emancipation—freedom from fear, freedom from want, and freedom for people to make their own decisions—inherent to the project of HS is thus denied, as new, state-centric priorities take their place. HS is also not a central tenet of US foreign policy. To the extent that it appears in a latent way within the war on terror or with the adoption of the counterinsurgency doctrine in Afghanistan and in Iraq, emancipation is also denied, as HS becomes a justification for war. And war, of course, leads to conditions of fear and insecurity, as Emery duly illustrates in chapter 9. Although HS aims to change international representations of and practices to ensure security, it has also, problematically, been used to justify the use of force during the war on terror era. In short, despite the initial promise of the innovative perspectives of HS, these paradoxes point to substantial limitations. They illustrate a militarization of HS in specific contexts of intervention, specifically those that relied on the humanitarian argument (in Kosovo) and the war of terror rhetoric (in the post-9/11 context in the United States).

All notions related to HS—such as intervention, human rights, and global justice—have a tragic dimension. In a context "where duties are in a radical conflict, we have to acknowledge that to act is to do wrong."[77] HS is not an exception to this rule. As Laura Neach has pointed out: "The genie cannot be put back in the bottle."[78] But it could generate both turbulence in world politics and tensions with the emancipation project that it promises. One of the most pressing challenges regarding the "ethics of HS" for the future is thus to reconnect strategic practices to this promise of emancipation.

NOTES

The epigraph is from Laura Neach, "The Future of Human Security," in *State Responses to Human Security*, ed. Countrey Hillbrecht, Tyler R. White, and Patrice C. McMahon (London: Routledge, 2014), 187.

1. Jorge Nef, quoted by David G. Haglund and Jennifer N. Ross, "La sécurité humaine sur le Champ de Bataille," in *La Sécurité Humaine: Une Nouvelle Conception des Relations Internationales*, ed. Charles-Philippe David and Jean-François Rioux (Montreal: L'Harmattan, 2001), 287.

2. Roland Paris, "Human Security: Hot Air or Paradigm Shift?" *International Security* 26, no. 2 (2001): 96.

3. Ibid., 102.

4. Barry Buzan, "A Reductionist, Idealistic Notion," *Security Dialogue* 35, no. 3 (2004): 369–70; and Edward Newman, "A Normatively Attractive but Analytically Weak Concept," *Security Dialogue* 35, no. 3 (2004): 358–59.

5. Oliver P. Richmond, "Post-Colonial Hybridity and the Return of Human Security," in *Critical Perspectives on Human Security: Rethinking Emancipation and Power in International Relations*, ed. David Chandler and Nik Hynek (London: Routledge, 2011), 43–55.

6. Mark Duffield and Nicholas Waddell, *Human Security and Global Danger: Exploring a Governmental Assemblage* (Lancaster: University of Lancaster, Department of Politics and International Relations, 2004); and Chandler and Hynek, *Critical Perspectives on Human Security.*

7. United Nations Development Program, *Human Development Report 1994* (New York: United Nations, 1994), http://hdr.undp.org/sites/default/files/reports/255/hdr_1994_en_complete_nostats.pdf.

8. Quentin Skinner, *Visions of Politics*, vol. 1 (Cambridge: Cambridge University Press, 2002).

9. Helge Jordheim and Iver Neumann, "Empire, Imperialism, and Conceptual History," *Journal of International Relations and Development* 14, no. 2 (2011): 153–85.

10. Otto Brunner, Werner Conze, and Reinhart Koselleck, *Geschichtliche Grundbegriffe: Lexikon zur historish-sozialen Sprache in Deutschland* (1972), xiv.

11. Jordheim and Neumann, "Empire, Imperialism, and Conceptual History," 157.

12. Skinner, *Visions of Politics*, 86–87.

13. Ibid., 85.

14. Ibid., 73.

15. Felix Berenskoetter, ed., *Concepts in World Politics* (London: Sage, 2016).

16. The idea of HS was already developed in the epistemic community, from Galtung to the constructivists. On the genealogy of HS, see Roland Paris, "Human Security: Paradigm Shift or Hot Air?" *International Security* 26, no. 2 (2001): 87–105, at 102–5; and David Bosold, "Development of the Human Security Field: A Critical Examination," in *Critical Perspectives on Human Security*, ed. Chandler and Hynek, 28–42, at 30–33.

17. See note 8.

18. HS is not new in the academic literature. See Amartya Sen, "Birth of a Discourse," in *The Routledge Handbook of Human Security*, ed. Mary Martin and Taylor Owen (London: Routledge, 2014), 17–27.

19. United Nations Development Program, *Human Development Report 1994*, 22.

20. Ibid., 24.

21. Ibid., 3.

22. Ibid., 33.

23. Ibid., 22.

24. Ibid., 39.

25. Lloyd Axworthy, "Now for a New Diplomacy to Fashion a New World," *International Herald Tribune*, October 21, 1998.

26. Lloyd Axworthy, "Canada and Human Security: The Need for Leadership," *International Journal* 52, no. 2 (1997): 183–96.

27. Fen Olser Hampson and Dean F. Oliver, "Pulpit Diplomacy: A Critical Assessment of the Axworthy Doctrine," *International Journal* 52, no. 3 (1998): 379–407.

28. Matthew S. Weinert, "From State Security to Human Security?" in *The Ashgate Research Companion Research in Ethics and International Relations*, ed. Patrick Hayden (Farnham, UK: Ashgate, 2009), 151–65.

29. Thomas Hobbes, *Leviathan* (Cambridge: Cambridge University Press, 1996), chap. 17.

30. Thomas Hobbes, *The Elements of Law* (Oxford: Oxford World's Classic, 2008), 108.

31. Tyler R. White, "The Emerging Picture of Human Security," in *State Responses to Human Security: At Home and Abroad*, ed. Courtney Hillebrecht, Tyler R. White, and Patrice C. McMahon (London: Routledge, 2014), 216.

32. Don Hubert, "An Idea That Works in Practice," *Security Dialogue* 35, no. 3 (2004): 351.

33. Amitav Acharya, "Human Security," in *The Globalization of World Politics: An Introduction to International Relations*, ed. John Baylis, Steve Smith, and Patricia Owens (Oxford: Oxford University Press, 2008), 492–505.

34. Mary Martin and Taylor Owen, "The Second Generation of Human Security: Lessons from the UN and the EU Experience," *International Affairs* 86, no. 1 (2010): 211–24.

35. Michael Ignatieff, "Peace, Order and Good Government: A Foreign Policy Agenda for Canada," O. D. Skelton Lecture, 2004, www.international.gc.ca/odskelton/ignatieff.aspx?lang=eng.

36. Ibid.

37. Premier Ministre du Canada, "Discours du premier ministre Jean Chrétien à l'occasion d'un déjeuner offert par le Cercle canadien de Winnipeg," *Discours*, Cabinet du Premier Ministre, Ottawa, March 25, 1999.

38. Ibid.

39. Ministère des Affaires Etrangères et du Commerce International, "Le Kosovo et le programme de sécurité humaine," speech by Lloyd Axworthy at the Woodrow Wilson School of Princeton University, *Déclarations et Discours* 99, no. 28 (Ottawa, April 7, 1999).

40. Wayne Nelles, "Canada's Human Security Agenda in Kosovo and Beyond: Military Intervention versus Conflict Prevention," *International Journal* 52, no. 3 (2002): 461.

41. Haglund and Ross, "La securite humaine," 294.

42. Ibid., 290–91.

43. Charles-Philippe David and Jean-François Rioux, "Le concept de sécurité humaine," in *La Sécurité Humaine*, ed. David and Rioux, 26.

44. Heather A. Smith, "Diminishing Human Security: The Canadian Case," in *A Decade of Human Security: Global Governance and New Multilateralisms*, ed. Sandra J. MacLean, Timothy M. Shaw, and David R. Black (Farnham, UK: Ashgate, 2006), 73–82.

45. Keith Krause, "Critical Perspectives on Human Security," in *Routledge Handbook of Human Security*, ed. Martin and Owen, 86.

46. Ibid., 87.

47. Smith, "Diminishing Human Security," 73.

48. "Evaluation of the Global Peace and Security Fund," *Foreign Affairs and International Trade Canada Executive Report*, February 2011, 3, www.international.gc.ca/about-a_propos/oig-big/2011/evaluation/gpsf_fpsm11.aspx?lang=eng.

49. Ibid., 29.

50. David Morin and Stéphane Roussel, "Autopsie de la politique étrangère de Stephen Harper: Un examen préliminaire," *Canadian Foreign Policy Journal* 20, no. 1 (2014): 1–8.

51. Smith, "Diminishing Human Security," 78–79.

52. Timothy E. Wirth, "Sustainable Development and National Security," address before the National Press Club, Washington, July 12, 1994, in *Dispatch* (US Department of State) 55, no. 30 (1994).

53. Kenneth H. MacKay, "Human Security in the Americas," Remarks to the 30th General Assembly of the Organization of American States, Windsor, Canada, June 4–6, 2000, www.state.gov/www/policy_remarks/2000/000605_mackay_oasga.html.

54. Hillary Clinton, "Manama Dialogue Opening Dinner," US Department of State, December 3, 2010, www.state.gov/secretary/20092013clinton/rm/2010/12/152354.htm.

55. Derek S. Reveron and Kathleen A. Mahoney-Norris, *Human Security in a Borderless World* (Boulder, CO: Westview Press, 2011), 18.

56. Tara McCormack, "The Limits to Emancipation in the Human Security Framework," in *Critical Perspectives on Human Security*, ed. Chandler and Hynek, 104.

57. "Department of Defense Bloggers Roundtable with Major Shannon Beebe, US Army, Office of the Deputy Chief of Staff for Intelligence Subject: African Security via Teleconference Time," US Department of Defense, 1:00 p.m. EDT, Wednesday, October 29, 2008.

58. "Counterinsurgency Guide," US Department of State, January 2009, 17, www.state.gov/t/pm/ppa/pmppt.

59. Ibid., 18.

60. United Nations Development Program, *Human Development Report 1994*, 22.

61. Mary Martin and Taylor Owen, "Introduction," in *Routledge Handbook of Human Security*, ed. Martin and Owen, 1–14.

62. Frédéric Ramel, "Political Philosophy and Human Security in the Light of Judith Shklar's Writing," *Human Security Journal* 5 (Winter 2007): 28–35.

63. Judith Shklar, "The Liberalism of Fear," in *Liberalism and the Moral Life*, ed. Nancy Rosenblum (Cambridge, MA: Harvard University Press, 1989), 29.

64. Eric Marclay, "La responsabilité de protéger: Un nouveau paradigme ou une boîte à outils?" November 2005, 9, www.institutidrp.org/contributionsidrp/eric%20marclay%202005.pdf.

65. ICISS, "The Responsibility to Protect: December," International Development Research Centre, Ottawa, 2004, 9, responsibilitytoprotect.org/ICISS%20Report.pdf.

66. Sandra Szurek, "La responsabilité de protéger: Mauvaises querelles et vraies questions," *Anuario Colombiano de Derecho Internacional* 4 (2011): 47–69.

67. James Turner Johnson, *Sovereignty: Moral and Historical Perspectives* (Washington, DC: Georgetown University Press, 2014).

68. Emmanuelle Tourme-Jouannet, *Le Droit international* (Paris: PUF, 2013), 10.

69. B. Badie, "1973: La situation Libyenne en Jamahiriya Arabe Libyenne," in *Les grandes résolutions du Conseil de sécurité des Nations Unies*, ed. Mélanie Albaret, Emmanuel Decaux, Nicolas Lemay-Hébert, and Delphine Placidi-Frot (Paris: Dalloz, 2012), 562.

70. UN Secretary-General, *Report on Human Security*, A/66/763 (New York: United Nations, 2012), www.un.org/humansecurity/sites/www.un.org.humansecurity/files/n1228537.pdf.

71. Mandy Turner, Neil Cooper, and Michael Pugh, "Why Human Security Has Lost Its Way," in *Critical Perspectives on Human Security*, ed. Chandler and Hynek, 86.

72. Severine Autesserre, *Peaceland: Conflict Resolution and the Everyday Politics of International Intervention* (Cambridge: Cambridge University Press, 2014).

73. McCormack, "Limits to Emancipation," 110.

74. Madeline Kristoff and Liz Panarelli, "Haiti: A Republic of NGOs?" United States Institute of Peace, April 26, 2010, www.usip.org/publications/haiti-republic-of-ngos.

75. UN Secretary-General, *Report on Human Security*; and Neach, "Future of Human Security."

76. Chandler and Hynek, *Critical Perspectives on Human Security*, 1.

77. Chris Brown, "Tragedy, Tragic Choices and Contemporary International Political Theory," *International Relations* 21, no. 1 (2007): 9.

78. Neach, "Future of Human Security," 187.

PART IV

Is Victory Really Enough?

13

Jus Post Bellum, Contested and Fragmented Sovereignty, and the Limits of Postwar Rehabilitation

BRIAN OREND

SINCE THE FALL OF THE BERLIN WALL in 1989, and the inauguration of an important new era in international relations, we have learned much. One of the topics connected with armed conflict about which we have learned the most—since that unforgettable moment twenty-five years ago—deals with the postwar situation, or *jus post bellum* (justice after war). This is to say: *What should we do as wars wrap up toward an end?* I have spent time trying to make sense of different postwar situations and policy options, and believe the past twenty-five years have witnessed a diverse range of postwar experiences, each of which has taught valuable lessons. Apart from studying historical cases, and just trying to analyze basic laws and concepts that might apply, my own intellectual advocacy has focused on suggesting that what I call "the rehabilitative model" of postwar justice is superior to its rival, "the retributive model." *I still believe this today, though I think the recent past in particular shows us some important limits to what we can expect of, and require from, postwar rehabilitation.* The point of this chapter is to provide a sense of the scope of these models, their pros and cons, giving some historical cases, but with a special focus on what we have recently learned (particularly in Iraq and Afghanistan) about the limits of postwar rehabilitation and what is actually possible during postwar reconstruction. These limits and lessons have much to do with the theme, and reality, of contested and fragmented sovereignty.

THREE POSTWAR MODELS, ACTUALLY

In the past, I made much of this fierce clash between the two rival models of postwar policy, retribution and rehabilitation.[1] On one hand, this is fine and true, as these models have dominated historical practice and are quite opposed conceptually, normatively, and in terms of the consequences they typically create. On the other hand, research and thinking during the recent past has led me to see, and better appreciate, that there is a robust and important *common ground between them*. Let us thus diagram the major postwar options in figure 13.1.

This threefold reality is important to note not merely for the sake of avoiding Big Bad Binaries (so to speak), but also especially for the following reason: I have published much on the need for there to be a new Geneva Convention dealing exclusively with postwar justice.[2] Sadly unregulated by international law,[3] the postwar situation cries out for the same kind of regulation that attends to the outbreak of war (*jus ad bellum*) and conduct during war (*jus in bello*).[4] But then I have further argued that the substance of such a new Geneva Convention should include the principles of the rehabilitative model.[5] Although I still believe this (in my heart of hearts), I now also believe that—as a result of the considerable difficulties with some recent high-profile cases of rehabilitation (e.g., in Iraq and Afghanistan)—there will be very little political appetite in the near future for including such substantial elements of postwar rehabilitation. Thus, my new, modified position is that *the most important thing is to*

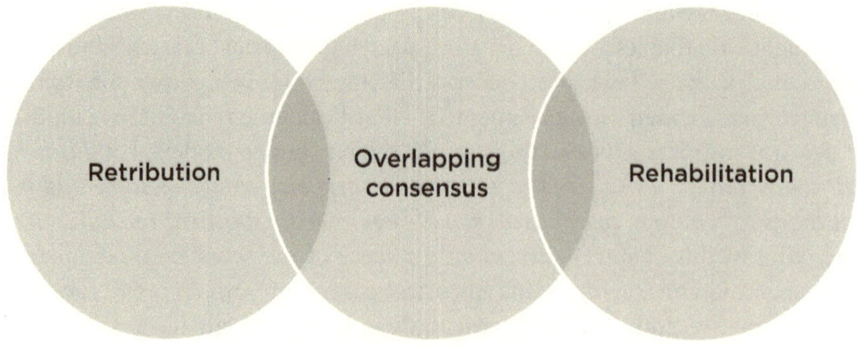

Figure 13.1 Three Postwar Models of Justice

fill in the law-of-war gap during the postwar moment—it is better to have some than none—because there *is* a common ground between the two rival theories. Let us call it "the overlapping consensus" or "thin theory of postwar justice." *This third model should serve as the most promising initial basis for any move to create new international laws regulating the postwar moment.* This is, to an extent, an admitted step down, yet (1) such would also mark progress over the status quo and (2) it is based on a realistic diagnosis of how the fracturing of those societies, even in spite of rehabilitation, has called into question how ambitious one can be about postwar reconstruction in our new and different time.

WHY REGULATE POSTWAR SITUATIONS?

Why does the postwar moment need to be regulated at all? There are at least six reasons. *The first is completion.* There are many international laws regulating both *jus ad bellum* and *jus in bello*. Moreover, many of these laws make sound strategic sense and good moral sense.[6] Thus, to complete our analysis of war's many effects on international life, we need to consider the ending phase of war. The bottom line: If it is important to guide both *the start* and *the middle*, it is just as important to guide *the end*.

The second reason is focus. The practical task of drafting and then ratifying a binding legal document on this issue would focus international attention on doing something constructive and improving about war in general, and take *jus post bellum* out of abstract theory and into the concrete reality of global politics. It would keep up the momentum regarding such recent reforms to the laws of armed conflict as the formation of the International Criminal Court, and the recent treaties banning land mines and the use of child soldiers.[7]

The third reason is guidance. The function of any kind of law is to guide behavior, hopefully in a way that is useful, advantageous, and improving for all.[8] The laws of *jus ad bellum* and *jus in bello* are designed to guide the behavior of all belligerents. The rules of *jus post bellum* could likewise guide both winner and loser in the aftermath of armed conflict. This is assuming there even *is* a clear-cut winner and loser, which sometimes *is not* the case, such as with the Iran-Iraq War of 1979–89, when the belligerents just stopped fighting after—eventually—realizing that neither of them could prevail.[9] *Both winners and losers would gain by there being clear postwar rules.* The losers, of course, could be assured that they would not be subjected to cruel, vindictive treatment at the hands of a gloating, arrogant winner. And the winners could get a clear understanding of their rights and obligations during the aftermath of war. In particular, winners would appreciate being able to point to such rules and say:

"Look, we've done what we're duty-bound to do, and now we are out of here." Rules provide assurances and expectations for everyone, plus clear ways of proceeding, and all parties benefit from such clarity and can put greater confidence in the process.[10]

The fourth reason is ending the fighting. Failure to regulate war termination probably prolongs fighting on the ground. Because belligerents have few assurances, or firm expectations, regarding the nature of the settlement, they will be sorely tempted to keep using force to jockey for position. And because international law imposes very few constraints on the winners of war, the losers can conclude it is reasonable for them to refuse to surrender and, instead, to continue to fight. Perhaps, they think: "We might get lucky and the military tide will turn. Better that than just throw ourselves at the mercy of our enemy." Many observers felt this reality plagued the Bosnian Civil War (1992–95), which had many failed negotiations and a three-year slow burn of continuous violence as the negotiations took place.[11]

The fifth reason is restraining the winner. Failure to construct principles of *jus post bellum* is to allow unconstrained war termination. And to allow unconstrained war termination is, indeed, to allow the winner to enjoy the spoils of war. This is dangerously permissive because winners have been known to exact peace terms that are draconian and vengeful (e.g., the Treaty of Versailles, terminating World War I in 1918–19).

And the sixth reason is preventing future wars. When wars are wrapped up badly, they sow the seeds for future bloodshed. Some people, for example, think that America's failure to remove Saddam Hussein from power after it first defeated him in 1991 prolonged a serious struggle and eventually necessitated the second war, of regime change, in 2003. *Would the second war have happened at all if the first one had ended differently*—that is, more properly and thoroughly, with a longer-range vision in mind? Many historians ask this exact same question of the two world wars and the more recent, related "Serb wars," first in Bosnia and then over Kosovo (1999).[12]

Peace treaties should still, of course, remain tightly tailored to the historical realities of the particular conflict in question. There is much nitty-gritty detail that is integral to each peace treaty. But admitting this is *not* to concede that the search for general guidelines, or universal standards, is futile or naive. There is no inconsistency, or mystery, in holding particular actors in complex local conflicts up to more general, even universal, standards of conduct. Judges and juries do this on a daily basis, evaluating the factual complexities of a given case in light of general moral and legal principles. We should do the same regarding war termination.[13]

STARTING ASSUMPTIONS, AND REPLIES TO INITIAL CHALLENGES

When does the end begin? The answer is not as simple as it may seem at first. Some have argued that the "termination phase" of war often does not have a clear starting point and/or that the notion of victory itself can be quite vague.[14] Daniel Brunstetter, in chapter 11 of this volume, correctly problematizes the first query, and Cian O'Driscoll, in chapter 14, does the same for the second one. These are important, interconnected issues: When will the norms of *jus post bellum* kick in? And kick out, as it were? Locating the exact "end" of war may, at times, be quite difficult; and it may turn out, as already noted, that victory is only one possible outcome (alongside defeat, indeterminacy, military victory but political loss, vice versa, etc.). Thus, *we should think of the war termination phase, crucially, as a kind of process*—along a continuum—wherein there are not razor-sharp distinctions between the *jus in bello* phase and the *jus post bellum* phase; and the end result may be a number of things, with victory for one side being only one—albeit important—option.[15]

The vagueness of victory is a significant conceptual challenge. O'Driscoll does a great job, in chapter 14, of problematizing the concept of victory and suggesting that its actual achievement is probably not the historical norm and is much mythologized and even "Disney-fied" (especially by political leaders keen on cloaking themselves in its triumphal garb). Though conceding such important points, the way I prefer to think of this issue is as follows. The reason why most conceptions of postwar justice focus on (or even assume) victory is not simplemindedness or a failure to realize that wars can end in truly messy and muddled ways. Rather, the focus is methodological; it is just easier to start with more ideal cases and then move to messier ones. Thus, when we talk about *jus post bellum*, it is just easier to take the ideal case where the just side (in terms of *jus ad bellum*, e.g., the Victim of an aggressive invasion) has achieved a clear victory (e.g., over the prior Aggressor, whose actions triggered the war), and then ask about rights and duties in those situations. This turns out to be surprisingly hard in itself, and laden with controversy (as is shown below). *But it needs to be done before moving on to the more complex cases.* Think of it as directly analogous to *jus ad bellum*: In the ideal case there, you have the vital, foundational concepts of (1) aggression and (2) defense from aggression. These two binary concepts are absolutely central in both the morality and law of *jus ad bellum*.[16] One thinks through the rights and duties in such an ideal case, and then uses them to wade into such trickier, more advanced concepts as preventive war and anticipatory attack, civil war, armed humanitarian intervention, asymmetrical war against nonstate actors, and so on.[17] We are here firmly in the realm of the ideal, trying to make sense of the best concepts and principles, and then to apply them to more muddled and difficult cases. Hence, it is useful to consider several simplifying starting assumptions (*already embedded in the existing laws of armed conflict*)[18] about Aggressor and Victim, loss and victory, and—as shown below—retribution versus rehabilitation as postwar policy.

As a helpful initial claim, spurred on by O'Driscoll's challenges, I would say that victory (if it has happened at all) has been achieved *when the goal for which the war was started has been achieved*; for example, if the goal was to repulse an Aggressor and kick it out of the Victim country that it had invaded, then the *post bellum* phase begins when this has been achieved. There may still be some actual fighting going on at that time, but clearly the victorious country will then move to shut down the violence after that point. This would be a gray area between *jus in bello* and *jus post bellum.* Once the violence has subsided (usually accompanied by a cease-fire or surrender)—and emphatically if the regime of the Aggressor has collapsed—then it becomes progressively clearer that we have entered an important new and different phase of war termination and possibly postwar occupation and regime transformation. Not to pretend that such is a complete definition of victory—merely a useful, prima facie one for the purposes of moving our discussion onward.[19]

Still another challenge is idealization. Conceptions of postwar justice make idealized assumptions about when the war termination process has begun and what victory might look like, and they take their initial cues from straightforward cases where the war has actually served the cause of justice—for example, by the Aggressor losing to the Victim and/or to any third-party Vindicators who have helped the Victim defend itself and its rights. Such circumstances might not actually occur in the real world, and it might even be only a minority of real-world cases where such a happy victory has been achieved (say, Nazi Germany losing World War II). However, in worst cases—say, where the Aggressor has won—we cannot meaningfully speak of postwar *justice*, so the war termination phase would be beyond the pale to begin with. *Any kind of law involves a kind of idealization, both of human behavior and social expectation.* This is the case because it is trying to hold people to a higher level of conduct than they might otherwise be tempted to display. The fact that such ideals are only imperfectly realized in the real world (e.g., not everyone obeys traffic speeding laws) is no reason to give up on the law or the improved behavior it sets out as its goal.[20]

WITH WHAT PRINCIPLES SHOULD ONE REGULATE POSTWAR SITUATIONS?

Thus, there is a legal vacuum in the postwar moment, and it should be filled—for the reasons stated above—but with what principles (as guided by the starting assumptions)? As stated and diagrammed, there are three basic models of postwar justice to choose from, and the "bird's-eye view" of their essences are as follows.

The first basic model is an *overlapping consensus, or the Thin Theory*. Its goal is vindicating the rights whose violation triggered the war, forcing the defeated Aggressor to accept a proportionate policy on surrender that includes a cease-fire and public terms of settlement; that there be a mutual exchange of prisoners of war (POWs); that the Aggressor apologize; that the Aggressor give up any unjust gains that it may have won during the war; that the Aggressor at least partially demilitarize; and that there be war crimes trials (*jus ad bellum* trials for the Aggressor; and *jus in bello* trials for all sides).

The second basic model is *Thick Theory 1: Retribution*. Its goal is to make the defeated Aggressor *worse off* than before the war (as backward-looking punishment). Its means include all the Thin Theory terms given above, plus compensation payments from the Aggressor to the Victim, and possibly to the international community more broadly; sanctions put on the Aggressor, to hamper its future economic growth; and no aid or assistance with postwar reconstruction, which is left up to the locals, with no forcible regime change imposed on the Aggressor.

The third basic model is *Thick Theory 2: Rehabilitation*. Its goal is to make the defeated Aggressor *better off* than before the war (as forward-looking reconstruction). Its means include all the Thin Theory terms given above, plus no compensation payments; no sanctions; aid and assistance with postwar reconstruction, possibly including forcible regime change imposed on the defeated Aggressor; and following a ten-step "rehabilitation recipe" (see below), with the best efforts over ten to fifteen years postwar, to realize in the defeated former Aggressor a new, and minimally just, society.

I have written extensively about the nature and justification of these three models, alongside relevant historical cases, and cannot replicate everything here.[21] However, apart from this initial bird's-eye encapsulation of the major policies, I need to provide more details about *the principles within* these models, and their pros and cons.

THE THIN THEORY'S SIX MAIN PRINCIPLES

The Thin Theory's first principle is a public peace treaty. Although it does not need to be nitpicky in detail, the basic elements of a peace agreement should be written down and publicly proclaimed so that everyone's expectations are clear, everyone knows the war is over, and everyone has an idea of what the general framework of the new postwar era will be.

Its second principle is an exchange of POWs. At war's end, all sides need to exchange all the POWs from the armed conflict.

Its third principle is an apology from the Aggressor. The Aggressor in war, like the criminal in domestic society, needs to admit fault and guilt for causing the war by committing aggression. This may seem quaint and elemental, yet it can be quite controversial. For example, Germany has offered many, and profuse, official apologies for World War II, and especially for the Holocaust. Indeed, Germany to this day still pays an annual reparations fee to Israel for the latter. By contrast, Japan has been nowhere near as forthcoming with a meaningful, official apology for World War II. This reticence enrages China, in particular, which suffered mightily from Japanese aggression and expansion in the 1930s.

Its fourth principle is that the Aggressor must give up any war gains. The thinking here is that the Aggressor, as the wrongdoer, cannot be rewarded for its aggression and be allowed to keep any gains it may have won for itself during its aggression. For instance, during its initial campaign in 1992–94, the Serb side of the Bosnian Civil War initially conquered 70 percent of Bosnia—way beyond the area traditionally occupied by ethnic Serbs. More dramatically, during the Blitzkrieg of 1939–40, Hitler's Germany conquered Austria, Czechoslovakia, France, Poland, and the Scandinavian countries. This principle requires that, at war's end, the Aggressor give back all such unjust gains.

Its fifth principle is that the Aggressor must be demilitarized to avoid a repeat. Because the Aggressor broke international trust, so to speak, by committing aggression, it *cannot* be trusted *not* to commit aggression again (at least in the short term, and in the absence of regime change). The international community is entitled to some added security. The tools the Aggressor has to commit aggression must thus be taken away from it, in a process known as demilitarization. This is to say that, often, defeated aggressors lose many of their military assets and weapons capabilities, and have caps placed on their ability to rebuild their armed forces over time.

And its sixth principle is that there must be war crimes trials for those responsible. The world's first postwar international war crimes trials were held after World War II, in 1945–46, in both Nuremberg and Tokyo. The vast majority of those tried were soldiers and officers charged with *jus in bello* violations, like torturing POWs and deliberately targeting civilians. But a handful of senior Nazis were also charged with the *jus ad bellum* violation of "committing crimes against peace," that is, of launching an aggressive war. In 1998 the international community passed the Treaty of Rome, creating the world's first *permanent* international war crimes tribunal. Situated mainly in The Hague, its ambitious mandate is to prosecute *all* war crimes committed by *all* sides in *all* wars, and to do so using lawyers and judges from countries that were *not* part of the war in question. Recently, this new court has heard many cases from the Bosnian Civil War and from various African wars.

Most everyone who takes international justice seriously agrees that such principles ought to be enshrined in any attempt to regulate postwar justice, as in a new Geneva Convention. Beyond this point, consensus breaks down, and a sharp division emerges.

RETRIBUTION: THICK THEORY 1

The core intuition behind retribution theory is that *the defeated Aggressor must be rendered worse off than before the start of the war.* This is thought to be required for proper punishment and the elemental demands of justice. Why must there be punishment at all? Why cannot we simply cancel the Aggressor's unjust war gains and then "live and let live"? Retribution theorists, such as Robert Nozick, articulate three reasons. First, there is the obvious—yet powerful—reason of *deterrence.* Punishing past aggression deters future aggression, or at least does so more than if we had no punishment at all. No punishment seems a lax policy, which actually invites future aggression. Second, it is thought that proper punishment can be *an effective spur to atonement and change* on the part of Aggressor (because presumably it does not want to suffer through such punitive measures again). Finally, and most powerfully, *failing to punish the Aggressor degrades and disrespects the worth, status, and suffering of the Victim.* Thus, it is not enough merely to take away the unjust gains of the Aggressor, and force it to apologize publicly. It must suffer some retribution as a matter of balance and fairness. This is the same reasoning, which explains and articulates criminal punishment in domestic society: If someone, for example, has stolen something, we do not just make him give it back and apologize to his victim; we make him suffer further—make him worse off than before his deed—for instance, by making him pay a fine or spend some time in jail.[22]

So, how do retribution theorists recommend that we should make the defeated Aggressor worse off than before the war? Demilitarization, as discussed above—yes. War crimes trials for those individuals complicit in aggression—absolutely.

But retribution theorists advocate two further things: (1) a backward-looking system of compensation payments, from the Aggressor to the Victim(s), and (2) a forward-looking system of sanctions, placed by the Victim and the international community on the Aggressor. The goal of the first is to offer some amendment to the Victim, to help it pay for the costs incurred during the fight for its rights. The second is to hamper, deliberately, the economic growth of the Aggressor, as a kind of fine for, and enduring lesson about, the commission of aggression.

The final distinctive aspect of the model of retribution—which may or may not be an expression of this desire to render the defeated Aggressor worse off—is a refusal to aid or assist the defeated country with regime change. The defeated regime is left in place, and the winning country, and/or allies, exits the defeated Aggressor as soon as they have firmly set into place the measures of postwar punishment.[23]

Two Historical Examples of Retribution, Leading to Its Pros and Cons

The two clearest examples of the retribution model in action, in modern times, are the end of World War I (1918–19) and the end of the Persian Gulf War of 1991. The Treaty of Versailles ended World War I (1914–18) and is widely deemed to be a controversial failure that sparked World War II. Germany was extensively demilitarized, had all its war gains taken away, and, furthermore, lost some valuable territory of its own as one aspect of punishment. Crushing reparations payments were levied on Germany, and they would have lasted into the 1980s (!) if the peace terms had stuck. The victorious powers also tried to force elections on Germany, but the only result was that the people there came to associate democracy with the huge economic problems, and they began to turn to radical, nondemocratic parties promising simple solutions in a time of complex crisis. Hitler was thus able to come to power and to undertake actions that led to World War II.[24]

The 1991 Treaty ending the Persian Gulf War—triggered by Iraq's aggressive invasion of Kuwait in 1990—was similarly punitive and also paved the way for a second war. After the war, Saddam was left in power, and no attempt was made either to change the regime or to bring anyone to trial on war crimes charges. But Iraq *was* to be extensively demilitarized and subject to extreme economic sanctions. Iraq had no-fly zones imposed on it, and the regime had to agree to a rigorous weapons inspections process sponsored by the United Nations. That said, the sanctions had little effect on the regime's behavior, and after Saddam kicked out the inspectors in 1998, this issue grew into a major factor in favor of a new "just" war in 2003.[25]

Considering these illustrative historical examples, and reflecting on principles described previously, many experts are inclined to view retribution with skepticism and opine that perhaps too great a weight is placed on the inexact analogy to individual criminal justice; for example, there is little evidence for "the deterrence argument," as second wars have often flowed out of retribution. Civilians suffer markedly under such policy, and arguably the cause of the problem—the decrepit regime—is left in place, and/or gets even more extreme, and must eventually be dealt with regardless.[26]

THE REHABILITATION MODEL: THICK THEORY 2

If the overall goal of the model of retribution is to make the defeated Aggressor *worse off* than before the war, the overall goal of rehabilitation is to make the defeated Aggressor *better off* than before the war. Where the models differ specifically is over three major issues. First, the rehabilitation model *generally rejects sanctions*, especially on grounds that they have been shown, historically, to harm civilians and thus to violate discrimination/noncombatant immunity.[27] Second, the rehabilitation model *rejects compensation payments* for the same reason. In fact, the model favors *investing in* a defeated Aggressor, to help it rebuild and to help smooth over the wounds of war.[28] Finally, the rehabilitation model *favors forcing regime change* on the defeated Aggressor, whereas the retribution model views that as too risky and costly. That it may be, but those who favor the rehabilitative model suggest that it can be worth it over the long term, leading to the creation of a new, better, nonaggressive—even progressive—member of the international community.[29] To those who scoff that such deep-rooted transformation simply cannot be done, supporters of the rehabilitative model reply: Not only *can* it be done, it *has* been done. The two leading examples are West Germany and Japan after World War II.

The details of these cases are well known and thus are not dwelt on here. (The interested reader is referred to the sources in the note appended here.[30]) For our purposes, we note the success of these two cases, and return below—in the section on "the rehabilitation recipe"—to the general principles that most rehabilitators believe can be inferred from the reconstruction of Japan and West Germany. We then compare these principles with the more recent, and contentious, cases of Afghanistan and Iraq.

The Idealized Ends and Means of Rehabilitation

The ideal goal of justified postwar regime change, according to supporters of the rehabilitation approach, is *the timely construction of a minimally just political community*. Such a community makes every reasonable effort to (1) avoid violating the rights of other minimally just communities (especially by not aggressing against them), (2) gain recognition as being legitimate in the eyes of the international community and its own people, and (3) realize the human rights of all its individual members.[31] The ideal of a human-rights-respecting, minimally just political community is a justified one to pursue because

- It is in every individual's self-interest.
- It respects everyone's potential for autonomy and self-direction.
- It thus has universal appeal.
- It already enjoys a very strong international consensus, both morally and legally.
- It is based on thin, reasonable, and accessible values like living a minimally good life.
- It generates good consequences, especially in terms of average quality of life.
- It promotes long-term international peace and stability.[32]

It is these values—their strength and moral resonance—that ground, for rehabilitators, regime-changing measures in a postwar environment. These are not extreme, narrow, "crusading," or "imperialistic" values; they are modest, secular, widely accepted, and based on appeal *to the first principle* of respecting individual human rights as well as *to after-the-fact considerations* of generating concrete, beneficial consequences for everyone. But how to achieve this goal?

According to sound empirical research analyzing the majority of historical cases since 1865 (and, emphatically, West Germany and Japan, 1945–55), the core blueprint for transforming defeated, rights-violating aggressor regimes into minimally just societies is something like the ten points that follow.[33] Quick, comparative references are made here to contemporary Afghanistan and Iraq, showing where, perhaps, some of the current difficulties there may have originated.

First, adhere diligently to the laws of armed conflict during the regime takedown and occupation. This is morally vital for its own sake, as well as to help win the hearts and minds of the locals. America, of course, ran afoul of this principle in Iraq, owing to the prisoner abuse scandal at the Abu Ghraib prison.

Second, purge much of the old regime, and prosecute its war criminals. This does not necessarily mean purging all. Clearly, anyone materially connected to aggression, tyranny, or atrocity cannot be permitted a substantial role in the new order. They have lost the right to govern. But others—say, middle-ranking civil servants—might be kept on for their local knowledge and bureaucratic expertise. There always needs to be some continuity, even in the face of a sea change in institutions.[34]

Third, disarm and demilitarize the society. The target military does need to be disarmed and demobilized—but then something needs to be done with them. Many critics of the American occupation of Iraq from 2003 to 2011 argue that a key decision that helped spark the insurgency was the United States' choice in mid-2003 to promptly disband the 400,000-strong Iraqi army—and then leave them to their own devices. Plans for employing these potentially dangerous men, providing them opportunity, should have been developed.[35] A related problem, in Afghanistan, is that it has always been a highly weaponized society, with most adult males having their own guns. Many groups—some organized into drug cartels, others into radical religious and political factions—thus have always retained formidable weaponry, which has posed serious and ongoing challenges to securing peace and stability in post-2001 Afghanistan.[36]

Fourth, provide effective military and police security for the whole country. Most experts suggest a two-stage approach here: Replace the successful "attack and overthrow" war divisions with other divisions *specifically trained* in post-combat peacekeeping and nation building. The transition should be as seamless as possible, and the ratios are crucial. *Nation-building research shows that about 20 soldiers are needed per 1,000 residents to stabilize and secure post-war populations.* Incidentally, and of particular importance, both the Afghanistan and Iraq occupation forces were always well short of this ratio, even after the "surges" in both cases. The moral is to go in big, with plenty of "boots on the ground," boots that have been tutored in what the Pentagon labels "stability operations." Show the locals strong—not hesitant—intentions to protect them and to provide a secure backdrop for the development of law and legitimacy.[37]

Fifth, work with a cross section of locals on a new, rights-respecting constitution that features checks and balances. Limited government is required to prevent regrowth of tyranny; legitimate government is needed both for moral fitness and for stability. The picture here is of a genuine political partnership between the war's winner and the local civilian population. The facts show that *the meaningful participation and support of both is absolutely necessary*, and usually more extensive international participation is desirable as well. Constitution making is a process, and so we cannot rationally expect perfection or closure the first time out. Even the most developed societies occasionally change their constitutions and/or take several tries before creating a workable one in the first place. So though the postwar atmosphere is pressured, and there is a desire to rapidly end foreign occupation, some patience is required on the part of everyone. Good things often take time. In terms of inclusion in the constitution-building process, Andrew Arato reminds us that every group must be included: (1) those whose nonparticipation could ruin any subsequent arrangement, and (2) those who are committed to the creation of a minimally just state. If these two conditions are met, all relevant groups—as guided by the war's winner—can develop an inclusive framework for limited, accountable, and rights-respecting government.[38]

In this regard, and to their credit, the Americans and other allies did struggle mightily during both recent occupations to engage in constitution making, including the holding of several democratic elections to ratify such changes. It is unclear, however, whether such changes will "stick," or rather have already become unglued. In Afghanistan, al-Qaeda and even remnants of the Taliban are still a force, especially in parts of Helmand Province, and are "bad-faith players," in terms of not being committed to a minimally just society. The same is true in Iraq, where recent local governments have failed to include crucial ethnic and religious groups, and where outsiders—such as the radical Islamic State group known as ISIS—have carved out huge chunks of northern Iraqi territory for themselves. Indeed, we can see how, in today's Iraq and Afghanistan—unlike in postwar Germany and Japan—bitter and persistent factionalism between groups has rendered very difficult the achievement of this crucial condition.

Sixth, allow other, nonstate associations, or "civil society," to flourish. Civil society associations refer to all groupings that do not involve the state. They range from chambers of commerce to little league sports associations, and from volunteer charities to online social media groups. Research stresses how important such associations are, not only to the enjoyment of life but also to people's commitment to their society. There is no denying that, in both Afghanistan and Iraq, there has been *some* success in this regard in the past twelve years, compared with the next-to-no-civil-society allowed at all, by either the Taliban or Saddam, in those two countries before that. That said, it is probably also fair to say that, in light of all the factionalism and continued serious security problems, civil society activity is nowhere near what it could, and should, be.[39] Here the paradox between human security and war discussed by Ramel in chapter 12 is illuminating.

Seventh, forgo compensation and sanctions in favor of investing in and rebuilding the economy. Many modern peace arrangements—notably, the Treaty of Versailles and the terms ending the Persian Gulf War, discussed above—unraveled or created perverse consequences when they included hefty compensation terms and sweeping sanctions. Punitive settlements do not seem to work, in this sense. The goal of proper regime change is the creation of stable, minimally just social conditions. This is difficult enough as it is; trying to achieve it while sucking resources *out* of the target country becomes nigh impossible. In both Iraq and Afghanistan, sanctions have been dropped, but in both cases, the political instability, and the long-term challenges of creating a good, probusiness infrastructure (e.g., with stable access to electricity and a clampdown on the violence), have prevented such an investment from being what it could—and certainly, in both cases, from being anything anywhere near approaching something like the Marshall Plan in post–World War II Germany.

Eighth, if necessary, revamp educational curricula to purge past propaganda and cement new values. The fascists in the 1930s used school systems to warp future citizens so that they would subscribe to highly destructive doctrines of racial and national supremacy, with the flip side being hatred and aggression against "Others." In Afghanistan under the Taliban, and elsewhere still in the Middle East, great controversy attaches to the teaching of Islamic extremism and its attitudes toward violence against Israel, the West, and women in particular. Much development research powerfully shows the beneficial effects of a massive commitment to the education of girls and women. Indeed, some have even pronounced this one of the few silver bullets in development, which correlates very strongly with such other desirable social outcomes as economic growth, higher life expectancy, lower crime rates, and internal political stability. There has been some progress on this in Afghanistan, at least relative to what education existed for females under the Taliban. However, the progress is mainly confined to urban cores and not throughout rural areas; and in any event, the ongoing security challenges undermine the smooth operation of these new institutions.[40]

Ninth, ensure that the benefits of the new order will be (1) concrete and (2) widely, not narrowly, distributed. As Michael Walzer says, you have got to increase *everyone's* stake in the new, developing order. In particular, you must avoid a situation where it seems that the foreign occupier is favoring one group above the rest, giving that group most of the power. That group will soon be marked as traitors and "foreign agents" and will lose legitimacy and popular support. Again, the persistent factionalism within both Iraq and Afghanistan shows that this condition of an apparent and real "fair distribution of concrete benefits" between all the relevant groups has, as yet, not been achieved.[41]

And tenth, follow an orderly, not-too-hasty exit strategy when the new regime can stand on its own two feet. This requires walking a fine line. On one hand, the foreign occupier cannot stay forever—that would be conquest, not reconstruction. The locals must see that occupation will come to an end and they will return to full sovereignty. This knowledge should diffuse some tension.

On the other hand, if you are going to do something as important as postwar rehabilitation, you should try to do it well. Plus, contra Biggar's nobel conclusion discussed in chapter 3, *there is a moral responsibility not to cut and run.* A botched reconstruction benefits no one, including impatient locals.

This ten-point "recipe for reconstruction," based on such best cases as West Germany and Japan, is only a general blueprint; clearly, in particular cases, some things will need to be emphasized over others. The best recipes always allow for individual variance and input, depending on time and the ingredients at hand. We should also note the heavy interconnectedness of many of these elements. US major-general William Nash is probably only exaggerating a bit when he declares: "The first rule of nation building is that everything is related to everything, and it's all political."[42] We also have noted, throughout this section, the degree of difference between what the ideal recipe, employed during the German and Japanese cases, would call for compared with what was sought after, and/or what has actually been achieved, in contemporary Afghanistan and Iraq. *It might thus be worth stressing how the suboptimal results in the two current cases need not be thought to have critical implications for the rehabilitative approach in general, given this very real degree of difference.*[43] Yet it admittedly may, as we revisit below, have practical political implications for what state governments and general publics have appetites for, regarding the legislating of postwar requirements.

Completing the Rehabilitation-versus-Retribution Comparison

This leads naturally into a summary of the pros and cons of the rehabilitation model, especially as contrasted with its main rival, retribution. The two main cons of rehabilitation are these: (1) It takes a ton of time, effort, and resources, and (2) there is controversy attached to the imposition of values. And, perhaps it should be noted how the more recent cases show that the ideal results are not always achieved. But rehabilitation also has four main pros.

First, in historical cases where it has worked well, the rehabilitation model has been an amazing success, well beyond what the retribution model could ever have dreamed of achieving. Indeed, in some historical cases, such as West Germany, the rehabilitation model has been employed *to clean up the messes left behind* by the retribution model.

Second, the rehabilitation model does not leave behind rights-violating regimes that often serve as the causal agents of a second, and worse, war. The rehabilitation model does not leave the aggressive regime in place, nor does it trust that measures of punishment and/or containment will suffice to handle the issue of the bad regime. It views the bad, rights-violating regime as itself the main problem, and thus as needing tackling, through such rehabilitative measures of political therapy, as defined above.

Third, rehabilitation cannot be accused of creating a new generation of enemies, nor can it plausibly be seen as sowing the seeds of a second war. Clearly, this model is trying to help the people in the defeated Aggressor country and, though complex emotions might be created by such actions, the desire for revenge is not typically one of them.

And fourth, against the accusation that rehabilitation involves the infliction of narrow or parochial values, the contention has already been made that rehabilitation ought to be limited to the construction only of a minimally just state, one characterized by values that are neither parochial nor narrow nor harmful—the values underlying the structure of a minimally just society.

Altogether, this adds up to a compelling case, suggesting strongly that rehabilitation is a superior model of postwar justice, as compared with retribution.

HOWEVER, . . . AFGHANISTAN AND IRAQ

Even though there are these compelling historical and conceptual grounds for still asserting—as I long have—that rehabilitation is generally better then retribution, I am realistic enough to note that the difficulties experienced with trying to impose rehabilitation in Afghanistan and Iraq over the past twelve years probably have put a damper on people's enthusiasm for this model. Let us update these two cases.

Afghanistan has been in a period of postwar reconstruction since early 2002, Iraq since mid-2003. These dates refer to when the regime fell in each society, as a result of American invasion, then leading to US military occupation.[44] It seems true that the international community, as led by America, has—more or less—been trying to construct a minimally just society in each instance. It has been a very difficult process, in both countries, and has seen a mixture of both successes and failures.

The major postwar successes, in both nations, have been the replacement of aggressive, rogue regimes with new governments. The old regimes have been purged, and these new governments enjoy some democratic legitimacy—through multiple elections, in both countries—and are based on written constitutions crafted by locals. The gains in personal freedom, in both societies, have also been significant. Finally, in Afghanistan anyway, the gains in gender equality have been substantial—with, for example, the international community building and staffing many new schools for girls and women.[45] These liberties have, however, come under fire as postwar reconstruction has blended with counterinsurgency campaigns aimed at rooting out remnants of the old regime.

The problem is that the evidence suggests that it is *not* things like individual liberty and gender equality that matter most when it comes to the success and durability of postwar reconstruction. Instead, the historical data suggest that *the most important things are physical security (i.e., personal safety) and economic growth.* Jim Dobbins, probably the leading scholar of this issue, has distilled all these data into one crystal-clear rule of thumb regarding postwar success: *The war-winning occupier, and the new local regime, have about ten years to form an effective partnership and to devote themselves in particular to making the average person in that society feel better off—more secure and more prosperous, especially—than they were before the outbreak of the war.* If they can do this, postwar reconstruction will probably succeed. If not, there will be failure, and a serious risk of backsliding into armed conflict.[46]

Using this rule of thumb, we note that the approximate deadline for achieving this in Afghanistan would have been 2012, and in Iraq, 2013. Now, the US occupation of Iraq has been declared "officially over" (as of December 2011), but the reality is that a substantial number of US troops remain indefinitely to help train the new Iraqi Army, and to protect the Iraqi oil infrastructure.[47] And, in Afghanistan, NATO troops were supposed to have completely withdrawn by the end of 2014. So, assuming a margin of error of a few years, might physical security and economic improvement in both societies clearly be achieved in the near future? It is hard to see this, given the serious sectarian violence still occurring in Iraq, the very disruptive presence of ISIS, and the bitter rivalry between the three main groups of Shi'a, Sunni, and Kurds. The same is true for Afghanistan, with substantial group divisions and, in fact, a resurgent Taliban in some rural parts of the country. The ongoing violence remains a massive drag on economic growth because businesses are of course unwilling to invest in such an unstable context. Moreover, in both countries, there are massive needs even with regard to simple infrastructure rebuilding of the sort needed for basic business activity, in light of the decades of war and dictatorship that have brought such ruin to these societies.

To cement all this with the book's overarching theme, in spite of very serious efforts at postwar rehabilitation, Iraq and Afghanistan are now profoundly fractured societies, and indeed might arguably be said to less resemble sovereign states in the normal sense and to more resemble broken, high-conflict zones, within which violence (and cycles of retribution) between various groups endure.[48] They are places where sovereignty is constantly contested, and consequently, ominously fragmented. To the extent that this is true, we can say that rehabilitation has not succeeded overall, in spite of sustained, committed efforts. The dis-analogies to the historical best cases of Japan and West Germany run too deep: America did not completely control Iraq and Afghanistan, postwar; there has been much foreign interference (Iran, Saudi Arabia, Turkey, and Pakistan) in the recent cases; and Iraq and Afghanistan feature bitter intercommunal divisions to the point of fracture, insurgency, and even questions of whether there is a will to have one ongoing, sovereign country. The "recipe" probably cannot work under such conditions; or perhaps, the most that can be done is to make all best efforts at such rehabilitation over ten to fifteen years, and then—again challenging Biggar's ultimate conclusion—manage potentially suboptimal results.

CONCLUSION

Since the fall of the Berlin Wall, we have seen the two basic models of postwar policy in action: the retribution model, in connection with the Persian Gulf War of 1991; and the rehabilitation model, in connection with Afghanistan and Iraq following the terrorist attacks of September 11, 2001. Exploring the concepts and values, and delving deeper into history and other cases (notably, of the two world wars), I have argued here that, in general, *the rehabilitation model still seems superior to the retribution model*, in spite of the recent difficulties trying to impose it on Afghanistan and Iraq. But I admitted that, because of these difficulties, it is unlikely that many people would now support the notion that we should try to legislate rehabilitation into any new Geneva Convention dealing with postwar justice. And thus, because *some* regulation of the postwar moment would be better than none, I am now of the view that any such reform of international law and practice should, first, focus on codifying the thin, overlapping consensus between retribution and rehabilitation. *We can keep our ultimate values and yet admit that baby steps, and lowered expectations, may be more appropriate for today's complex postwar situations.*

NOTES

1. Brian Orend, *The Morality of War* (Peterborough, UK: Broadview Press, 2006), 160–222.
2. Brian Orend, "La justice après la guerre," *Raisons politiques* 45 (2012): 163–86; and Brian Orend, *The Morality of War*, 2nd ed. (Peterborough, UK: Broadview Press, 2013), 185–250; all subsequent references to *Morality* are to this second edition.
3. Brian Orend, *War and International Justice: A Kantian Perspective* (Waterloo, ON: Wilfrid Laurier University Press, 2000).
4. Michael Walzer, *Just and Unjust Wars* (New York: Basic Books, 1977); and Brian Orend, "*Jus Post Bellum*: The Perspective of a Just-War Theorist," *Leiden Journal of International Law* 20 (2007): 571–91.

5. Brian Orend, "Justice after War: Towards a New Geneva Convention," in *Ethics Beyond War's End*, ed. E. Patterson (Washington, DC: Georgetown University Press, 2012), 175–96.

6. Michael Reisman and Antoniou Christos, eds., *The Laws of War* (New York: Vintage, 1994); Adam Roberts and Richard Guelff, eds., *Documentation on the Laws of War*, 3rd ed. (Oxford: Oxford University Press, 2000); and Gary Solis, *The Law of Armed Conflict* (Cambridge: Cambridge University Press, 2010).

7. Gerd Oberleitner, *Human Rights in Armed Conflict: Law, Practice, Policy* (Cambridge: Cambridge University Press, 2015).

8. Raymond Wacks, *Understanding Jurisprudence*, 3rd ed. (Oxford: Oxford University Press, 2012).

9. Willamson Murray and Kevin Woods, *The Iran-Iraq War* (Cambridge: Cambridge University Press, 2014).

10. Antonio Cassese, *International Law*, 2nd ed. (Oxford: Oxford University Press, 2005); and Malcolm Shaw, *International Law* (Cambridge: Cambridge University Press, 2008).

11. David Reiff, *Slaughterhouse: Bosnia and the Failure of the West* (New York: Simon & Schuster, 1995).

12. William Martel, *Victory in War* (Cambridge: Cambridge University Press, 2011).

13. Fen O. Hampson, *Nurturing Peace: Why Peace Settlements Succeed or Fail* (Washington, DC: US Institute of Peace Press, 1996).

14. I am indebted to Michael Walzer of Princeton University for pushing me on this. See also Gabriella Blum, "The Fog of Victory," *European Journal of International Law* 24, no. 1 (2013): 391–421.

15. Paul R. Pillar, *Negotiating Peace: War Termination as a Bargaining Process* (Princeton, NJ: Princeton University Press, 1983).

16. Consult, e.g., note 6. Of particular relevance is Article 51 of the UN Charter.

17. For more on nontraditional forms of armed conflict, see, e.g., Orend, *Morality*, 71–110.

18. Reisman and Antoniou, *Laws*.

19. But then note how, if such an initial definition is compelling, it calls into question whether, as O'Driscoll opines in chapter 14 of this volume, the notion of victory is of necessity at odds with just war theory and its values. As I have sketched it, there need be no *logical* tension at all: victory, indeed a just victory, is achieved when the just cause that triggered the war has been secured, and in an enduring way.

20. Wacks, *Jurisprudence*.

21. Orend, *Morality*, 185–250.

22. Robert Nozick, *Anarchy, State and Utopia* (Cambridge, MA: Harvard University Press, 1974).

23. Orend, *Morality*, 185–214.

24. Margaret MacMillan, *Paris 1919: Six Months That Changed the World* (New York: Random House, 2001); John Keegan, *The First World War* (New York: Vintage, 1994); and John Keegan, *The Second World War* (New York: Penguin Books, 1989).

25. Daniel Brunstetter, "Trends in Just War Thinking during the US Presidential Debates 2000–12: Genocide Prevention and the Renewed Salience of Last Resort," *Review of International Studies* 4, no. 1 (2014): 77–99.

26. For more, see Orend, *Morality*, 185–248.

27. Gary C. Hufbauer, Jeffrey J. Schott, Kimberly Ann Elliott, and Barbara Oegg, *Economic Sanctions Reconsidered*, 3rd ed. (Washington, DC: Peterson Institute for International Economics, 2009).

28. Jon Miller and Rahul Kumar, *Reparations: Interdisciplinary Inquiries* (Oxford: Oxford University Press, 2007).

29. Julie Mertus and Jeffrey Helsing, eds., *Human Rights and Conflict: Exploring the Links between Rights, Law, and Peacebuilding* (Washington, DC: US Institute of Peace Press, 2006).

30. Leon V. Segal, *Fighting to the Finish: The Politics of War Termination in America and Japan* (Ithaca, NY: Cornell University Press, 1989); and Eugene Davidson, *The Death and Life of Germany: An Account of the American Occupation* (Saint Louis: University of Missouri Press, 1999).

31. Brian Orend, *Human Rights: Concept and Context* (Peterborough, UK: Broadview Press, 2002), 15–36; Orend, *Morality*, 37–43; and Allen Buchanan, *Human Rights, Legitimacy and the Use of Force* (Oxford: Oxford University Press, 2010).

32. Michael Doyle, *Liberal Peace* (New York: Routledge, 2011); and M. Brown, ed., *Debating the Democratic Peace* (Cambridge, MA: MIT Press, 1996).

33. James Dobbins and Rollie Lal, *America's Role in Nation-Building: From Germany to Iraq* (Santa Monica, CA: RAND Corporation, 2003); James Dobbins, Seth G. Jones, Keith Crane, James Dobbins, Andrew Rathmell, and Brett Steele, *The United Nations' Role in Nation-Building: From Congo to Iraq* (Santa Monica, CA: RAND Corporation, 2005); James Dobbins and Seth G. Jones, *Europe's Role in Nation-Building: From the Balkans to Congo* (Santa Monica, CA: RAND Corporation, 2008); and James Dobbins, Seth G. Jones, Keith Crane, and Beth Cole, *The Beginner's Guide to Nation-Building* (Santa Monica, CA; RAND Corporation, 2009).

34. Francis Fukuyama, *State-Building: Governance and World Order in the 21st Century* (Ithaca, NY: Cornell University Press, 2004).

35. Rowan Scarborough, *Rumsfeld's War* (New York: Regnery, 2004); and US Special Inspector General, *Hard Lessons: The Iraq Reconstruction Experience* (Washington, DC: US Independent Agencies and Commissions, 2009).

36. US Government, *Afghanistan Reconstruction* (Washington, DC: Bibliogov, 2011); Matteo Tondini, *Statebuilding and Justice Reform: Post-Conflict Reconstruction in Afghanistan* (New York: Routledge, 2010); and Dov Zakheim, *A Vulcan's Tale: How the Bush Administration Mismanaged the Reconstruction of Afghanistan* (Washington, DC: Brookings Institution Press, 2011).

37. James Traub, "Making Sense of the Mission," *New York Times Magazine*, April 11, 2004, 36; and Roland Paris, *The Dilemmas of Statebuilding* (New York: Routledge, 2009).

38. Andrew Arato, "Constitution-Making in Iraq," *Dissent*, Spring 2004, 32–36; and C. Zelizer, *Integrated Peacebuilding* (Boulder, CO: Westview Press, 2013).

39. Michael Edwards, *Civil Society*, 2nd ed. (London: Polity, 2009).

40. Martha Nussbaum, *Women and Human Development: The Capabilities Approach* (Chicago: University of Chicago Press, 2001).

41. Michael Walzer, *Arguing about War* (New Haven, CT: Yale University Press, 2004), 164–65.

42. W. Nash, quoted by Traub, "Making Sense," 35.

43. Jeff Bridoux, *American Foreign Policy and Post-War Reconstruction: Comparing Japan and Iraq* (New York: Routledge, 2012).

44. Eric Carlton, *Occupation* (London: Routledge, 1995).

45. See notes 35 and 36.

46. See note 33.

47. This was widely reported in December 2011 by the Associated Press, along with the following figures: Iraq War lasted nine years (2003–11), costing more than $800 billion and involving 4,500 US military dead and 32,000 US military wounded.

48. I am grateful to an anonymous reviewer for this point.

14

After Disneyland

The (Hollow) Victory of Just War

CIAN O'DRISCOLL

THE LATE JEAN BETHKE ELSHTAIN'S 2003 monograph, *Just War against Terror: The Burden of American Power in a Violent World*, was one of the more controversial books on the ethics of war in recent years.[1] Critics railed at Elshtain's robust support for the military interventionism of the George H. W. Bush administration and grumbled about the tendentious reading of Augustinian political theology that anchored her position.[2] In the midst of this furor, the signal contribution and most startling element of this book was somehow overlooked. Buried under the polemic, Elshtain put her finger on one issue that would shape the post–Cold War world more than any other: the apparent reemergence of the use of military force as a viable tool for a foreign and security policy. With the collapse of the Soviet Union, the subsequent empowerment of the United Nations Security Council led by a newly emboldened United States, and the advent of smart munitions, the accepted wisdom that the "scale and horror of modern warfare—whether nuclear or not—makes it totally unacceptable as a means of settling differences between nations" was seemingly debunked.[3]

The reality of this development has dawned on scholars of the just war tradition in the decade that has passed since the publication of Elshtain's *Just War against Terror*. A profusion of work has appeared on the subject of when and how states, either acting alone or in concert with one another on behalf of the international community, may use limited force to advance what Mary Kaldor has termed a "cosmopolitan law enforcement" agenda.[4] As part 1 of this volume demonstrates, a vast amount of ink has thus been spilled on, among other things, the threshold conditions for humanitarian intervention, the rights and wrongs of the deployment of unmanned aerial vehicles (UAVs) to carry out targeted killings, the use of military force to punish violations of international law and United Nations Security Council resolutions, and the legitimacy of preventive defense.[5] Alongside this, the move spearheaded by Brian Orend, among others, to develop a *jus post bellum* strand of just war thought has ensured that scholarly attention has also been fixed on the moral and legal rights and responsibilities that belligerents acquire in the aftermath of violent conflict.[6] At the same time, with very few exceptions, scant attention has been paid to the question of what military victory might encompass in the context of post–Cold War military interventions. That is to say, though scholars have devoted a great deal of attention to when and how communities may wage wars, and have even detailed the obligations they accrue once a war is over, scant attention has been paid to the question of what constitutes winning such a war. Indeed, the absence of victory in recent wars has been a major contributing factor to the notion of contested and fragmented sovereignty discussed in the introduction, as it has spawned new conflicts—the ISIS conflict comes to mind—that both transcend borders, just as states like Syria and Iraq seek to restore their own borders.

This challenge must lead us to consider two very obvious questions: What does it mean to *win* a just war? And is it even possible to speak sensibly about such an idea? Lifting the lid on this Pandora's box, these apparently straightforward questions do not elicit any easy answers, but rather reveal a host of conundrums. What might winning a just war actually entail? Would it, for instance, require the achievement of a durable and just peace? Or should the bar be set rather lower, at, say, the institution of some minimal form of order that approximates Saint Augustine's *tranquilitas ordinas*? Whichever option we select, further questions inevitably arise regarding how to establish whether victory, thus conceived, has in fact been achieved in any given war. Is there a standard metric to assist us in this task? Should such a metric incorporate the possibility of "moral victories"—that is, military losses that nevertheless yield a modicum of prestige for the vanquished on account of their display of honor in defeat? Turning this on its head, if so-called moral victories are conceivable, can we also countenance the possibility of "winning dirty"—that is, achieving victory by dubious means? Or is this a contradiction in terms? Would such a victory necessarily be tarnished by the fact that it was won by foul means? Finally, and most fundamentally, is the ideal of victory compatible with the notion of just war, or does an uneasy tension define their relation to one another? This chapter seeks to unpack these questions with a view to developing an agenda for further research.

The chapter proceeds in a straightforward manner. Its first section considers the place of victory vis-à-vis contemporary warfare. It argues that victory appears to be both an idea whose time has come and whose time has passed. The second section examines how victory is treated in contemporary just war thinking, paying particular attention to *jus post bellum* scholarship. The third section then presents a case for a particular way of approaching the relation between victory and just war. It argues that the notion of victory is both essential to but in tension with the just war ethos. The conclusion brings the discussion to a close by returning to the writings of Jean Elshtain and the challenges that the next generation of just war scholars will confront as they face the second quarter century following the fall of the Berlin Wall. It suggests that, in the absence of any clear sense of what winning a war actually entails, scholars would do well to take as the starting point of their ethical analysis of warfare the values of political judgment, authority, and sovereignty.

NO SUBSTITUTE FOR VICTORY?

"War's very object is victory, not prolonged indecision," Gen. Douglas MacArthur once famously declared. "In war there is no substitute for victory."[7] Indeed, ever since Aristotle, and after him Cicero, defined victory as the *telos* of military science, the idea that war is all about winning and that "every war has a winner" has been deeply lodged in the popular imaginary.[8] It is even set in stone in the motto extolled above the main entrance to the French military academy at Saint-Cyr: "They teach themselves to be victorious."[9] When the occasion has demanded it, political as well as military leaders have demonstrated a laser-like focus on victory. This was certainly the case when Prime Minister Winston Churchill responded vigorously to parliamentary questions about Allied war objectives in May 1940: "You ask, what is our aim? I can answer in one word: victory—victory, victory at all costs, victory however long and hard the road may be; for without victory, there is no survival."[10] More recently, Senator John McCain made similar remarks about the 2003 Iraq War, declaring that the only acceptable "exit strategy" for the United States from this particular conflict is "victory."[11]

At the same time, many people have wondered whether victory is an appropriate term to apply to modern war. Aristide Briand, prime minister of France for periods on either side of the Great War, remarked: "In modern war there is no victor. Defeat reaches out its heavy hand to the uttermost corners of the

Earth, and lays its burdens on victor and vanquished alike."[12] Writing after World War II, Basil Liddell Hart observed that nuclear weapons had rendered traditional strategic principles nonsensical: "To aim at winning a war, to take victory as your object, is no more than a state of lunacy."[13] This view was famously echoed by Bernard Brodie, who argued that whereas thus far, the chief purpose of military establishments had been to "win wars," their principal aim from now on must be to avoid wars.[14] Moving into the mainstream of international relations theory, Kenneth Waltz put the matter concisely: In modern war, "there is no victory, but only varying degrees of defeat."[15] These general sentiments are also discernible in the manner by which wars are both commemorated—a timely issue, given the program of events devoted to the centenary of World War I. War memorials seldom depict scenes of triumph in war, preferring instead to offer a site of mourning and reflection, though most modern novelists and artists who dwell on the subject of war also treat it in a somber or grimly ironic rather than celebratory fashion.[16]

The pressure to declare victory an obsolete concept is arguably more pronounced today than ever before. As Robert Mandel notes, the historical record indicates that there has been an observable decline in the proportion of wars that conclude with a "clean, decisive victory for one side or the other."[17] Contemporary wars seldom end with a clear-cut winner and loser, but instead tend to degenerate into stalemate, quagmire, or low-intensity conflict. Armies may sometimes melt away, apparently defeated, but often reemerge to carry on the fight by irregular means. But even if we refute the assertion that modern wars rarely give rise to decisive victories, we are still left with the tricky question of how to determine victory in practice in today's wars. According to the standard Clausewitzian view, victory requires the imposition of one's will on the enemy.[18] Yet there are no longer any obvious criteria by which to gauge the accomplishment of this end. Although command of the battlefield once served as just such a yardstick, it is of little help in an era defined by protracted campaigns and amorphous battle spaces. In its place, commentators have measured military victories variously on the basis of body counts, capital cities captured, hearts and minds won, or strategic objectives accomplished. Among the problems that arise in light of these rival metrics, there is no easy way to choose between them when they produce different answers to the question of who won a particular war.[19] Thus, Saddam could claim that, contrary to appearances, Iraq won the 1991 Gulf War.[20]

The problem is magnified when we view it in light of the "war on terror." As the then–secretary of defense, Donald Rumsfeld, observed in 2003, "We lack a metrics to know if we are winning or losing the global war on terror."[21] Four years later, Gen. David Petraeus echoed Rumsfeld's consternation. It is hard to know if you are winning the fight against al-Qaeda, because "this is not the sort of struggle where you take a hill, plant the flag, and go home with a victory parade."[22] Writing as late as 2010, Andrew Bacevich remarked that policymakers still "do not have the foggiest notion of what victory would look like, how it would be won, and what it might cost."[23] In chapter 13 of this volume, Brian Orend comments on the "vagueness" that necessarily attaches to the concept of victory with respect to contemporary warfare. And in chapter 4, Kerstin Fisk and Jennifer Ramos suggest that the shift on the part of the United States toward the use of UAVs and preventive force evinces a form of warfare that is anathema to the pursuit of decisive victory. President Barack Obama signaled his awareness of these issues when he initiated a shift in the "war on terror" discourse away from "victory" and toward less freighted terms, such as "success."[24] Indeed, Obama confessed anxiety "about using the word 'victory,' because, you know, it invokes this notion of Emperor Hirohito coming down and signing a surrender to MacArthur."[25]

Nevertheless, the language of victory still pervades the "war on terror," and modern armed conflict more generally. Then–UK prime minister David Cameron demonstrated the enduring appeal of "victory talk" in December 2013, when he repeated President George W. Bush's now-infamous "mission accomplished" boast in a speech on the war in Afghanistan.[26] Beyond this, the language of victory has featured prominently in recent debates about conflicts in Libya, Syria, Gaza, and Iraq. On one hand, the 2011 NATO intervention in Libya was hailed, at least initially, as a "model" victory.[27] On the other hand, some commentators have questioned what victory over the Islamic State in Iraq and Syria would look like in practice, while others have queried whether the notion of "victory" is even applicable to Gaza.[28] Victory, then, is apparently both an enduring idea and one whose time has passed.

THE (HOLLOW) VICTORY OF JUST WAR

If victory appears both integral to our understanding of war but also curiously out of step with the realities of contemporary armed conflict, there is arguably no such ambiguity where the notion of just war is concerned. The just war tradition supplies a moral grammar, arguably the predominant one in the Western world, for thinking about the rights and wrongs of war. It is typically understood today as consisting of three discrete but interlocking sets of principles bearing on the conditions that justify the recourse to force (*jus ad bellum*), the limits that pertain to the conduct of force (*jus in bello*), and the desiderata that should guide its conclusion (*jus post bellum*). Scholars occasionally clash over how different principles should be interpreted, as well as the relative weighting assigned to them, but there is a consensus that *jus ad bellum* matters revolve around the principles of just cause, proper authority, and right intention; that *jus in bello* concerns focus on the principles of discrimination and proportionality; and that *jus post bellum* treats the moral responsibilities of victors and vanquished in the aftermath of conflict. Scholars who in the past may have dismissed the just war tradition as an obscure hobby pursued by Catholic theologians will have been given cause to sit up and take notice by its recent prominence in the discourse of political and military leaders, including prime ministers Tony Blair and David Cameron, as well as presidents George W. Bush and Barack Obama, among others.[29] Recent years have also seen the emergence of a new pole of just war reasoning, the *jus ad vim*, which focuses on the use of force short of war. Because this new proposal is treated elsewhere in this volume (in chapter 11), I do not treat it here. Suffice it to say that this is an intriguing notion that merits further attention.

The emergence of just war discourse as the lingua franca of international politics has been acknowledged by a number of scholars. Most influentially, Michael Walzer has written about what he calls "the triumph of just war theory." According to Walzer, having been a minority pursuit during the latter decades of the nineteenth century and first half of the twentieth century, the moral vocabulary of just war came to the fore in the aftermath of the Vietnam War. It continued to gather momentum until it was tripping off the tongues of generals and politicians alike in the 1990s.[30] Writing in his own national context, Mark Totten echoes Walzer's comments, noting that the just war tradition now "provides the grammar for how the vast majority of Americans discuss, debate, and make decisions about war." Concepts such as last resort and just cause, he elaborates, increasingly "structure the way we think about war, from weighty discussions in the Roosevelt Room to water fountain conversations on the job."[31] Such concepts provide, as Brunstetter puts it in chapter 11 of this volume, a "moral framework" that provides guidance to military and political leaders as well as scholars and civilians.

The increased usage of just war vocabulary reflects its renaissance in the academic literature—a renaissance that Walzer traces to the Vietnam War, but that may just as easily be dated to the writings of Paul Ramsey in the early 1960s or even the conclusion of World War II.[32] In particular, the past decade has seen a surge of interest in just war ideas, and a high volume of monographs, edited books, and journal articles is now appearing every year. Many of these texts address the realities of contemporary armed conflict vis-à-vis a wide range of issues bearing on both when it is justified to resort to war and how to wage it. Yet, generally speaking, there has been no adequate treatment of what it means to actually win a just war in the twenty-first century.

There is, however, one possible exception to this, one area of just war scholarship where victory at least appears to enjoy the limelight: the *jus post bellum*, dedicated to questions of postwar justice. Understood as a discrete area of investigation, the idea of *jus post bellum* is itself a recent development. It may be traced to Michael J. Schuck's influential 1994 essay in the *Christian Century*.[33] Appalled by the triumphalism displayed by the United States in the wake of the 1991 Gulf War, Schuck argued that a triumphalist victory parade down Main Street of Disneyland conducted by veterans of the war, including Gen. Norman Schwarzkopf, showed a lack of both humility and remorse for the losses that the war had occasioned on both sides. More deeply, he claimed, it exposed the general lack of thought devoted to the question of how states ought to comport themselves in the aftermath of war. As a remedy, Schuck coined the phrase *jus post bellum* and proffered it as the missing element of just war theory.

The concept of victory is ubiquitous within the *jus post bellum*—a number of influential scholars have even posited it as the pivot of *jus post bellum* analysis. Louis Iasiello equates the remit of *jus post bellum* with the task of determining the responsibilities that victors in war incur with respect to the societies that have fallen under their sway. He writes that the job of *jus post bellum* theorists is to devise "moral precepts to guide the *post bellum* activities of victors."[34] Alex Bellamy proposes that the principal division in the *jus post bellum* field is between minimalist and maximalist approaches, a distinction that rests on whether one apportions minor or extensive responsibilities to victors for the vanquished.[35] Larry May claims that the key question for *jus post bellum* theorists is "what difference should there be between victors and vanquished in terms of post war responsibilities?"[36] Finally, Darren Mollendorf submits that the function of *jus post bellum* theory is to clarify "the limitations on the terms that a victorious warring party can impose on the vanquished."[37]

Within this rubric, the character of victory achieved in any given war is viewed as significant insofar as it makes an impact on the prospects for a durable peace: The more legitimate the victory, the greater the odds are that a sustainable peace will ensue. It is in this spirit that Orend argues—both in chapter 13 of this volume and elsewhere—that victories marked by a vengeful spirit pave the way, not for reconciliation, but for bitterness and recrimination. "We know," he writes, "that when wars are wrapped up badly, they sow the seeds for future bloodshed."[38] Conversely, a number of scholars have cited the conduct of the commanders of the Union Army in the US Civil War as an example of how humility in victory—exactly what Schuck alleges was absent in the United States in 1991—can play a pivotal role in facilitating peace. The magnanimity displayed by Gen. Ulysses Grant at Appomattox is often cited as a case of best practice in this respect.[39] Cognizant that bad winners create bad losers, Grant and his men tempered their behavior accordingly, and reaped the benefits. Other scholars have remarked that it is not only *bad* winners that hinder peacemaking. Citing Afghanistan, Eric Patterson has argued that *unconvincing* winners also cause problems. For example, the inability of the United States and its allies to achieve an emphatic victory over the Taliban has, he observes, undermined all subsequent efforts to usher in a meaningful peace by creating a strategic environment conducive to festering hostilities.[40] Perhaps this has much to do with a failure to accurately read what Kelsay calls in chapter 8 the "signs of the times."

This intimate relationship between considerations of victory and *jus post bellum* theorizing should come as no surprise, given that the latter is rooted in the former. This is evidently true with respect to how *jus post bellum* has been constituted as a field of inquiry. As a recent addition to just war thinking, *jus post bellum* analysis has its disciplinary origins in Schuck's writings on victory and for Orend and others the goal of discerning the moral responsibilities of victors in the aftermath of conflict. In this respect, *jus post bellum* is an outgrowth of a broader interest in the ethics of victory. But the observation that *jus post bellum* is rooted in victory is also true conceptually. As a body of thought dedicated to guiding victors with respect to their postwar obligations, it assumes the achievement of victory as its point of departure. That is to say, victory is posited as a threshold for the commencement of *jus post bellum* theorizing.

Herein lies the rub. Although the concept of victory pervades *jus post bellum* analysis, it is rarely interrogated. None of the sources cited thus far offer a convincing definition of what is meant by "victory." The reason for this is because, despite its prominence in the literature, victory is not the central concern of conventional *jus post bellum* analysis. Rather, as David Rodin has pointed out, the majority of *jus post bellum* scholars are actually interested in discerning only what moral and legal principles should obtain *after* victory has been achieved and the transition to peace has already begun.[41]

This should not be waved away as a mere semantics. The proclivity to treat victory as the point of departure for *jus post bellum* analysis miscasts a substantive issue as a premise. If, as seems sensible to suppose, the determination of winners and losers is part and parcel of the endgame phase of war, rather than preceding it, our analytical framework should reflect this. This is because the manner in which a war is ended primes the prospects for a durable peace in its aftermath. By contrast, the prevailing tendency to treat the category of victory as a given brackets the very questions we should be asking. Consider, for instance, the following statements by Gen. Tommy Franks and Michael Walzer. Interviewed by *The National Interest* in 2006, Franks emphasized the importance of subjecting the concept of victory itself to scrutiny: "What constitutes victory? I think that is a fundamental question, and it is good for each of us in this country to ask ourselves that from time to time. When we try to decide whether or not we've been victorious, we have to think, for just a second, what the term 'victory' means."[42] But six years later, Walzer bypassed these valid concerns in an essay on *jus post bellum*: "I am going to *assume* the *victory* of just warriors," he writes, "and ask what their responsibilities are *after victory*" (emphasis added).[43] To assume, as Walzer and does on this occasion, that the distinction between winner and loser prefigures *jus post bellum* analysis is to foreclose precisely the matters we should be interrogating—that is, how victory itself is understood, produced, and consolidated.

FROM TRIUMPH TO TRAGEDY

The failure to address the relation between victory and just war in the contemporary security environment is a significant omission. After all, the failure to develop a clear conception of what victory requires has hampered the efforts of Western powers to terminate what they presented as just wars in, among other places, Afghanistan, Iraq, and Libya.[44] This chapter thus argues that there is a pressing, but also fundamental, need to reconsider the relation between just war and victory.

The notion of victory, understood in its fullest sense, is essential to but also in tension with the just war ethos. On one hand, the ideal of victory is clearly presupposed by the idea of just war. For a war to be regarded as just, it must be vital to win it, and it would be a *non sequitur* to think otherwise. Walzer expresses this point of view in a characteristically astute observation in his classic book *Just and Unjust Wars*: "There must be purposes that are worth dying for, outcomes for which soldiers' lives are not too high a price. The idea of a just war requires the same assumption. A *just war is one that is morally urgent to win*, and a soldier who dies in a just war does not die in vain" (emphasis added).[45] According to this perspective, the notion of victory is integral to the very idea of war. To pretend otherwise or to ignore this fact would be to disregard what is in plain sight. So, though just war scholars—and indeed, then-president Obama—may feel some measure of discomfort with the term "victory," and wish to use other terms instead, any effort to do so will recode rather than resolve the issue. The point here, then, is that rather than pretending it does not exist, or simply steering around it, just war scholars should acknowledge the inescapability of the concept of victory and engage with it in a constructive fashion. To do anything else would be to ignore the elephant in the room.

On the other hand, the ideal of victory arguably encourages a dangerous "eyes-on-the-prize" disposition that discounts humility and respect for constraints in war. The former tendency was evident, for instance, in General Schwarzkopf's stroll down Main Street in Disneyland as well as President George W. Bush's boastful assertion of "mission accomplished" after the 2003 invasion of Iraq. The latter tendency was apparent in Prime Minister Churchill's uncompromising statement of Allied war objectives. The aim of the United Kingdom and its allies in this war was, he said, "victory *at all costs, in spite of all terror, and no matter how long and hard the road*" (emphasis added).[46] These sentiments belie a tension with the tragic vision of just war articulated by Saint Augustine and other key thinkers. If Augustine famously declared that "it is the iniquity on the part of the adversary that forces a just war upon the wise man," he also lamented the use of force as a source of evils, manifold disasters, and dire necessities.[47] Just war, on this view, is not a solution to injustice and disorder, but a part of the problem. This should not be read as an invitation to withdrawal, but as a clarification that war, even when unavoidable and waged with just cause, is a source of ill that damages all it touches. Hugo Grotius echoed this view when he quoted Plutarch to the effect that "war is a most cruel thing and brings with it an ocean of calamities and violence."[48] The point here is that, whereas the just war ethos emphasizes humility, restraint, and temperance, the ideal of victory threatens to subvert this agenda by nourishing a "winner takes all" credo.

If the discussion of victory is unsettling, this is because it presses directly on an uncomfortable truth: that the very idea of just war assumes, but struggles to accommodate, the notion of winning. This is not something that should be swept under the rug. Rather, it is something that should be openly debated. For it is precisely the question of what winning means, and whether it is possible to win justly (or "not win" with honor—as, in chapter 3, Biggar concludes might be necessary), that is at stake in war zones from Gaza to Damascus today. Not only this, the question of what winning means, and whether it is possible to win justly, also has the potential to reveal the tragic character of the just war idea itself—and, by extension, to cast a critical light on the hubristic way in which it is often used today.

Identifying the issue is the easy part; treating it is much harder. It might be useful, then, to set down some preliminary thoughts in this regard. Engaging the question of victory and its relation to just war would require scholars to commit to a very involved program of work that will involve an ontological and epistemological, as well as a normative, component. Taking these elements in turn, scholars will first be obliged to reflect on what the notion of victory encompasses in the context of contemporary armed conflict. Second, there is a need for scholars to develop a reliable set of indicators, so that we can identify victory when we encounter it. Engaging with the concept of human security, discussed by Ramel in chapter 12, could offer some insights. Progress on these issues will provide a solid base for the third task: unpacking the normative dimensions of victory and understanding its relation to just war.

There are, of course, different ways in which one could pursue this undertaking. One could, for instance, treat it in the mode of analytical philosophy by developing an account of "just victory" from first principles. Alternatively, one could strive to construct a genealogy of victory. The approach I propose is different yet again. I aim to develop an account of the relation between just war and victory by examining its historical development and trajectory. The reasoning behind this way of proceeding is clear: If we are to grasp the full meaning of the connection between victory and just war, the trick is not to abstract away from these concepts to generalized norms, but to situate them within the evolving body of thought and practice that gave rise to them. It is only by acquainting ourselves with the specific ways that the relation between victory and just war was conceived and practiced in different historical milieu that we can acquire a full sense of its dimension, reference, and possibilities.[49] It is important to stress, then, that this is not history purely for history's sake. Rather, it is history as philosophy, teaching by examples. As such, it assumes that the study of the past provides a commanding vantage point on the present, enabling us to look beyond and call into question the contingencies and commonplaces of current thinking on victory and just war.

Once one adopts such a perspective, it swiftly becomes apparent that the problem of thinking about victory in light of warfare is even more entrenched than one might have initially supposed. The issue is that the challenges that the concept of victory raises, though perhaps more obvious today than ever before, are nothing new. There has seldom if ever been a time when either participants or observers could say with cast-iron certainty how a given war would end, and what state of affairs it would bequeath to the world in its aftermath.[50] The problem, stated bluntly, is that one can never truly predict with any degree of accuracy whether victory is achievable in a given conflict and what it would look like. A combination of what Clausewitz referred to as friction and Reinhold Niebuhr called the irony of history has a way of confounding our expectations. In light of these factors, it is incumbent on us to think about what victory might mean in a just war as a matter of, among other things, great complexity and contingency. This places the onus on anyone who wishes to think about these issues to treat them as a question of political judgment, a term that in turn leads to considerations of authority and sovereignty—precisely the issues under review in this book.[51] In the absence of certainty regarding the outcomes of our actions (military and otherwise), and indeed their moral character, we must acknowledge that making the tough decisions regarding war and peace is not a precise science that any commentator can second-guess, but an existential leap in the dark that the political leader orders on behalf of his or her community.

CONCLUSION

As Walzer notes, even if "it is sometimes urgent to win, it is not always clear what winning is."[52] Nor, we may add, is it clear that the aim of winning is compatible with the notion of just war. At the very least, there are tensions about how these ideals relate to and bear on one another. The ideal of victory seems simultaneously essential to but in tension with the just war ethos. Recent years have, however, witnessed the emergence of a division of labor wherein just war scholars simply surrendered the notion of victory to strategists. Even where just war theorists have cited victory—most notably, with respect to *jus post bellum*—they have failed to truly engage with it. With recent events in Gaza, Libya, Syria, Iraq, and Afghanistan fresh in our minds, there is now a timely opportunity to address how the notion of victory haunts just war thinking. This chapter has suggested that if and when we do so, we will discover that the notion of victory provides a prism for a tragic reading of just war.

This leads us back to our starting point. If Elshtain did more than most to identify the development whereby the use of military force has once again become a viable tool of foreign policy, her writings also reveal the need to think more carefully and more deeply about what victory can mean in relation to just war in today's security environment. Thus, as the next generation of just war scholars, we should be asking questions about the whither, as well as the when and the how, of the recourse to force. What does, or could, victory mean with respect to a just war? How will we know it when we see it? What ethical challenges does it presuppose? How does it color or inform our understanding of the requirements of just war? Is the shift toward preventive force and the use of UAVs anathema to the pursuit of victory? And what might victory look like in relation to what Brunstetter has termed the *jus ad vim*? Attention to these questions will both steer just war scholars away from the unthinking triumphalism represented by General Schwarzkopf's Disney parade and President Bush's "mission accomplished" moment, and remind us anew of the limits of military power in a violent world. Moreover, in a world where one simply cannot see around the corner, nor anticipate all the outcomes of one's actions (military or otherwise), nor even ascertain with cast-iron certainty the merit of one's cause, any serious reflection on the challenges we confront must take as its starting point a renewed attention to the values of political judgment, authority, and sovereignty. Thus, even if we do not know what victory might mean in any given war, we at least know where our moral evaluation should begin.

NOTES

1. Jean Bethke Elshtain, *Just War against Terror: The Burden of American Power in a Violent World*, rev. ed. (New York: Basic Books, 2004).

2. Nicholas J. Rengger, "Just a War against Terror? Jean Bethke Elshtain's Burden and American Power," *International Affairs* 80, no. 1 (2004): 107–16; Maja Zehfuss, "The Tragedy of Violent Justice: The Danger of Elshtain's *Just War against Terror*," *International Relations* 21, no. 4 (2007): 493–502; and Peter Lee, "Scarred Souls, Weary Warriors, and Military Intervention: The Emergence of the Subject in the Just War Writings of Jean Bethke Elshtain," *Review of International Studies* 39, no. 4 (2013): 859–80.

3. Pope John Paul II, quoted by National Conference of Catholic Bishops, "The Challenge of Peace: God's Promise and Our Response—The Pastoral Letter on War and Peace," in *Just War Theory*, ed. Jean Bethke Elshtain (Oxford: Blackwell, 1992), 93.

4. Mary Kaldor, *New and Old Wars: Organized Violence in a Global Era* (Cambridge: Polity, 2001), 124. Aidan Hehir's chapter 1 in this volume, and indeed his body of work as a whole, offers an incisive commentary on this agenda.

5. Many of these issues are tackled in detail elsewhere in this volume. On the limited use of force, see chapter 11 by Daniel Brunstetter. On UAVs, see chapter 4 by Kerstin Fisk and Jennifer Ramos. And Nigel Biggar examines preventive defense in chapter 3. Also see Caron E. Gentry and Amy E. Eckert, eds., *The Future of Just War: New Critical Essays* (Athens: University of Georgia Press, 2014).

6. Brian Orend, "Jus Post Bellum," *Journal of Social Philosophy* 31, no. 1 (2000): 117–37. Orend returns to and develops his account of *jus post bellum* in chapter 13 of this volume.

7. Gen. Douglas MacArthur, "Farewell Address to Congress," April 19, 1951, www.americanrhetoric.com/speeches/douglasmacarthurfarewelladdress.html.

8. Aristotle, *Nicomachean Ethics*, trans. Harris Rackham (London: Wordsworth Classics, 1996), 3; Also see Cicero, *The Republic and The Laws*, trans. Niall Rudd (Oxford: Oxford University Press, 1998), 83; and Robert Mandel, *The Meaning of Military Victory* (Boulder, CO: Lynne Rienner, 2006), 12.

9. John I. Alger, *The Quest for Victory: The History of the Principles of War* (Westport, CT: Greenwood Press, 1982), 173.

10. Quoted by Brian Bond, *The Pursuit of Victory: From Napoleon to Saddam Hussein* (Oxford: Oxford University Press, 1996), 142.

11. John McCain, "Our Exit Strategy in Iraq Is Victory," November 5, 2003, www.mccain.senate.gov/public/index.cfm/speeches?ID=2d7dce5e-ff99-4a07-8436-36bf310fc60b.

12. Quoted by Richard Hobbs, *The Myth of Victory: What Is Victory in War?* (Boulder, CO: Westview Press, 1979), 477.

13. Quoted by Beatrice Heuser, *The Evolution of Strategy: Thinking War from Antiquity to the Present* (Cambridge: Cambridge University Press, 2010), 454.

14. Bernard Brodie, *The Absolute Weapon* (New York: Harcourt Brace, 1946), 76.

15. Kenneth Waltz, *Man, the State, and War: A Theoretical Analysis* (New York: Columbia University Press, 2001), 1; this is redolent of a line from the popular HBO television series *The Wire*: "Nobody wins; one side loses more slowly is all."

16. On war memorials, see Jay Winter, *Sites of Memory, Sites of Mourning: The Great War in European Cultural History* (Cambridge: Cambridge University Press, 1998); on literature and art, see Paul Fussell, *The Great War and Modern Memory* (Oxford: Oxford University Press, 1975).

17. Robert Mandel, "Defining Postwar Victory," in *Understanding Victory and Defeat in Contemporary War*, ed. Jan Angstrom and Isabelle Duyvesteyn (Abingdon, UK: Routledge, 2007), 18.

18. Carl von Clausewitz, *On War*, trans. Michael Howard and Peter Paret (Oxford: Oxford University Press, 2007), 13.

19. This argument is elaborated by Dominic P. Johnson and Dominic Tierney, *Failing to Win: Perceptions of Victory and Defeat in International Politics* (Cambridge, MA: Harvard University Press, 2006).

20. Lawrence Freedman and Efraim Karsh, *The Gulf Conflict 1990–1991: Diplomacy and War in the New World Order* (Princeton, NJ: Princeton University Press, 1993), 410.

21. Quoted by Mandel, *Meaning of Military Victory*, 135.

22. Mark Tran, "General David Petraeus Warns of Long Struggle Ahead for US in Iraq," *The Guardian*, September 11, 2008, www.theguardian.com/world/ 2008/sep/11 /iraq.usa.

23. Andrew J. Bacevich, *Washington Rules: America's Path to Permanent War* (New York: Henry Holt, 2010), 10.

24. William C. Martel, *Victory in War: Foundations of Modern Strategy—Revised and Expanded Edition* (Cambridge: Cambridge University Press, 2011), 17; evidencing this shift, the word "victory" appears only three times in Gen. Stanley McChrystal's 2009 strategic review of US operations in Afghanistan. This is in marked contrast to President George W. Bush's frequent recourse to the idiom of victory.

25. Quoted by Gabriella Blum, "The Fog of Victory," *European Journal of International Law* 24, no. 1 (2013): 421.

26. Rowena Mason, "Mission Accomplished in Afghanistan, Declares David Cameron," *The Guardian*, December 16, 2013, www.theguardian.com/uk-news/2013 /dec/16/afghanistan-mission-accomplished-david-cameron. Indeed, senior officials of the Bush administration perceived that their key challenge in 2003 was to ensure that when Iraq was defeated militarily, "there would be no ambiguity about victory." Bob Woodward, *Plan of Attack* (London: Simon & Schuster, 2004), 402; Bush endorsed this focus when he instructed the National Security Council that "only one thing matters: winning." The "big picture," he elaborated, was not about timetables, "it's a matter of victory." Quoted by Martel, *Victory in War*, 329.

27. Ivo H. Daalder and James G. Stavridis, "NATO's Victory in Libya: The Right Way to Run an Intervention," *Foreign Affairs* 91, no. 2 (2012): 2–7.

28. Spencer Ackerman, "Degrade and Destroy?" *The Guardian*, September 17, 2014, www.theguardian.com/world/2014/sep/17/degrade-destroy-isis-obama-unclear -military-goals; and Amira Hass, "Israel's Moral Defeat Will Haunt Us for Years,"

Haaretz, July 28, 2014, www.haaretz.com/mobile/.premium-1.607550?v=B844E2B91 34251232410386CC5A070D8.

29. On Bush and Blair, see Cian O'Driscoll, *The Renegotiation of the Just War Tradition and the Right to War in the 21st Century* (New York: Palgrave, 2008); on Obama, see Barack Obama, "Remarks by the President at the Acceptance of the Nobel Peace Prize," December 10, 2009, www.whitehouse.gov/the-press-office/remarks-president-acceptance-nobel-peace-prize; On Cameron, see David Cameron, "Prime Minister's Statement on Libya," March 19, 2011, www.gov.uk/government/speeches/prime-ministers-statement-on-libya.

30. Michael Walzer, "The Triumph of Just War Theory (and the Dangers of Success)," in *Arguing about War* (New Haven, CT: Yale University Press, 2004), 3–22.

31. Mark Totten, *First Strike: America, Terrorism, and Moral Tradition* (New Haven, CT: Yale University Press, 2010), 80, 82.

32. Paul Ramsey, *War and the Christian Conscience: How Shall Modern War Be Conducted Justly?* (Durham, NC: Duke University Press, 1961).

33. Michael J. Schuck, "When the Shooting Stops: Missing Elements in Just War Theory," *Christian Century*, October 26, 1994, 982–83.

34. Louis V. Iasiello, "Jus Post Bellum: The Moral Responsibilities of Victors in War," *Naval War College Review* 57, nos. 3–4 (2004): 40.

35. "Minimalists envisage *jus post bellum* as a series of restraints on what it is permissible for victors to do once the war is over. By contrast, maximalists argue that victors acquire certain additional responsibilities that must be fulfilled for the war as a whole to be considered just." Alex J. Bellamy, "The Responsibilities of Victory: Jus Post Bellum and the Just War," *Review of International Studies* 34, no. 4 (2008): 601–25, at 602.

36. Larry May, *After War Ends: A Philosophical Perspective* (Cambridge: Cambridge University Press, 2012), 1.

37. Darren Mollendorf, "Jus Ex Bello," *Journal of Political Philosophy* 16, no. 2 (2008): 130.

38. Orend, chapter 13 of this volume; Also see Brian Orend, "Justice after War," *Ethics & International Affairs* 16, no. 1 (2002): 43.

39. David A. Crocker, "Ending the US Civil War Well: Reconciliation and Transitional Justice," in *Ethics beyond War's End*, ed. Eric D. Patterson (Washington, DC: Georgetown University Press, 2012), 145–74.

40. Eric D. Patterson, *Ending Wars Well: Order, Justice, and Conciliation in Contemporary Post-Conflict* (New Haven, CT: Yale University Press, 2012), 174.

41. David Rodin, "Two Emerging Issues of *Jus Post Bellum*: War Termination and the Liability of Soldiers for Crimes of Aggression," in *Jus Post Bellum: Towards a Law of Transition from Conflict to Peace*, ed. Carsten Stahn and Jann K. Kleffner (The Hague: TMC Asser Press, 2008), 53–77.

42. General Tommy Franks, "The Meaning of Victory: A Conversation with Tommy Franks," *The National Interest* 86 (November–December 2006): 8.

43. Michael Walzer, "The Aftermath of War: Reflections on Jus Post Bellum," in *Ethics beyond War's End*, ed. Patterson, 37.

44. Gideon Rose, *How Wars End: Why We Always Fight the Last Battle* (New York: Simon & Schuster, 2011).

45. Michael Walzer, *Just and Unjust Wars: A Moral Argument with Historical Illustrations*, 2nd ed. (New York: Basic Books, 1992), 110.

46. Quoted by Bond, *Pursuit of Victory*, 142.

47. "But how many great wars, what slaughter of men, what outpourings of human blood have been necessary to bring [the current 'peace'] about! Those wars are now over; but the misery of these evils has not yet come to an end." Augustine, *The City of God against the Pagans*, trans. R. W. Dyson (Cambridge: Cambridge University Press, 1998), 928–29.

48. Hugo Grotius, *The Rights of War and Peace*, ed. Richard Tuck (Indianapolis: Liberty Fund, 2005), 1148.

49. This approach draws on James Turner Johnson, "Contemporary Just War Thinking: Which Is Worse, to Have Friends or Critics?" *Ethics & International Affairs* 27, no. 1 (2013): 25–45; and John Kelsay, "Just War, Jihad, and the Study of Comparative Ethics," *Ethics & International Affairs* 24, no. 3 (2010): 227–38.

50. One can think here of Xenophon's ironical conclusion to the *Hellenica* (VII.5.26–27): "The result of this battle was just the opposite of what everyone expected it would be. Nearly the whole of Greece had been engaged on one side or the other, and everyone imagined that, if a battle had been fought, the winner would become the dominant power and the losers would be their subjects. . . . In fact, there was even more uncertainty and confusion in Greece after the battle than there had been previously"; Xenophon, *A History of My Times*, trans. Rex Warner (London: Penguin, 1979).

51. For more on this theme, see James Turner Johnson, *Sovereignty: Moral and Historical Perspectives* (Washington, DC: Georgetown University Press, 2014); Chris Brown, "Just War and Political Judgement," in *Just War: Tradition, Authority, Practice*, ed. Anthony F. Lang Jr., Cian O'Driscoll, and John Williams (Washington, DC: Georgetown University Press, 2013), 25–48; and Nicholas Rengger, "On the Just War Tradition in the Twenty-First Century," *International Affairs* 78, no. 2 (2002): 353–63.

52. Walzer, *Just and Unjust Wars*, 110.

Conclusion

Toward the Future of the Ethics of War and Peace

DANIEL R. BRUNSTETTER AND JEAN-VINCENT HOLEINDRE

THIS PROJECT BEGAN with a very broad question: What have we learned about the ethics of intervention from the conflicts that have led us from a time when sovereignty was seen as inviolable to an era of contested and fragmented sovereignty? Although the book's contributing authors do not always agree, there are several common features across all its chapters. First and foremost is the recognition that lethal force is a necessary, albeit tragic, feature of statecraft. And given this tragic inevitability, there is a sense of moral responsibility that pushes us to continually reevaluate the paradigms we use to justify and judge recourse to war. Being critical of war for the sake of being critical or supportive of war for the sake of being supportive betrays the responsibility of academic engagement with matters of civil and international discord. Rather, the authors leveled criticism with a view toward pointing out the ethical shortcomings of the paradigms frequently used to evaluate options for the use of force (including the Responsibility to Protect, R2P, and the just war doctrine) and offering insights for improvements; or they proffered support of doctrines modified to correct shortcomings evident from recent conflicts; or they proposed more appropriate, sometimes new, paradigms (including human security and *jus ad vim*). And sometimes they pointed out conceptual lacunae, like the elusiveness of victory, and offered a road map to address the relevant issues.

In this conclusion, we offer tentative answers to the three questions that have animated the book as a whole, attempting to take into account the insights of the various contributors. To refresh the reader's memory, these questions were:

- Assuming that we live in a world wherein the notion of sovereignty is, and has been, evolving, what do we really know about the relationship between military intervention and ethics?
- How has the concept of war evolved amid changing notions of sovereignty? And what might war (and war ethics) look like in the future?
- As we look forward in time, what are the most pressing challenges regarding the ethics of war and peace for the future, and how can the lessons learned from the past (assuming there are any) help us to navigate these challenges in new and innovative ways (or old and time-tested ways)?

By offering tentative answers to these questions, we seek to highlight the insights from this collective enterprise and offer a road map to future research and scholarly engagement with international affairs.

CONTESTED AND FRAGMENTED SOVEREIGNTY, ETHICS, AND WAR

The contributions to this volume suggest that the major paradigms used to think about the relationship between morality and the use of force—R2P and the just war tradition—are useful, but are in need of reevaluation, and perhaps supplementing with alternative paradigms. They are useful because they provide a shared means to talk about conflicts—whether past or forthcoming. This is true in spite of shortcomings that become readily apparent when a critical gaze is cast on how, when applied, they are mapped onto real-world conflicts.

With regard to R2P, Hehir offered a negative analysis of the fate of humanitarian advocacy but also sought to forestall total resignation by sketching out the parameters of a viable alternative. His proposal advances the creation of a new judicial body independent of states that would have the military capacity to act in a way to enforce preexisting human rights. Recognizing that this is an ideal, but not utopian, Hehir defends the core idea that force can be used to protect human beings facing massive human rights abuses, but that the mechanisms of R2P are too prone to abuses by states gripped by their own material and national interests. Lindemann and Giacomelli's use of recognition theory points to a way to supplement R2P by employing an alternative framework for looking at humanitarian intervention that emphasizes the significance of emotions. Doing so sheds light on two mechanisms that can distort the intentions of R2P: the hero-protector syndrome, which enables intervention, and the minimization of the Other, which allows for disengagement from human suffering. Recognition theory supplements our understanding of the dynamic of humanitarian intervention—including decisions to not intervene—by identifying the emotional elements that affect the war–ethics relationship. Rather than purely ethical motives dictating the decision to use military force, the emotional baggage that statesmen and citizens alike bring to the table muddies the waters. This points to the need to further untangle the role of emotions in the decision about whether to use force, and how emotion enhances or diminishes the feeling of ethical responsibility. Finally, Holeindre's explanation of French postcolonial responsibility offers alternative insights into a possible future for the R2P norm compared with Hehir, while also explaining some of the selectivity concerns raised by Lindemann and Giacomelli.

Regarding the just war tradition, the sentiment that the Bush administration overly relaxed the impetus of restraint inherent in some readings of the tradition (e.g., Walzer's contra Johnson's historical readings of the tradition, and Elshtain's controversial Augustinian rendering) gave way to hope, following the Obama administration's embracing of a more restrictive view of just war. But the conflicts of the Obama era, too, have raised concerns, notably with the advent of preventive drone strikes and the blurring of the lines between law enforcement and war when it comes to fighting terrorism. Such concerns, raised in the chapters by Fisk and Ramos as well as by Brunstetter, are significant, especially if they are adopted by other states, but they do not mean that we should jettison just war thinking altogether.

Biggar's chapter reveals the limits on exercising retrospective judgment regarding the costs and benefits of past wars in order to judge the paradigms themselves. Rather than read history as a series of events that came to pass with the application of flawed principles, we should take into account that history is made of contingencies. Regarding the principles of just war, Biggar's reflections remind us that the practice of ethical war is not an exact science or realm of abstract morality but rather a realm of judgment defined by uncertainty and governed by ethical concerns as well as state-centric national interests. To divorce ethics from the interests of states is to overlook something very significant. To marry them, as Biggar thinks we must, complicates the relationship between ethics and war by making it contingent on a particular state's (or group of states') position in the international system. To this end, augmenting war ethics by balancing uncertainty with risk and security is one of the key themes of Emery's chapter on fighting terrorist groups. According to Emery, we can better understand the challenges of fighting ethically if we supplement just war thinking not by marrying national interest and ethics but through a better understanding of the enemy and the limits of our actions. Although terrorist groups may not play by the rules, overreaction and the call to "do something" (militarily) in response to the uncertainty posed by terrorist groups—for example, the reactions of the United States and France—can result in the opposite of the intended outcome—that is, an increased risk of future attacks as well as an undermining of liberal democratic values at home.

The relationship between war and war ethics is further complicated by the prudential "lessons of history"—namely, that leaders should always plan for costs to exceed their estimates and that wars do not always lead to hopes of victory (a point O'Driscoll brings to the fore). Regarding the former, we are left to contemplate the efficacy of evaluating war through a consequentialist lens, and how the art of predicting consequences has an impact on our turn to ethics. Here, Vilmer's chapter is illustrative. As France debates whether to acquire and use armed drones, it faces public opinion shaped by the postcolonial philosopher Grégoire Chamayou's critical rejection of the US defense of drones. Chamayou's analysis, based deeply in critical theory, dismisses the turn to the principles of just war theory as a "death ethics." Vilmer reminds us that ethical principles, such as those of *jus in bello* (discrimination and proportionality), necessarily involve death, but that does not mean they should be dismissed. Rather, the principles offer a marker—perhaps imperfect—to evaluate drone strikes. Vilmer's support of drones because the outcome is efficacious is at odds with the argument furthered by Fisk and Ramos. The latter are concerned with how judging consequences positively can promote a problematic norm in the international arena—in this case, that of preventive force. To supplement our understanding of ethical principles such as those of the just war, the conversations between these chapters highlight the importance of normative evolution, as shaped by paying particular attention to consequences. For drones, the perception that they satisfy the *jus in bello* principles better than other weapons may have enabled a shift in the normative practice of war not simply by lowering the threshold to use force, but enabling preventive force. Although preventive war was widely discredited after the Bush doctrine and the Iraq War debacle, the fear is that something of the preventive force norm war has stuck. In a world of fragmented and contested sovereignty, this may come to alter the way leaders understand the *jus ad bellum* decisions. Here is where Kelsay's call to better understand the "signs of the times" takes on greater significance.

For Kelsay, the practice of just war thinking has suffered from an undisciplined attempt to understand the complex dynamics of current conflicts, particularly in the Middle East. His concern is that the importance of timing—which is central to just war thinking but is often misunderstood when linked to the modern concept of last resort—has lost its centrality when responding to current crises. The rise of the preventive force norm that Fisk and Ramos describe offers some evidence, as do the insights that Lindemann and Giacomelli's turn to recognition theory about the selectivity of humanitarian intervention. Kelsay's astute rendering of jihadi discourse—particularly that of ISIS—is an attempt to show the level of detail and understanding of the dynamics required to prudently use force, and grasp the limitations thereof. Kelsay's ultimate conclusion, which he reaches by pointing us in the direction of prudence as understood in the classical just war tradition, is that obtaining this level of complexity will necessarily temper the hopes of war as statecraft. Here he points to the art of statecraft as finding a fit between long-term goals and the requirements of the moment. Rather than victory, just war practice that reads correctly the signs of the times might have to settle for tactical and strategic success—an objective that would severely challenge even the "thin" version of *jus post bellum* aspired to by Orend.

Even if the manner in which the *jus ad bellum* and *jus in bello* principles are understood is subject to change, they still offer a powerful starting point for thinking about the use of force and the moral challenges it entails. Avant's chapter delimits how just war principles, supplemented by pragmatism, can have a positive effect on how private military and security companies (PMSCs) can be brought into the category of legitimate and ethical actors. Avant recognizes that the state's legitimacy as the sole procurer of force is fast dwindling, but argues that the just war tradition can still offer insights into how to incorporate some nonstate actors. She attempts to marry just war principles with a form of pragmatism to draw PMSCs into the just war tradition by focusing less on who they are and more on what they do. French, Sisk, and Bass build from the basis of *jus in bello* principles to enhance our understanding of how drones make an impact on the way we fight. They see the need for a consistent set of rules as fundamental to the warrior ethos, but argue that our understanding of the particularities of drones needs to be enhanced by taking into account the power hierarchies they embody. To this end, a turn to traditional psychological experiments—such as the Milgram experiments—is revealing. In other words, how drone-wielding warriors implement *jus in bello* principles can be supplemented by research about deference to authority drawn from other fields.

A final way just war thinking can be supplemented is by viewing the responsibility inherent in military ethics through a different lens. In Vilmer's chapter, we saw how critical French theory served as a basis for criticizing drone use as a form of postcolonial imperialism—a view Vilmer rejects. One could, rather, think about a country's postcolonial legacy as entailing a sense of responsibility that affects the military ethos. Holeindre's chapter demonstrates how the notion of postcolonial responsibility has made an impact on how France sees its military role. As we think about just war principles, tempering their universalist appeal with the particularities of a state's historical and ethical ethos, not to mention its national interest (e.g., Biggar's argument), can provide insight into the deliberations about entering into a conflict and decisions made during it, and maybe even afterward. Of course, postcolonial responsibility may just be a veiled way of pursuing a state's national interest. Such a slippery slope is obvious; but Holeindre concludes that this should not necessarily discount the ethical possibility. However, he warns that there is also a domestic element in postcolonial responsibility—that of ensuring the integration of immigrants and their descendants from former colonies. France's struggle in this domain has implications for the fight against jihadist groups such as ISIS, as some alienated French nationals have been radicalized.

THE CHANGING FACE OF WAR, AND THE PARADIGMS USED TO EVALUATE IT

Scholars have noted various trends about war in the past few decades: that today's wars have fewer overall casualties compared with the general history of warfare; that war is less and less between states, but now tends to pit states against nonstate actors or groups within a state against each other in a civil war; that powerful states are becoming more reliant on air power and less prone to put ground troops in harm's way; and that what we call war—for example, the drone campaign against terrorist groups—is not really war at all. If war is changing, then the question of whether ethics must adapt, too, takes on urgent significance. This is a question about whether existing frameworks like the just war tradition or R2P are good enough, or whether they fail to deliver the needed moral purchase to guide leaders on certain questions about the use of force.

The just war tradition can serve as a language of debate—for scholars to argue about and evaluate the use of force. It can also provide the language for statesmen to persuade the public and international community that war to address an international crisis is just (or unjust if, for example, the threshold of last resort has not been crossed). In these instances, there is room for change in how certain principles come to be interpreted, but not necessarily for the betterment of the international system. Fisk and Ramos warn of the negative consequences of a potential shift in light of new types of threats and new means of waging war. The emerging norm of preventive force has, problematically for them, allowed two successive US presidents to mislead the public and make the world more dangerous. Bush rested his argument on the view that just war thinking needed to adapt to the post-9/11 times; Obama argued that we needed a return to a more traditional reading of just war principles—except when it comes to using drones to combat terrorism. Fisk and Ramos argue that Obama has succeeded in grafting the Bush notion of preventive force onto the particularities of drone strikes, which may have engendered a global preventive force norm. Their point is that reinterpreting just war principles in light of new conflicts and technologies can, despite an initial international outcry—much of the world was against the United States' 2003 Iraq War, and global public opinion on US drone strikes has a significantly negative bend to it—alter the normative structures of the international system as other powerful states claim the right to act in the same way. Fisk and Ramos provide evidence that some states have preliminarily endorsed their right to use preventive force. Will this be the case for all states, as lethal drone technology spreads? Their discussion of India and South Korea suggests a worrisome trend, though Vilmer's consequentialist argument in the context of France offers an alternative viewpoint insofar as he seems to reject the preventive force argument.

But the just war tradition also serves as part of the pedagogical bedrock on which military ethics is laid. French, Sisk, and Bass reject the idea that the just war tradition—or at least its *jus in bello* elements—is somehow outdated. They forcefully argue that for soldiers to be able to function honorably, a consistent standard needs to be woven into the military ethos—what they call the warrior's code; departing from this standard risks making honorable action all the more difficult to achieve. Although new technologies such as drones magnify some of the challenges to acting honorably—for example, living up to the *jus in bello* restraints—this does not mean there is a need to reject or reformulate the just war principles. Their conclusion runs counter to that of Brunstetter, who argues that the propensity to use force short of war suggests the need for a new ethical framework calibrated to limited force (*jus ad vim*). Brunstetter attempts to elucidate the limitations of law enforcement and just war thinking when it comes to evaluating the moral dilemmas associated with using force short of war. He does not insist that these frameworks should be rejected outright but rather argues that in certain circumstances neither one offers the moral leverage necessary to work through the dilemmas statesmen face. A theory of just and unjust limited force, he purports, could fill the moral space between peace and war where force short of war (including drone strikes) lies. Whether this framework could come to be part of the warrior's code, or the moral vocabulary of statesmen, is an open question.

Ramel's contribution marks an example of how new frameworks have already enriched the ethical discussions about global issues—namely, the research developed around the concept of human security. Ramel considers the normative effects of human security in the international arena in relation to the use of force. Despite the good intentions conceptualized in the 1994 United Nations Development Program's report, Ramel shows how any new framework can suffer from ambiguities that lead to alternative—and sometimes problematic—interpretations. Although this paradigm had the intention of challenging traditional notions of security and raising awareness about alternative security concerns, it had the effect of justifying wars that undermined the very backbone of the concept of human security. Ramel's discussion warns us to be wary of the paradoxes that new paradigms may engender, and how their eventual adaptation into mainstream discourse could lead to unintended results, or even bolster already-existing and morally problematic global power structures. For those engaging with the *jus ad vim* research agenda, the lessons from the evolution of the human security paradigm offer fruitful ground to probe.

It may simply be the case that we need only revaluate existing paradigms, and revise them in such a way that derives achievable standards from the ideal. Orend's contribution on *jus post bellum* attempts to do just this. Taking into account the difficulties of recent *post bellum* situations—in Afghanistan and Iraq—Orend revises his previous views on *jus post bellum* to offer a more realistic paradigm. He does not want to abandon *jus post bellum* based on rehabilitation, but recognizes that holding to this ideal can be problematic. Abandoning the ideal, however, has consequences; and this is an important point to keep in mind as we consider how ethical frameworks evolve. If the ideal is not applicable, or if attempts to apply it lead to deep problems, we may need to blend the ideal with less-than-ideal alternatives. Ultimately for Orend, this means finding what he calls the thin, overlapping consensus between rehabilitation (the ideal) and retribution (the problematic alternative).

That being said, the contested and fragmentary nature of sovereignty in some parts of the world raises deeper conceptual questions. What if we are in a time when the very notion of war has been called into question, as Brunstetter's argument about the space that limited force occupies between peace and war suggests? Or what if, as O'Driscoll claims, the notion of victory has become so elusive that we are, for all intents and purposes, in some kind of state of perpetual war? For example, consider a blending of one conflict (Iraq in 1991) into another (Iraq in 2003), into another (ISIS in 2014). If the evolution of war is moving in the direction of exploding the traditional notion of war as having a beginning, middle, and end, then this raises some serious concerns about how we evaluate the use of force in the future.

LOOKING TOWARD THE FUTURE: WHERE THEORY MEETS PRACTICE

Making ethical judgments, whether in the decision leading to the use of force, during the military campaign, or after the conflict is over is not a science. Adapting tried-and-tested frameworks channels the power of moral tradition to make sense of, and navigate through, the practice of war. But old frameworks have gaps of knowledge and make assumptions that need further unpacking, while new frameworks—despite the challenges they pose—can also be helpful.

In these concluding remarks, we identify several areas of future inquiry, which we have divided into three general categories: meta-theoretical, conceptual, and practical. These categories, of course, blend into each other; however, in keeping with the theme of fluidity with which we have organized the volume, we invite the reader to think of points of overlap between them, and draw his or her own conclusions regarding the contributions of the authors to each.

Meta-theoretical: One of the implicit conclusions drawn from reading the contributions as a whole is that the frameworks used to persuade domestic and international publics to support or reject a specific intervention, to criticize state leaders for their decisions, or to evaluate any use of military force are vulnerable to the crisis of the moment. The crisis in Syria is interpreted through the lens of Libya. The potential for preventive strikes against Iran is read through the 2003 Iraq War. Drone strikes against ISIS are viewed through the problematic signature strike program against multifaceted militants along the Afghanistan/Pakistan border. And so on, and so forth. One theme that connects the chapters is an underlying inquiry about the life cycle of ethical paradigms. As current conflicts undergo a metamorphosis, such as the one against ISIS, and we ponder once again about the validity of existing paradigms, we would be keen to cast our gaze beyond the crisis of the moment into the deeper history of these paradigms. How do new paradigms come into being? How do existing paradigms change? What leads to their evolution? Or devolution? What could make them obsolete? This is particularly relevant in an era of contested and fragmented sovereignty, when it seems that the hard-and-fast rules of where one can intervene, which were once linked to the notion of inviolable sovereignty, are no longer the guiding force they once were.

As international conditions continue to evolve, these questions will no doubt be applicable to the future importance of just war thinking, R2P, human security, and the *jus ad vim* project. The contributions in this volume point to several specific areas of inquiry.

The preventive force norm, thought to be repudiated after the Bush doctrine inspired the Iraq War, has found fertile ground for support. Under what conditions might preventive force come to be internationally accepted? At the level of drones? In a limited strike to thwart the spread of weapons of mass destruction? Or even in a return to full-scale preventive war?

The legitimacy of humanitarian intervention, inspired by the principles of R2P, has suffered what some see as a decisive blow since the flawed Libya campaign. How could it be refashioned by linking responsibility to a notion of postcolonial responsibility that empowers the former colonial population and limits the former colonial power to a supporting role? Can one conceive of humanitarian intervention through the lens of limited force instead of the quantum of force (and postwar commitment) needed to provoke democratic reconstruction? Can human security, if revised to overcome its shortcomings, provide an alternative framework?

The just war tradition has put great stock in the tripartite framework of *jus ad bellum*, *jus in bello*, and *jus post bellum*. However, as war changes with the advent of new technologies, with the difficulty of winning traditional wars, and with the global threat of nonstate actors that contest and fragment sovereignty, how will the just war tradition evolve? Will it hold firm, and reject the push for a theory of force short of war such as *jus ad vim*, which seeks to track a middle ground between law enforcement and war? Can the just war tradition enter into a constructive dialogue with such a framework to push our conceptual knowledge forward? What about a framework that seeks to balance uncertainty, risk, and security—could it add fresh concepts to the ethical debates? How might classical notions, from before the era of Westphalian sovereignty, contribute?

Conceptual: Cian O'Driscoll's illuminating chapter identifies perhaps the most telling challenge when thinking about the future of war: identifying what it means to win a war, and unraveling the tension between the notion of victory and the just war ethos. O'Driscoll reminds us that the impetus to wage just—and necessary—wars can also be part of future problems if the pursuit of victory undermines the humility and restraint supposedly inherent in just war thinking. Conceptually, O'Driscoll sets out a future research agenda to ascertain what victory means in the context of just war, highlighting alternative paths of inquiry. One could look for first principles, pursue a genealogy of victory, or examine the relation between just war and victory by tracing its historical trajectory.

Part of the challenge of identifying victory lies in understanding what war means today—that is, identifying where a war begins and ends, and what counts as war. This is especially true in the generational struggle against groups such as al-Qaeda and ISIS, which takes place both abroad and at home. It is also true given that victory is no longer linked to nominally restoring sovereignty, as Kelsay's discussion of jihadist groups that contest this notion makes clear. As existing paradigms continue to evolve, they will need to address the question of what war is. In many ways, this is exacerbated by the prolonged use of limited force, or instances of force short of war. The *jus ad vim* research agenda discussed in the conclusion of Brunstetter's chapter points to one way to conceptually reframe the debates: for proponents of *jus ad vim* to develop new conceptual tools to address current challenges, and for proponents of just war thinking (in its various guises) to show how their paradigms do (or could do) a more adequate job. Among the key challenges to address are delimiting a clearer boundary between law enforcement and war and the ethical rules that apply in each, theorizing about the risk of escalation from law enforcement to force short of war to war, and conceptualizing what justice looks like after the use of limited force. Here, further probing into the relationship between risk, uncertainty, and security explored by Emery is fertile ground for future research. How do the ways in which we construct the terrorist enemy as a homogenous and hierarchical structure influence the way terrorist groups are fought (by law enforcement, force short of war, aerial bombing, or full-scale war)? In what ways have shifting rules of engagement and a sliding scale for ethics increased risk and insecurity at home? To civilians abroad who must bear the brunt of our generational conflict against al-Qaeda and ISIS? In the end, both Emery's and Brunstetter's contributions highlight the necessity of a new conceptual tool kit for thinking about law enforcement, war, and ethics, to fight terrorism justly in an era of fragmented and contested sovereignty.

A final conceptual development concerns exploring questions relating to who is fighting, for what reasons, and by what rules. If humanitarian interventions are problematic because they do not systematically resolve the humanitarian crises they set out to fix, how do we think about who should intervene and what propels them to accept the responsibility? How do we incorporate the voice of the Other, whether as a combatant or victim, into our ethical frameworks? And how can understanding the Other help us to better read the "signs of the times" and make more morally sound choices? Can new actors—for example, PMSCs—become legitimate if they play by old rules? Although it is contested whether emerging technologies such as drones alter the rules of war (particularly *jus in bello*)—how drones alter the chain of command and the ability of drone operators to follow the rules is, if we believe French, Sisk, and Bass, a cause of deep concern. Even if the rules remain the same, we need to better understand the power structures that underlie them.

This conceptual development can enrich our moral vocabulary—that is to say, how we talk about the relationship between ethics and violence. Enriching our conceptual language can, in turn, have practical implications.

Practical: Moral frameworks, and the conceptual developments to which they are subject, have practical implications. The paradigms of just war and R2P help frame international norms and international laws as well as the decisions made by leaders related to the use of force; key documents that communicate how force might be used in the international sphere—such as, to name a few recent examples, Obama's US National Security Strategy and UN Resolution

1973 regarding Libya—are imbued with their language. These principles also enter into the classrooms of those who may be called one day to take up arms, as education tools to inform the warrior's code or to guide the actions of PMSCs. In other words, the insights of future conceptual developments can cross over into the sphere of statecraft and warfare.

The development of a richer moral language to talk about victory and force short of war can alert leaders (and citizens) to the (new?) dilemmas of using force in today's world. The practical reforms proposed for the concept of human security and the norm of R2P (coupled with the insights from recognition theory) can make an impact on the way leaders and institutions invoke their core principles in response to future international crises. A better conception of who the enemy is and how they understand their struggle by grappling with the myriad of jihadi discourses can lend important insights that may lead to more prudent uses of force.

Finally, taking stock of how war and the principles used to morally evaluate its spaces have evolved is key to educating those who are part of Anglo and French societies that seem so prone to wield force today. These include future combatants, in order that they better navigate the complex space of the modern battlefield. It also means educating citizens and statesmen, to empower debates marked by a mutually understood vocabulary. Part of this, in France at least, is grappling with its postcolonial identity, and coming to grips with the banes and boons of the American example. Given France's aspiring role as a global force, this holds true for implementing R2P, fighting terrorism with or without armed drones, and attending to its postcolonial responsibility in its sphere of influence. To this end, the conceptual developments suggested in this conclusion should be pursued not only to contribute to scholarly debates (the meta-theoretical avenues of inquiry) but also with an eye for their practical implications—whether in the classroom, in public discourse, or on the battlefield.

CONTRIBUTORS

Deborah Avant is a political scientist and Sié Chéou-Kang Chair at the Joseph Korbel School of International Studies at the University of Denver, where she also directs the Sié Chéou-Kang Center for International Security and Diplomacy. Her research focuses on civil–military relations and the roles of state and nonstate actors in controlling violence and governing security. She is the author of dozens of articles and four books, including *Who Governs the Globe?* and *The Market for Force*. She also engages frequently in policy and public outreach on these issues. She founded and maintains the Private Security Monitor (http://psm.du.edu/) and is an observer member of the International Code of Conduct Association. She also edits the International Studies Association's newest journal, *The Journal of Global Security Studies*.

Caroline Bass received a BA in philosophy and political science and an MA in bioethics from Case Western Reserve University. Her research interests include health, law, and bioethics. She completed internships in bioethics at Yale University and with the American Medical Association Ethics Group, and she is the coauthor of "Conflicts of Interest for Physicians Treating Egg Donors," which was published in the *AMA Journal of Ethics*. She is currently a business technology consultant for Deloitte.

Nigel Biggar is Regius Professor of Moral and Pastoral Theology at Oxford University, where he is also director of the McDonald Centre for Theology, Ethics, and Public Life. He is also a canon of Christ Church Cathedral, Oxford. Among his current research interests are the theology and ethics of empire, national loyalty and nationalism, war, assisted suicide, forgiveness, and burying the past after civil conflict. He has published numerous books, including *In Defence of War* and *Burying the Past: Making Peace and Doing Justice after Civil Conflict*.

Daniel R. Brunstetter is an associate professor in the Department of Political Science at the University of California, Irvine. His first book, *Tensions of Modernity*, explores early human rights debates in the context of European encounters with the New World. He has published numerous articles on the ethics of war in leading journals, including *Ethics & International Affairs*, *Political Studies*, *International Relations*, *The Atlantic*, *Review of International Studies*, *Journal of Military Ethics*, and *International Journal of Human Rights*. He also coedited a special edition of *Raisons politiques* on the theme *guerre juste* (just war), as well as the book *Just War Thinkers: From Cicero to the 21st Century* (coedited with Cian O'Driscoll).

John R. Emery is a PhD candidate in the Department of Political Science at the University of California, Irvine. He is also a lecturer on issues in national security at Chapman University. His research focuses on issues of terrorism and counterterrorism, US foreign policy, and the ethics of technology in warfare. His work has been published in *Ethics & International Affairs*, *Peace Review*, and *Political Psychology*.

Kerstin Fisk is an assistant professor of political science at Loyola Marymount University in Los Angeles. Her research focuses on issues of security, peace, and conflict, with emphases on changes in international warfare and civil war dynamics. Her research has been published in the *Journal of Conflict Resolution*, *International Studies Perspectives*, and *Civil Wars*. She is also coeditor (with Jennifer Ramos) of the book *Preventive Force: Drones, Targeted Killing, and the Transformation of Contemporary Warfare*.

Shannon E. French is the Inamori Professor of Ethics at Case Western Reserve University, where she is also the director of the Inamori International Center for Ethics and Excellence, a professor in the Philosophy Department, and a professor in the School of Law. She is also the General Hugh Shelton Distinguished Visiting Chair in Ethics for the US Army Command and General Staff College. Before starting at Case Western in 2008, she taught ethics for eleven years as an associate professor of philosophy at the US Naval Academy in Annapolis, where she also served as associate chair of the Department of Leadership, Ethics, and Law. Her main area of research is military ethics, especially conduct-of-war issues, ethical leadership, command climate, sacrifice and responsibility, warrior transitions, ethical responses to terrorism, and the future of war. She is the author of many publications—including *The Code of the Warrior: Exploring Warrior Values, Past and Present*—and is an associate editor for the *Journal of Military Ethics*.

Alex Giacomelli is a Brazilian career diplomat. He received master's degrees in public administration from the John F. Kennedy School of Government at Harvard University and in political science from the Université Paris I Panthéon–Sorbonne. He received bachelor's degrees in diplomacy from the Instituto Rio Branco and in law from the Centro Universitário de Brasília.

Aidan Hehir is a reader in international relations at the University of Westminster in London. His research interests include humanitarian intervention, the Responsibility to Protect, and international human rights law. He is the author of three books: *Humanitarian Intervention After Kosovo*; *Humanitarian Intervention: An Introduction*; and *The Responsibility to Protect: Rhetoric, Reality and the Future of Humanitarian Intervention*. He is currently part of a two-year project funded by Britain's Economic and Social Research Council on "The Responsibility to Protect and Prosecute: The Political Sustainability of Liberal Norms in an Age of Shifting Power Balances."

Jean-Vincent Holeindre is a professor of political science at the Université Paris 2 Panthéon-Assas and scientific director of the Institute for Strategic Research of the French Ministry of Defense. His recent publications include three books—*La ruse et la force: Une autre histoire de la stratégie* (*Cunning and Force: A History of Strategy*); *La fin des guerres majeures* (*The End of Major Wars*), with Frédéric Ramel; and *La Democratie et la guerre: De la paix democratique aux guerres irregulières* (*Democracy and War: From Democratic Peace to Irregular Wars*), with Geoffroy Murat—as well as numerous articles on war and peace. He has organized several conferences in France on war, including one in 2008 co-organized with Daniel R. Brunstetter, whose proceedings were published in a special edition of the journal *Raisons politiques* on the theme *guerre juste* (just war).

John Kelsay holds the positions of Richard L. Rubenstein Professor of Religion and the Bristol Distinguished Professor of Ethics at Florida State University. His research focuses on religious ethics, particularly in relation to the perspectives of the Islamic and Christian traditions on war and peace. He is the author of dozens of articles on the theme of religion and war, and numerous books, including *Arguing the Just War in Islam*; *Islam and War: A Study in Comparative Ethics*; and *Human Rights and the Conflict of Cultures*.

Thomas Lindemann is a professor of political science at Versailles University Saint-Quentin and the École Polytechnique in France. He is an elected member of the Conseil de l'Administration de l'Association Française de Science

Politique. His research focuses on the intersection of identity, war, and peace, with a particular focus on the problematics of recognition and perceptions of the enemy. He is the author of numerous books, including *Causes of War: The Struggle for Recognition*; *The Struggle for Recognition in International Relations* (with Erik Ringmar); and *La guerre*.

Cian O'Driscoll is senior lecturer in politics at the University of Glasgow. His work focuses on the just war tradition and the ethics of war more generally. He has published articles in *International Studies Quarterly*, *Ethics & International Affairs*, *Review of International Studies*, and *Journal of Military Ethics*. He also published a monograph, *The Renegotiation of the Just War Tradition and the Right to War in the Twenty-First Century*. He has coedited three volumes: *Just War: Authority, Tradition, Practice* (with John Williams and Anthony F. Lang Jr.); *Just War Thinkers: From Cicero to the 21st Century* (with Daniel R. Brunstetter); and *Moral Victories: The Ethics of Winning Wars* (with Andrew Hom and Kurt Mills). He is the coconvener of the Glasgow Global Security Network, and a fellow of the Royal Society of Edinburgh's Young Academy.

Brian Orend is the director of international studies, and a professor of philosophy, at the University of Waterloo in Canada. He has taught at Columbia University in New York and the University of Lund in Sweden (where he was Distinguished Visiting Professor of Human Rights). His research focuses on human rights and the ethics of war, with a particular focus on the importance of *jus post bellum* (justice after war). He is the author of six books, including *Human Rights: Concept and Context*, which was named an outstanding academic title by *Choice* magazine, and *The Morality of War*, which critics consider one of the most authoritative books on the ethics of war today.

Frédéric Ramel is a professor and head of the Department of Political Science at Sciences Po, and a member of the Centre d'Études et de Recherches Internationales (Center for International Study and Research). He is the author of dozens of articles on international relations, peacekeeping, and the concept of the enemy in a post-9/11 world, as well as four books, including *Philosophie des relations internationales* (*Philosophy of International Relations*).

Jennifer M. Ramos is an associate professor of political science at Loyola Marymount University in Los Angeles. Her research focuses on peacebuilding in divided societies, public opinion and US foreign policy, and the evolution of international norms. Her work has appeared in the *Journal of Politics*, *Public Opinion Quarterly*, *International Studies Perspectives*, *Journal of Political Ide-*

ologies, *Foreign Policy Analysis*, and *Human Rights Review*. Her recent books include *Preventive Force: Drones, Targeted Killing, and the Transformation of Contemporary Warfare* (coedited with Kerstin Fisk); *Changing Norms through Actions: The Evolution of Sovereignty*; and *iPolitics: Citizens, Elections, and Governing in the New Media Era* (coedited with Richard L. Fox).

Victoria Sisk received a BA in philosophy and psychology from Case Western Reserve University. Her main areas of interest are applied ethics and social psychology. She has worked on several significant research projects, including one that examines the role of stress mind-sets in the quality-of-life and medical outcomes of breast cancer patients. She is currently working in Washington and plans to pursue a PhD in psychology.

Jean-Baptiste Jeangène Vilmer is director of the Institut de Recherche Stratégique de l'École Militaire of the French Ministry of Defense. He is also lecturer on the laws of war at Sciences Po (the Paris School of International Affairs) and the École spéciale militaire de Saint-Cyr (Special Military School at Saint Cyr). His book *La Guerre au nom de l'humanité: Tuer ou laisser mourir* (*War in the Name of Humanity: To Kill or Let Die*) won the Prix du Maréchal Foch. In France, he is one of the principal leaders of the drone debate, which was the focus of the recent special issue "Les drones dans la guerre" (Drones in War) of the journal *Politique étrangère*.

INDEX

www.ingramcontent.com/pod-product-compliance
Lightning Source LLC
LaVergne TN
LVHW050148080826
844660LV00002B/113

* 9 7 8 1 6 2 6 1 6 5 0 6 9 *